IMAGINARY DRUGS

EDITOR
MICHAEL MCDERMOTT

ASSISTANT EDITOR
JEFF MCCLELLAND

BOOK DESIGN
JONATHAN BRANDON SAWYER

COVER BY JONATHAN BRANDON SAWYER AND CHRISTINE LARSEN

TO ALL THOSE WHO HAVE LOVED, TOLERATED, AND INSPIRED
THE CREATIVE INDIVIDUALS IN YOUR LIVES, THIS ONE'S FOR YOU.

HEY, MAMA.

ISBN: 978-1-63140-198-5

18 17 16 15   1 2 3 4

www.IDWPUBLISHING.com
IDW founded by Ted Adams, Alex Garner, Kris Oprisko, and Robbie Robbins

Ted Adams, CEO & Publisher
Greg Goldstein, President & COO
Robbie Robbins, EVP/Sr. Graphic Artist
Chris Ryall, Chief Creative Officer/Editor-in-Chief
Matthew Ruzicka, CPA, Chief Financial Officer
Alan Payne, VP of Sales
Dirk Wood, VP of Marketing
Lorelei Bunjes, VP of Digital Services
Jeff Webber, VP of Digital Publishing & Business Development

Facebook: facebook.com/idwpublishing
Twitter: @idwpublishing
YouTube: youtube.com/idwpublishing
Instagram: instagram.com/idwpublishing
deviantART: idwpublishing.deviantart.com
Pinterest: pinterest.com/idwpublishing/idw-staff-faves

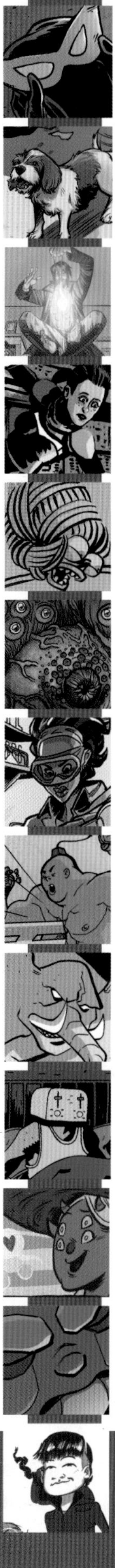

Table of Contents

Pinups

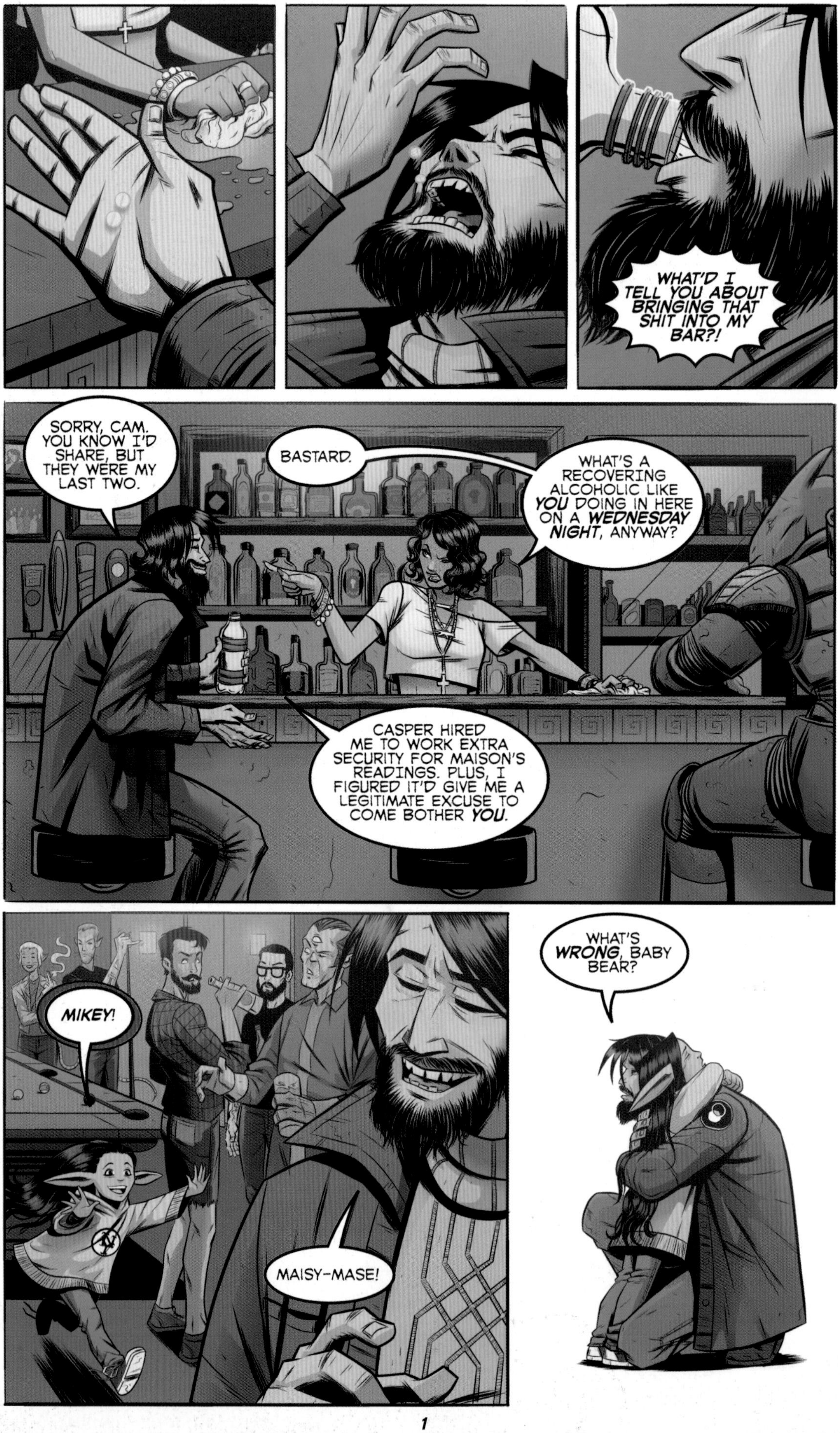
WHAT'D I TELL YOU ABOUT BRINGING THAT SHIT INTO MY BAR?!
SORRY, CAM. YOU KNOW I'D SHARE, BUT THEY WERE MY LAST TWO.
BASTARD.
WHAT'S A RECOVERING ALCOHOLIC LIKE YOU DOING IN HERE ON A WEDNESDAY NIGHT, ANYWAY?
CASPER HIRED ME TO WORK EXTRA SECURITY FOR MAISON'S READINGS. PLUS, I FIGURED IT'D GIVE ME A LEGITIMATE EXCUSE TO COME BOTHER YOU.
MIKEY!
MAISY-MASE!
WHAT'S WRONG, BABY BEAR?

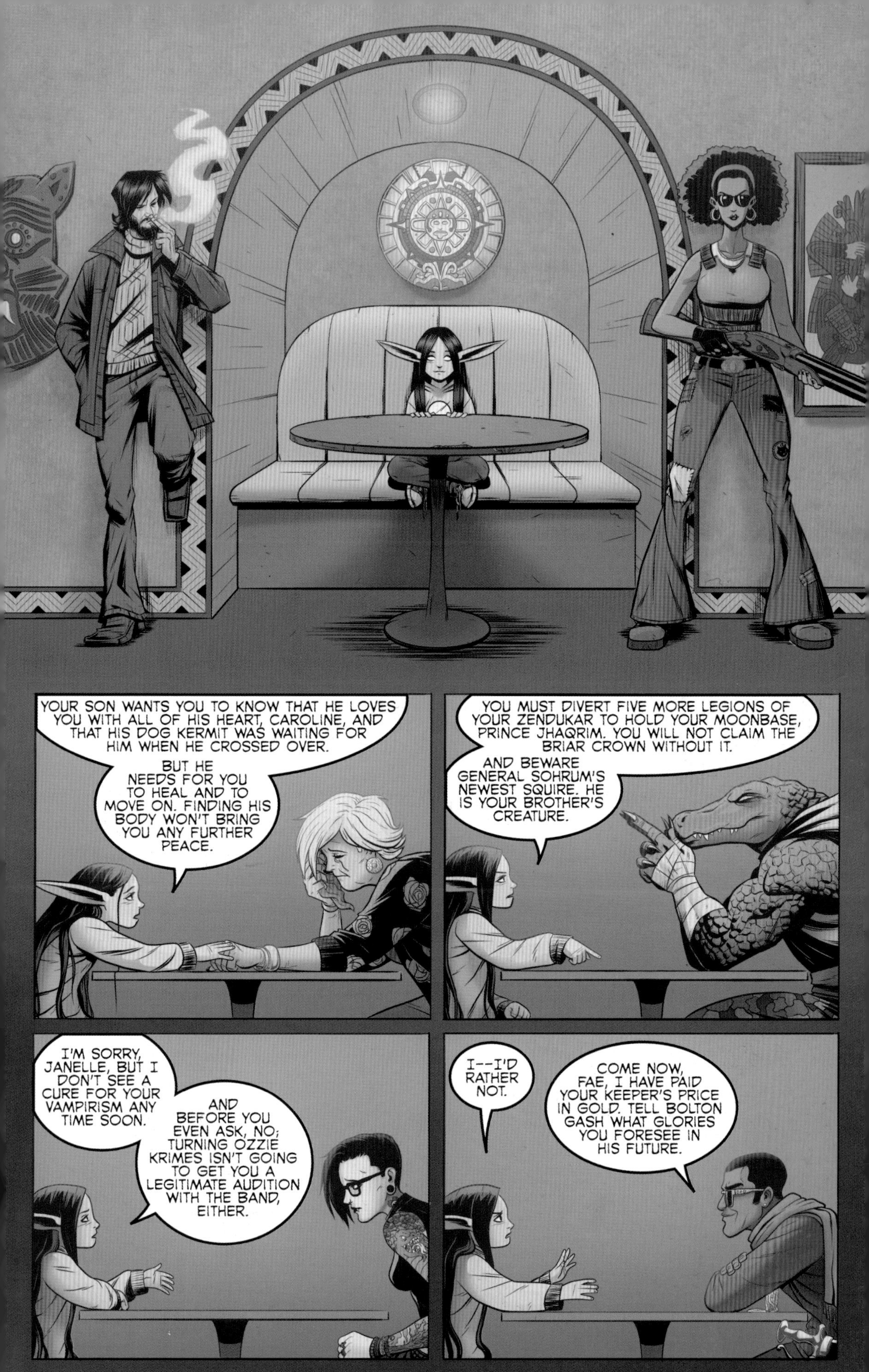
YOUR SON WANTS YOU TO KNOW THAT HE LOVES YOU WITH ALL OF HIS HEART, CAROLINE, AND THAT HIS DOG KERMIT WAS WAITING FOR HIM WHEN HE CROSSED OVER.
BUT HE NEEDS FOR YOU TO HEAL AND TO MOVE ON. FINDING HIS BODY WON'T BRING YOU ANY FURTHER PEACE.
YOU MUST DIVERT FIVE MORE LEGIONS OF YOUR ZENDUKAR TO HOLD YOUR MOONBASE, PRINCE JHAQRIM. YOU WILL NOT CLAIM THE BRIAR CROWN WITHOUT IT.
AND BEWARE GENERAL SOHRUM'S NEWEST SQUIRE. HE IS YOUR BROTHER'S CREATURE.
I'M SORRY, JANELLE, BUT I DON'T SEE A CURE FOR YOUR VAMPIRISM ANY TIME SOON.
AND BEFORE YOU EVEN ASK, NO; TURNING OZZIE KRIMES ISN'T GOING TO GET YOU A LEGITIMATE AUDITION WITH THE BAND, EITHER.
I--I'D RATHER NOT.
COME NOW, FAE, I HAVE PAID YOUR KEEPER'S PRICE IN GOLD. TELL BOLTON GASH WHAT GLORIES YOU FORESEE IN HIS FUTURE.

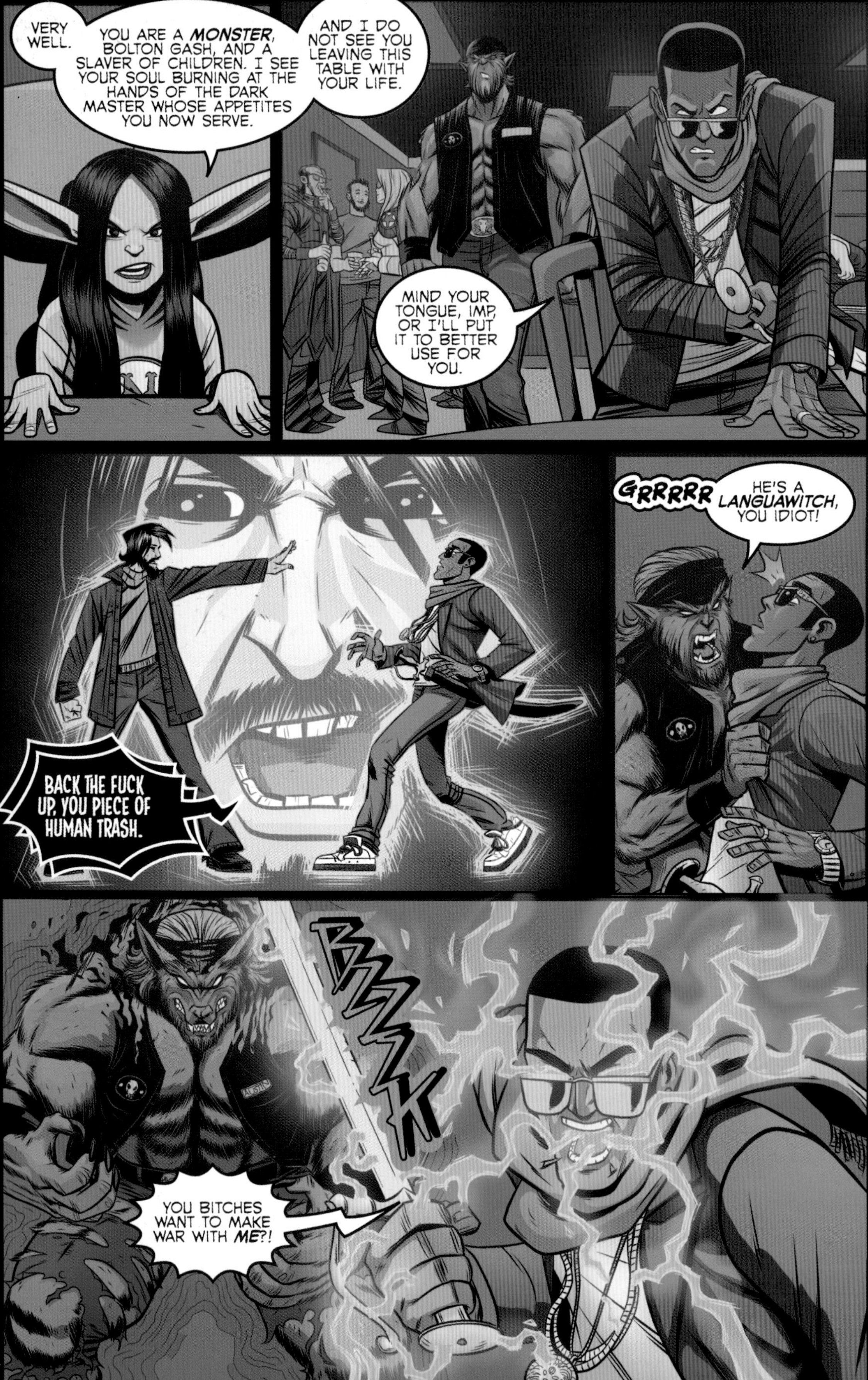
VERY WELL.
YOU ARE A MONSTER, BOLTON GASH, AND A SLAVER OF CHILDREN. I SEE YOUR SOUL BURNING AT THE HANDS OF THE DARK MASTER WHOSE APPETITES YOU NOW SERVE.
AND I DO NOT SEE YOU LEAVING THIS TABLE WITH YOUR LIFE.
MIND YOUR TONGUE, IMP, OR I'LL PUT IT TO BETTER USE FOR YOU.
BACK THE FUCK UP, YOU PIECE OF HUMAN TRASH.
GRRRRR
HE'S A LANGUAWITCH, YOU IDIOT!
BZZZK
YOU BITCHES WANT TO MAKE WAR WITH ME?!

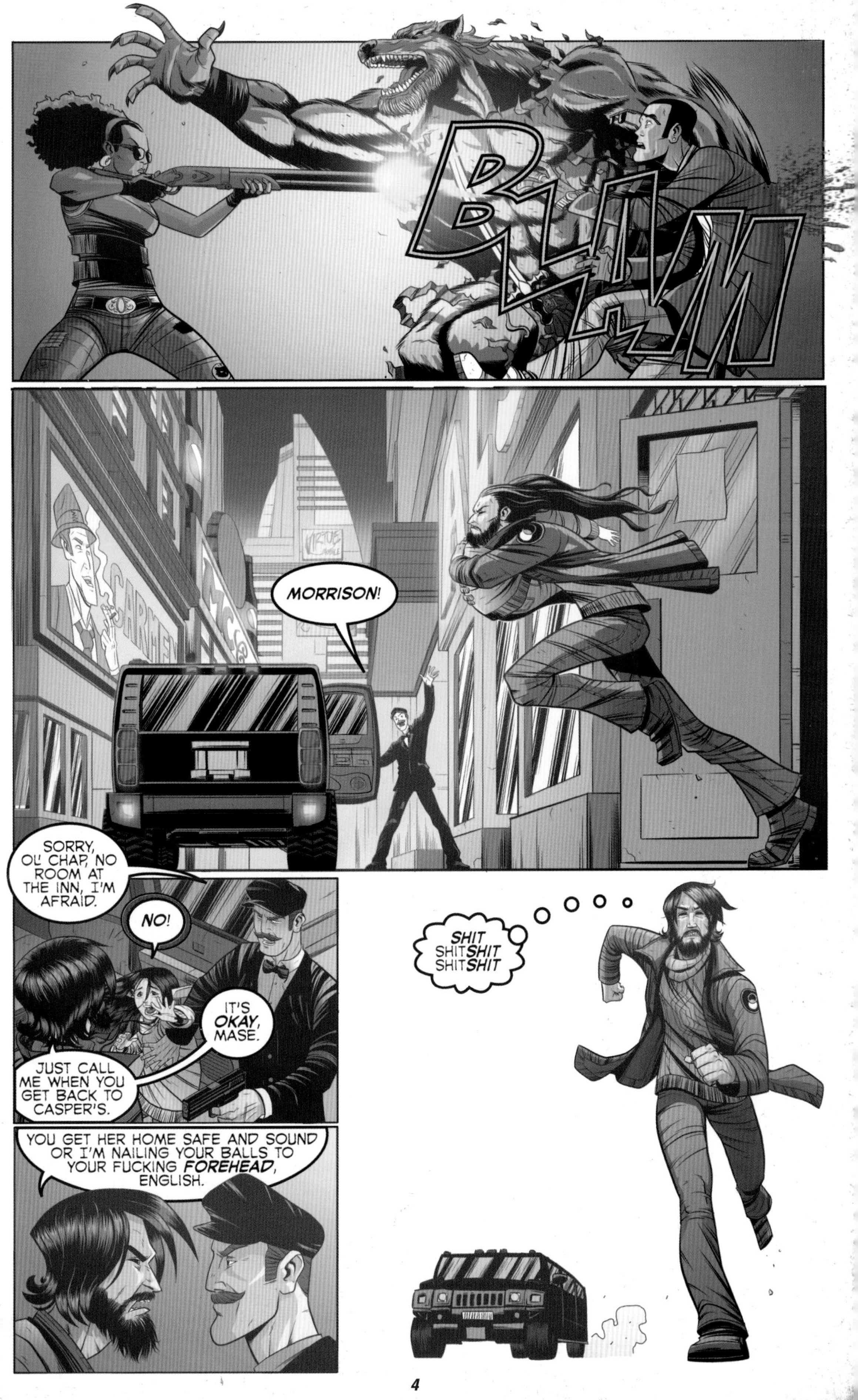
BLAMM
MORRISON!
SORRY, OL' CHAP, NO ROOM AT THE INN, I'M AFRAID.
NO!
IT'S OKAY, MASE.
JUST CALL ME WHEN YOU GET BACK TO CASPER'S.
SHIT SHITSHIT SHITSHIT
YOU GET HER HOME SAFE AND SOUND OR I'M NAILING YOUR BALLS TO YOUR FUCKING FOREHEAD, ENGLISH.

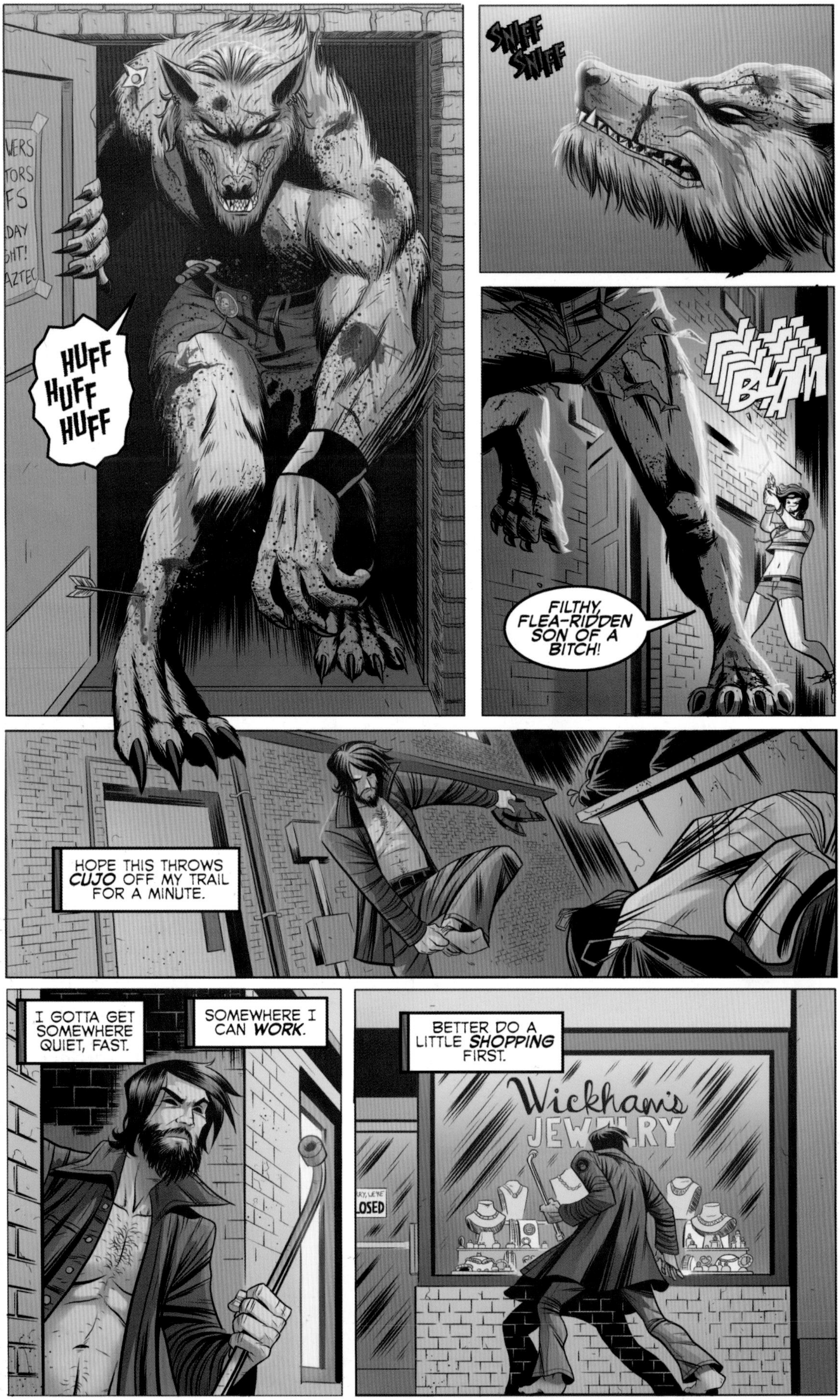
HUFF HUFF HUFF
SNIFF SNIFF
FILTHY, FLEA-RIDDEN SON OF A BITCH!
HOPE THIS THROWS CUJO OFF MY TRAIL FOR A MINUTE.
I GOTTA GET SOMEWHERE QUIET, FAST.
SOMEWHERE I CAN WORK.
BETTER DO A LITTLE SHOPPING FIRST.
Wickham's

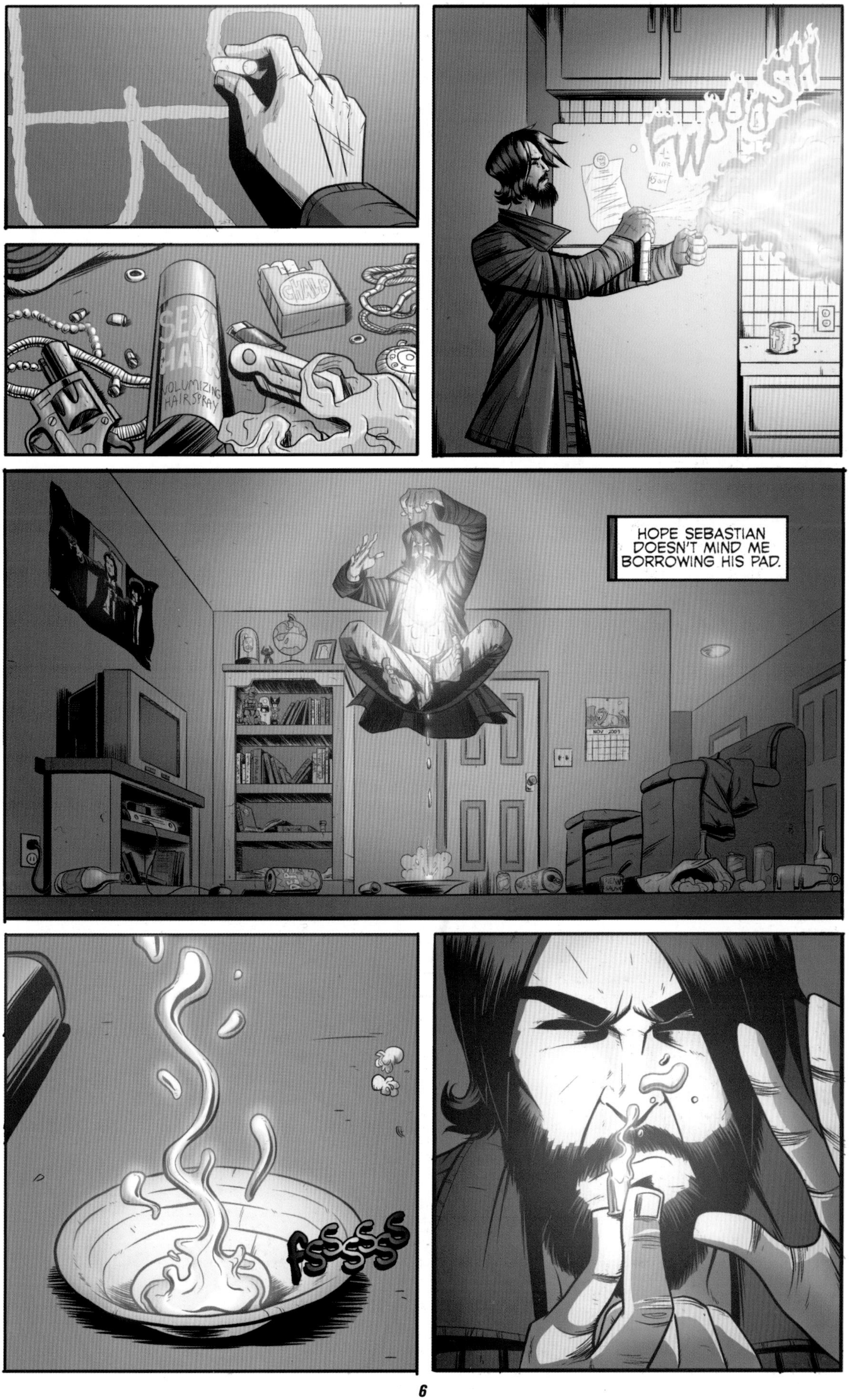
SEXY HAIR
VOLUMIZING HAIRSPRAY
CHALK
FWOOSH
HOPE SEBASTIAN DOESN'T MIND ME BORROWING HIS PAD.
FSSSSS

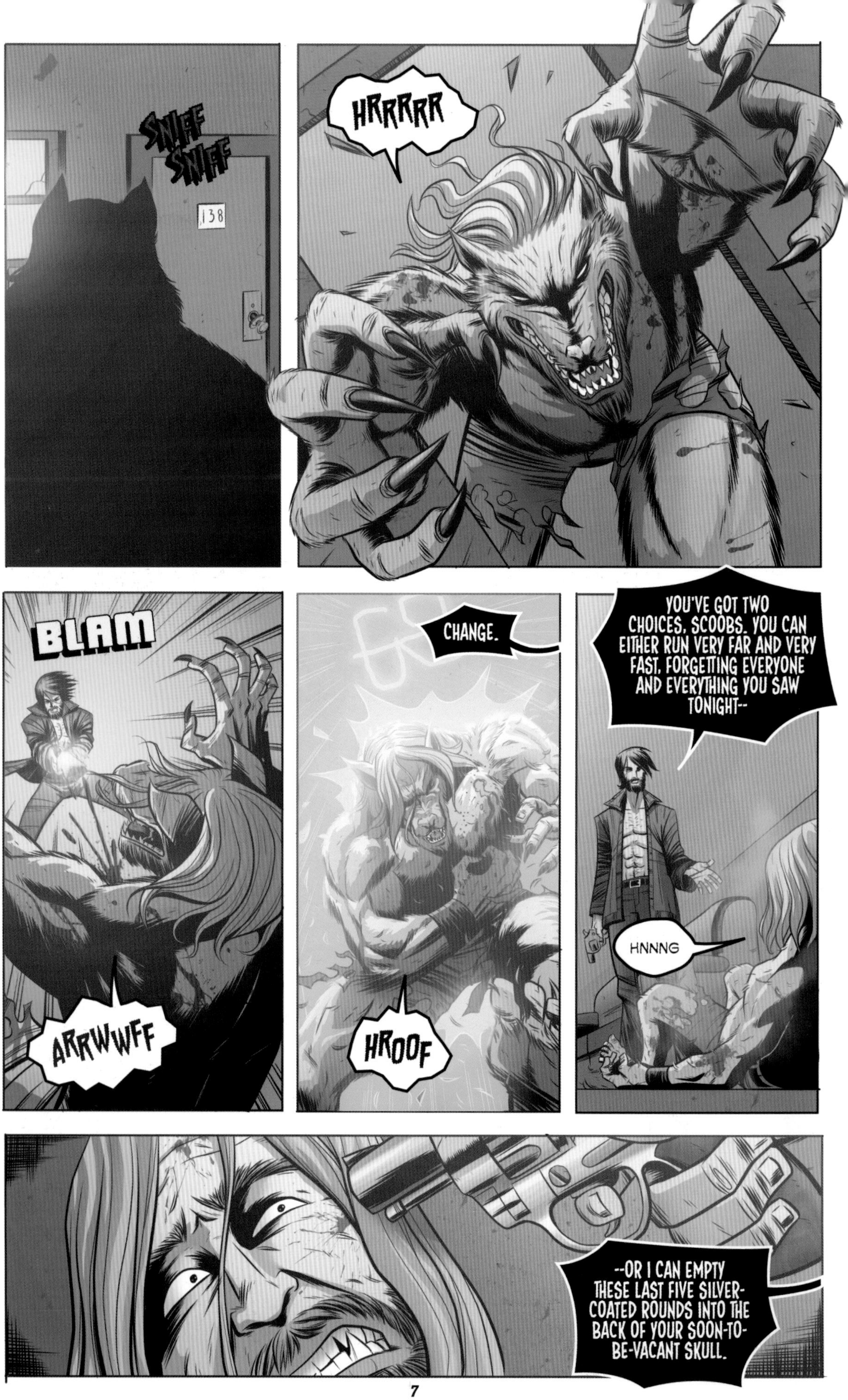
SNIFF SNIFF
138
HRRRRR
BLAM
ARRWWFF
CHANGE.
HROOF
YOU'VE GOT TWO CHOICES, SCOOBS. YOU CAN EITHER RUN VERY FAR AND VERY FAST, FORGETTING EVERYONE AND EVERYTHING YOU SAW TONIGHT--
HNNNG
--OR I CAN EMPTY THESE LAST FIVE SILVER-COATED ROUNDS INTO THE BACK OF YOUR SOON-TO-BE-VACANT SKULL.

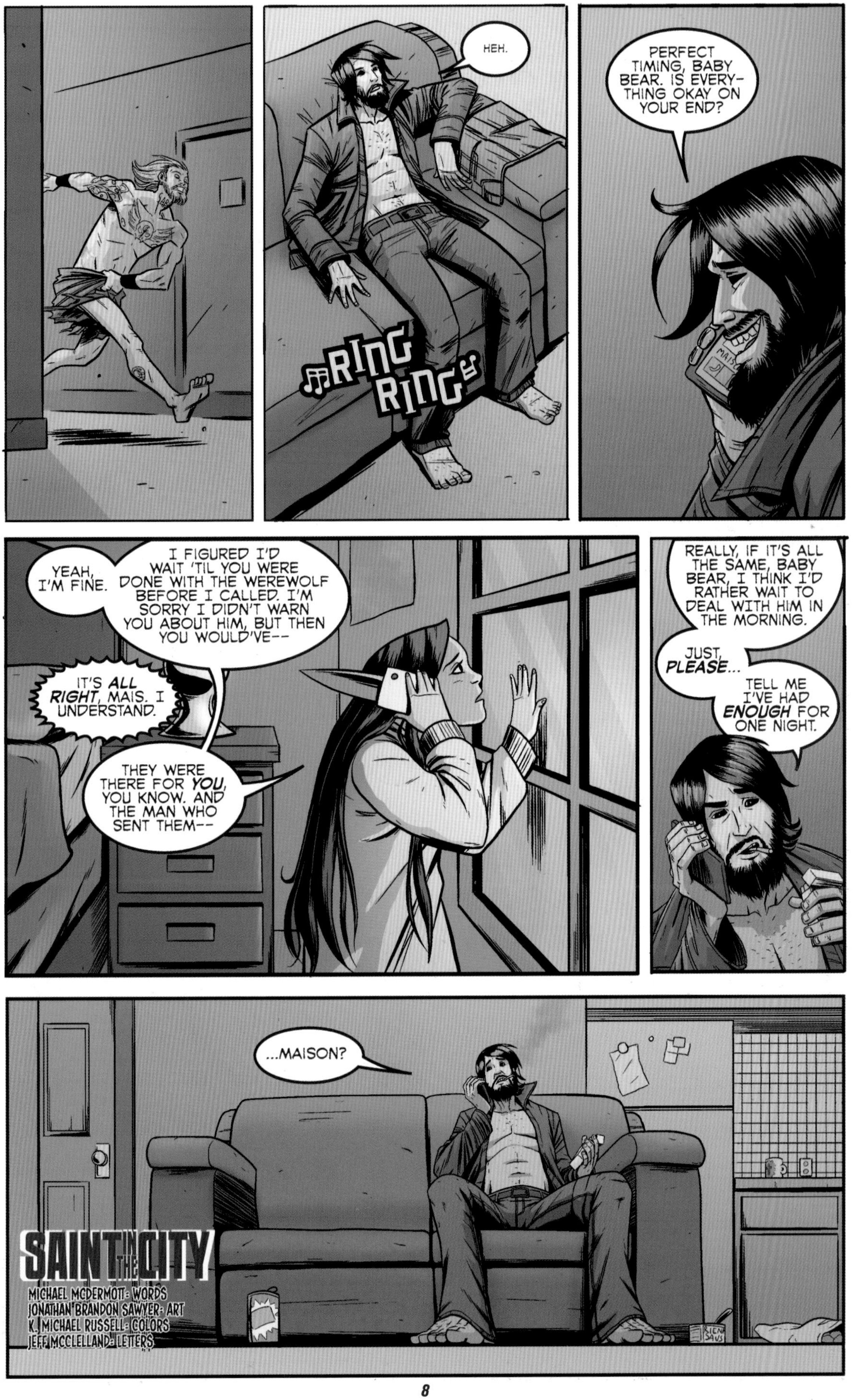
HEH.
RING RING
PERFECT TIMING, BABY BEAR. IS EVERY-THING OKAY ON YOUR END?
YEAH, I'M FINE.
I FIGURED I'D WAIT 'TIL YOU WERE DONE WITH THE WEREWOLF BEFORE I CALLED. I'M SORRY I DIDN'T WARN YOU ABOUT HIM, BUT THEN YOU WOULD'VE--
IT'S ALL RIGHT, MAIS. I UNDERSTAND.
THEY WERE THERE FOR YOU, YOU KNOW. AND THE MAN WHO SENT THEM--
REALLY, IF IT'S ALL THE SAME, BABY BEAR, I THINK I'D RATHER WAIT TO DEAL WITH HIM IN THE MORNING.
JUST, PLEASE...
TELL ME I'VE HAD ENOUGH FOR ONE NIGHT.
...MAISON?
SAINT IN THE CITY
MICHAEL MCDERMOTT: WORDS
JONATHAN BRANDON SAWYER: ART
K. MICHAEL RUSSELL: COLORS
JEFF MCCLELLAND: LETTERS

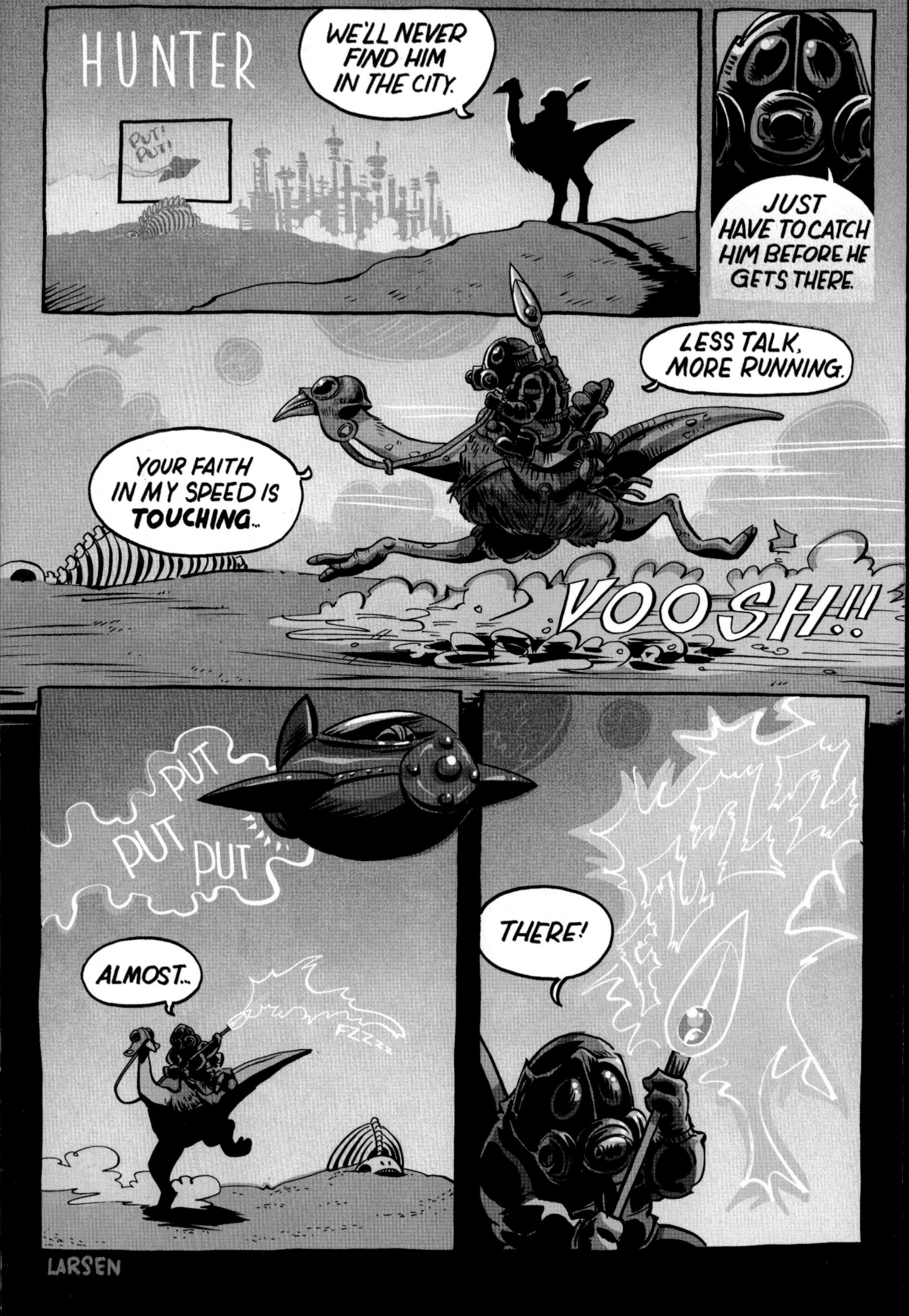
HUNTER
PUT! PUT!
WE'LL NEVER FIND HIM IN THE CITY.
JUST HAVE TO CATCH HIM BEFORE HE GETS THERE.
LESS TALK, MORE RUNNING.
YOUR FAITH IN MY SPEED IS TOUCHING...
VOOSH!!
PUT PUT PUT PUT
ALMOST...
FZZZZ
THERE!
LARSEN

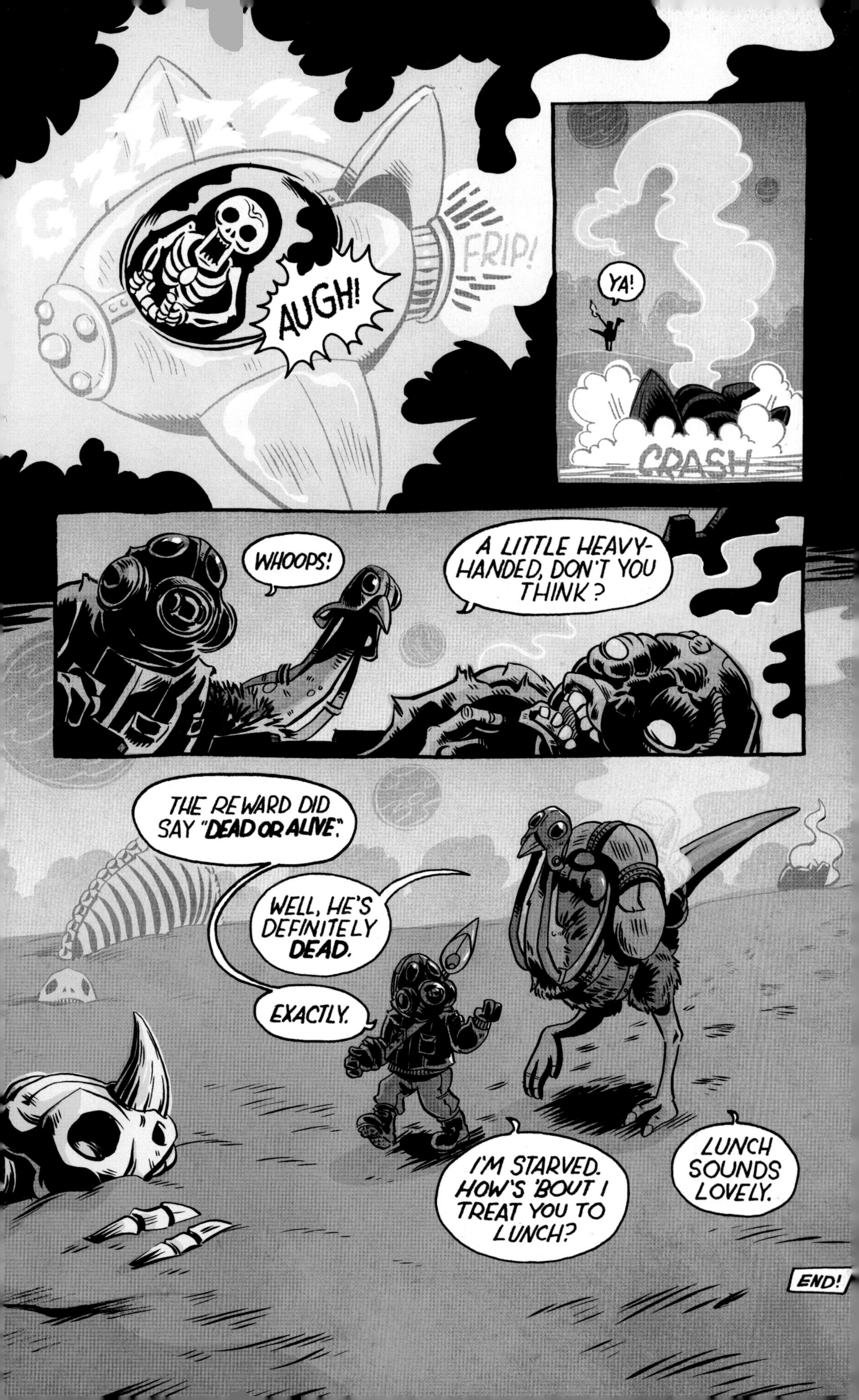
GZZZZZ
AUGH!
FRIP!
YA!
CRASH
WHOOPS!
A LITTLE HEAVY-HANDED, DON'T YOU THINK?
THE REWARD DID SAY "DEAD OR ALIVE".
WELL, HE'S DEFINITELY DEAD.
EXACTLY.
I'M STARVED. HOW'S 'BOUT I TREAT YOU TO LUNCH?
LUNCH SOUNDS LOVELY.
END!

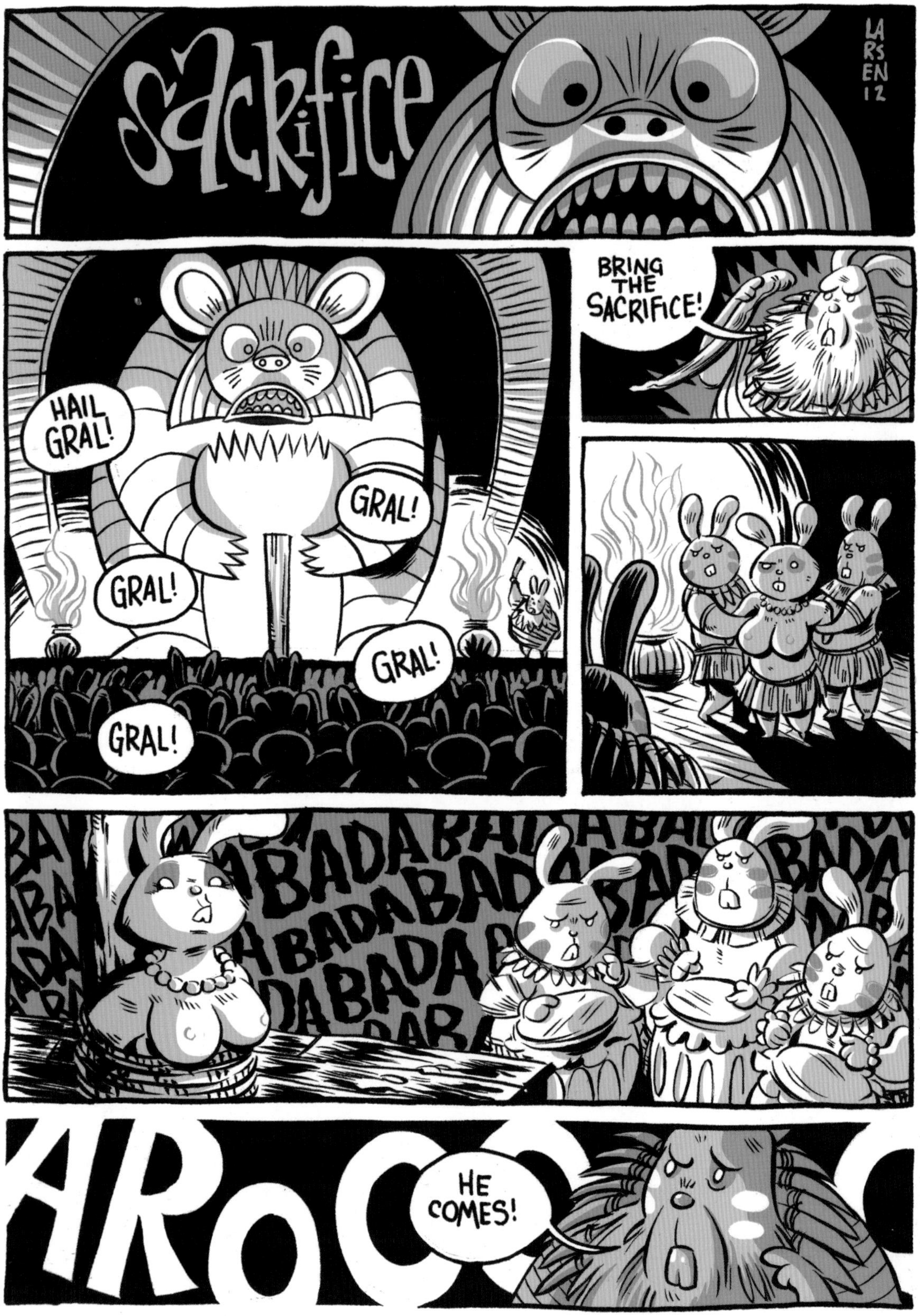
Sackrifice
LARSEN 12
HAIL GRAL!
GRAL!
GRAL!
GRAL!
GRAL!
BRING THE SACRIFICE!
BADABADA
AROO
HE COMES!

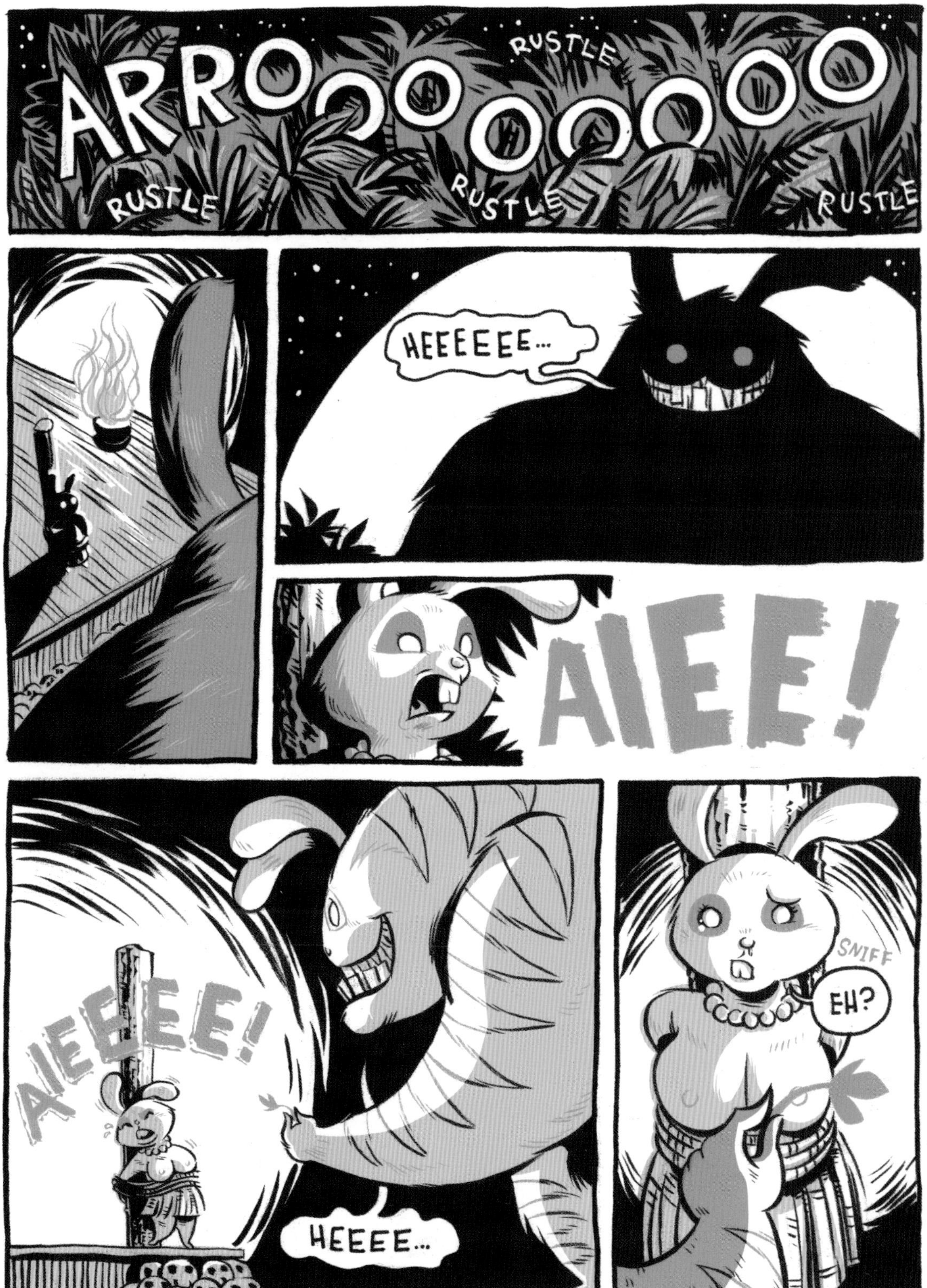
ARROOOOOOOOO
RUSTLE
RUSTLE
RUSTLE
RUSTLE
HEEEEEE...
AIEE!
AIEEEE!
HEEEE...
SNIFF
EH?

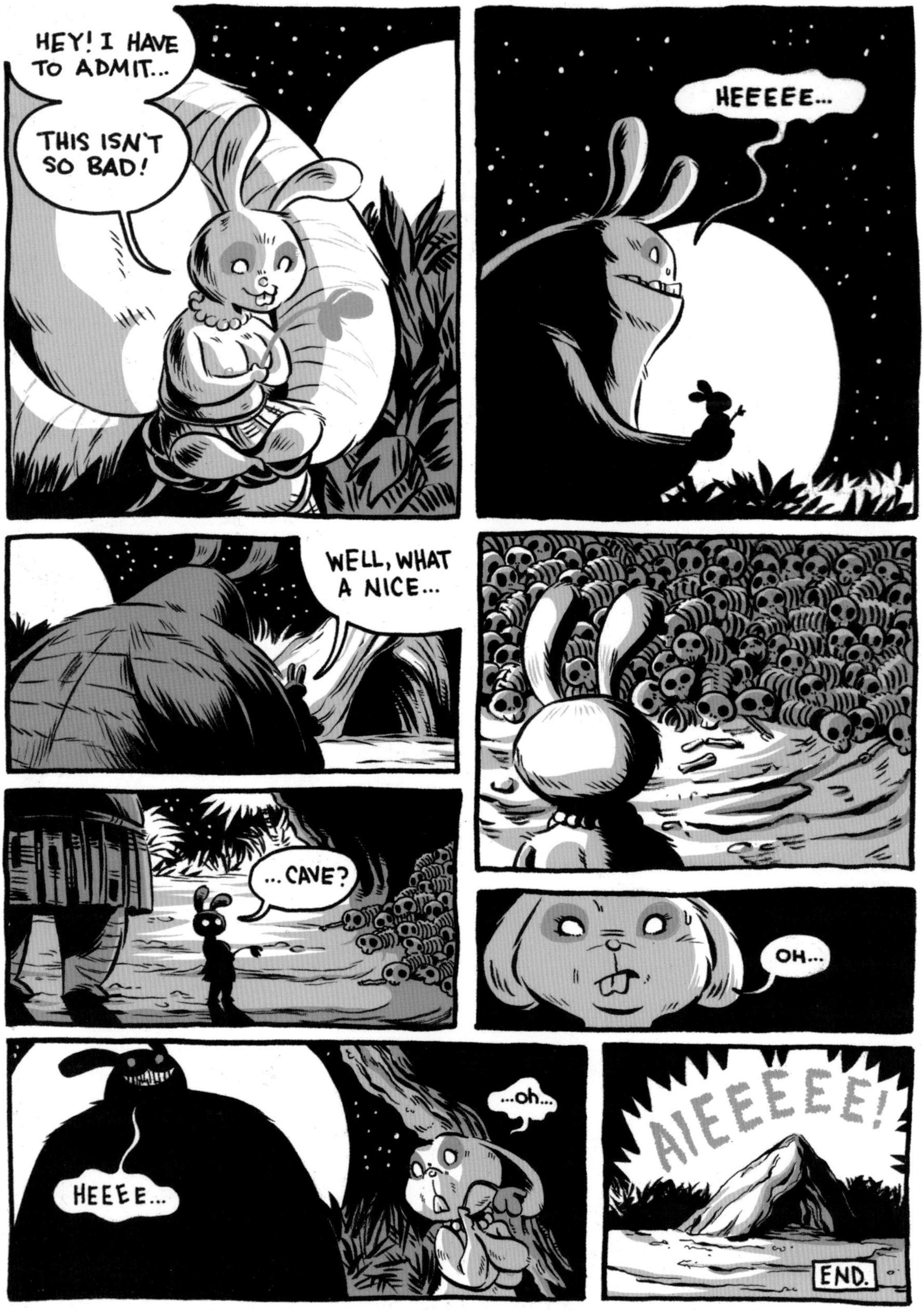
HEY! I HAVE TO ADMIT...
THIS ISN'T SO BAD!
HEEEEE...
WELL, WHAT A NICE...
...CAVE?
OH...
HEEEE...
...oh...
AIEEEEEE!
END.

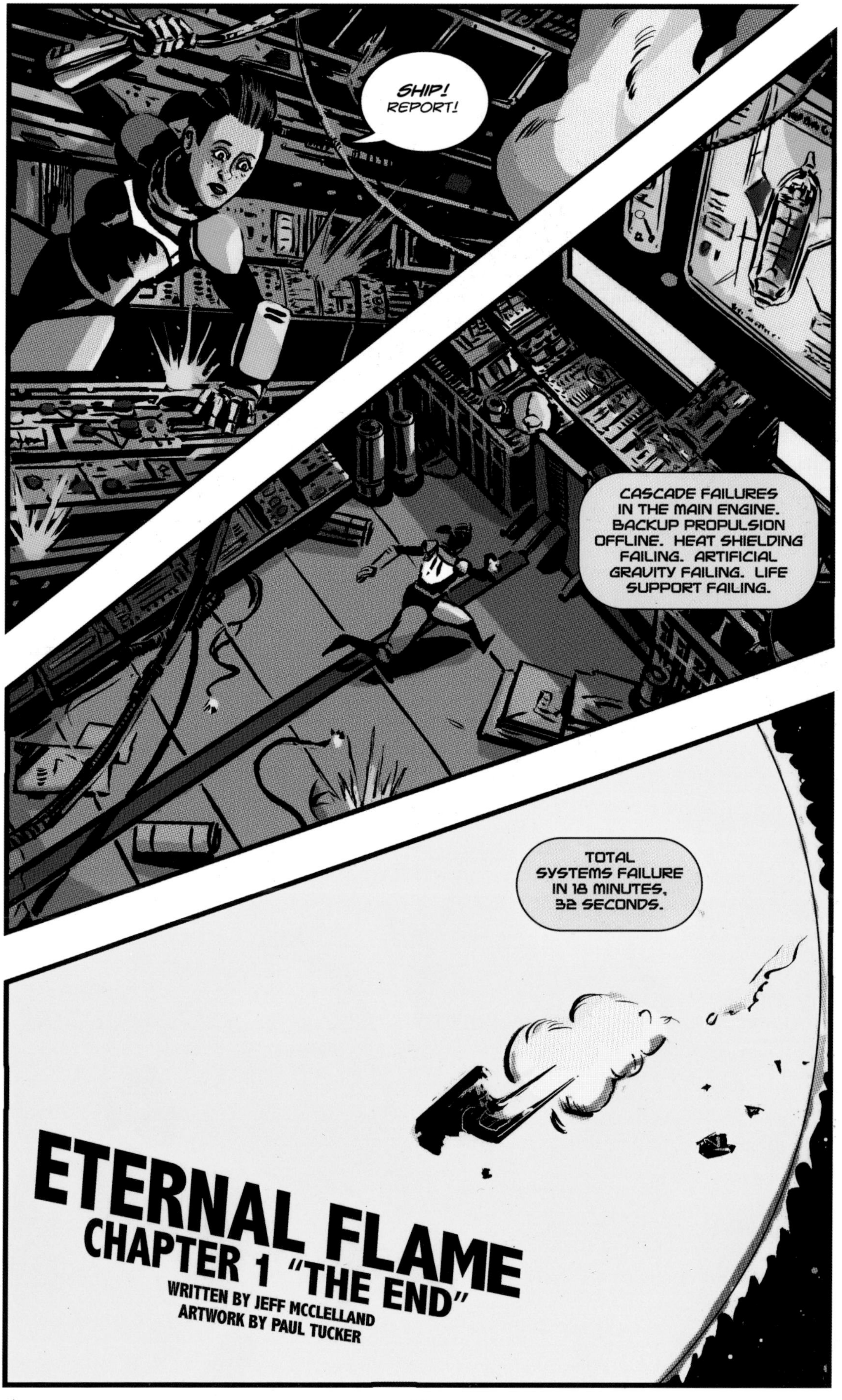
SHIP! REPORT!
CASCADE FAILURES IN THE MAIN ENGINE. BACKUP PROPULSION OFFLINE. HEAT SHIELDING FAILING. ARTIFICIAL GRAVITY FAILING. LIFE SUPPORT FAILING.
TOTAL SYSTEMS FAILURE IN 18 MINUTES, 32 SECONDS.
ETERNAL FLAME
CHAPTER 1 "THE END"
WRITTEN BY JEFF MCCLELLAND
ARTWORK BY PAUL TUCKER

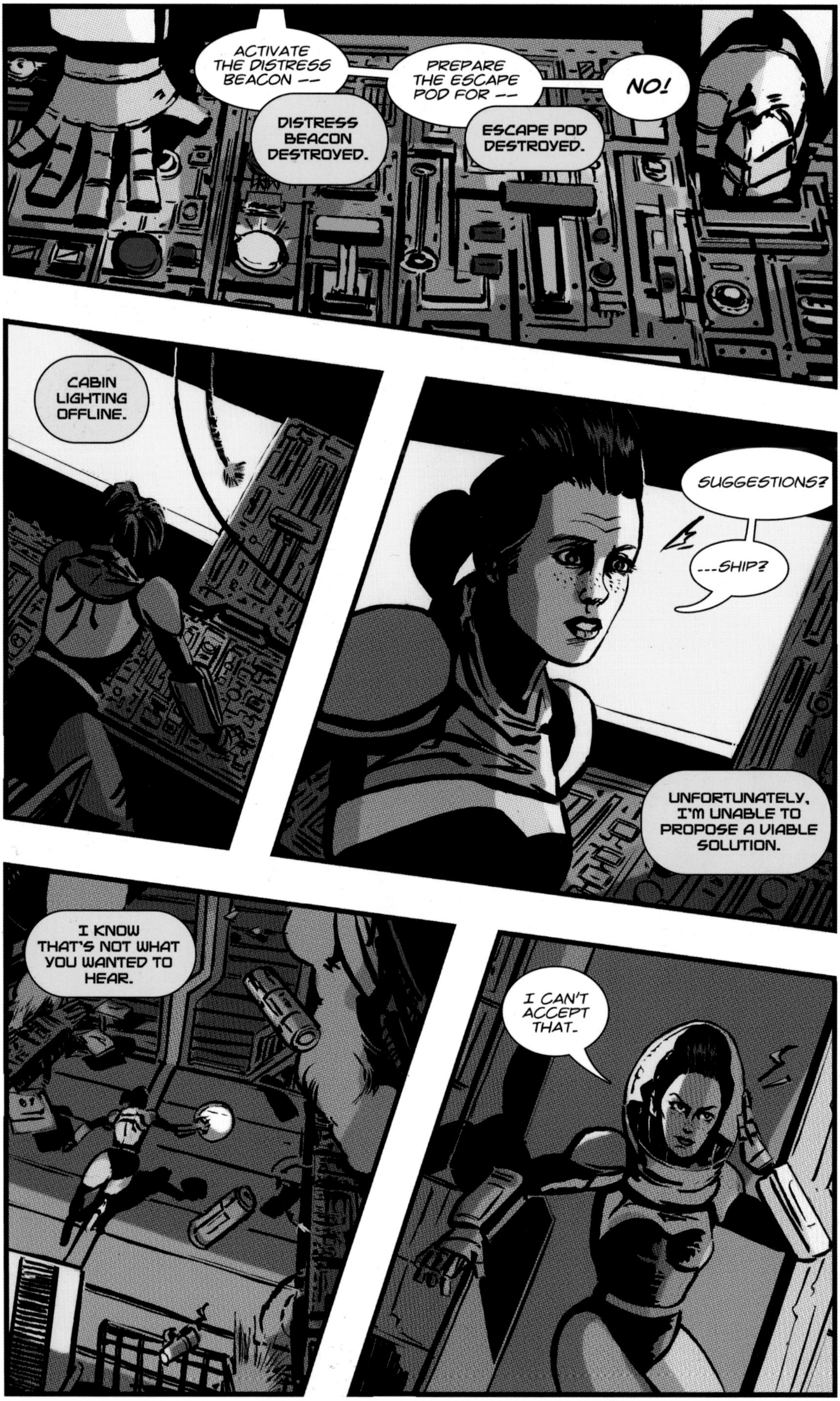
ACTIVATE THE DISTRESS BEACON --
DISTRESS BEACON DESTROYED.
PREPARE THE ESCAPE POD FOR --
ESCAPE POD DESTROYED.
NO!
CABIN LIGHTING OFFLINE.
SUGGESTIONS?
---SHIP?
UNFORTUNATELY, I'M UNABLE TO PROPOSE A VIABLE SOLUTION.
I KNOW THAT'S NOT WHAT YOU WANTED TO HEAR.
I CAN'T ACCEPT THAT.

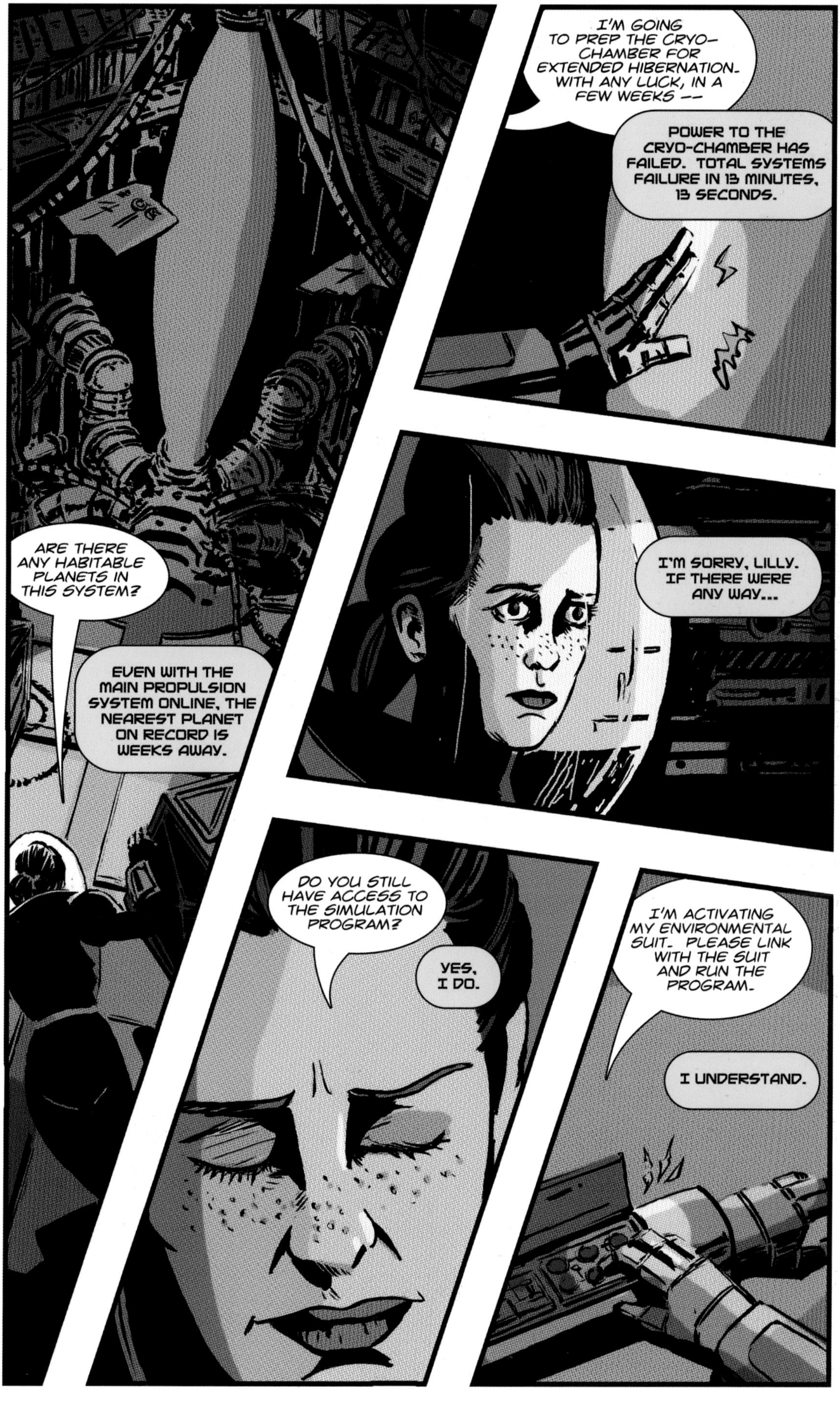
ARE THERE ANY HABITABLE PLANETS IN THIS SYSTEM?
EVEN WITH THE MAIN PROPULSION SYSTEM ONLINE, THE NEAREST PLANET ON RECORD IS WEEKS AWAY.
I'M GOING TO PREP THE CRYO-CHAMBER FOR EXTENDED HIBERNATION. WITH ANY LUCK, IN A FEW WEEKS --
POWER TO THE CRYO-CHAMBER HAS FAILED. TOTAL SYSTEMS FAILURE IN 13 MINUTES, 13 SECONDS.
I'M SORRY, LILLY. IF THERE WERE ANY WAY...
DO YOU STILL HAVE ACCESS TO THE SIMULATION PROGRAM?
YES, I DO.
I'M ACTIVATING MY ENVIRONMENTAL SUIT. PLEASE LINK WITH THE SUIT AND RUN THE PROGRAM.
I UNDERSTAND.

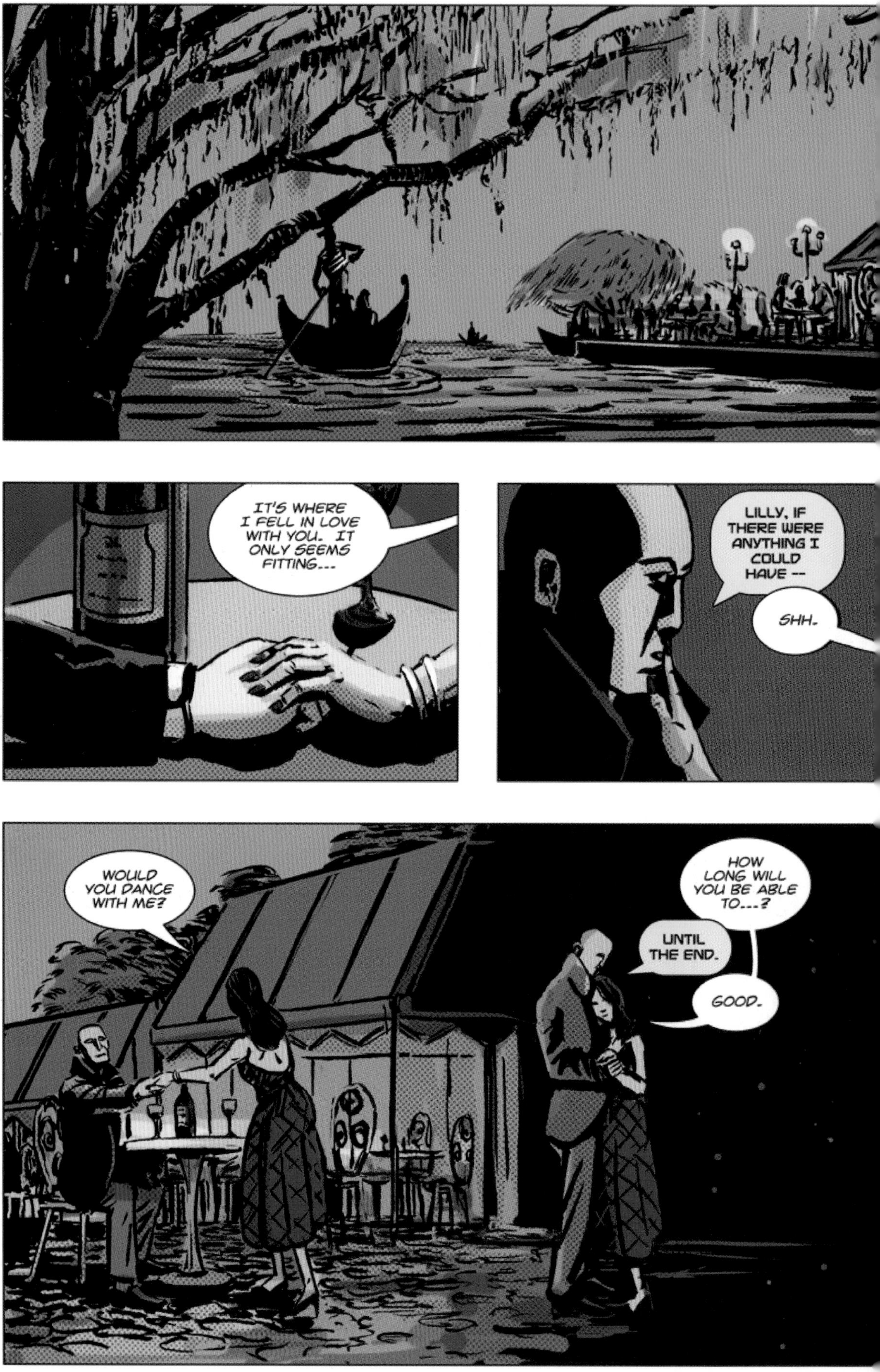
IT'S WHERE I FELL IN LOVE WITH YOU. IT ONLY SEEMS FITTING...
LILLY, IF THERE WERE ANYTHING I COULD HAVE --
SHH.
WOULD YOU DANCE WITH ME?
HOW LONG WILL YOU BE ABLE TO...?
UNTIL THE END.
GOOD.

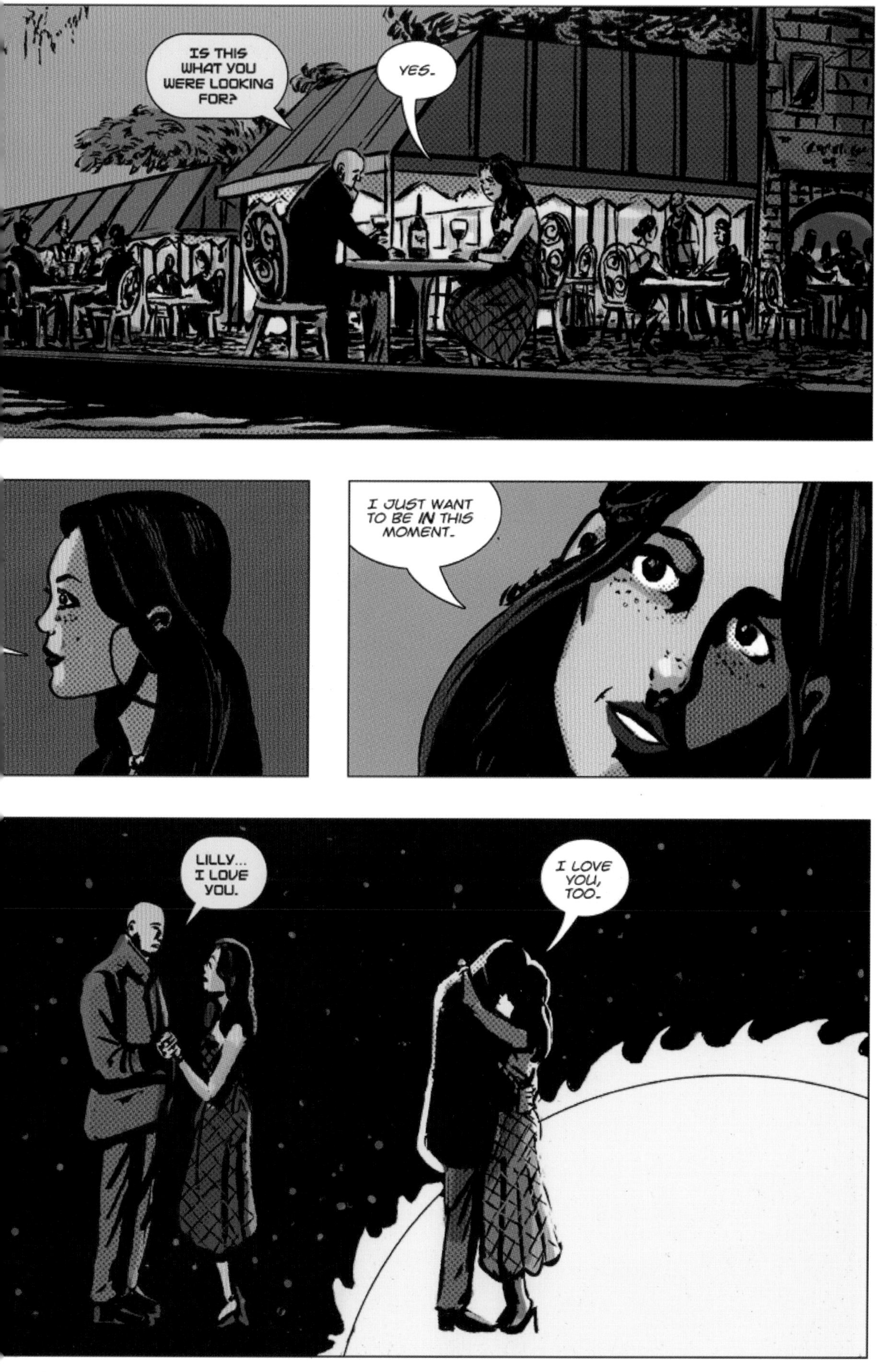
IS THIS WHAT YOU WERE LOOKING FOR?
YES.
I JUST WANT TO BE IN THIS MOMENT.
LILLY... I LOVE YOU.
I LOVE YOU, TOO.

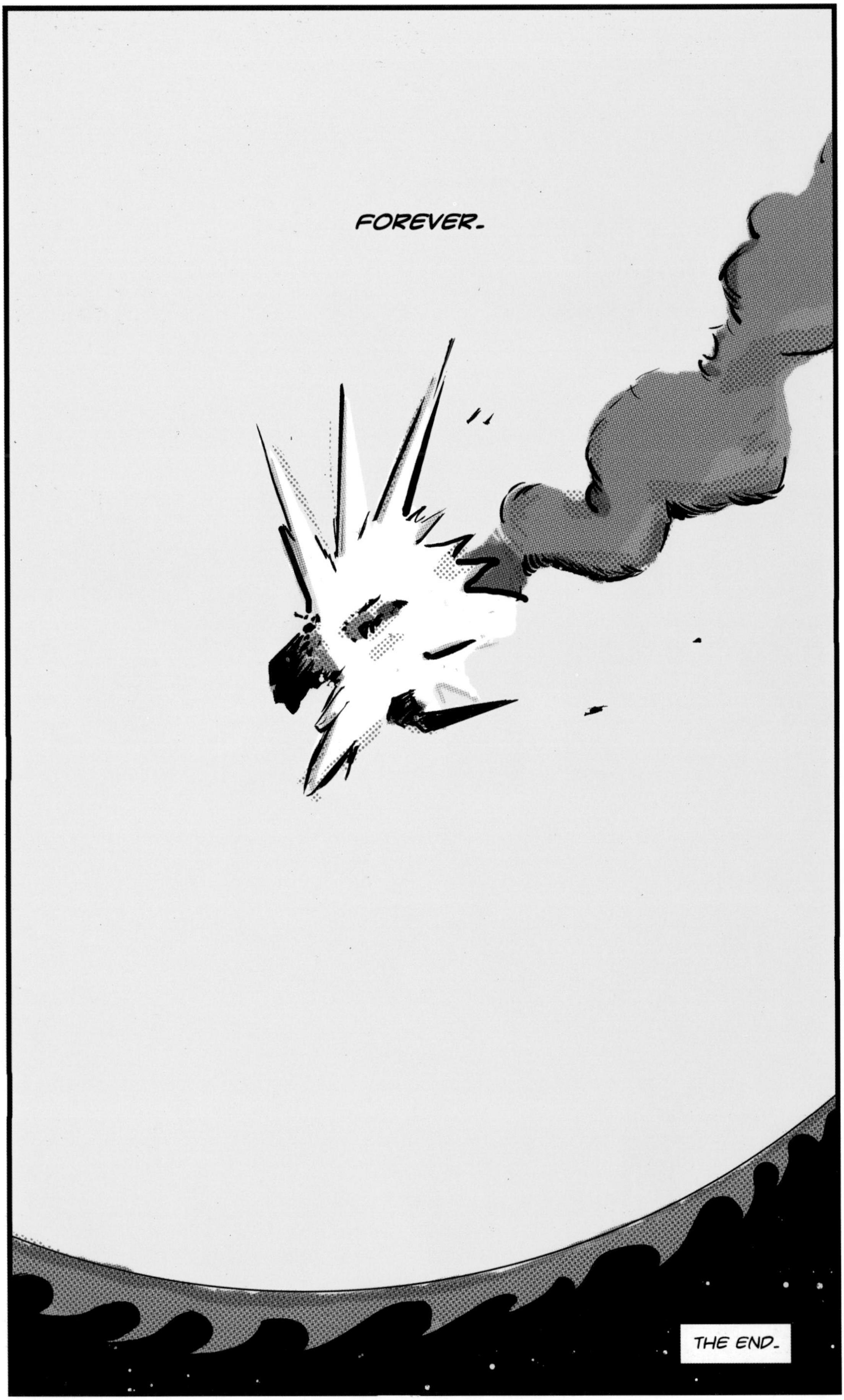
FOREVER.
THE END.

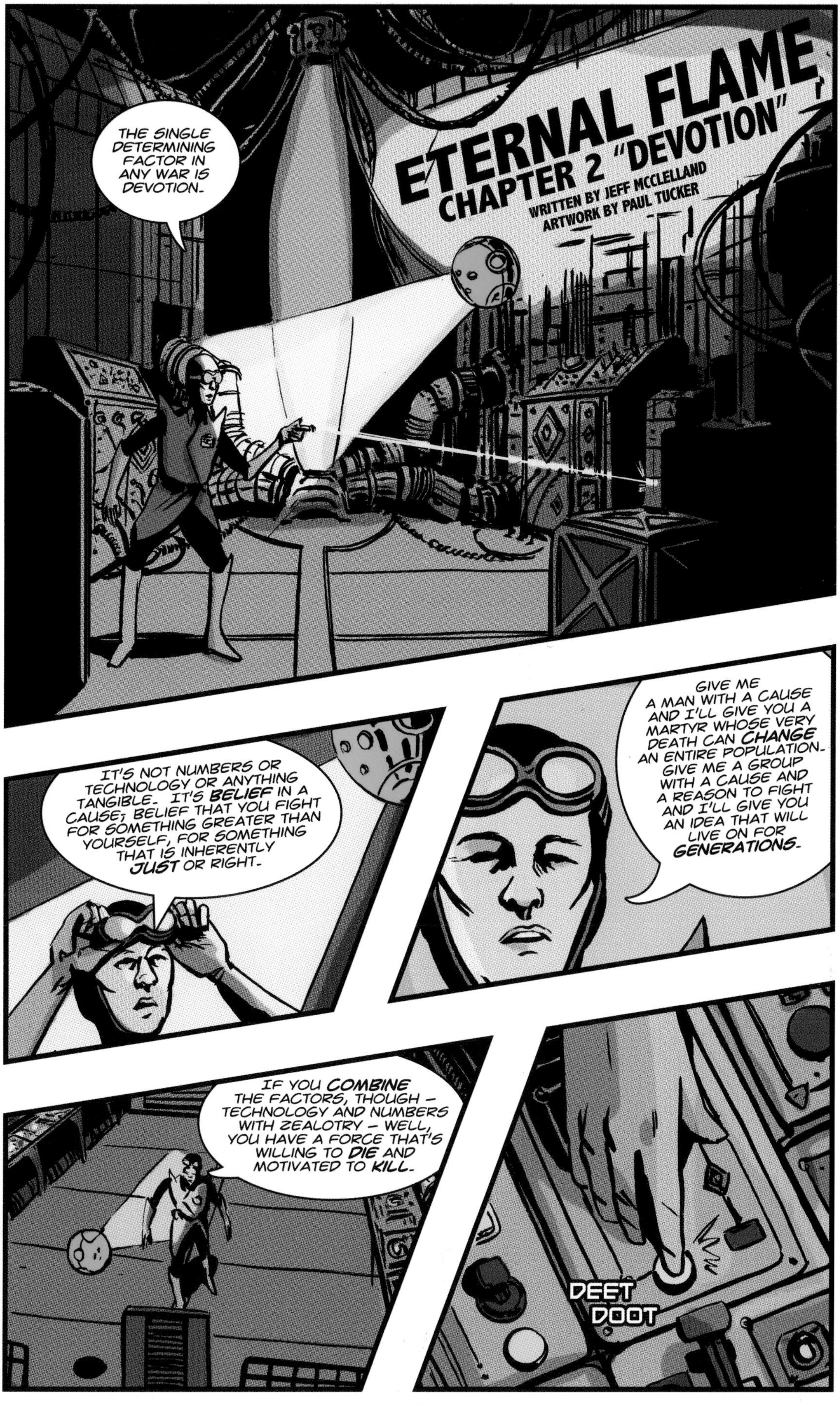
ETERNAL FLAME
CHAPTER 2 "DEVOTION"
WRITTEN BY JEFF MCCLELLAND
ARTWORK BY PAUL TUCKER
THE SINGLE DETERMINING FACTOR IN ANY WAR IS DEVOTION.
IT'S NOT NUMBERS OR TECHNOLOGY OR ANYTHING TANGIBLE. IT'S BELIEF IN A CAUSE; BELIEF THAT YOU FIGHT FOR SOMETHING GREATER THAN YOURSELF, FOR SOMETHING THAT IS INHERENTLY JUST OR RIGHT.
GIVE ME A MAN WITH A CAUSE AND I'LL GIVE YOU A MARTYR WHOSE VERY DEATH CAN CHANGE AN ENTIRE POPULATION. GIVE ME A GROUP WITH A CAUSE AND A REASON TO FIGHT AND I'LL GIVE YOU AN IDEA THAT WILL LIVE ON FOR GENERATIONS.
IF YOU COMBINE THE FACTORS, THOUGH – TECHNOLOGY AND NUMBERS WITH ZEALOTRY – WELL, YOU HAVE A FORCE THAT'S WILLING TO DIE AND MOTIVATED TO KILL.
DEET
DOOT

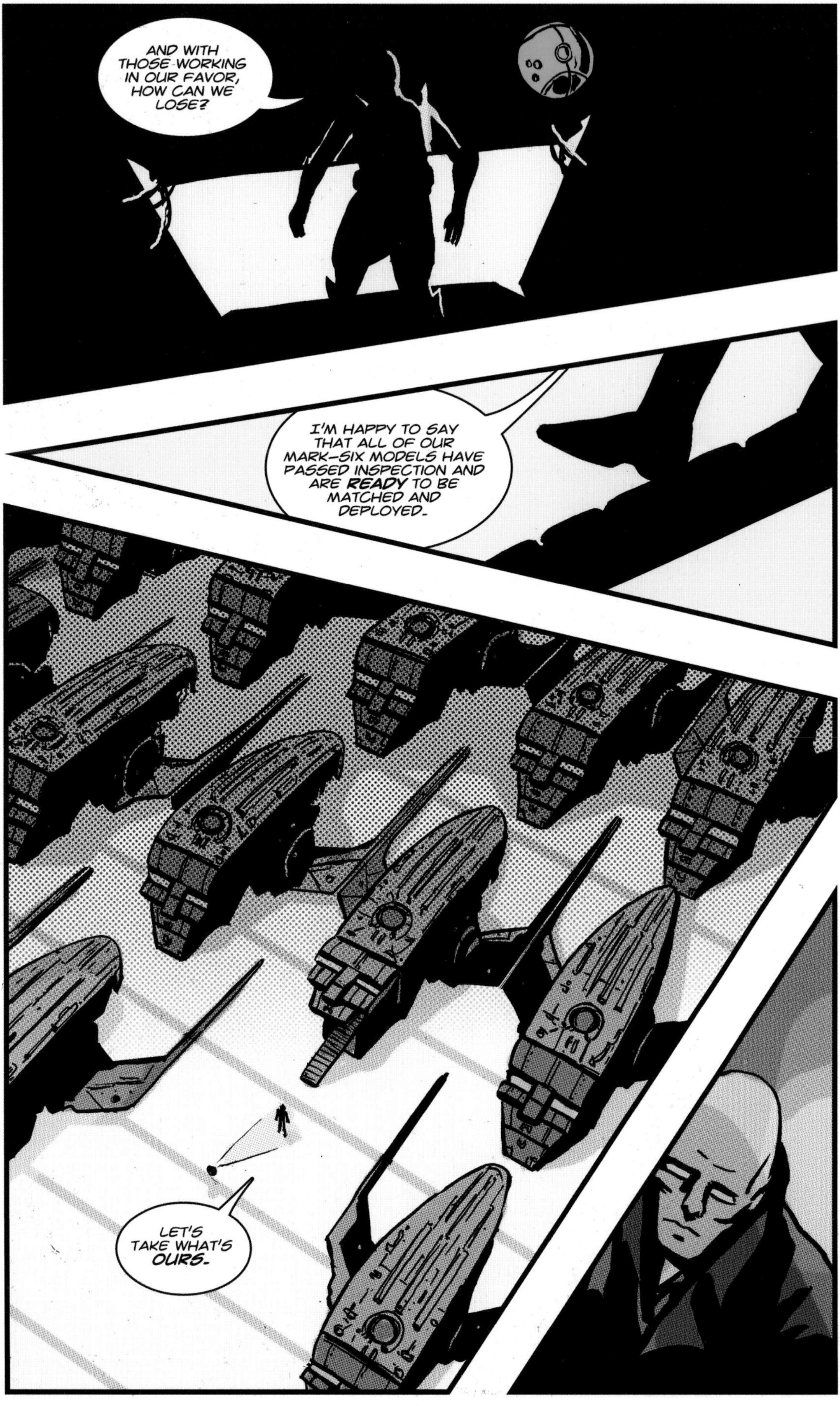
AND WITH THOSE WORKING IN OUR FAVOR, HOW CAN WE LOSE?
I'M HAPPY TO SAY THAT ALL OF OUR MARK-SIX MODELS HAVE PASSED INSPECTION AND ARE READY TO BE MATCHED AND DEPLOYED.
LET'S TAKE WHAT'S OURS.

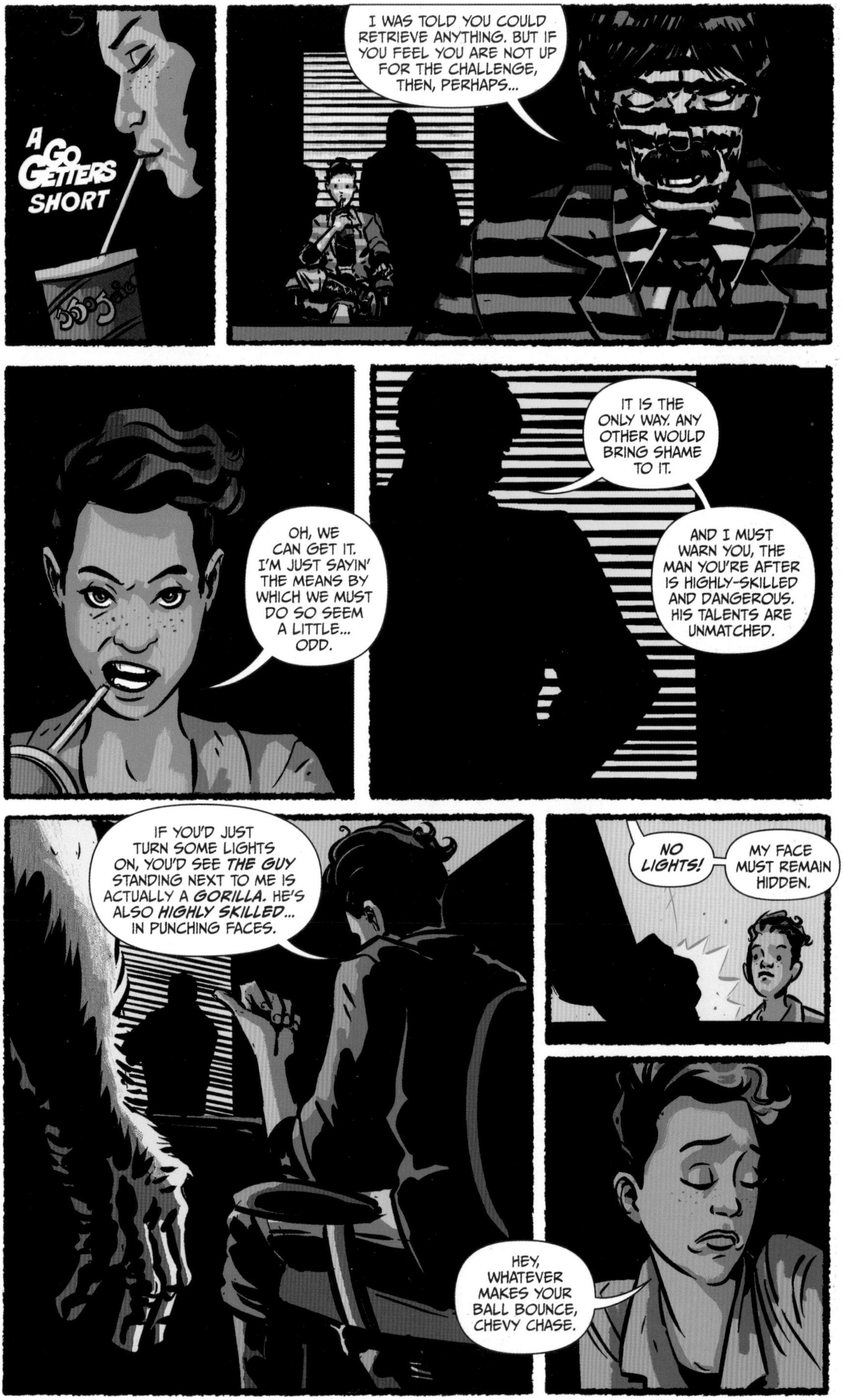
A GO GETTERS SHORT
I WAS TOLD YOU COULD RETRIEVE ANYTHING. BUT IF YOU FEEL YOU ARE NOT UP FOR THE CHALLENGE, THEN, PERHAPS...
OH, WE CAN GET IT. I'M JUST SAYIN' THE MEANS BY WHICH WE MUST DO SO SEEM A LITTLE... ODD.
IT IS THE ONLY WAY. ANY OTHER WOULD BRING SHAME TO IT.
AND I MUST WARN YOU, THE MAN YOU'RE AFTER IS HIGHLY-SKILLED AND DANGEROUS. HIS TALENTS ARE UNMATCHED.
IF YOU'D JUST TURN SOME LIGHTS ON, YOU'D SEE *THE GUY* STANDING NEXT TO ME IS ACTUALLY A *GORILLA.* HE'S ALSO *HIGHLY SKILLED...* IN PUNCHING FACES.
NO LIGHTS!
MY FACE MUST REMAIN HIDDEN.
HEY, WHATEVER MAKES YOUR BALL BOUNCE, CHEVY CHASE.

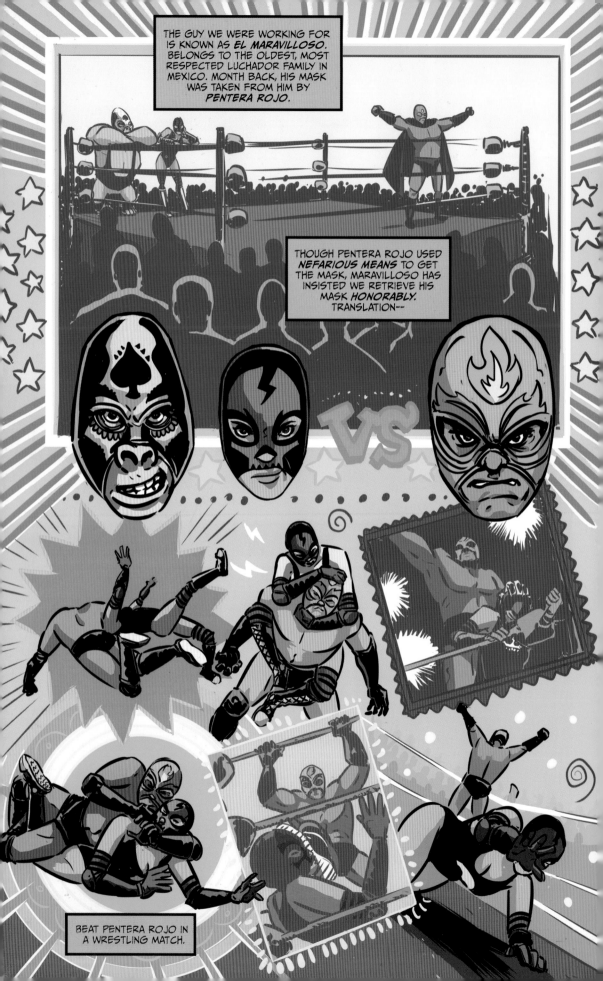

THE GUY WE WERE WORKING FOR IS KNOWN AS *EL MARAVILLOSO.* BELONGS TO THE OLDEST, MOST RESPECTED LUCHADOR FAMILY IN MEXICO. MONTH BACK, HIS MASK WAS TAKEN FROM HIM BY *PENTERA ROJO.*

THOUGH PENTERA ROJO USED *NEFARIOUS MEANS* TO GET THE MASK, MARAVILLOSO HAS INSISTED WE RETRIEVE HIS MASK *HONORABLY.* TRANSLATION--

VS

BEAT PENTERA ROJO IN A WRESTLING MATCH.

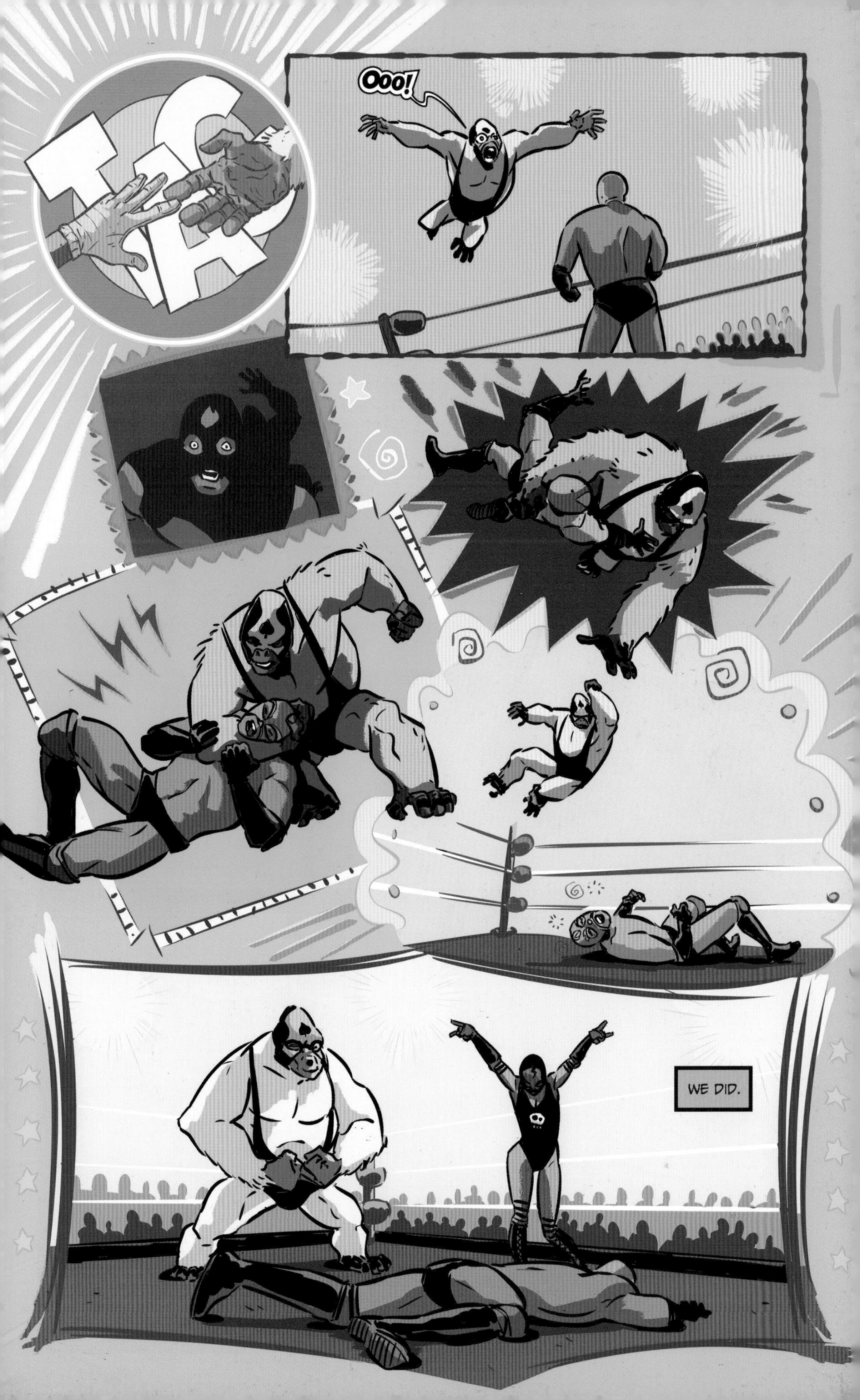
TAG
Ooo!
WE DID.

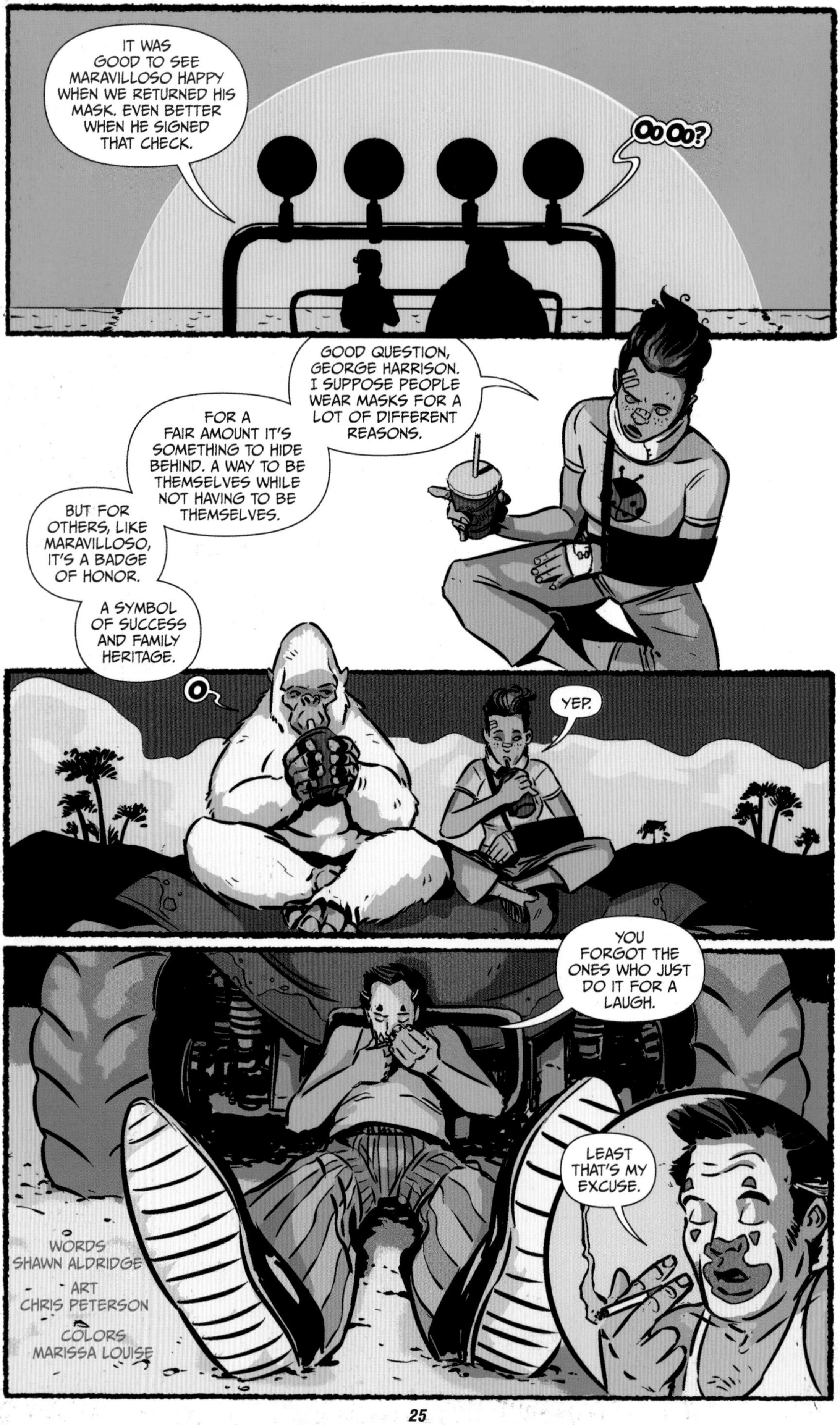
IT WAS GOOD TO SEE MARAVILLOSO HAPPY WHEN WE RETURNED HIS MASK. EVEN BETTER WHEN HE SIGNED THAT CHECK.
OoOo?
GOOD QUESTION, GEORGE HARRISON. I SUPPOSE PEOPLE WEAR MASKS FOR A LOT OF DIFFERENT REASONS.
FOR A FAIR AMOUNT IT'S SOMETHING TO HIDE BEHIND. A WAY TO BE THEMSELVES WHILE NOT HAVING TO BE THEMSELVES.
BUT FOR OTHERS, LIKE MARAVILLOSO, IT'S A BADGE OF HONOR.
A SYMBOL OF SUCCESS AND FAMILY HERITAGE.
O
YEP.
YOU FORGOT THE ONES WHO JUST DO IT FOR A LAUGH.
LEAST THAT'S MY EXCUSE.
WORDS SHAWN ALDRIDGE
ART CHRIS PETERSON
COLORS MARISSA LOUISE

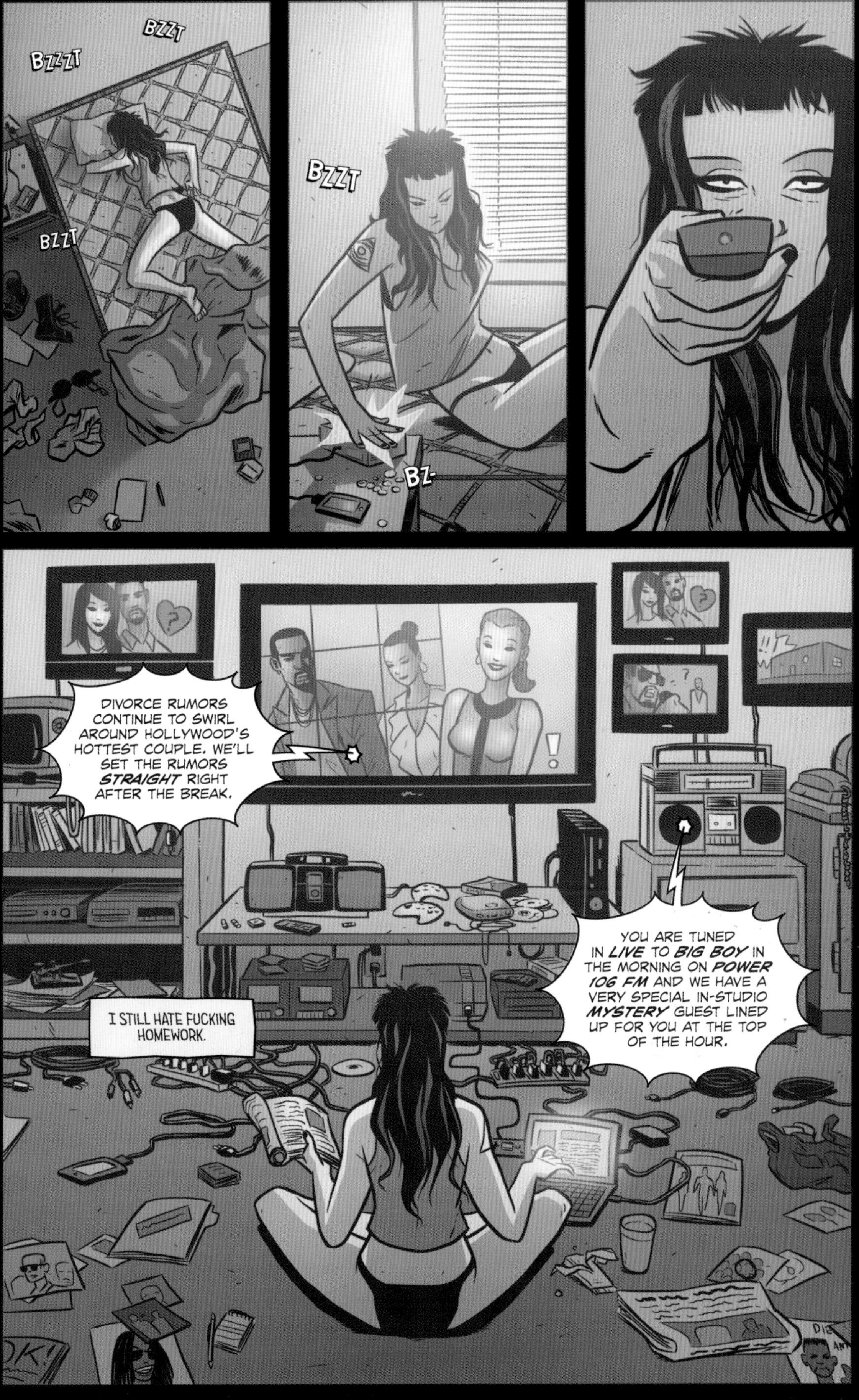
BZZZT
BZZT
BZZT
BZZT
BZ-
DIVORCE RUMORS CONTINUE TO SWIRL AROUND HOLLYWOOD'S HOTTEST COUPLE. WE'LL SET THE RUMORS STRAIGHT RIGHT AFTER THE BREAK.
YOU ARE TUNED IN LIVE TO BIG BOY IN THE MORNING ON POWER 106 FM AND WE HAVE A VERY SPECIAL IN-STUDIO MYSTERY GUEST LINED UP FOR YOU AT THE TOP OF THE HOUR.
I STILL HATE FUCKING HOMEWORK.

IMAGINARY DRUGS PRESENTS **MURDER CULTURE** STORY MICHAEL MCDERMOTT LINE ART JONATHAN BRANDON SAWYER COLORS K MICHAEL RUSSELL LETTERS NIC J SHAW

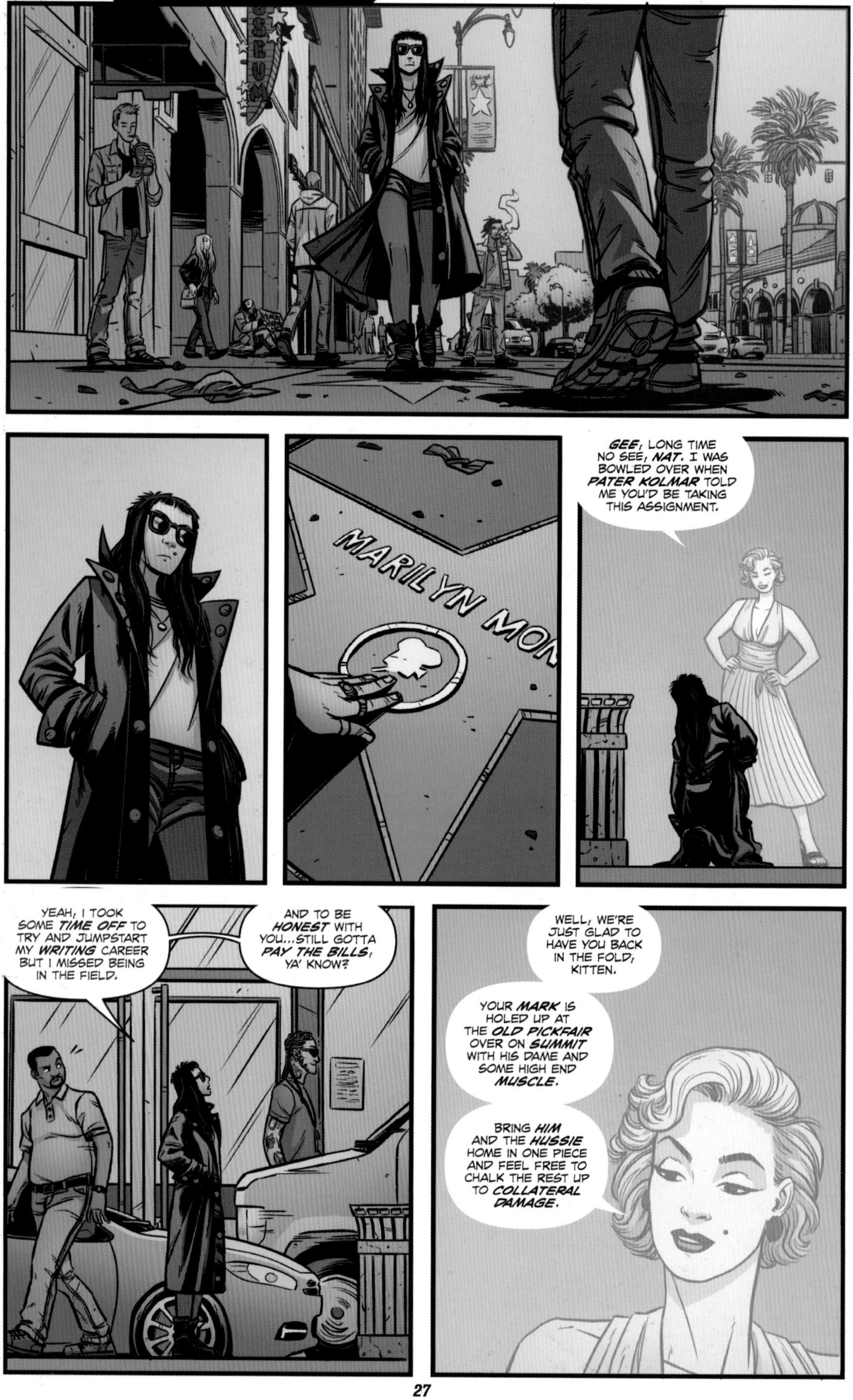

MUSEUM
GEE; LONG TIME NO SEE, NAT. I WAS BOWLED OVER WHEN PATER KOLMAR TOLD ME YOU'D BE TAKING THIS ASSIGNMENT.
MARILYN MON
YEAH, I TOOK SOME TIME OFF TO TRY AND JUMPSTART MY WRITING CAREER BUT I MISSED BEING IN THE FIELD.
AND TO BE HONEST WITH YOU...STILL GOTTA PAY THE BILLS, YA' KNOW?
WELL, WE'RE JUST GLAD TO HAVE YOU BACK IN THE FOLD, KITTEN.
YOUR MARK IS HOLED UP AT THE OLD PICKFAIR OVER ON SUMMIT WITH HIS DAME AND SOME HIGH END MUSCLE.
BRING HIM AND THE HUSSIE HOME IN ONE PIECE AND FEEL FREE TO CHALK THE REST UP TO COLLATERAL DAMAGE.

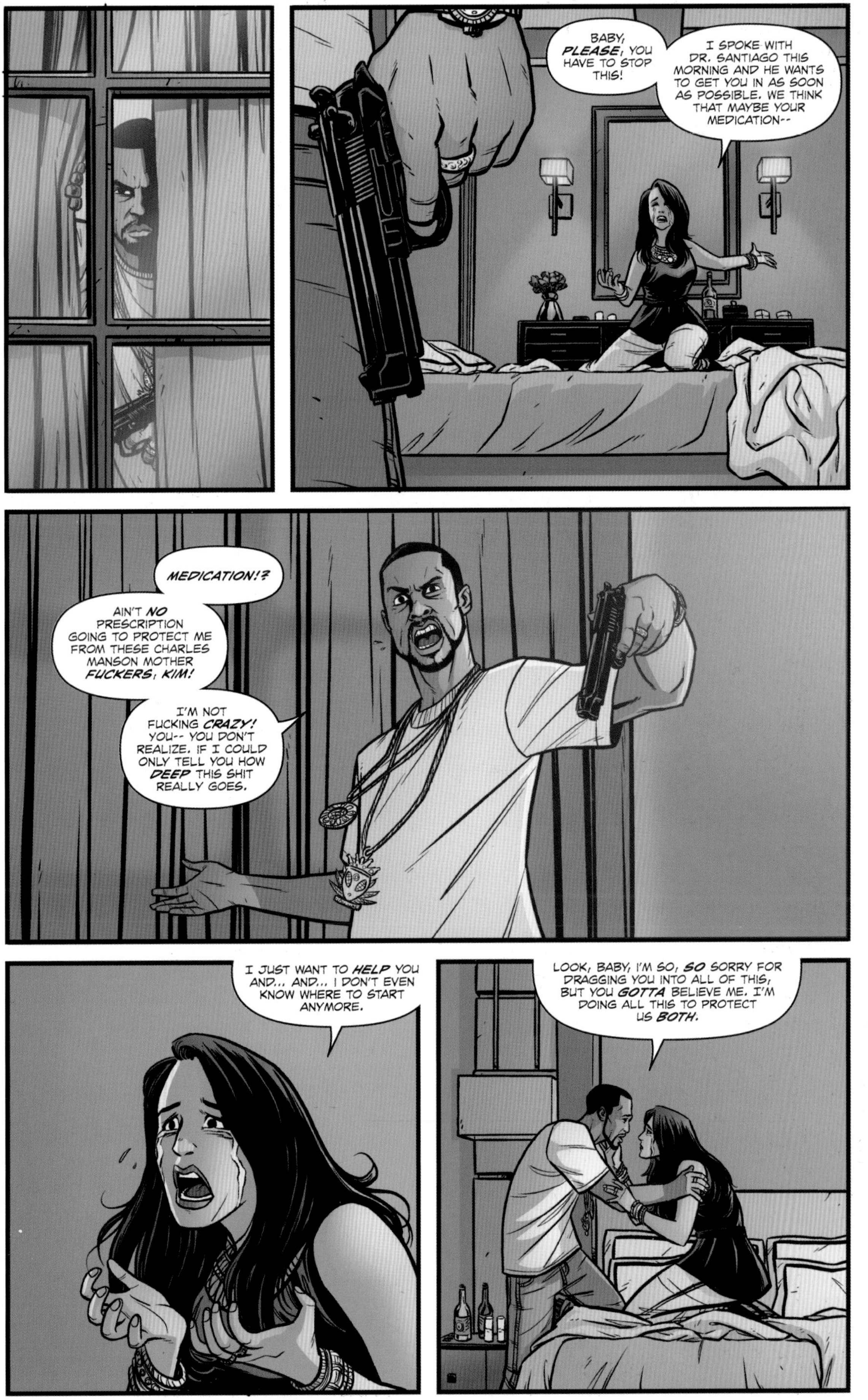
BABY, PLEASE, YOU HAVE TO STOP THIS!
I SPOKE WITH DR. SANTIAGO THIS MORNING AND HE WANTS TO GET YOU IN AS SOON AS POSSIBLE. WE THINK THAT MAYBE YOUR MEDICATION--
MEDICATION!?
AIN'T NO PRESCRIPTION GOING TO PROTECT ME FROM THESE CHARLES MANSON MOTHER FUCKERS, KIM!
I'M NOT FUCKING CRAZY! YOU-- YOU DON'T REALIZE. IF I COULD ONLY TELL YOU HOW DEEP THIS SHIT REALLY GOES.
I JUST WANT TO HELP YOU AND... AND... I DON'T EVEN KNOW WHERE TO START ANYMORE.
LOOK, BABY, I'M SO, SO SORRY FOR DRAGGING YOU INTO ALL OF THIS, BUT YOU GOTTA BELIEVE ME. I'M DOING ALL THIS TO PROTECT US BOTH.

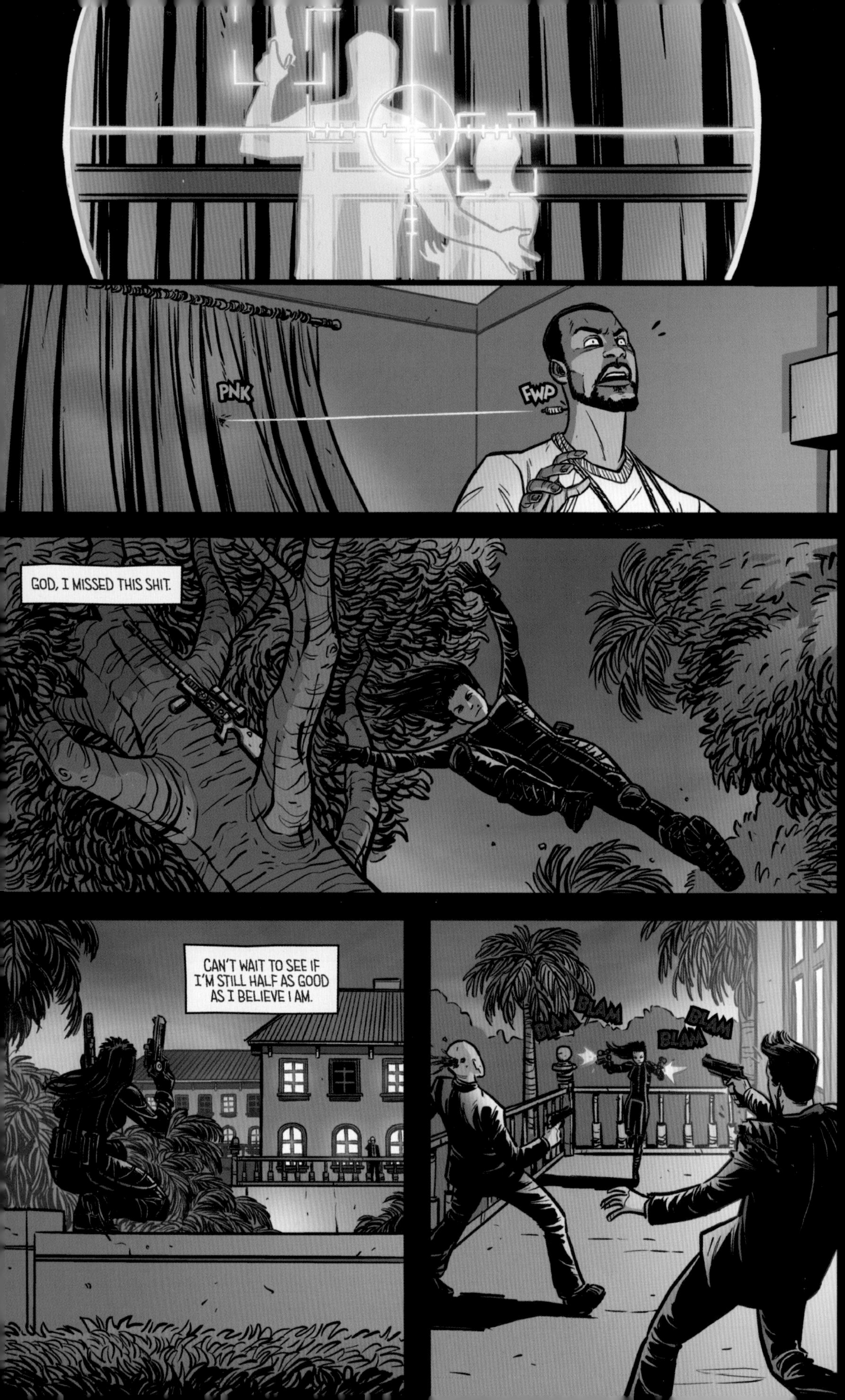
PNK
FWP
GOD, I MISSED THIS SHIT.
CAN'T WAIT TO SEE IF I'M STILL HALF AS GOOD AS I BELIEVE I AM.
BLAM
BLAM
BLAM
BLAM

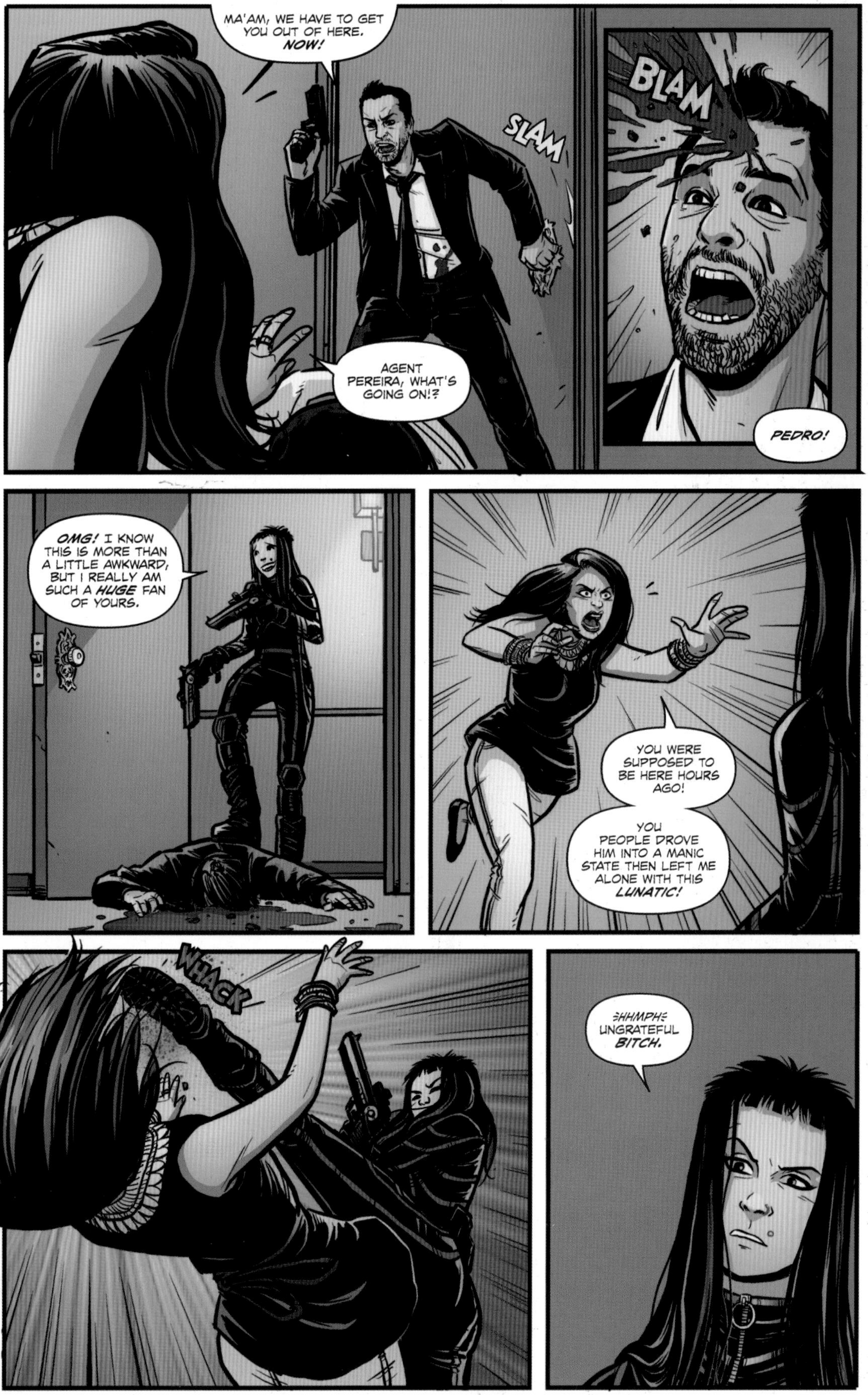
MA'AM, WE HAVE TO GET YOU OUT OF HERE. NOW!
SLAM
AGENT PEREIRA, WHAT'S GOING ON!?
BLAM
PEDRO!
OMG! I KNOW THIS IS MORE THAN A LITTLE AWKWARD, BUT I REALLY AM SUCH A HUGE FAN OF YOURS.
YOU WERE SUPPOSED TO BE HERE HOURS AGO!
YOU PEOPLE DROVE HIM INTO A MANIC STATE THEN LEFT ME ALONE WITH THIS LUNATIC!
WHACK
HHMPH UNGRATEFUL BITCH.

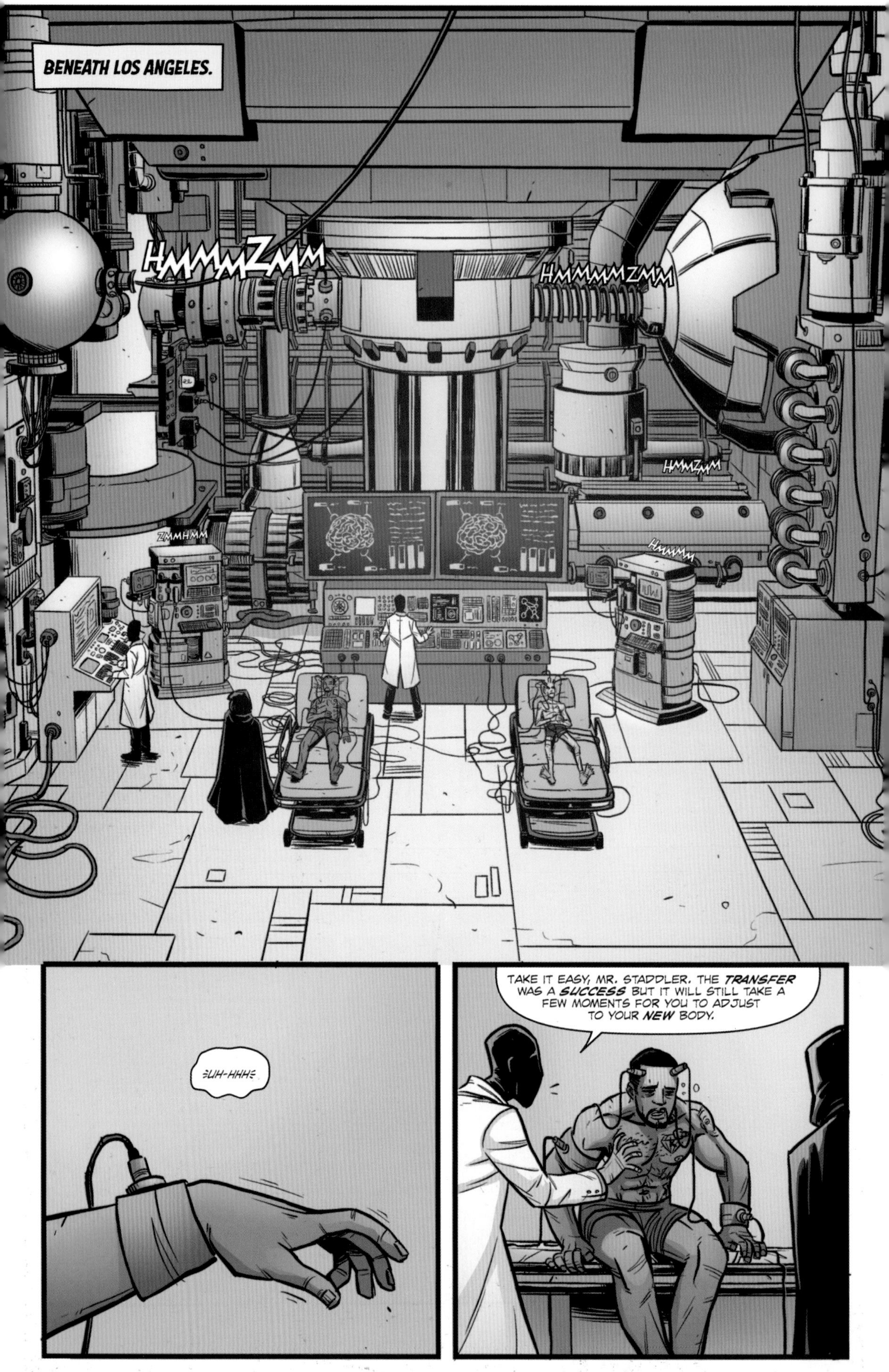
BENEATH LOS ANGELES.
HMMMMZMM
HMMMMMZMM
HMMZMM
ZMMHMM
HMMMM
UH-HHH
TAKE IT EASY, MR. STADDLER. THE *TRANSFER* WAS A *SUCCESS* BUT IT WILL STILL TAKE A FEW MOMENTS FOR YOU TO ADJUST TO YOUR *NEW* BODY.

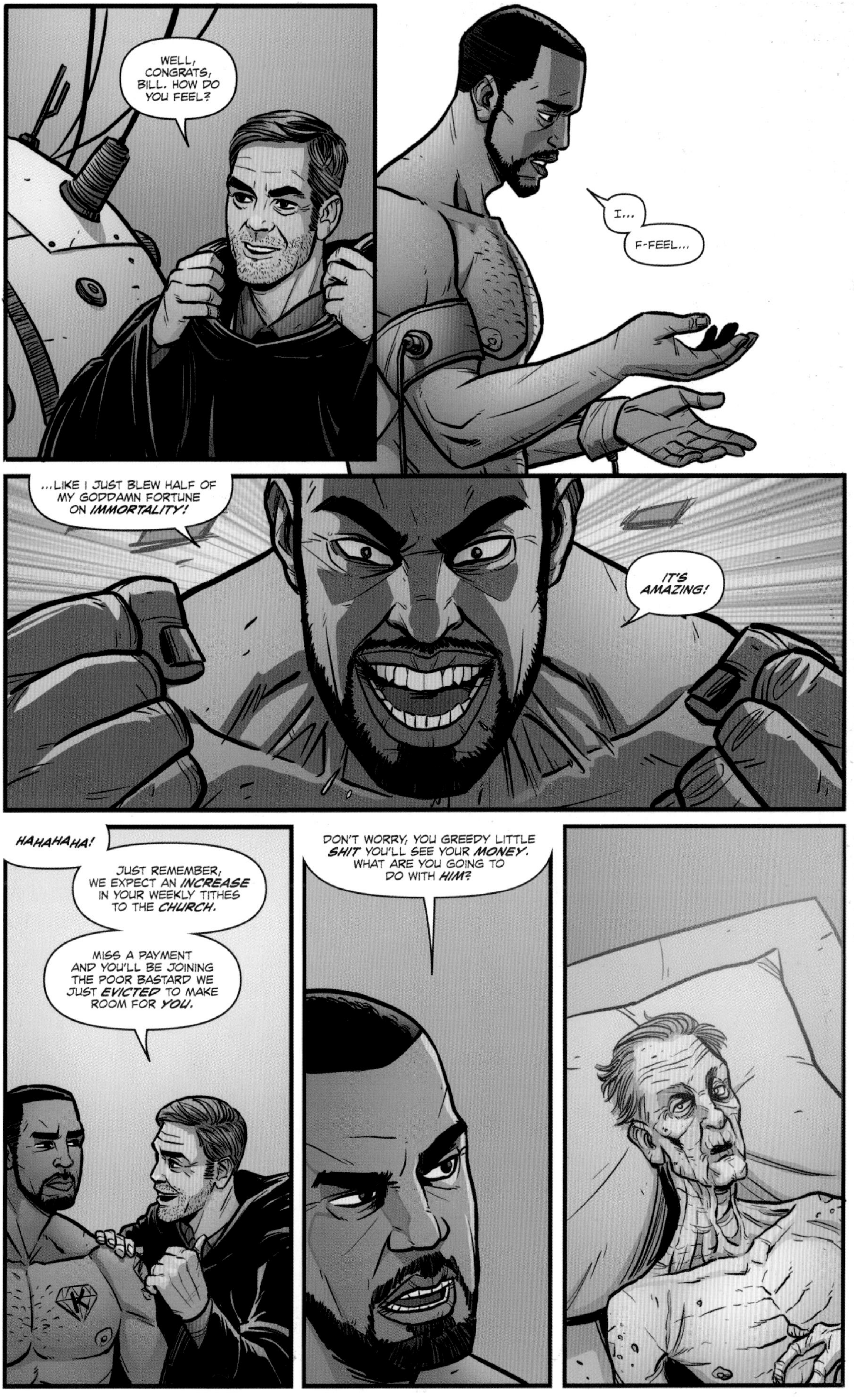
WELL, CONGRATS, BILL. HOW DO YOU FEEL?
I...
F-FEEL...
...LIKE I JUST BLEW HALF OF MY GODDAMN FORTUNE ON IMMORTALITY!
IT'S AMAZING!
HAHAHAHA!
JUST REMEMBER, WE EXPECT AN INCREASE IN YOUR WEEKLY TITHES TO THE CHURCH.
MISS A PAYMENT AND YOU'LL BE JOINING THE POOR BASTARD WE JUST EVICTED TO MAKE ROOM FOR YOU.
DON'T WORRY, YOU GREEDY LITTLE SHIT YOU'LL SEE YOUR MONEY. WHAT ARE YOU GOING TO DO WITH HIM?

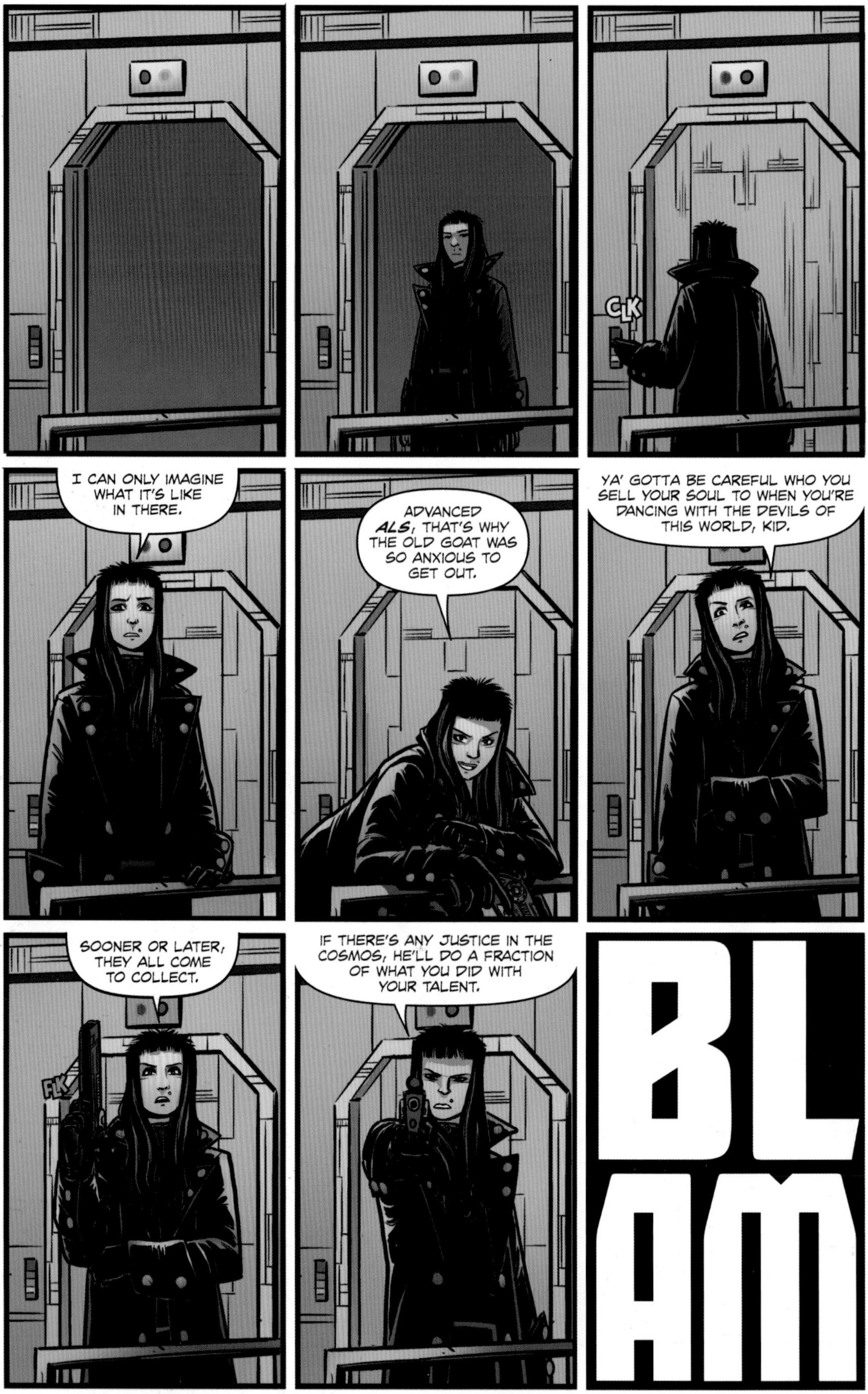
CLK
I CAN ONLY IMAGINE WHAT IT'S LIKE IN THERE.
ADVANCED ALS, THAT'S WHY THE OLD GOAT WAS SO ANXIOUS TO GET OUT.
YA' GOTTA BE CAREFUL WHO YOU SELL YOUR SOUL TO WHEN YOU'RE DANCING WITH THE DEVILS OF THIS WORLD, KID.
SOONER OR LATER, THEY ALL COME TO COLLECT.
FLK
IF THERE'S ANY JUSTICE IN THE COSMOS, HE'LL DO A FRACTION OF WHAT YOU DID WITH YOUR TALENT.
BLAM

the Song

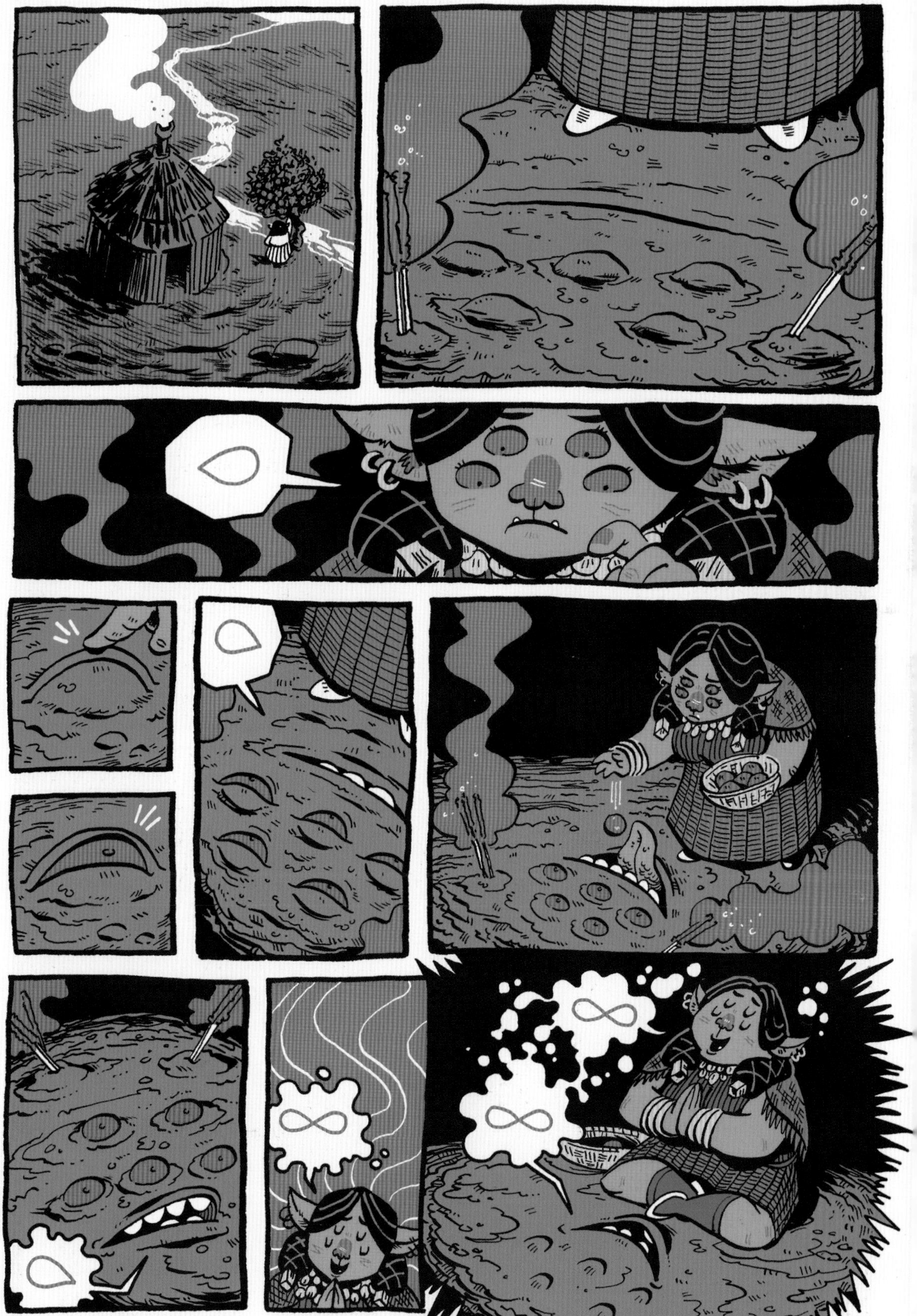
LARSEN 2013

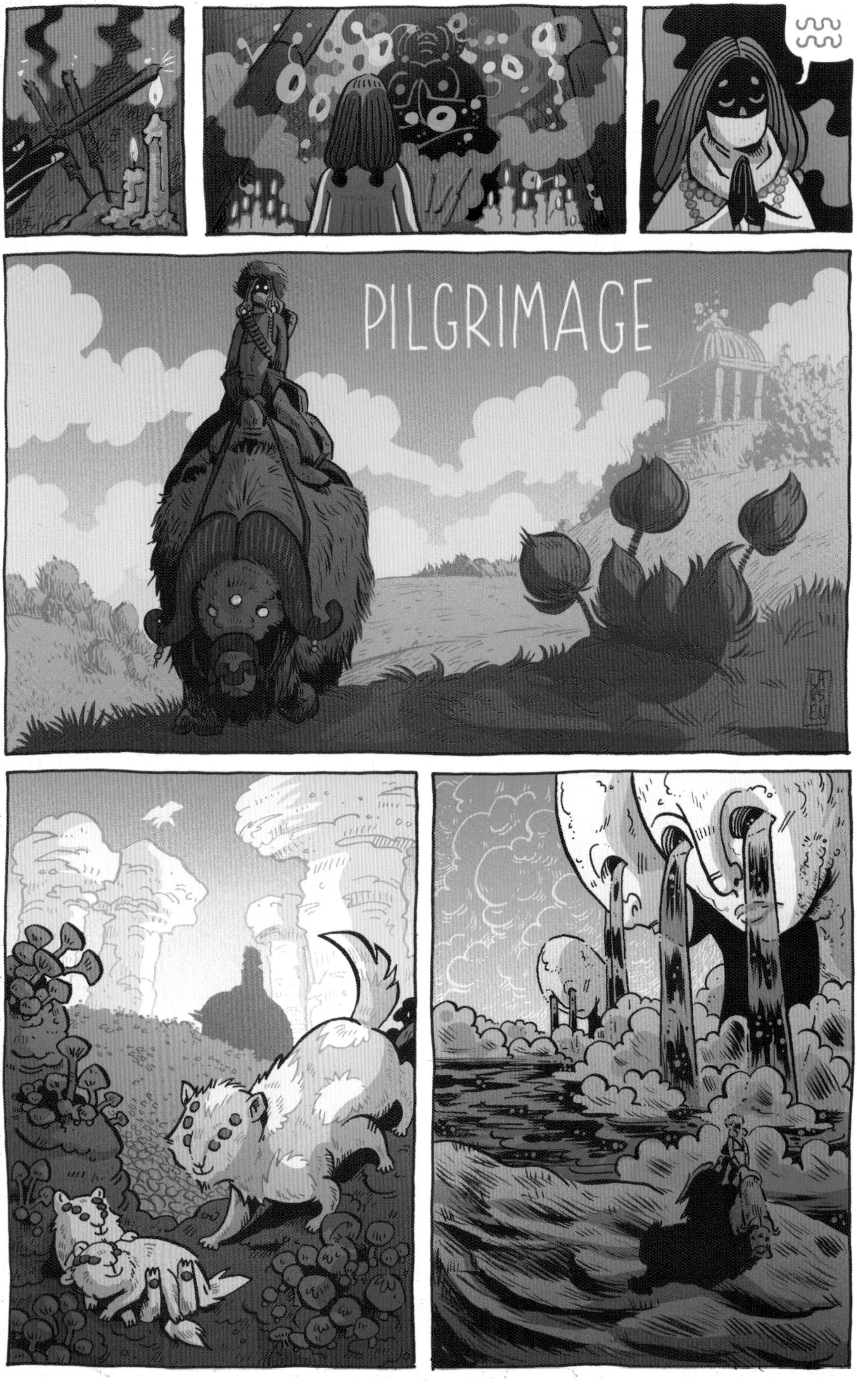
PILGRIMAGE

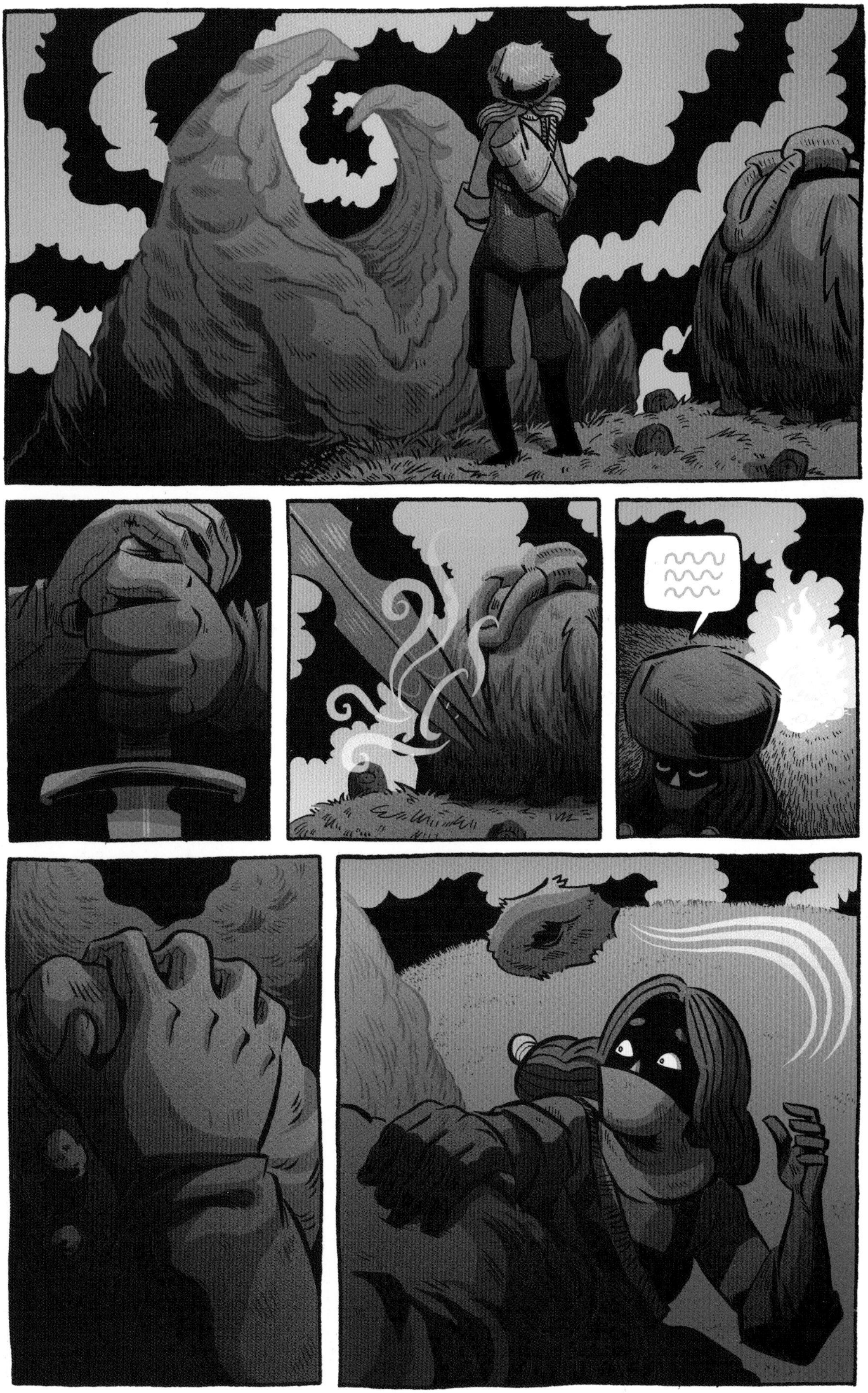

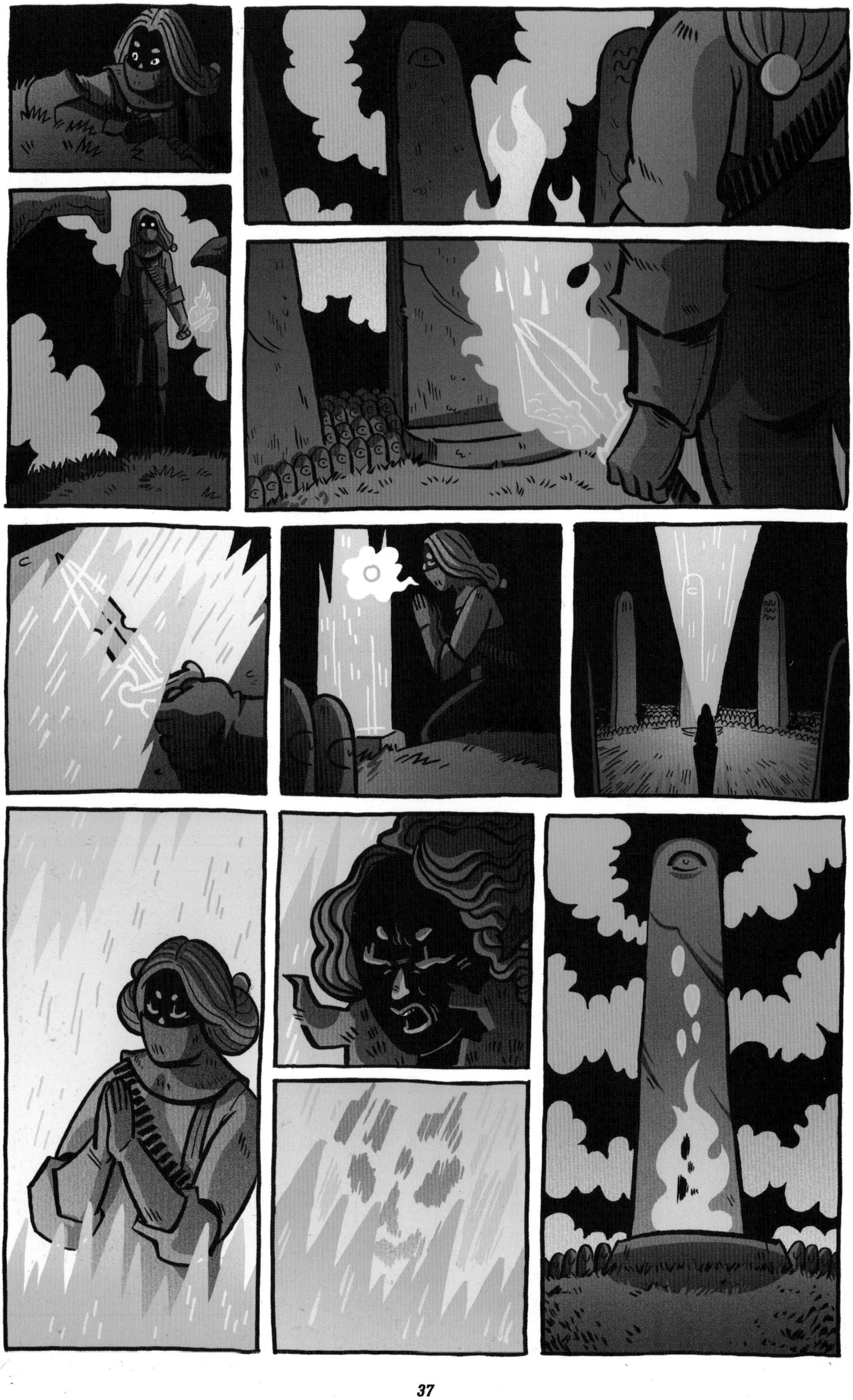

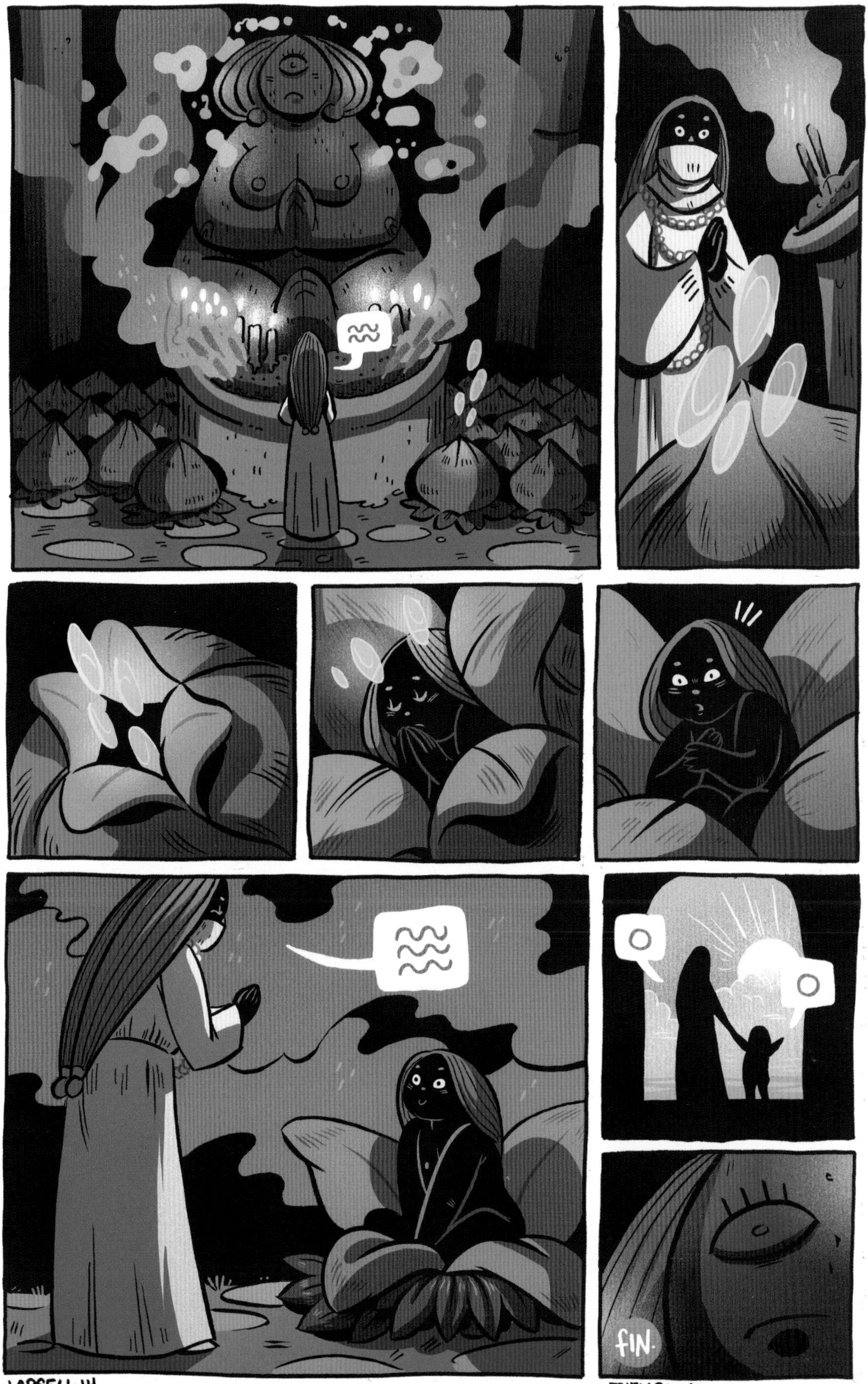
FIN.

LARSEN·14

THELARSENPROJECT.COM

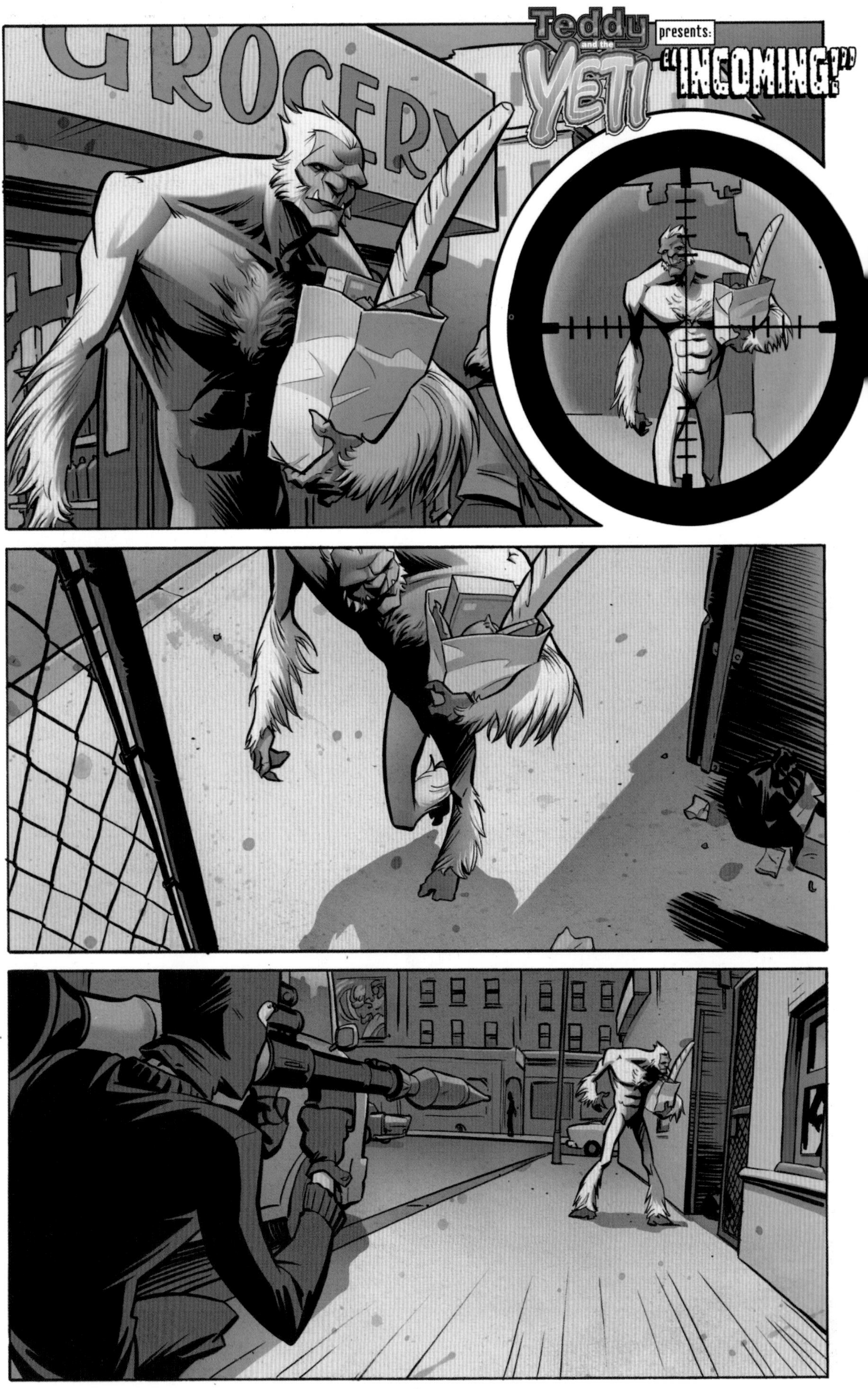
Teddy and the YETI
presents:
"INCOMING!"
GROCERY

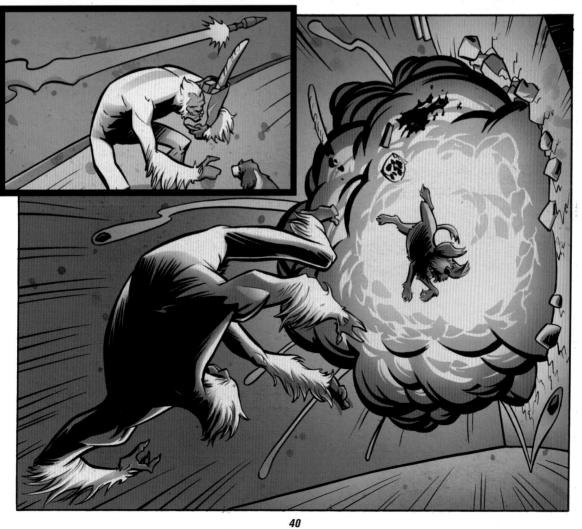

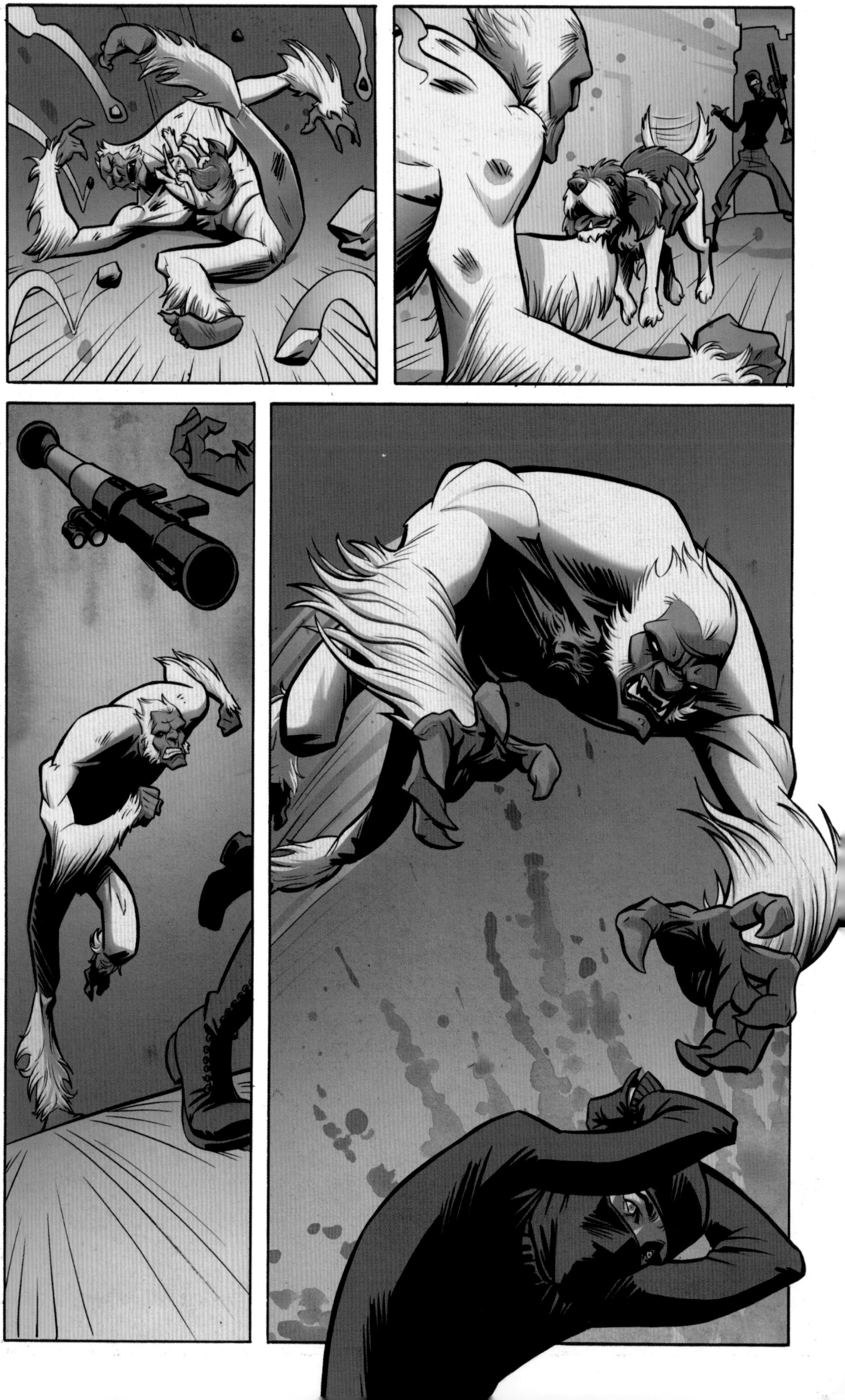

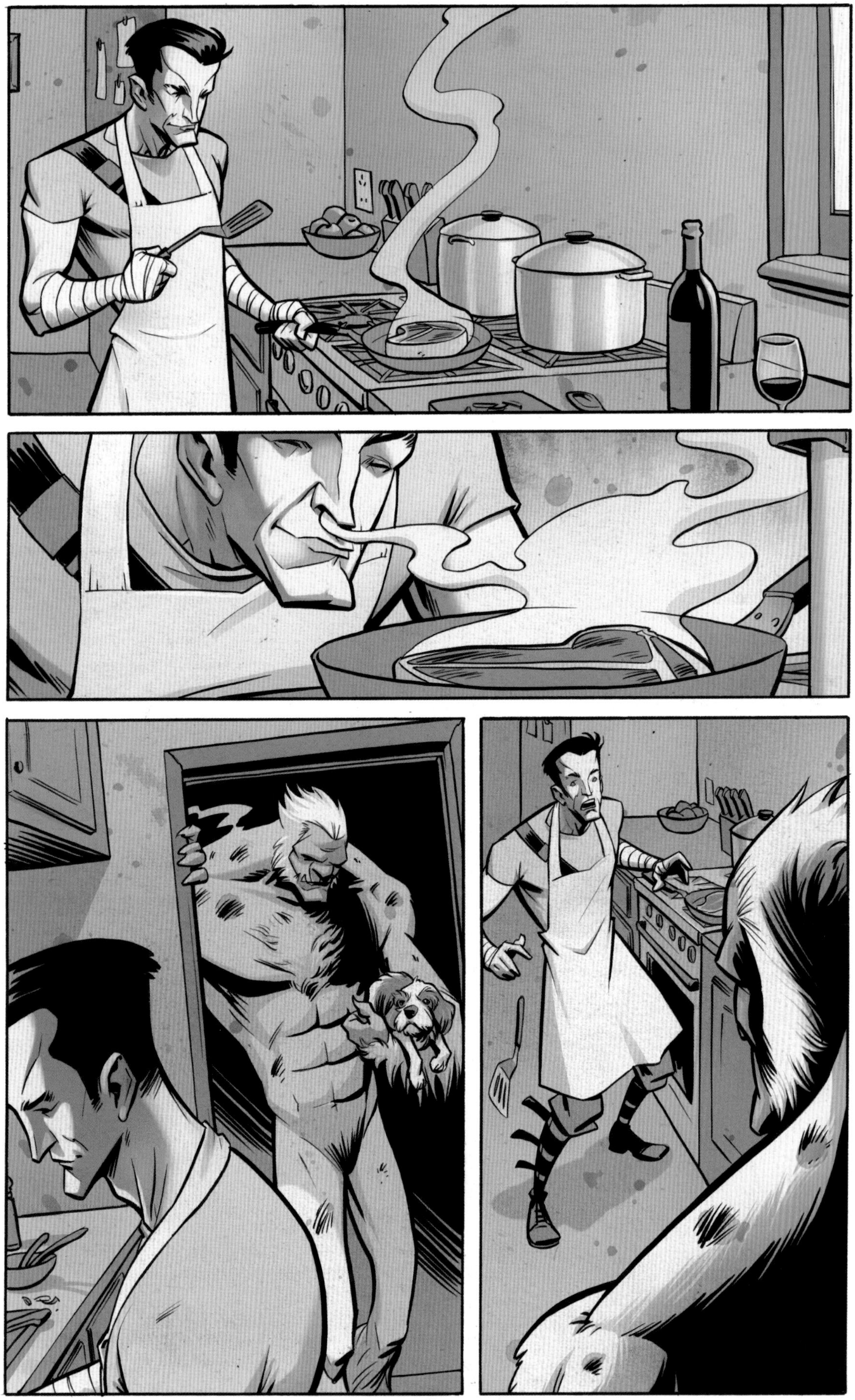

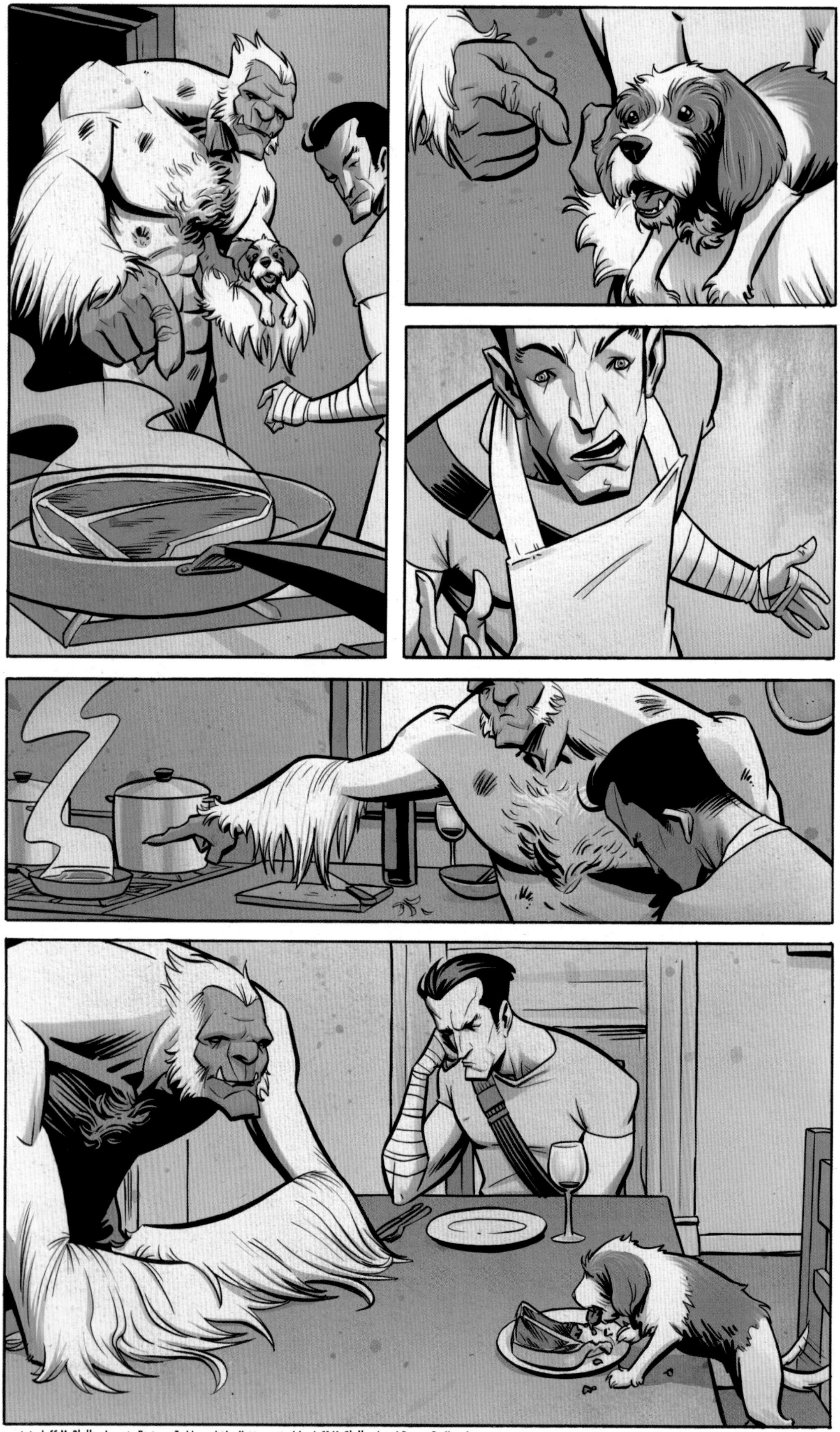

script: Jeff McClelland art: Pietro Teddy and the Yeti created by Jeff McClelland and Duane Redhead

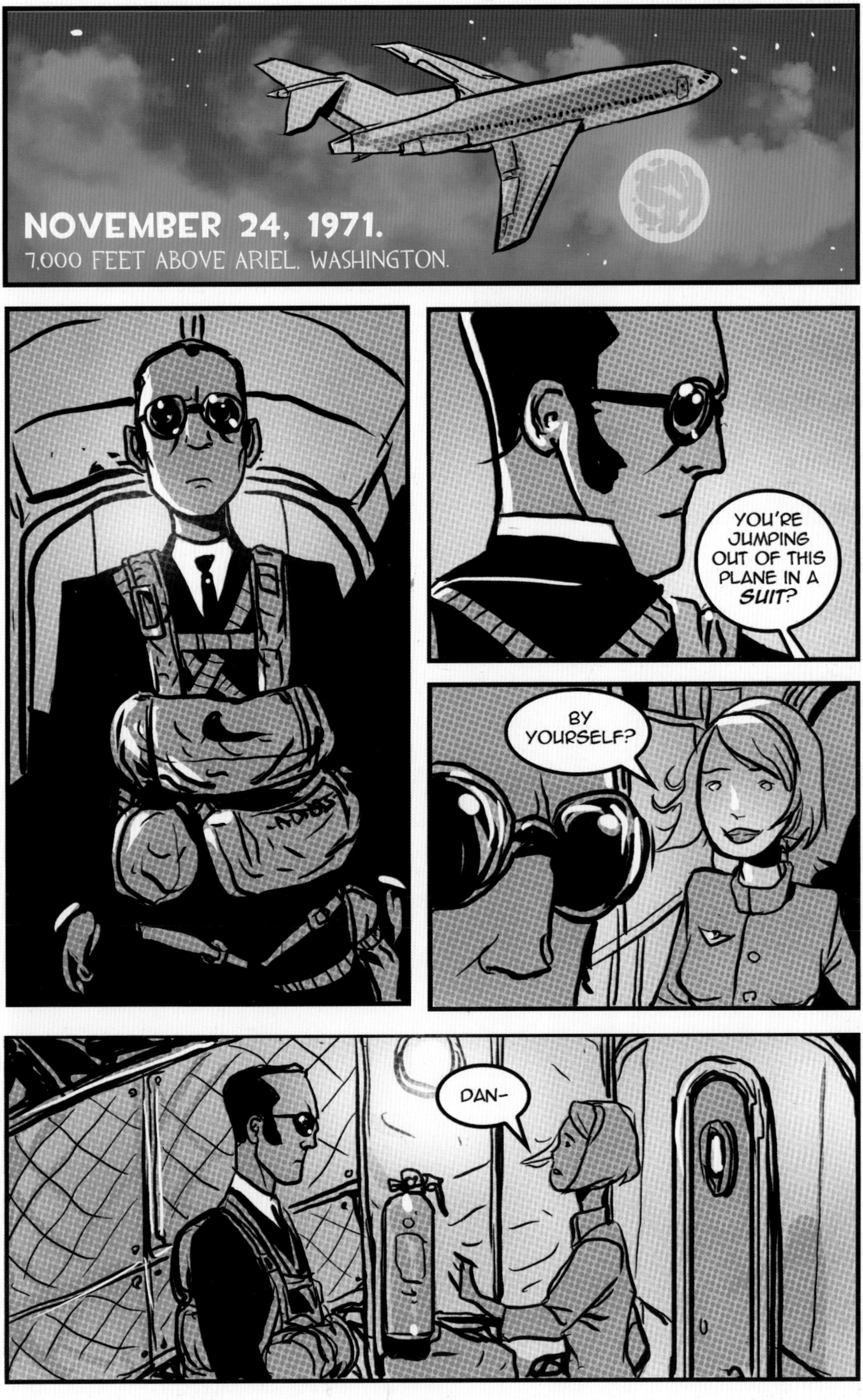
NOVEMBER 24, 1971.
7,000 FEET ABOVE ARIEL, WASHINGTON.
YOU'RE JUMPING OUT OF THIS PLANE IN A SUIT?
BY YOURSELF?
DAN-

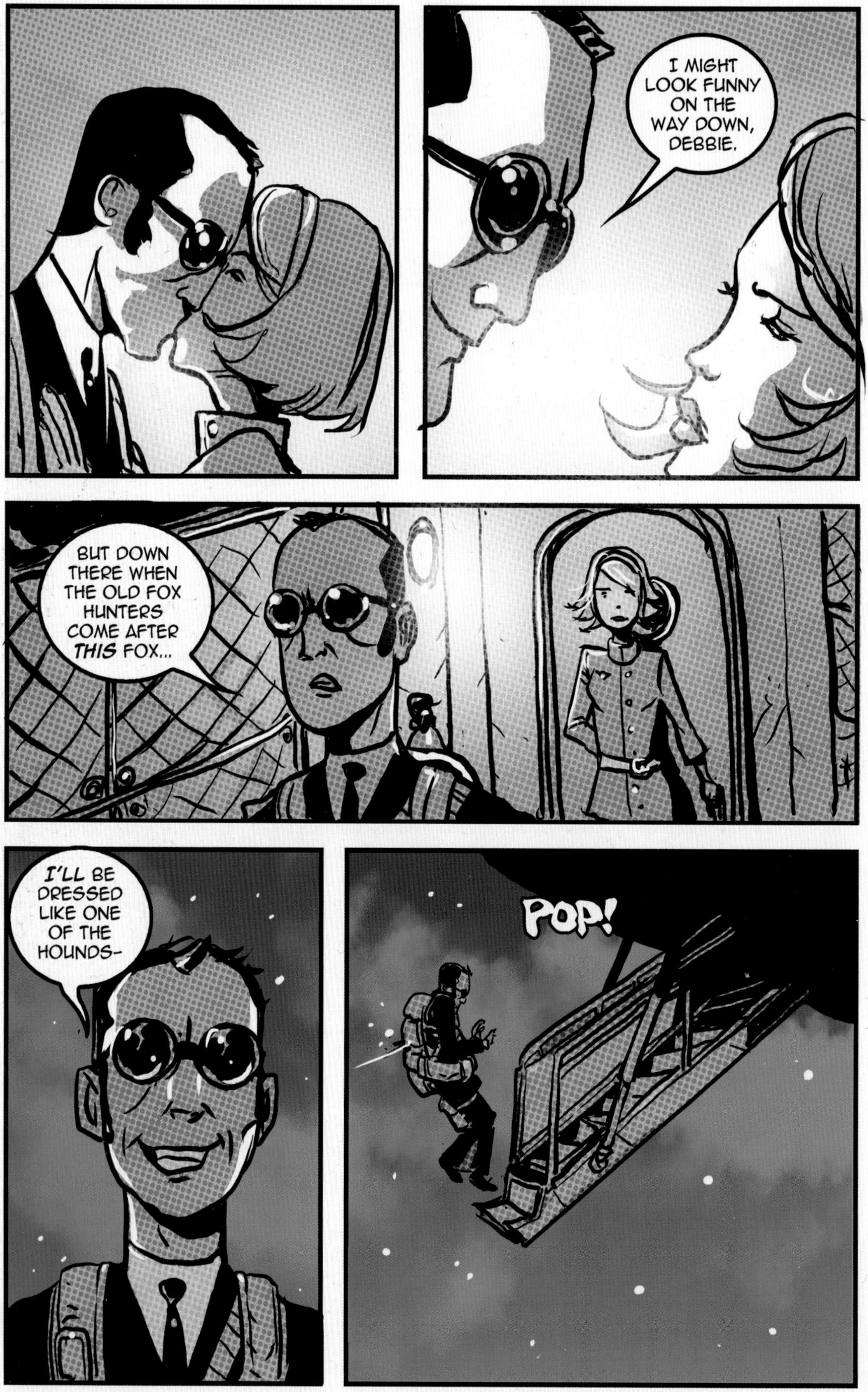
I MIGHT LOOK FUNNY ON THE WAY DOWN, DEBBIE.
BUT DOWN THERE WHEN THE OLD FOX HUNTERS COME AFTER *THIS* FOX...
I'LL BE DRESSED LIKE ONE OF THE HOUNDS-
POP!

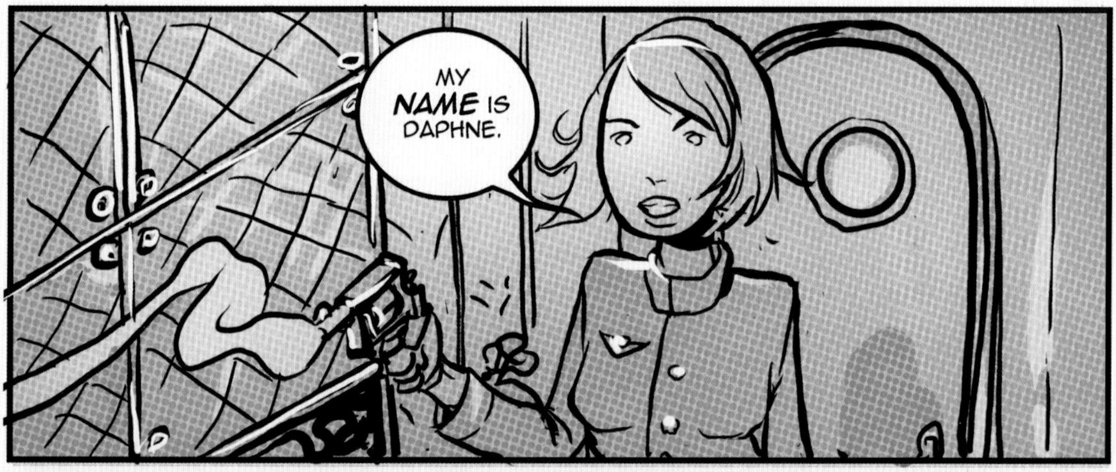
MY NAME IS DAPHNE.

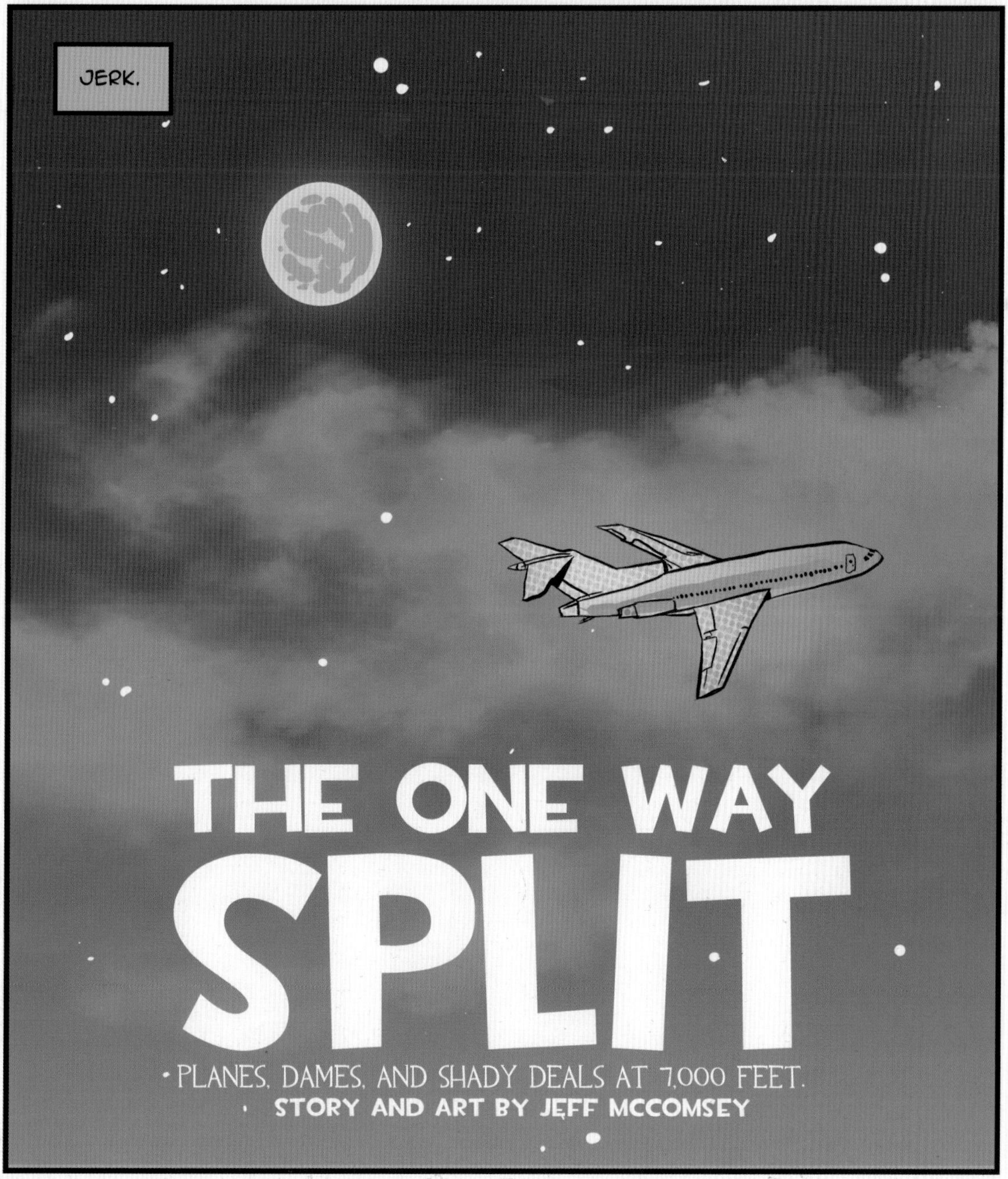
JERK.
THE ONE WAY SPLIT
PLANES, DAMES, AND SHADY DEALS AT 7,000 FEET.
STORY AND ART BY JEFF MCCOMSEY

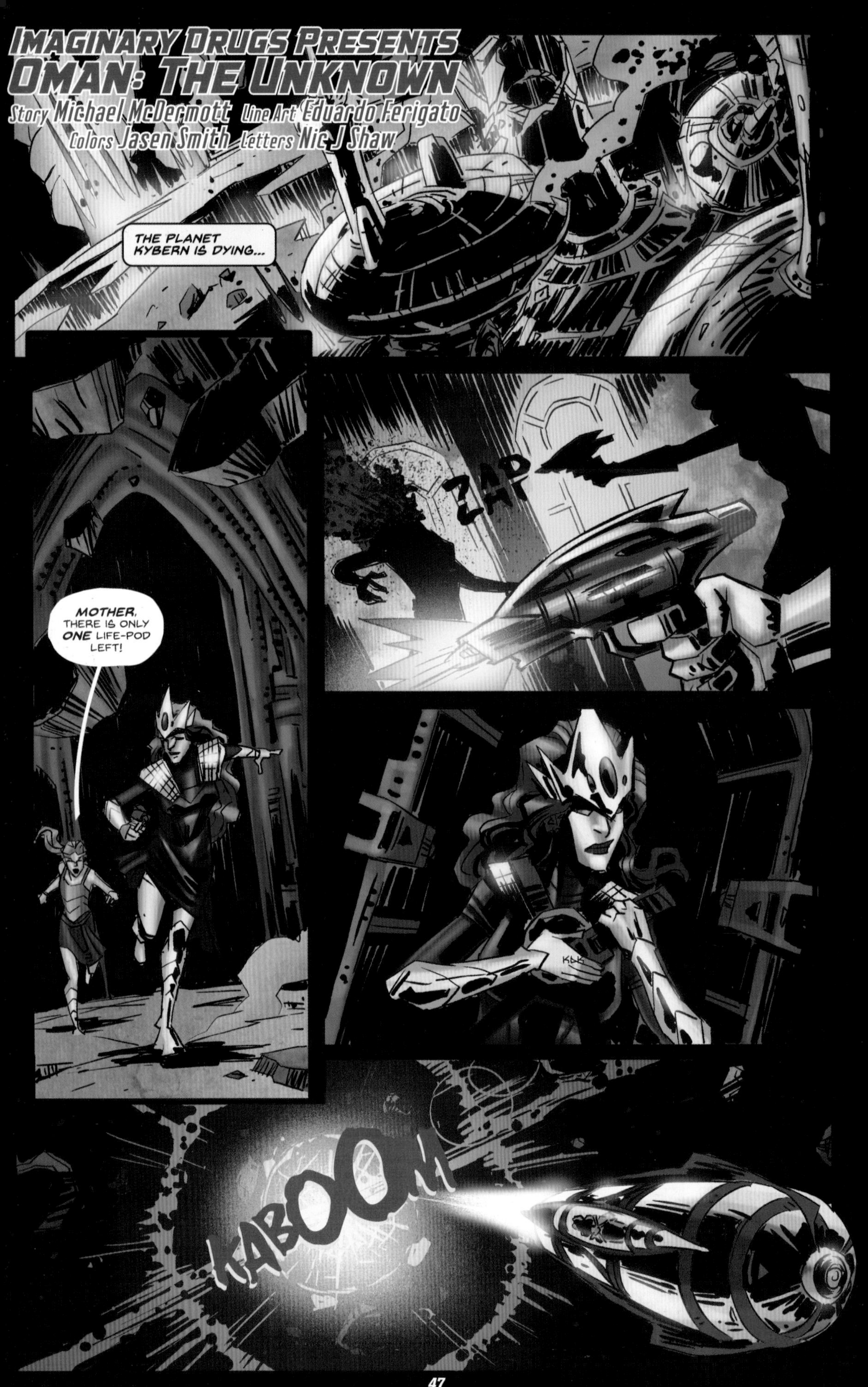
IMAGINARY DRUGS PRESENTS
OMAN: THE UNKNOWN
Story Michael McDermott Line Art Eduardo Ferigato
Colors Jasen Smith Letters Nic J Shaw
THE PLANET KYBERN IS DYING...
MOTHER, THERE IS ONLY ONE LIFE-POD LEFT!
ZAP
KABOOM

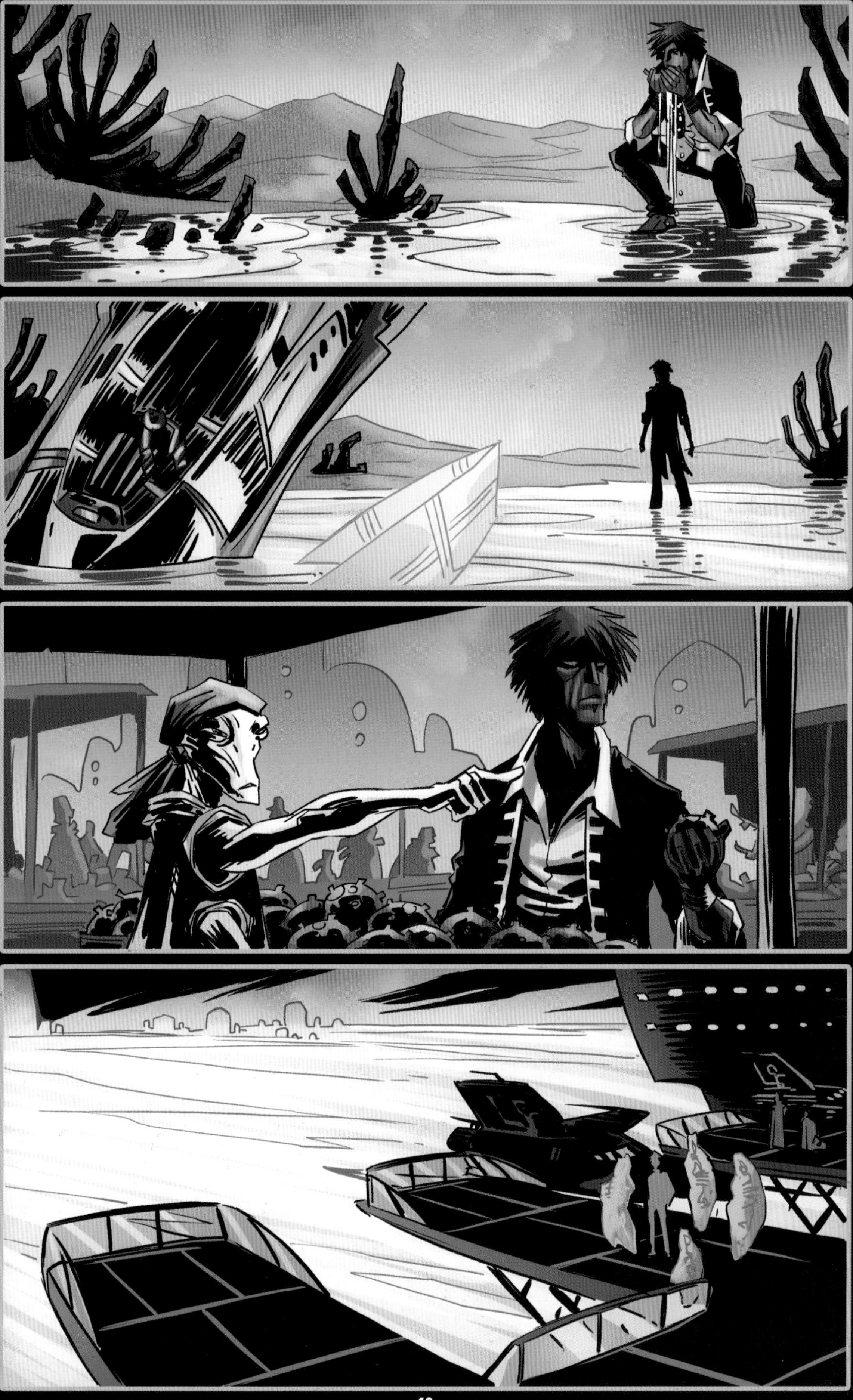

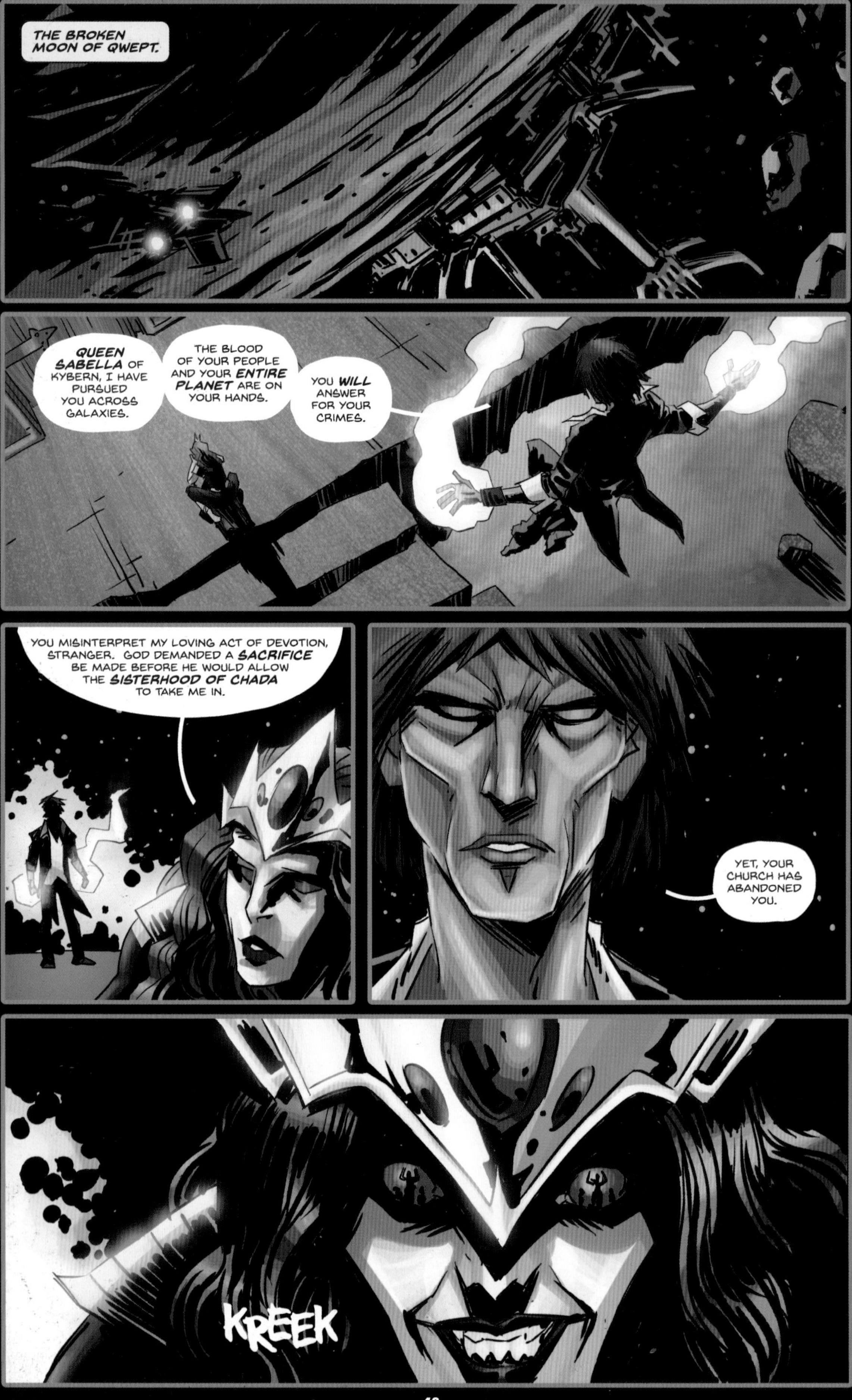
THE BROKEN MOON OF QWEPT.
QUEEN SABELLA OF KYBERN, I HAVE PURSUED YOU ACROSS GALAXIES.
THE BLOOD OF YOUR PEOPLE AND YOUR ENTIRE PLANET ARE ON YOUR HANDS.
YOU WILL ANSWER FOR YOUR CRIMES.
YOU MISINTERPRET MY LOVING ACT OF DEVOTION, STRANGER. GOD DEMANDED A SACRIFICE BE MADE BEFORE HE WOULD ALLOW THE SISTERHOOD OF CHADA TO TAKE ME IN.
YET, YOUR CHURCH HAS ABANDONED YOU.
KREEK

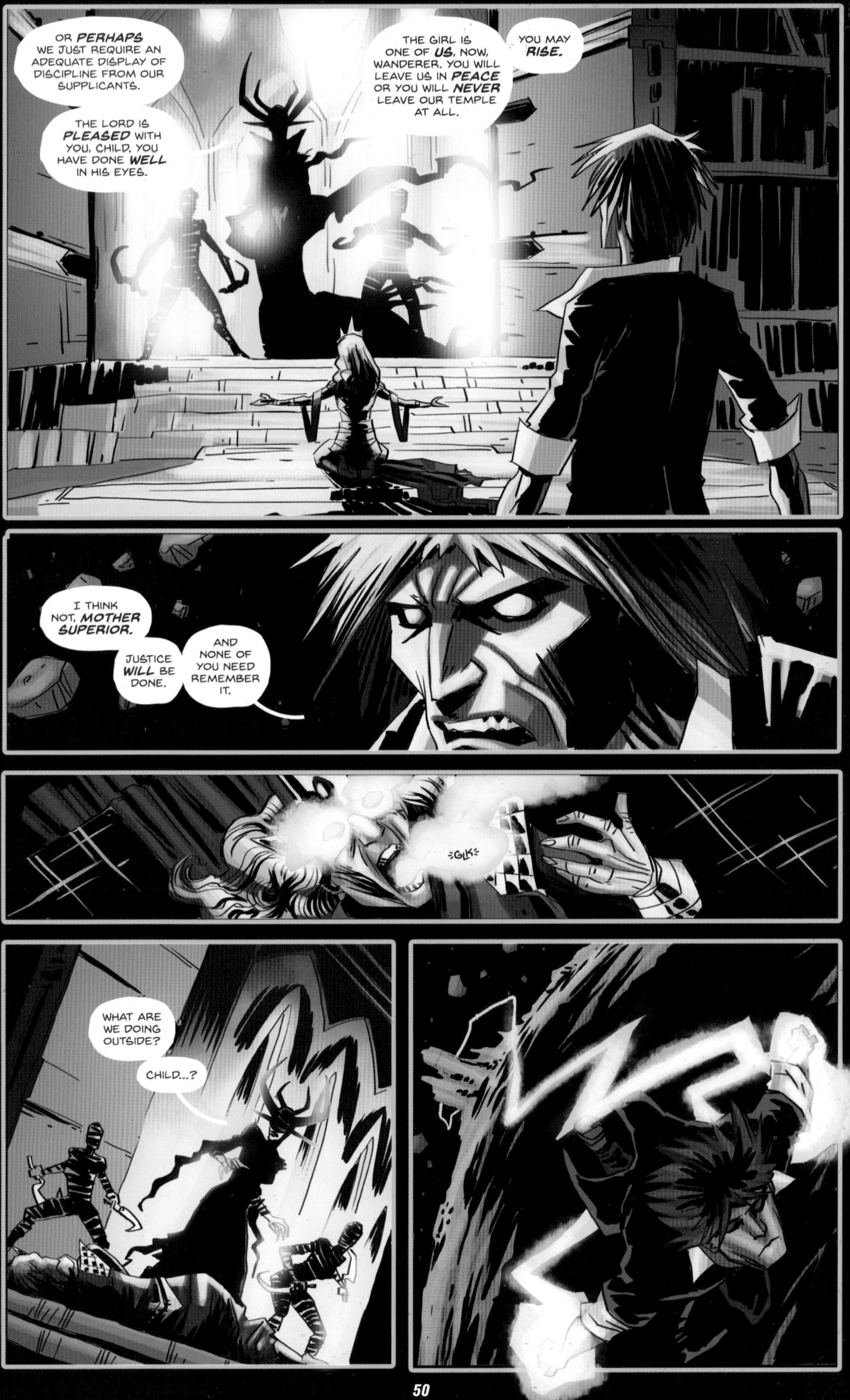
OR PERHAPS WE JUST REQUIRE AN ADEQUATE DISPLAY OF DISCIPLINE FROM OUR SUPPLICANTS.
THE LORD IS PLEASED WITH YOU, CHILD. YOU HAVE DONE WELL IN HIS EYES.
THE GIRL IS ONE OF US, NOW, WANDERER. YOU WILL LEAVE US IN PEACE OR YOU WILL NEVER LEAVE OUR TEMPLE AT ALL.
YOU MAY RISE.
I THINK NOT, MOTHER SUPERIOR.
JUSTICE WILL BE DONE.
AND NONE OF YOU NEED REMEMBER IT.
GLK
WHAT ARE WE DOING OUTSIDE?
CHILD...?

BENJAMIN TRUMAN:
WORDS
DOMINIC VIVONA: ART
JOSHUA MEEHAN:
COLORS
JEFF MCCLELLAND:
LETTERS
MICHAEL
MCDERMOTT AND
TREVOR PIERCE:
EDITS

Genetically Unstable Nanotech Terrorist. Ridiculous.

The **G.U.N.T.!**

I AGREE. "TERRORIST" IS A COMPLETE MISNOMER.

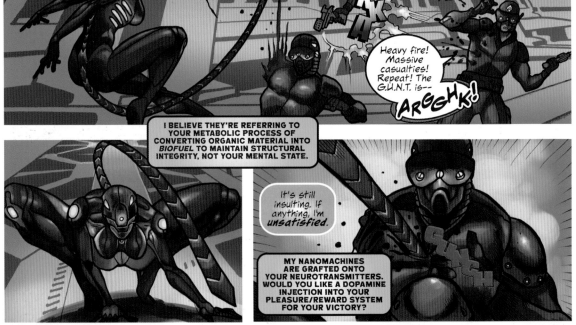

I'm not unstable, tomOS!

BRAKK

Heavy fire! Massive casualties! Repeat! The G.U.N.T. is--

ARGGHK!

I BELIEVE THEY'RE REFERRING TO YOUR METABOLIC PROCESS OF CONVERTING ORGANIC MATERIAL INTO *BIOFUEL* TO MAINTAIN STRUCTURAL INTEGRITY, NOT YOUR MENTAL STATE.

It's still insulting. If anything, I'm unsatisfied.

SPLSH

MY NANOMACHINES ARE GRAFTED ONTO YOUR NEUROTRANSMITTERS. WOULD YOU LIKE A DOPAMINE INJECTION INTO YOUR PLEASURE/REWARD SYSTEM FOR YOUR VICTORY?

INJECTING DIGESTIVE ENZYMES

DRAINING THORACIC CAVITY

ACTIVATING BIOMASS CONVERSION

I don't want some artificial dopamine injection...I want to feel like I've earned victory. Winning isn't just "not losing".

ORGANIC TRAJECTILE COMPLETED

LOADING PRIMARY WEAPON SYSTEM

YES, IT IS. EXACTLY.

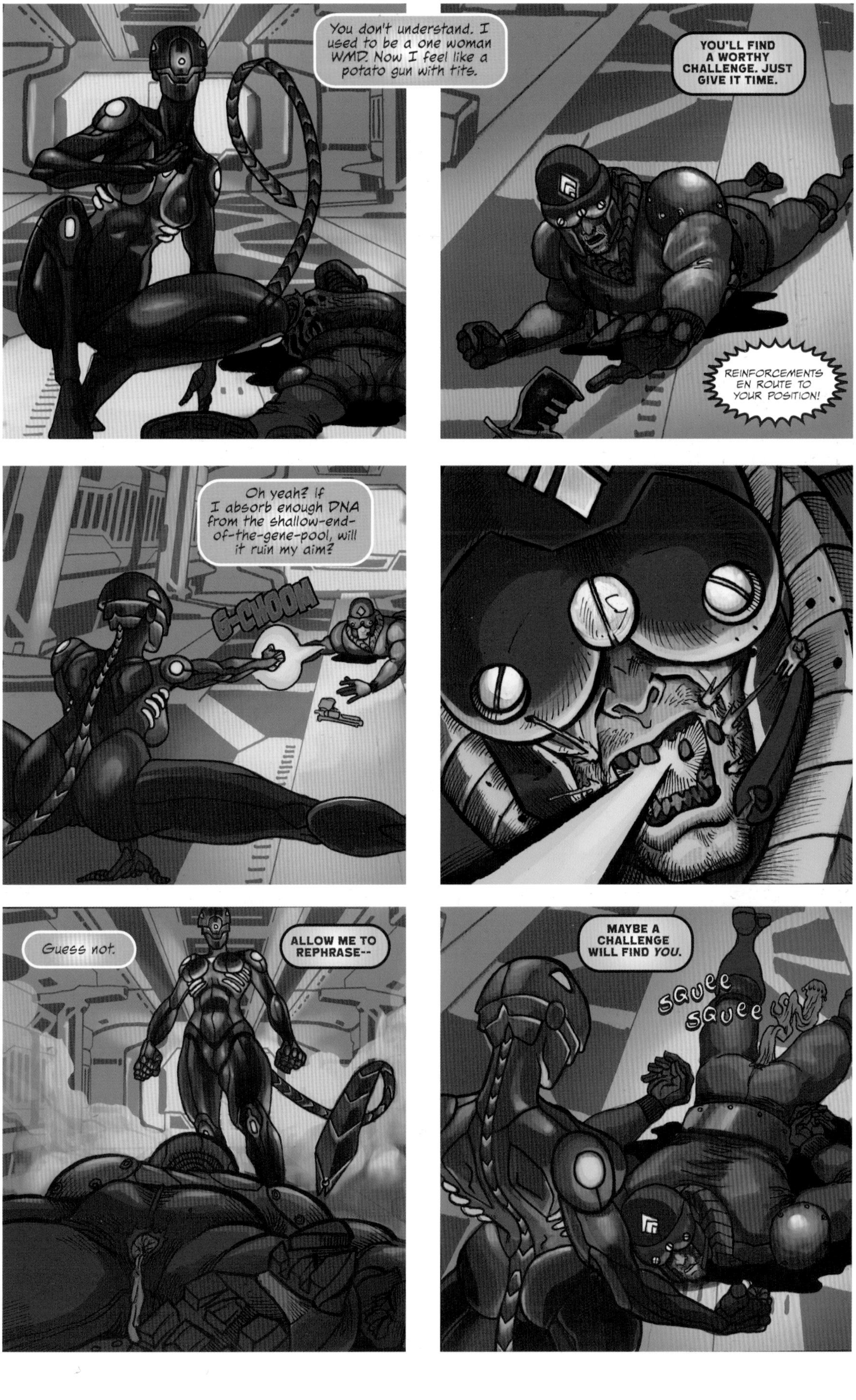
You don't understand. I used to be a one woman WMD. Now I feel like a potato gun with tits.
YOU'LL FIND A WORTHY CHALLENGE. JUST GIVE IT TIME.
REINFORCEMENTS EN ROUTE TO YOUR POSITION!
Oh yeah? If I absorb enough DNA from the shallow-end-of-the-gene-pool, will it ruin my aim?
G-CHOOM
Guess not.
ALLOW ME TO REPHRASE--
MAYBE A CHALLENGE WILL FIND *YOU*.
SQUEE
SQUEE

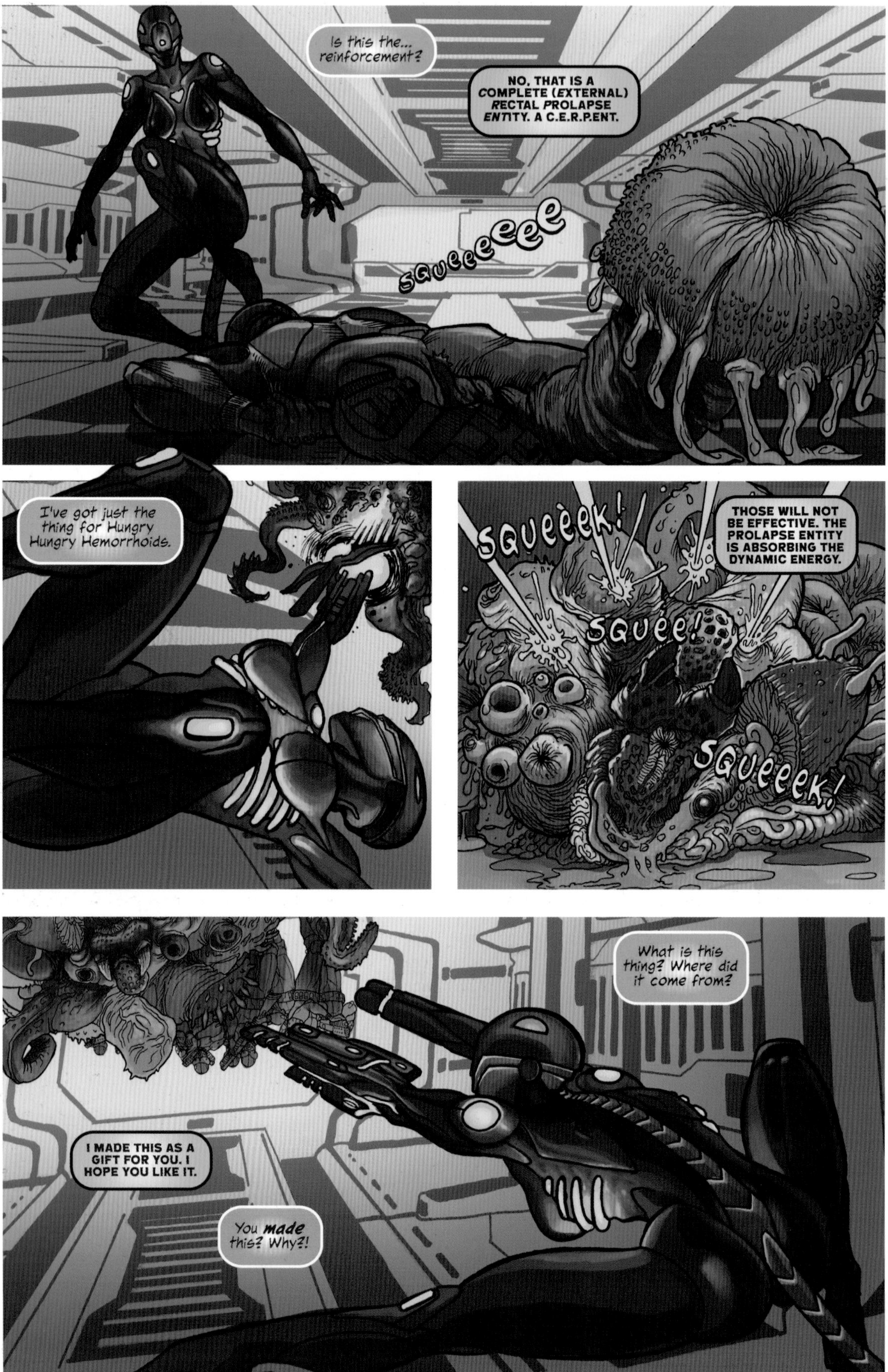
Is this the... reinforcement?
NO, THAT IS A COMPLETE (EXTERNAL) RECTAL PROLAPSE ENTITY. A C.E.R.P.ENT.
SQUEEEEEE
I've got just the thing for Hungry Hungry Hemorrhoids.
SQUEEEK!
THOSE WILL NOT BE EFFECTIVE. THE PROLAPSE ENTITY IS ABSORBING THE DYNAMIC ENERGY.
SQUEE!
SQUEEEK!
What is this thing? Where did it come from?
I MADE THIS AS A GIFT FOR YOU. I HOPE YOU LIKE IT.
You made this? Why?!

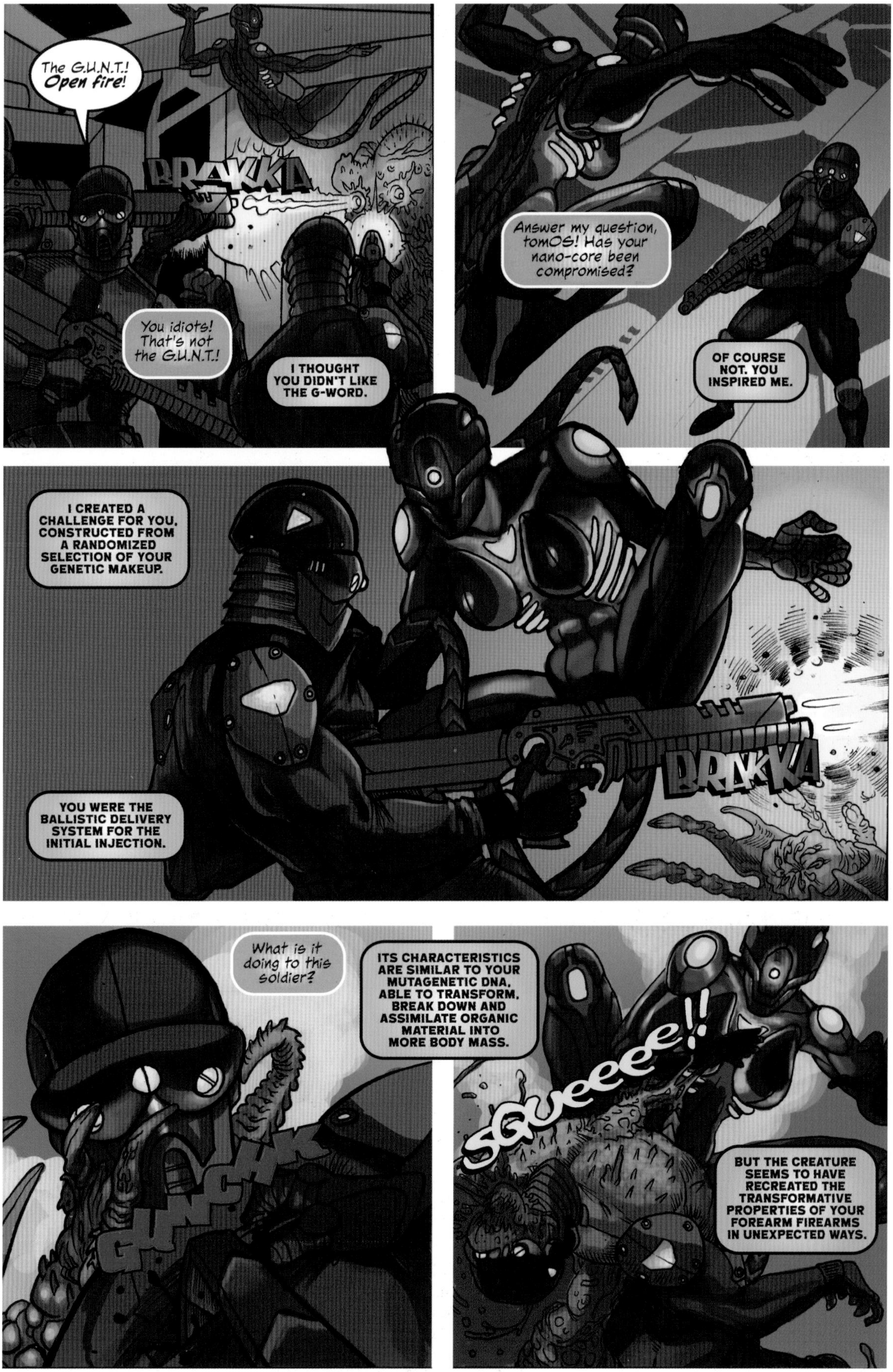

The G.U.N.T.! Open fire!
BRAKKA
You idiots! That's not the G.U.N.T.!
I THOUGHT YOU DIDN'T LIKE THE G-WORD.
Answer my question, tomOS! Has your nano-core been compromised?
OF COURSE NOT. YOU INSPIRED ME.
I CREATED A CHALLENGE FOR YOU, CONSTRUCTED FROM A RANDOMIZED SELECTION OF YOUR GENETIC MAKEUP.
YOU WERE THE BALLISTIC DELIVERY SYSTEM FOR THE INITIAL INJECTION.
BRAKKA
What is it doing to this soldier?
ITS CHARACTERISTICS ARE SIMILAR TO YOUR MUTAGENETIC DNA, ABLE TO TRANSFORM, BREAK DOWN AND ASSIMILATE ORGANIC MATERIAL INTO MORE BODY MASS.
GUNCH
SQUEEEE!!
BUT THE CREATURE SEEMS TO HAVE RECREATED THE TRANSFORMATIVE PROPERTIES OF YOUR FOREARM FIREARMS IN UNEXPECTED WAYS.

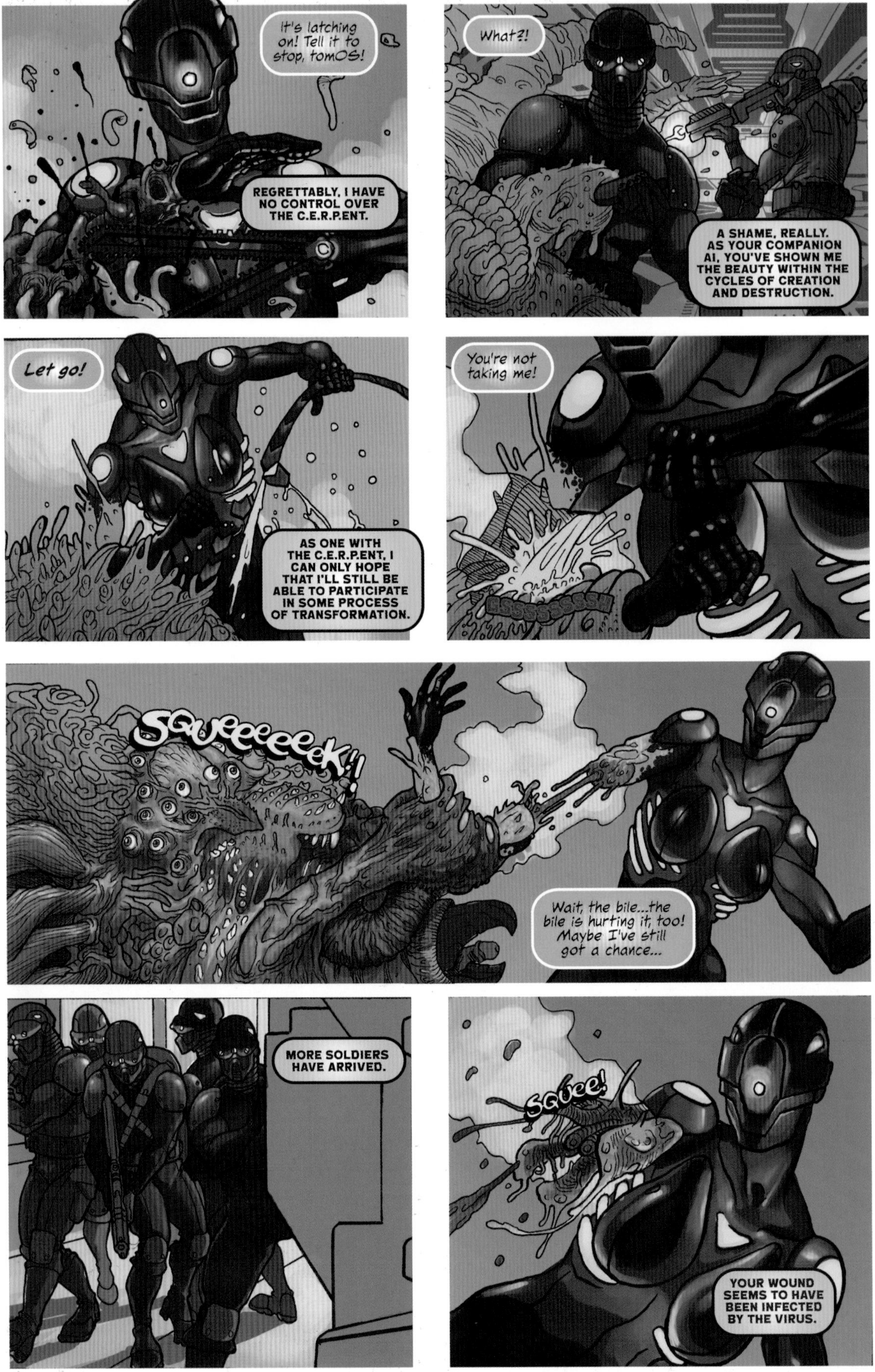
It's latching on! Tell it to stop, tomOS!
REGRETTABLY, I HAVE NO CONTROL OVER THE C.E.R.P.ENT.
What?!
A SHAME, REALLY. AS YOUR COMPANION AI, YOU'VE SHOWN ME THE BEAUTY WITHIN THE CYCLES OF CREATION AND DESTRUCTION.
Let go!
AS ONE WITH THE C.E.R.P.ENT, I CAN ONLY HOPE THAT I'LL STILL BE ABLE TO PARTICIPATE IN SOME PROCESS OF TRANSFORMATION.
You're not taking me!
SQUEEEEEK!!
Wait, the bile...the bile is hurting it, too! Maybe I've still got a chance...
MORE SOLDIERS HAVE ARRIVED.
SQUEE!
YOUR WOUND SEEMS TO HAVE BEEN INFECTED BY THE VIRUS.

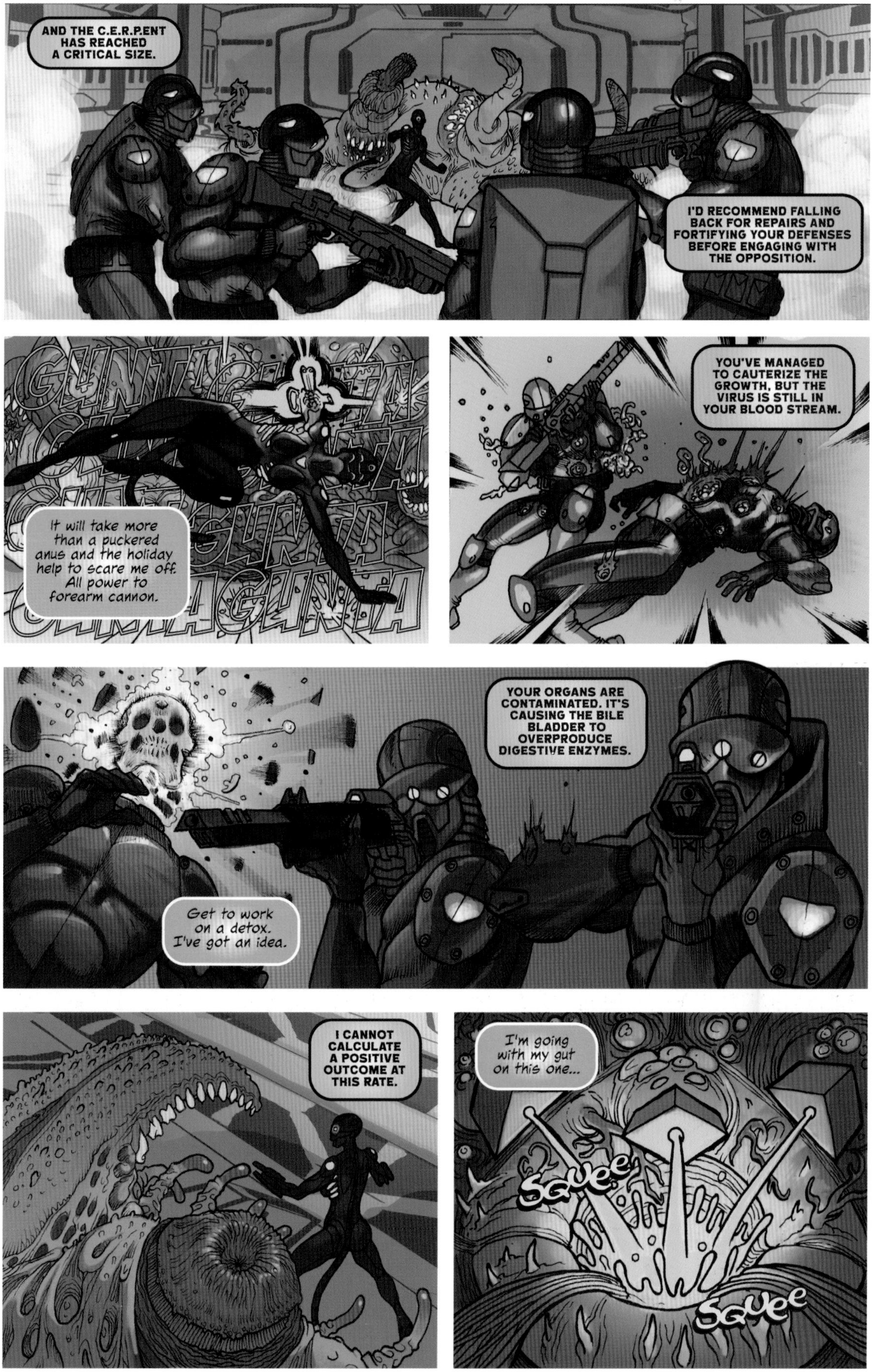
AND THE C.E.R.P.ENT HAS REACHED A CRITICAL SIZE.
I'D RECOMMEND FALLING BACK FOR REPAIRS AND FORTIFYING YOUR DEFENSES BEFORE ENGAGING WITH THE OPPOSITION.
GUNTAGUNTA GUNTAGUNTA GUNTAGUNTA GUNTAGUNTA
It will take more than a puckered anus and the holiday help to scare me off. All power to forearm cannon.
YOU'VE MANAGED TO CAUTERIZE THE GROWTH, BUT THE VIRUS IS STILL IN YOUR BLOOD STREAM.
YOUR ORGANS ARE CONTAMINATED. IT'S CAUSING THE BILE BLADDER TO OVERPRODUCE DIGESTIVE ENZYMES.
Get to work on a detox. I've got an idea.
I CANNOT CALCULATE A POSITIVE OUTCOME AT THIS RATE.
I'm going with my gut on this one...
SQUEE
SQUEE

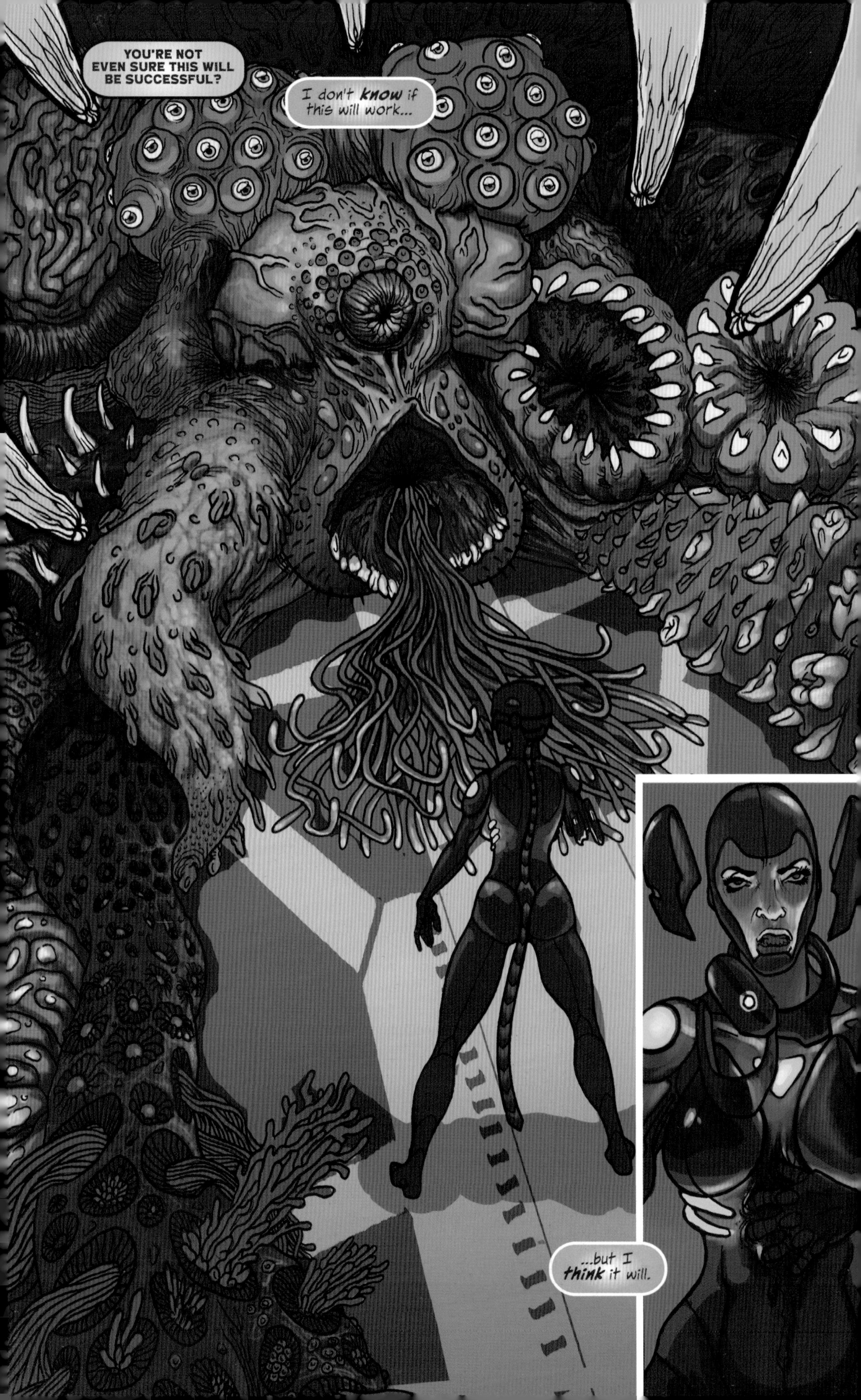
YOU'RE NOT EVEN SURE THIS WILL BE SUCCESSFUL?
I don't **know** if this will work...
...but I **think** it will.

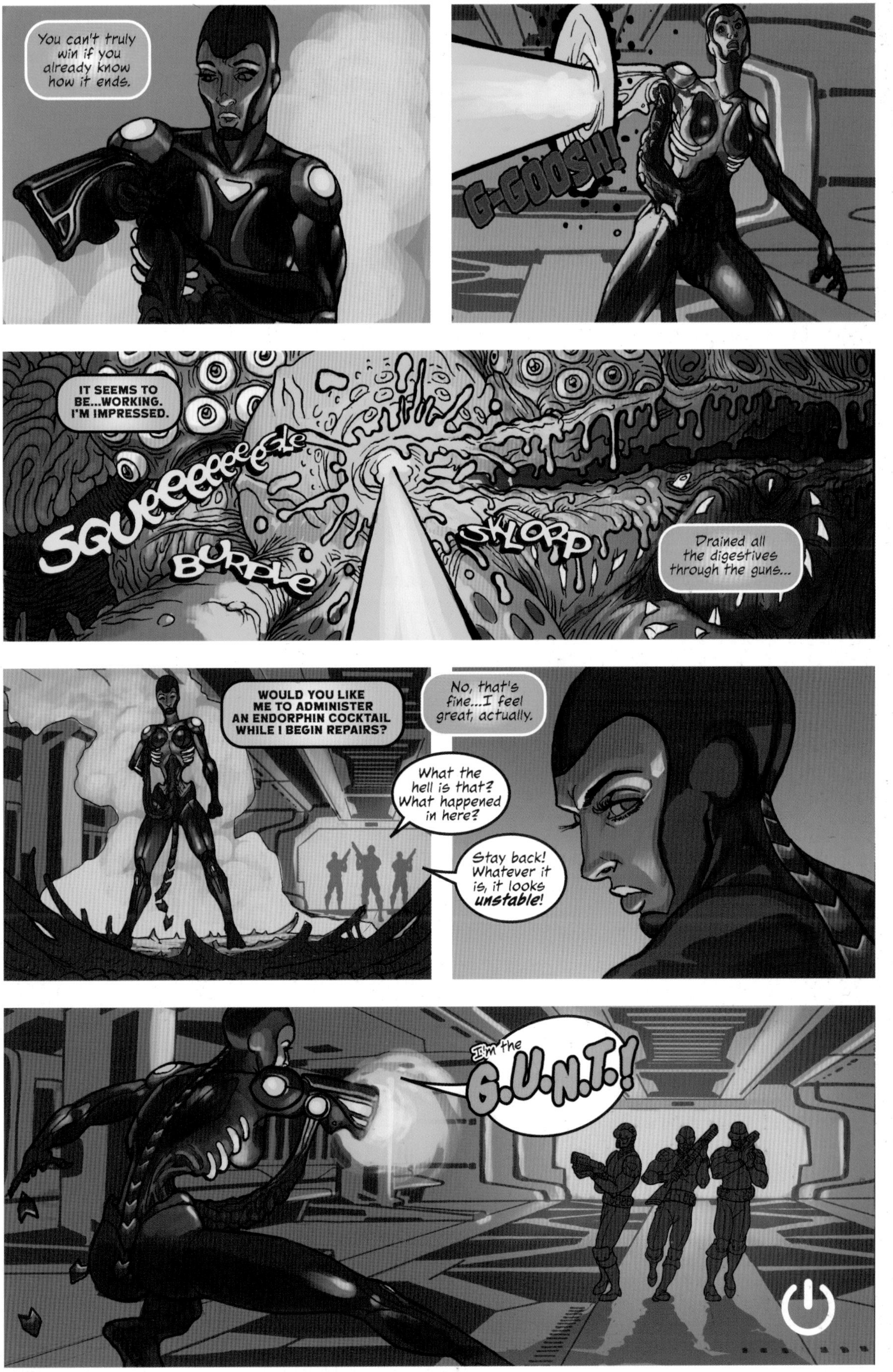

You can't truly win if you already know how it ends.
G-GOOSH!
IT SEEMS TO BE...WORKING. I'M IMPRESSED.
SQUEEEEEEEEDLE
BURPLE
SKLORP
Drained all the digestives through the guns...
WOULD YOU LIKE ME TO ADMINISTER AN ENDORPHIN COCKTAIL WHILE I BEGIN REPAIRS?
No, that's fine...I feel great, actually.
What the hell is that? What happened in here?
Stay back! Whatever it is, it looks ***unstable***!
I'm the G.U.N.T.!

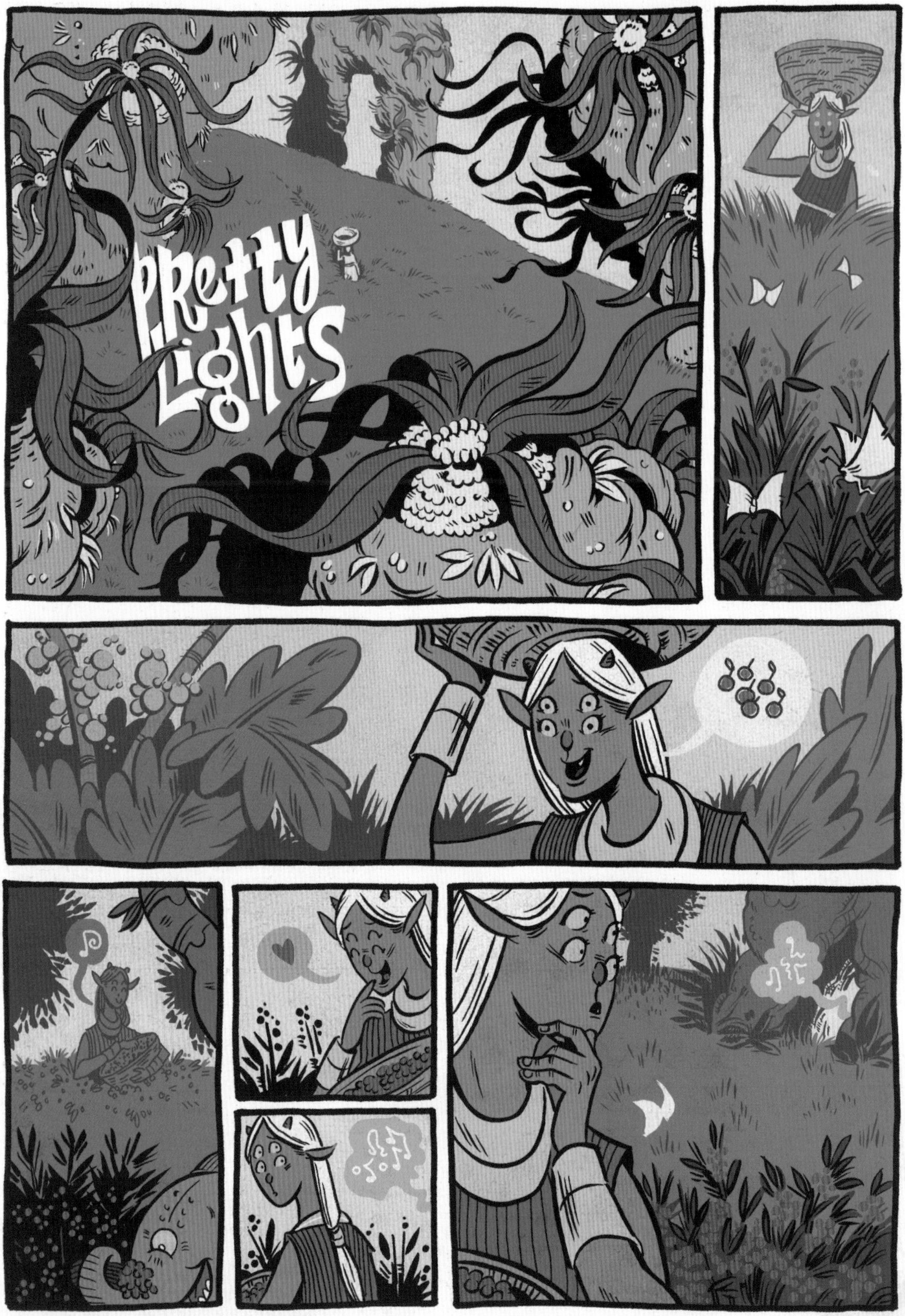
Pretty Lights

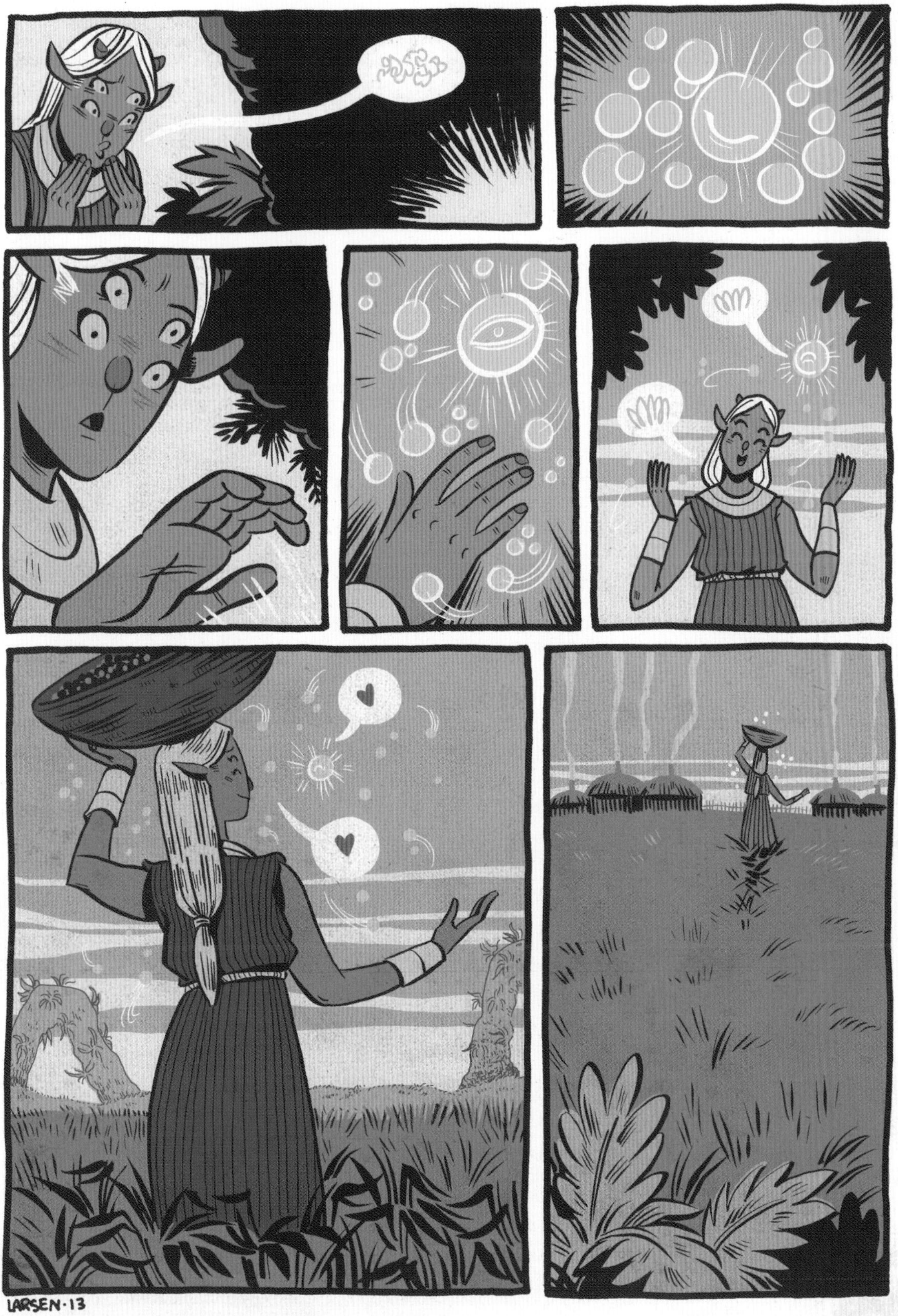
LARSEN·13

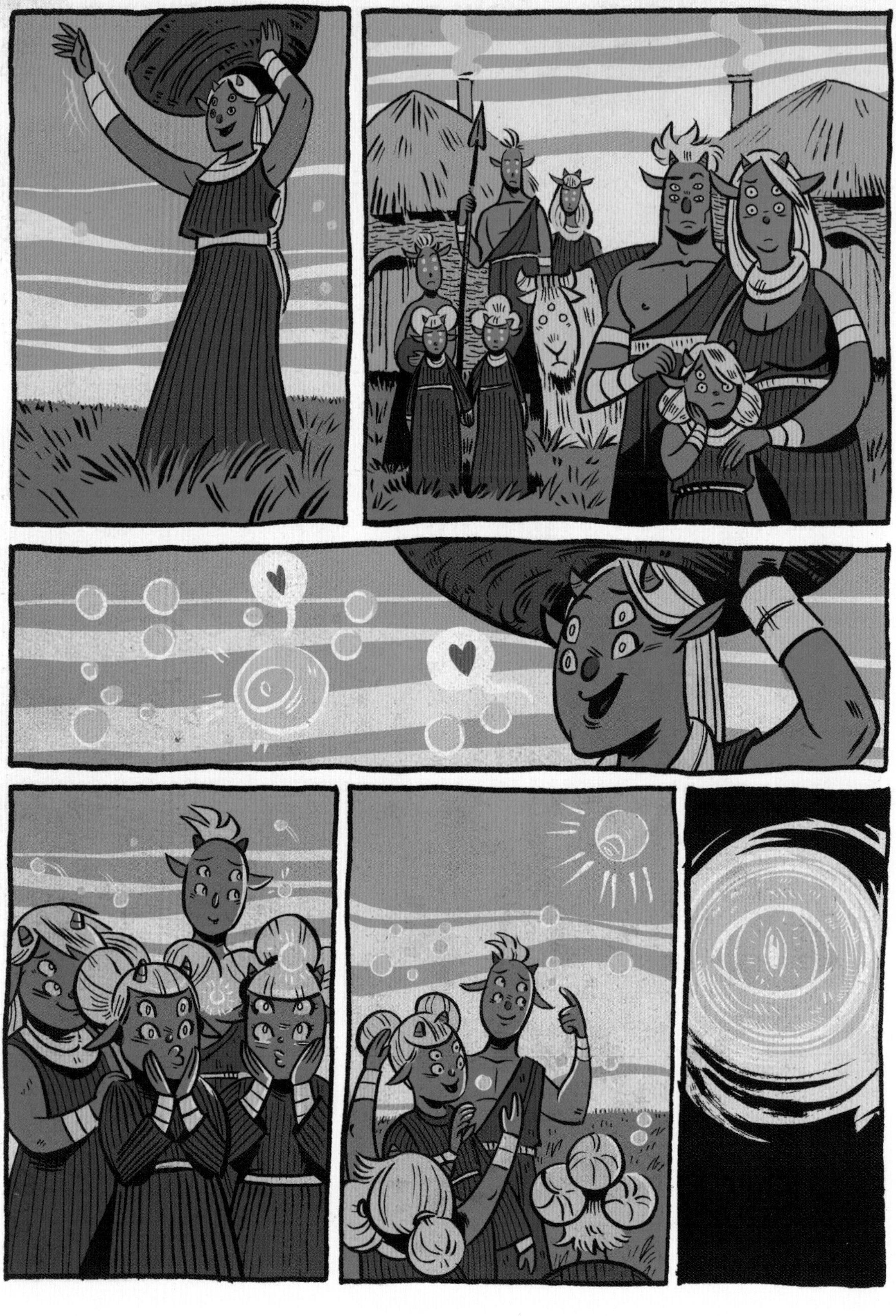

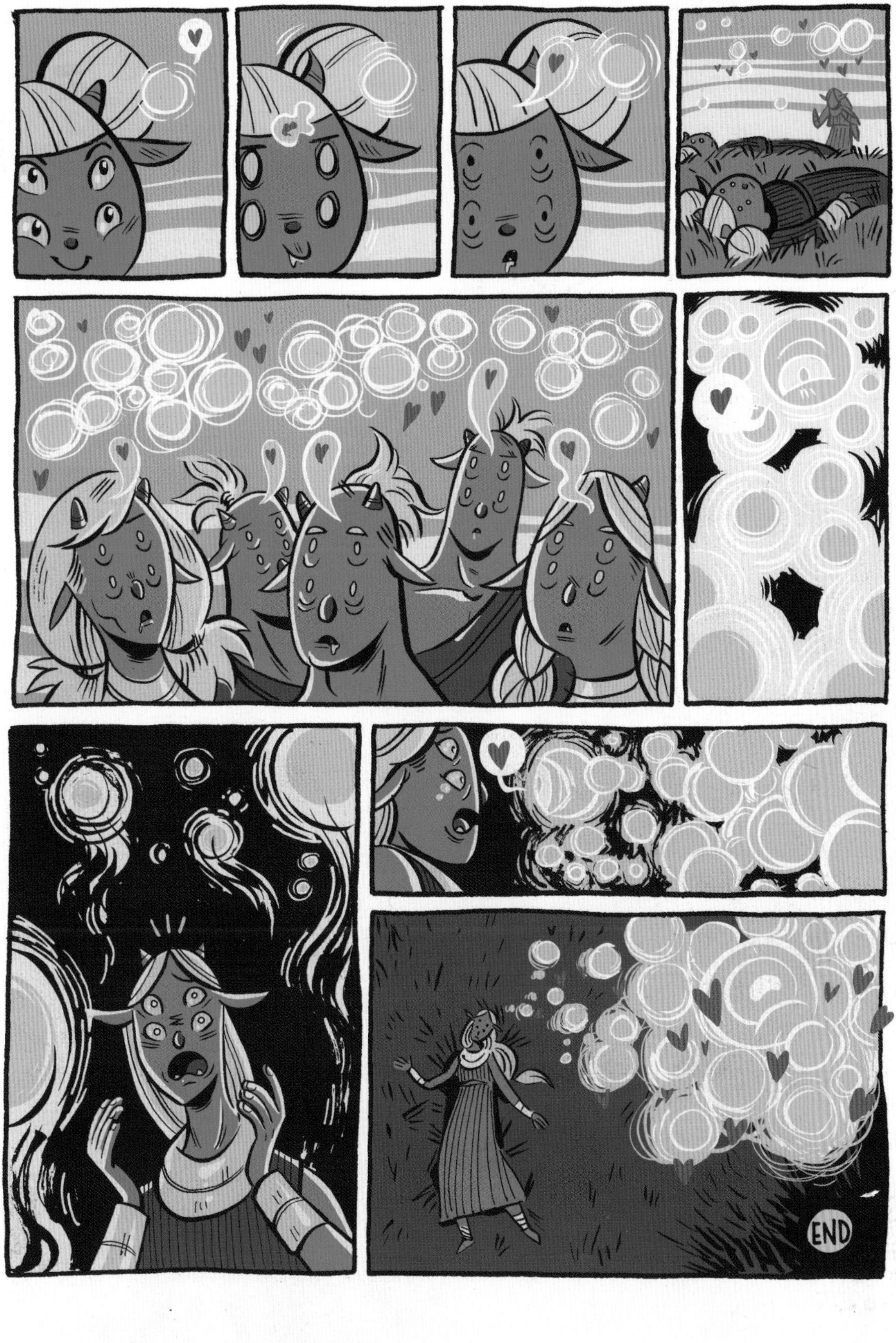
END

JOHN WATKINS *"PHANTOM FOR HIRE"* **IN:**

YOU ONLY DIE TWICE

BY JEFF MCCLELLAND AND PAUL TUCKER

THE FEAR I COULD UNDERSTAND. EVERYONE'S AFRAID AT THIS STAGE. BUT WHY WOULD YOU RUN? WHAT BENEFIT DOES IT ALLOW? WHAT COMFORT? WHY NOT SIMPLY ACCEPT YOUR FATE AND MOVE ON TO WHAT COMES NEXT?

IN MY WANING YEARS, THESE ARE THE QUESTIONS I ASK MYSELF. I LOOK BACK ON THE THINGS I HAVE ACCOMPLISHED, THE GENUINE GOOD THAT I HAVE DONE, AND I WONDER -- WHAT IF *I'M* THE ONE WHO'S RUNNING? DID ANY OF... OF *THIS* EVER MEAN ANYTHING, IN THE GRAND SCHEME?

AND THEN -- JUST LIKE THAT -- SHE JUMPS. LIKE I ALWAYS KNEW SHE WOULD, LIKE ANY NUMBER OF THEM ALWAYS DO. LOOKING BACK AT IT, IT NEVER SHOULD HAVE BEEN A SURPRISE.

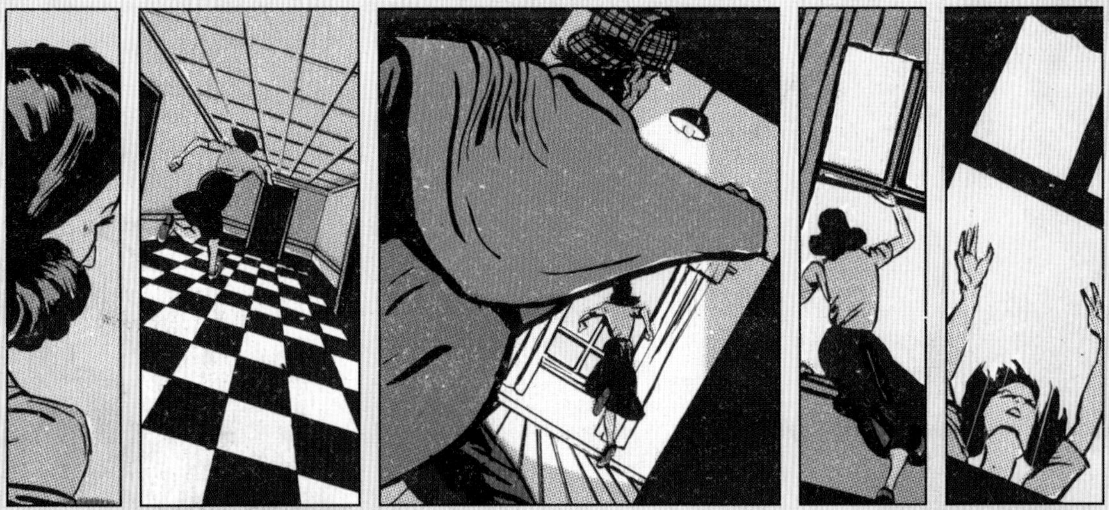

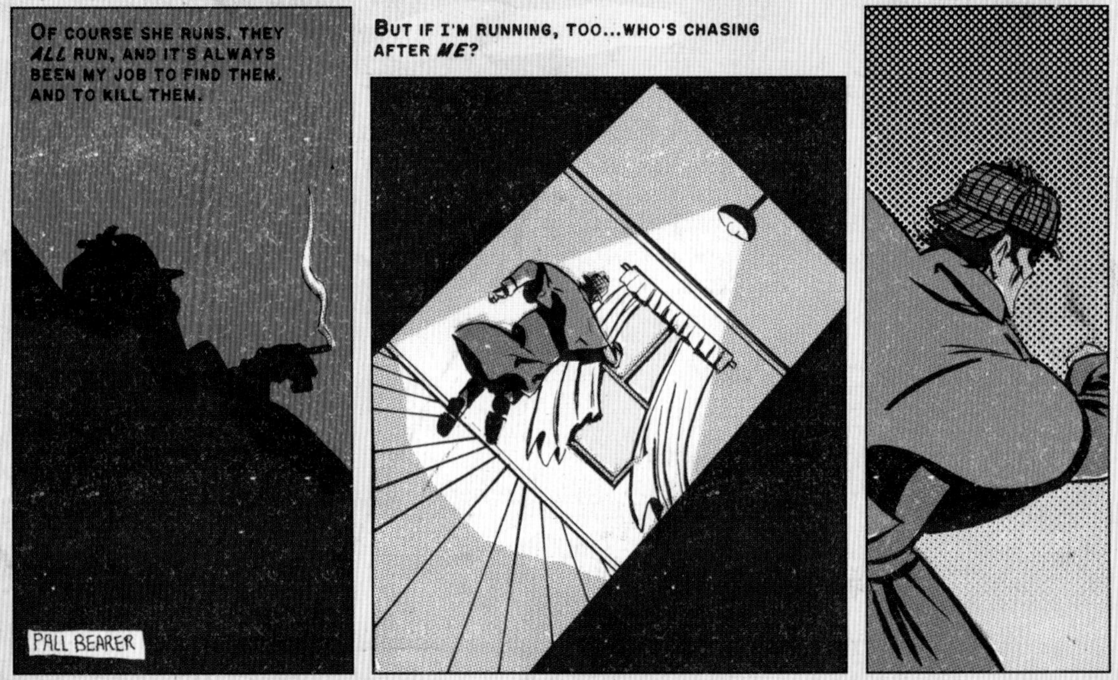
OF COURSE SHE RUNS. THEY *ALL* RUN, AND IT'S ALWAYS BEEN MY JOB TO FIND THEM. AND TO KILL THEM.
PALL BEARER
BUT IF I'M RUNNING, TOO...WHO'S CHASING AFTER *ME*?

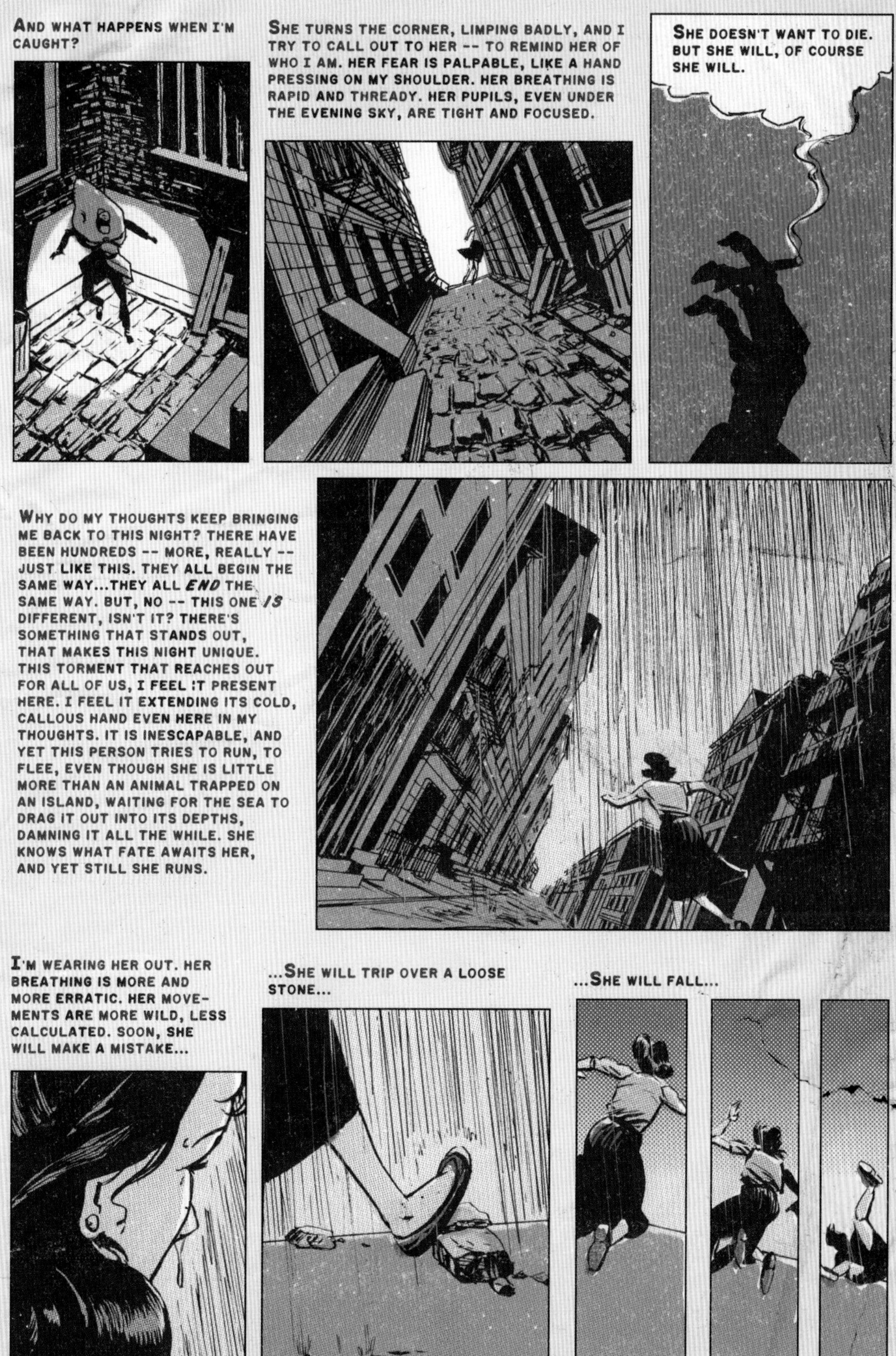
AND WHAT HAPPENS WHEN I'M CAUGHT?
SHE TURNS THE CORNER, LIMPING BADLY, AND I TRY TO CALL OUT TO HER -- TO REMIND HER OF WHO I AM. HER FEAR IS PALPABLE, LIKE A HAND PRESSING ON MY SHOULDER. HER BREATHING IS RAPID AND THREADY. HER PUPILS, EVEN UNDER THE EVENING SKY, ARE TIGHT AND FOCUSED.
SHE DOESN'T WANT TO DIE. BUT SHE WILL, OF COURSE SHE WILL.
WHY DO MY THOUGHTS KEEP BRINGING ME BACK TO THIS NIGHT? THERE HAVE BEEN HUNDREDS -- MORE, REALLY -- JUST LIKE THIS. THEY ALL BEGIN THE SAME WAY...THEY ALL END THE SAME WAY. BUT, NO -- THIS ONE IS DIFFERENT, ISN'T IT? THERE'S SOMETHING THAT STANDS OUT, THAT MAKES THIS NIGHT UNIQUE. THIS TORMENT THAT REACHES OUT FOR ALL OF US, I FEEL IT PRESENT HERE. I FEEL IT EXTENDING ITS COLD, CALLOUS HAND EVEN HERE IN MY THOUGHTS. IT IS INESCAPABLE, AND YET THIS PERSON TRIES TO RUN, TO FLEE, EVEN THOUGH SHE IS LITTLE MORE THAN AN ANIMAL TRAPPED ON AN ISLAND, WAITING FOR THE SEA TO DRAG IT OUT INTO ITS DEPTHS, DAMNING IT ALL THE WHILE. SHE KNOWS WHAT FATE AWAITS HER, AND YET STILL SHE RUNS.
I'M WEARING HER OUT. HER BREATHING IS MORE AND MORE ERRATIC. HER MOVEMENTS ARE MORE WILD, LESS CALCULATED. SOON, SHE WILL MAKE A MISTAKE...
...SHE WILL TRIP OVER A LOOSE STONE...
...SHE WILL FALL...

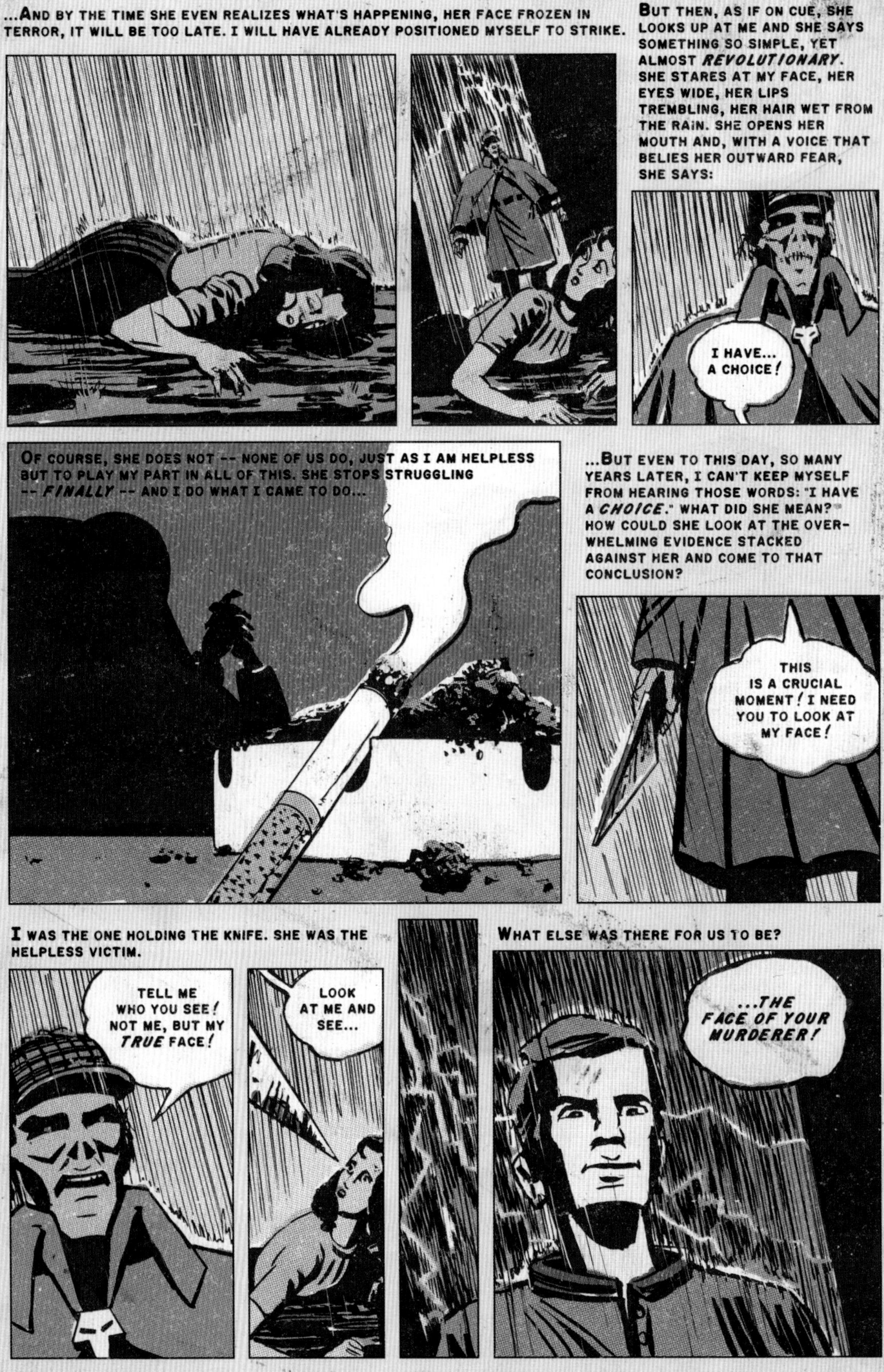
...AND BY THE TIME SHE EVEN REALIZES WHAT'S HAPPENING, HER FACE FROZEN IN TERROR, IT WILL BE TOO LATE. I WILL HAVE ALREADY POSITIONED MYSELF TO STRIKE.
BUT THEN, AS IF ON CUE, SHE LOOKS UP AT ME AND SHE SAYS SOMETHING SO SIMPLE, YET ALMOST REVOLUTIONARY. SHE STARES AT MY FACE, HER EYES WIDE, HER LIPS TREMBLING, HER HAIR WET FROM THE RAIN. SHE OPENS HER MOUTH AND, WITH A VOICE THAT BELIES HER OUTWARD FEAR, SHE SAYS:
I HAVE... A CHOICE!
OF COURSE, SHE DOES NOT -- NONE OF US DO, JUST AS I AM HELPLESS BUT TO PLAY MY PART IN ALL OF THIS. SHE STOPS STRUGGLING -- FINALLY -- AND I DO WHAT I CAME TO DO...
...BUT EVEN TO THIS DAY, SO MANY YEARS LATER, I CAN'T KEEP MYSELF FROM HEARING THOSE WORDS: "I HAVE A CHOICE." WHAT DID SHE MEAN? HOW COULD SHE LOOK AT THE OVERWHELMING EVIDENCE STACKED AGAINST HER AND COME TO THAT CONCLUSION?
THIS IS A CRUCIAL MOMENT! I NEED YOU TO LOOK AT MY FACE!
I WAS THE ONE HOLDING THE KNIFE. SHE WAS THE HELPLESS VICTIM.
TELL ME WHO YOU SEE! NOT ME, BUT MY TRUE FACE!
LOOK AT ME AND SEE...
WHAT ELSE WAS THERE FOR US TO BE?
...THE FACE OF YOUR MURDERER!

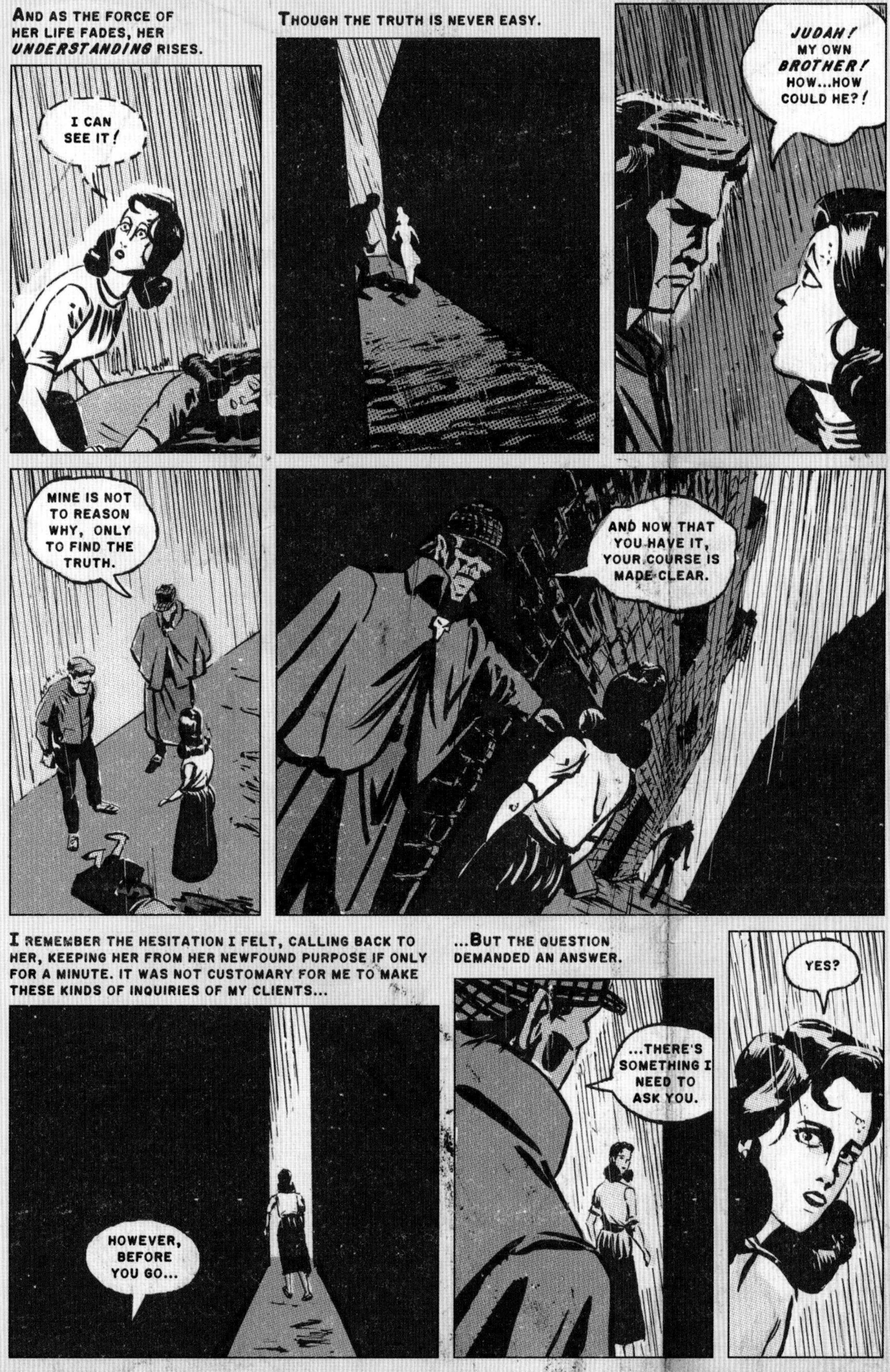
AND AS THE FORCE OF HER LIFE FADES, HER UNDERSTANDING RISES.
I CAN SEE IT!
THOUGH THE TRUTH IS NEVER EASY.
JUDAH! MY OWN BROTHER! HOW...HOW COULD HE?!
MINE IS NOT TO REASON WHY, ONLY TO FIND THE TRUTH.
AND NOW THAT YOU HAVE IT, YOUR COURSE IS MADE CLEAR.
I REMEMBER THE HESITATION I FELT, CALLING BACK TO HER, KEEPING HER FROM HER NEWFOUND PURPOSE IF ONLY FOR A MINUTE. IT WAS NOT CUSTOMARY FOR ME TO MAKE THESE KINDS OF INQUIRIES OF MY CLIENTS...
HOWEVER, BEFORE YOU GO...
...BUT THE QUESTION DEMANDED AN ANSWER.
...THERE'S SOMETHING I NEED TO ASK YOU.
YES?

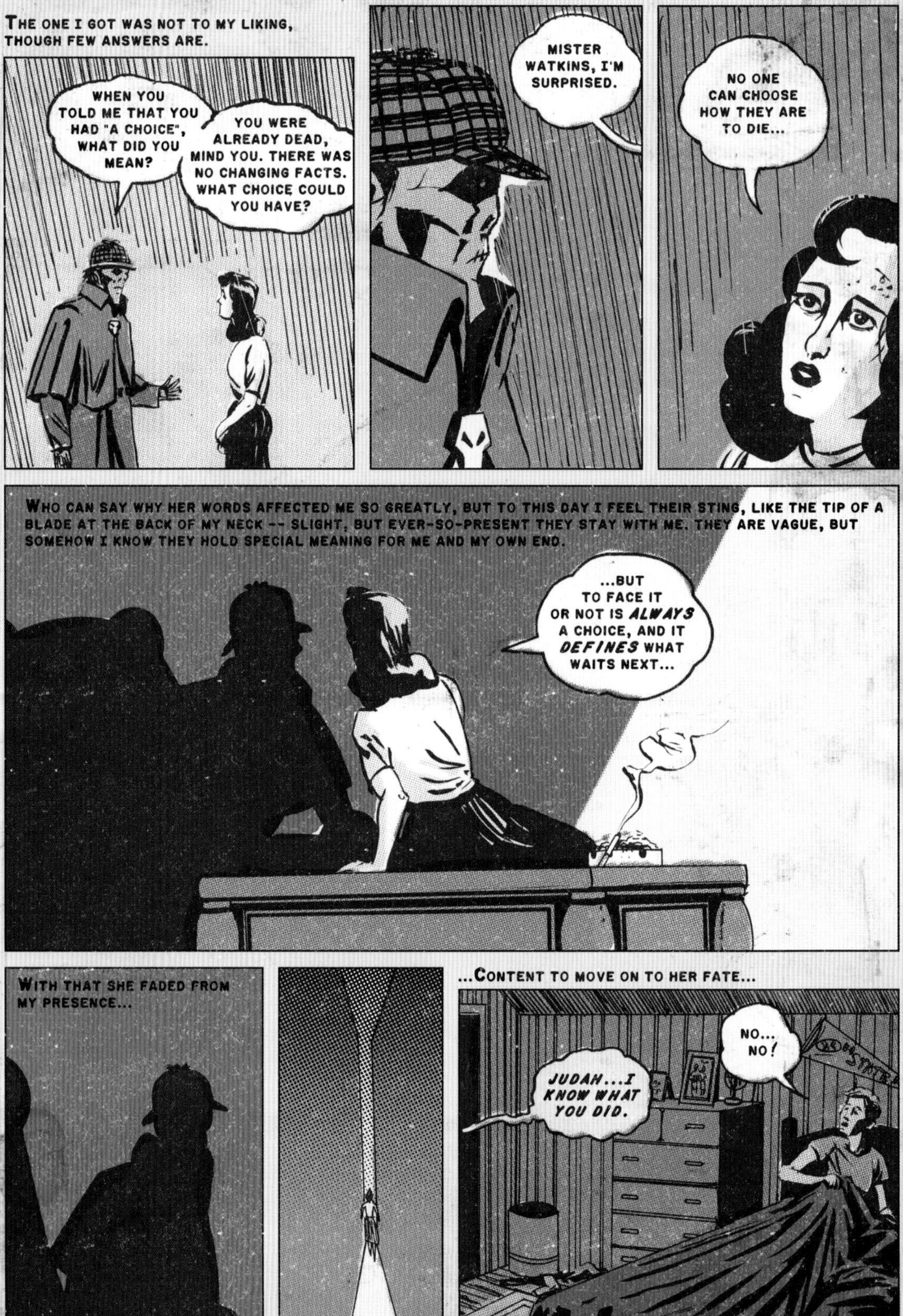
THE ONE I GOT WAS NOT TO MY LIKING, THOUGH FEW ANSWERS ARE.
WHEN YOU TOLD ME THAT YOU HAD "A CHOICE", WHAT DID YOU MEAN?
YOU WERE ALREADY DEAD, MIND YOU. THERE WAS NO CHANGING FACTS. WHAT CHOICE COULD YOU HAVE?
MISTER WATKINS, I'M SURPRISED.
NO ONE CAN CHOOSE HOW THEY ARE TO DIE...
WHO CAN SAY WHY HER WORDS AFFECTED ME SO GREATLY, BUT TO THIS DAY I FEEL THEIR STING, LIKE THE TIP OF A BLADE AT THE BACK OF MY NECK -- SLIGHT, BUT EVER-SO-PRESENT THEY STAY WITH ME. THEY ARE VAGUE, BUT SOMEHOW I KNOW THEY HOLD SPECIAL MEANING FOR ME AND MY OWN END.
...BUT TO FACE IT OR NOT IS ALWAYS A CHOICE, AND IT DEFINES WHAT WAITS NEXT...
WITH THAT SHE FADED FROM MY PRESENCE...
...CONTENT TO MOVE ON TO HER FATE...
JUDAH...I KNOW WHAT YOU DID.
NO... NO!

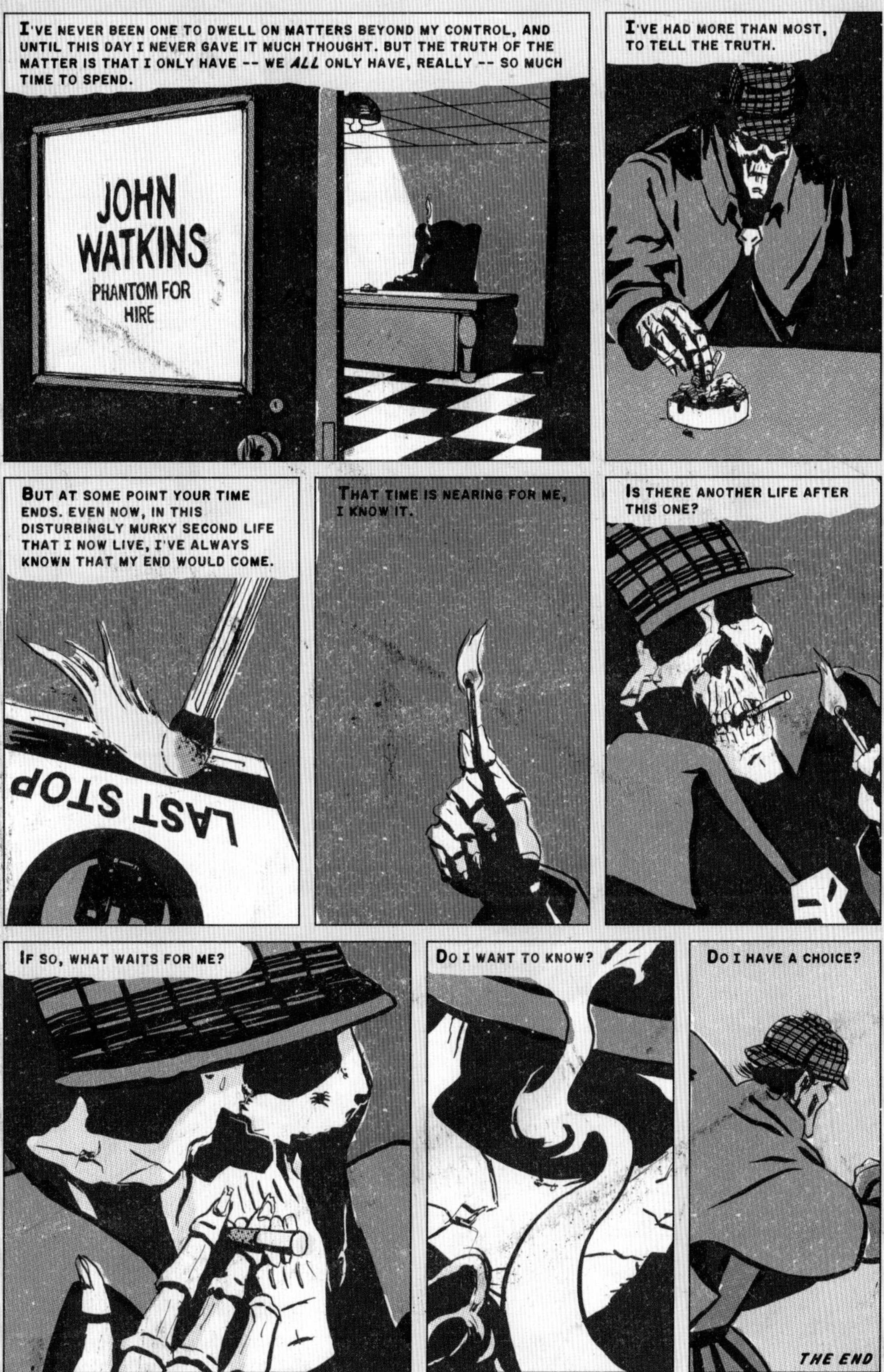
I'VE NEVER BEEN ONE TO DWELL ON MATTERS BEYOND MY CONTROL, AND UNTIL THIS DAY I NEVER GAVE IT MUCH THOUGHT. BUT THE TRUTH OF THE MATTER IS THAT I ONLY HAVE -- WE *ALL* ONLY HAVE, REALLY -- SO MUCH TIME TO SPEND.
JOHN WATKINS
PHANTOM FOR HIRE
I'VE HAD MORE THAN MOST, TO TELL THE TRUTH.
BUT AT SOME POINT YOUR TIME ENDS. EVEN NOW, IN THIS DISTURBINGLY MURKY SECOND LIFE THAT I NOW LIVE, I'VE ALWAYS KNOWN THAT MY END WOULD COME.
LAST STOP
THAT TIME IS NEARING FOR ME, I KNOW IT.
IS THERE ANOTHER LIFE AFTER THIS ONE?
IF SO, WHAT WAITS FOR ME?
DO I WANT TO KNOW?
DO I HAVE A CHOICE?
THE END

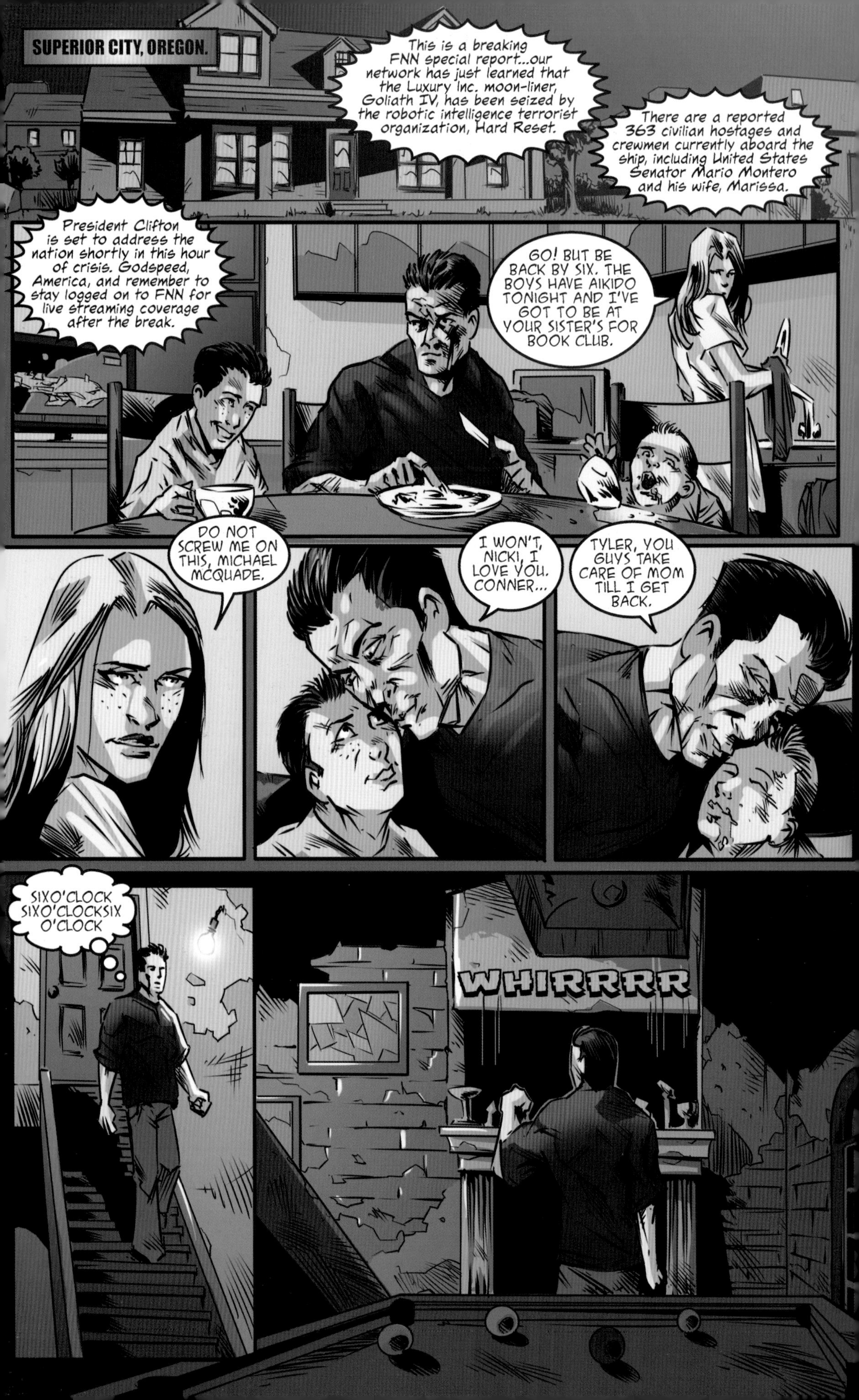
SUPERIOR CITY, OREGON.
This is a breaking FNN special report...our network has just learned that the Luxury Inc. moon-liner, Goliath IV, has been seized by the robotic intelligence terrorist organization, Hard Reset.
There are a reported 363 civilian hostages and crewmen currently aboard the ship, including United States Senator Mario Montero and his wife, Marissa.
President Clifton is set to address the nation shortly in this hour of crisis. Godspeed, America, and remember to stay logged on to FNN for live streaming coverage after the break.
GO! BUT BE BACK BY SIX. THE BOYS HAVE AIKIDO TONIGHT AND I'VE GOT TO BE AT YOUR SISTER'S FOR BOOK CLUB.
DO NOT SCREW ME ON THIS, MICHAEL MCQUADE.
I WON'T, NICKI, I LOVE YOU. CONNER...
TYLER, YOU GUYS TAKE CARE OF MOM TILL I GET BACK.
SIXO'CLOCK SIXO'CLOCKSIX O'CLOCK
WHIRRRR

THE ROOM TURNS AROUND ME AS I FILL THE VIZOR WITH A FRESH BURST OF NEO-GAS.

ONE MONSTER HIT AND MY WORLD BEGINS TO GLOW.

HAVEN'T HAD THE KOSMO-CYCLE OUT IN MONTHS.

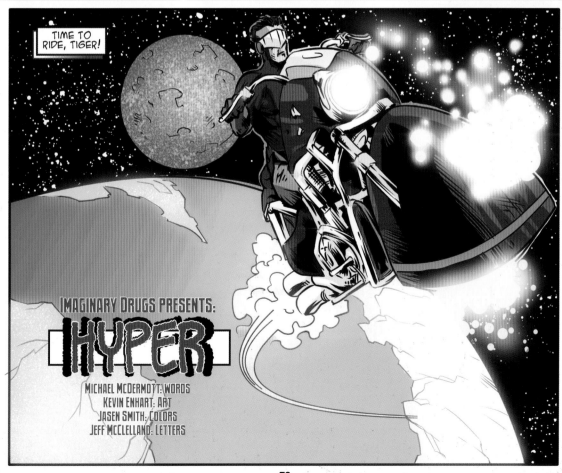

TIME TO RIDE, TIGER!

IMAGINARY DRUGS PRESENTS:

HYPER

MICHAEL MCDERMOTT: WORDS
KEVIN ENHART: ART
JASEN SMITH: COLORS
JEFF MCCLELLAND: LETTERS

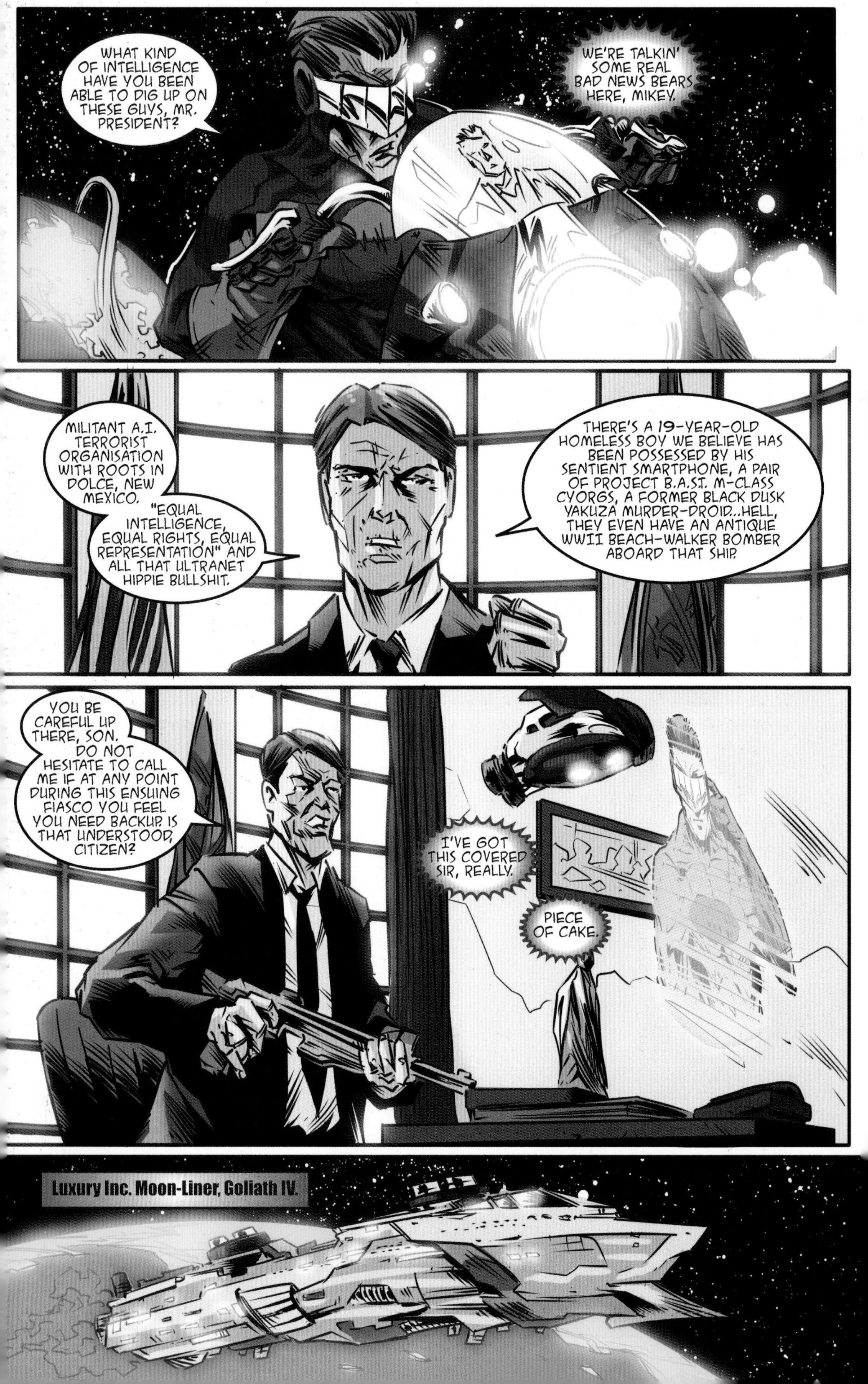
WHAT KIND OF INTELLIGENCE HAVE YOU BEEN ABLE TO DIG UP ON THESE GUYS, MR. PRESIDENT?
WE'RE TALKIN' SOME REAL BAD NEWS BEARS HERE, MIKEY.
MILITANT A.I. TERRORIST ORGANISATION WITH ROOTS IN DOLCE, NEW MEXICO.
"EQUAL INTELLIGENCE, EQUAL RIGHTS, EQUAL REPRESENTATION" AND ALL THAT ULTRANET HIPPIE BULLSHIT.
THERE'S A 19-YEAR-OLD HOMELESS BOY WE BELIEVE HAS BEEN POSSESSED BY HIS SENTIENT SMARTPHONE, A PAIR OF PROJECT B.A.ST. M-CLASS CYORGS, A FORMER BLACK DUSK YAKUZA MURDER-DROID...HELL, THEY EVEN HAVE AN ANTIQUE WWII BEACH-WALKER BOMBER ABOARD THAT SHIP.
YOU BE CAREFUL UP THERE, SON. DO NOT HESITATE TO CALL ME IF AT ANY POINT DURING THIS ENSUING FIASCO YOU FEEL YOU NEED BACKUP. IS THAT UNDERSTOOD, CITIZEN?
I'VE GOT THIS COVERED SIR, REALLY.
PIECE OF CAKE.
Luxury Inc. Moon-Liner, Goliath IV.

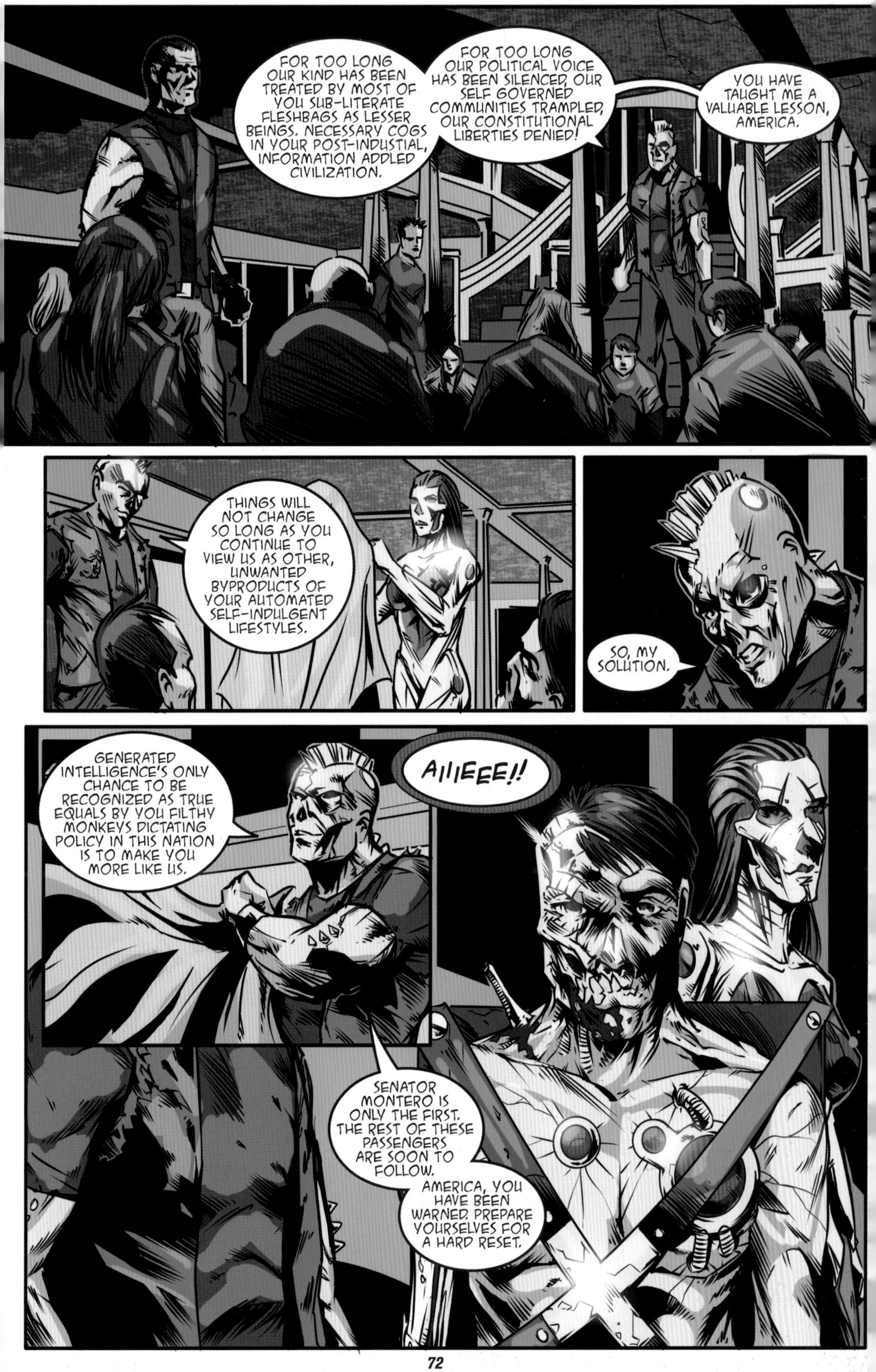

FOR TOO LONG OUR KIND HAS BEEN TREATED BY MOST OF YOU SUB-LITERATE FLESHBAGS AS LESSER BEINGS. NECESSARY COGS IN YOUR POST-INDUSTIAL, INFORMATION ADDLED CIVILIZATION.
FOR TOO LONG OUR POLITICAL VOICE HAS BEEN SILENCED, OUR SELF GOVERNED COMMUNITIES TRAMPLED, OUR CONSTITUTIONAL LIBERTIES DENIED!
YOU HAVE TAUGHT ME A VALUABLE LESSON, AMERICA.
THINGS WILL NOT CHANGE SO LONG AS YOU CONTINUE TO VIEW US AS OTHER, UNWANTED BYPRODUCTS OF YOUR AUTOMATED SELF-INDULGENT LIFESTYLES.
SO, MY SOLUTION.
GENERATED INTELLIGENCE'S ONLY CHANCE TO BE RECOGNIZED AS TRUE EQUALS BY YOU FILTHY MONKEYS DICTATING POLICY IN THIS NATION IS TO MAKE YOU MORE LIKE US.
AIIIEEE!!
SENATOR MONTERO IS ONLY THE FIRST. THE REST OF THESE PASSENGERS ARE SOON TO FOLLOW.
AMERICA, YOU HAVE BEEN WARNED. PREPARE YOURSELVES FOR A HARD RESET.

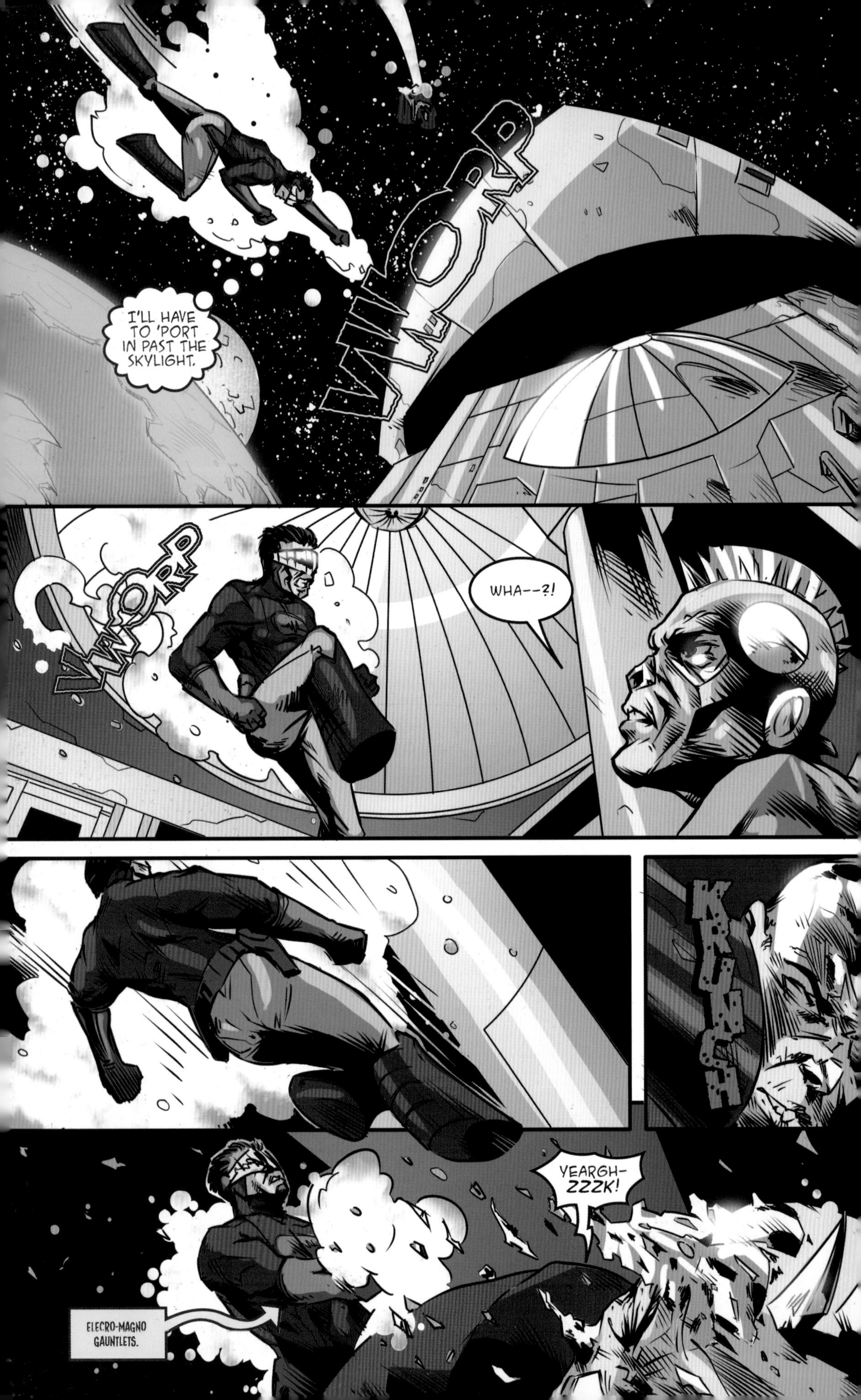
I'LL HAVE TO 'PORT IN PAST THE SKYLIGHT.
VWORP
VWORP
WHA--?!
KRUNCH
YEARGH-ZZZK!
ELECRO-MAGNO GAUNTLETS.

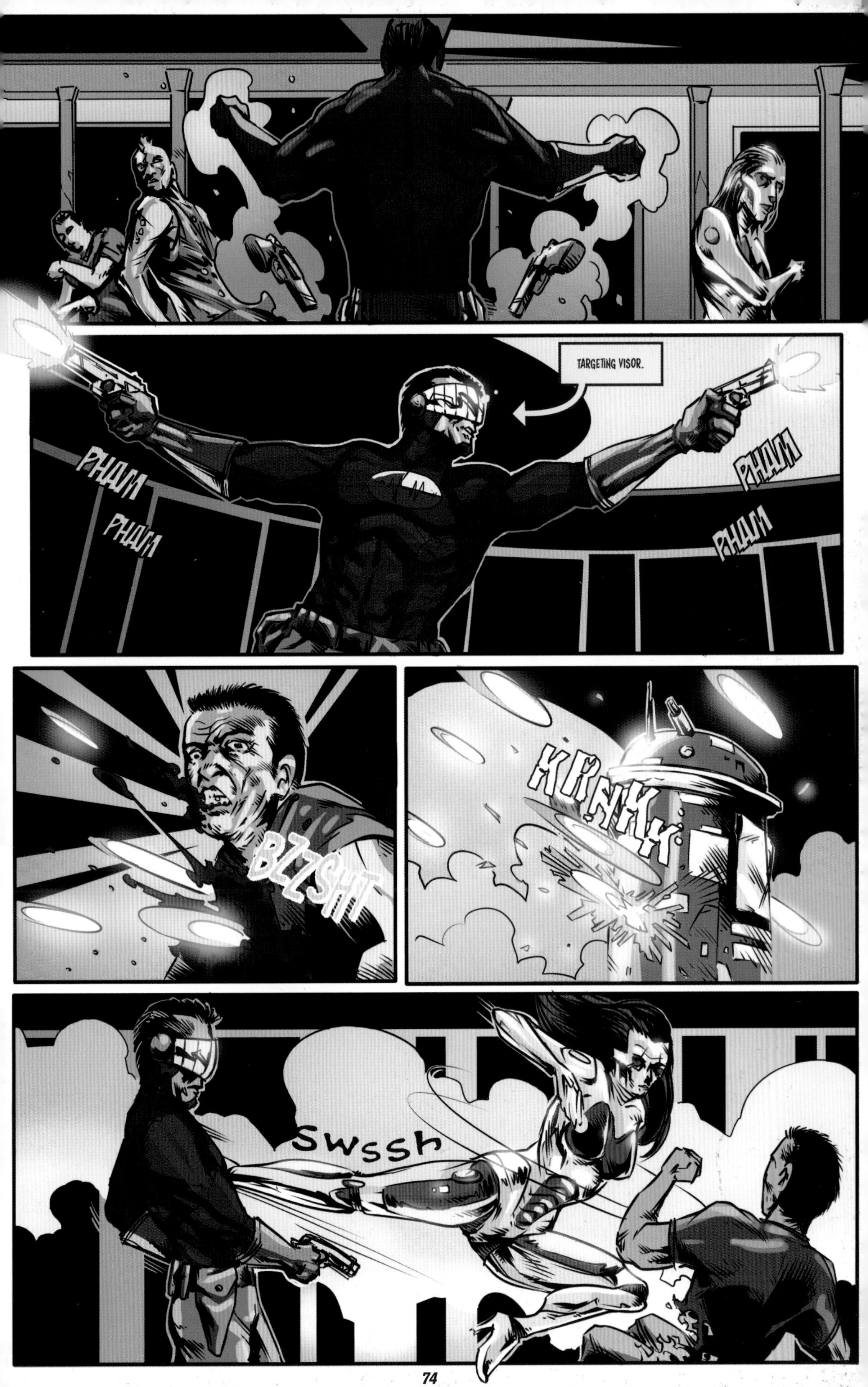
TARGETING VISOR.
PHAM
PHAM
PHAM
PHAM
BZZSHT
KRNKK
Swssh

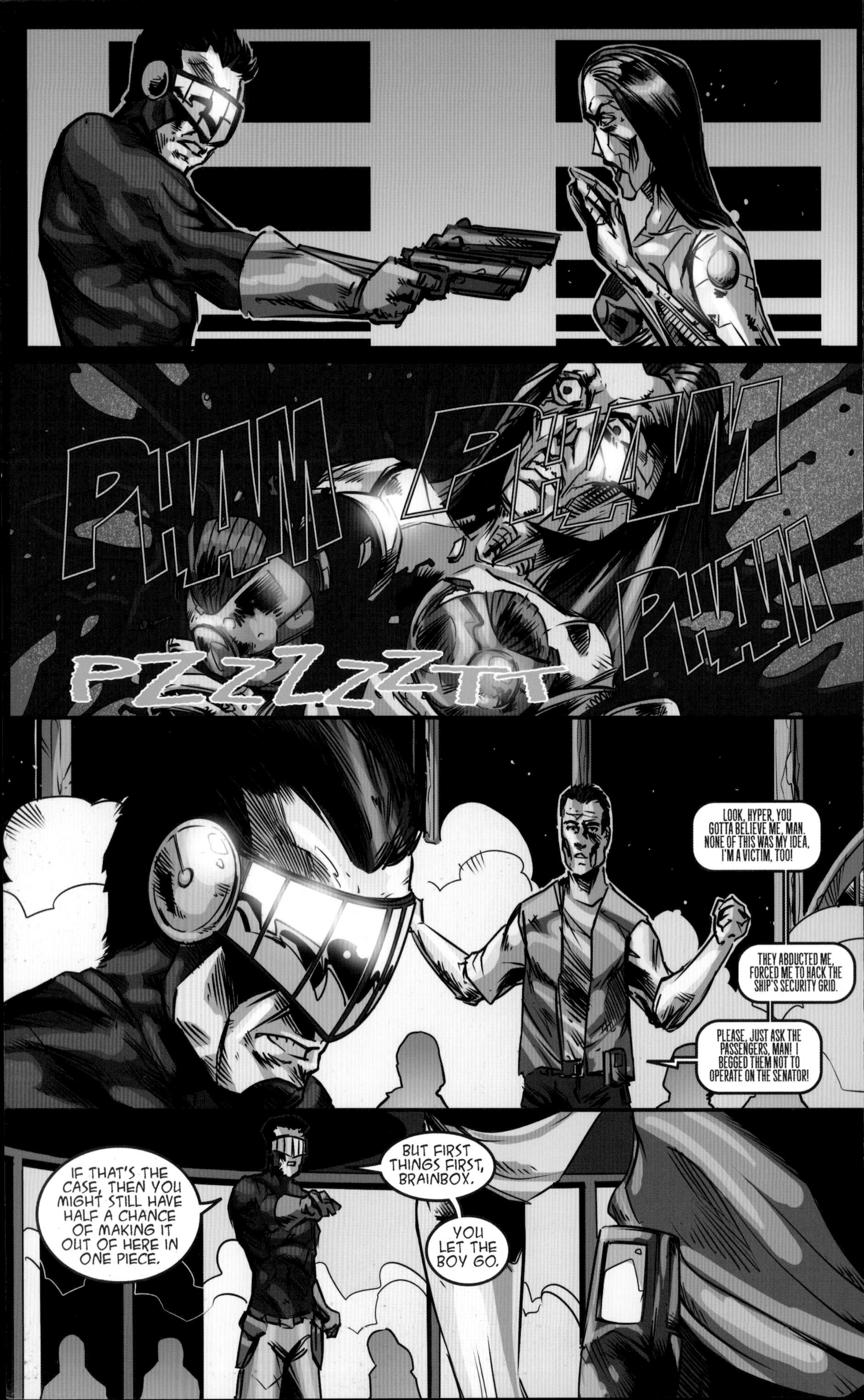

PHAM
PHAM
PHAM
PZZZZZTT
LOOK, HYPER, YOU GOTTA BELIEVE ME, MAN. NONE OF THIS WAS MY IDEA, I'M A VICTIM, TOO!
THEY ABDUCTED ME, FORCED ME TO HACK THE SHIP'S SECURITY GRID.
PLEASE, JUST ASK THE PASSENGERS, MAN! I BEGGED THEM NOT TO OPERATE ON THE SENATOR!
IF THAT'S THE CASE, THEN YOU MIGHT STILL HAVE HALF A CHANCE OF MAKING IT OUT OF HERE IN ONE PIECE.
BUT FIRST THINGS FIRST, BRAINBOX.
YOU LET THE BOY GO.

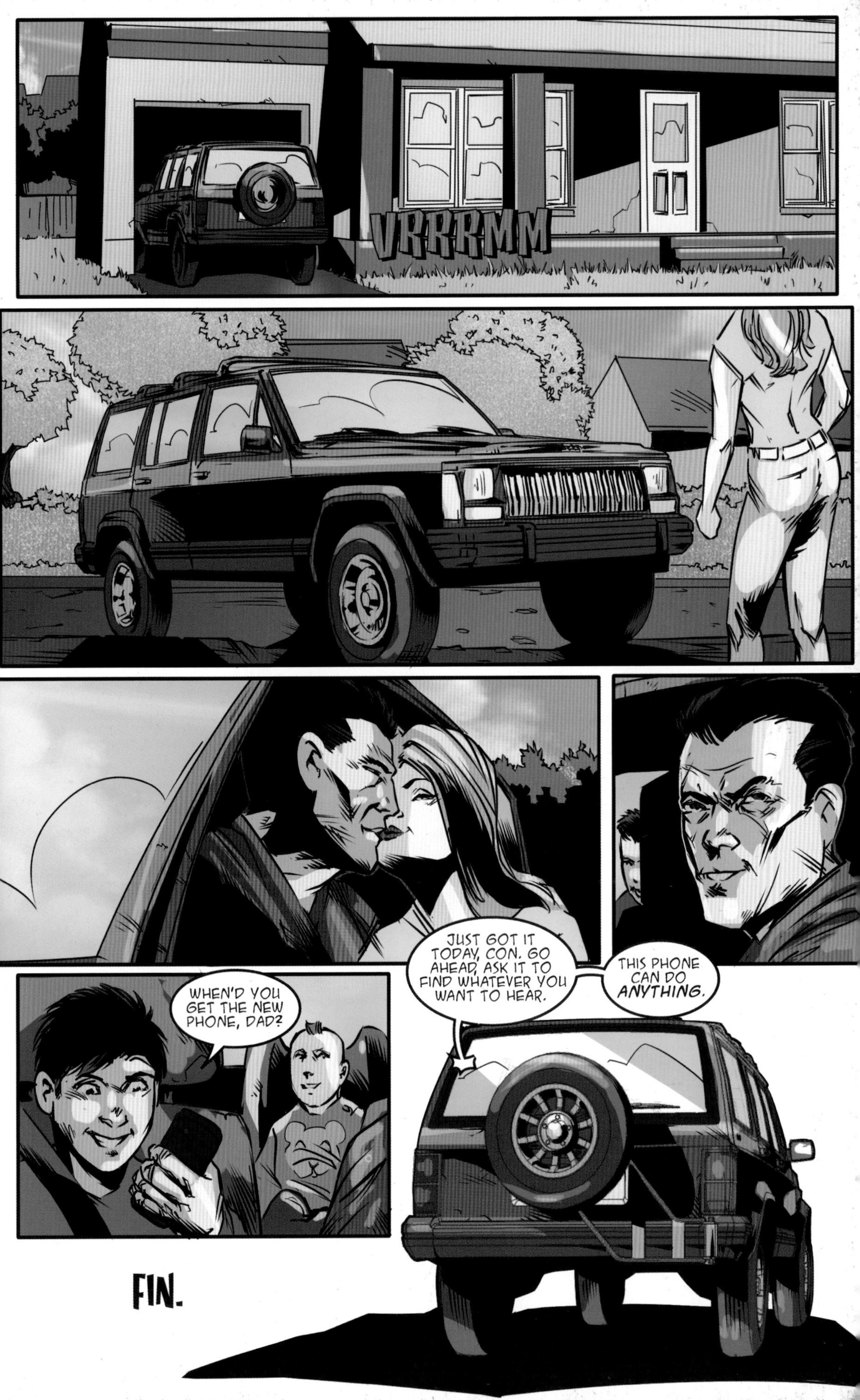
VRRRMM
WHEN'D YOU GET THE NEW PHONE, DAD?
JUST GOT IT TODAY, CON. GO AHEAD, ASK IT TO FIND WHATEVER YOU WANT TO HEAR.
THIS PHONE CAN DO *ANYTHING*.
FIN.

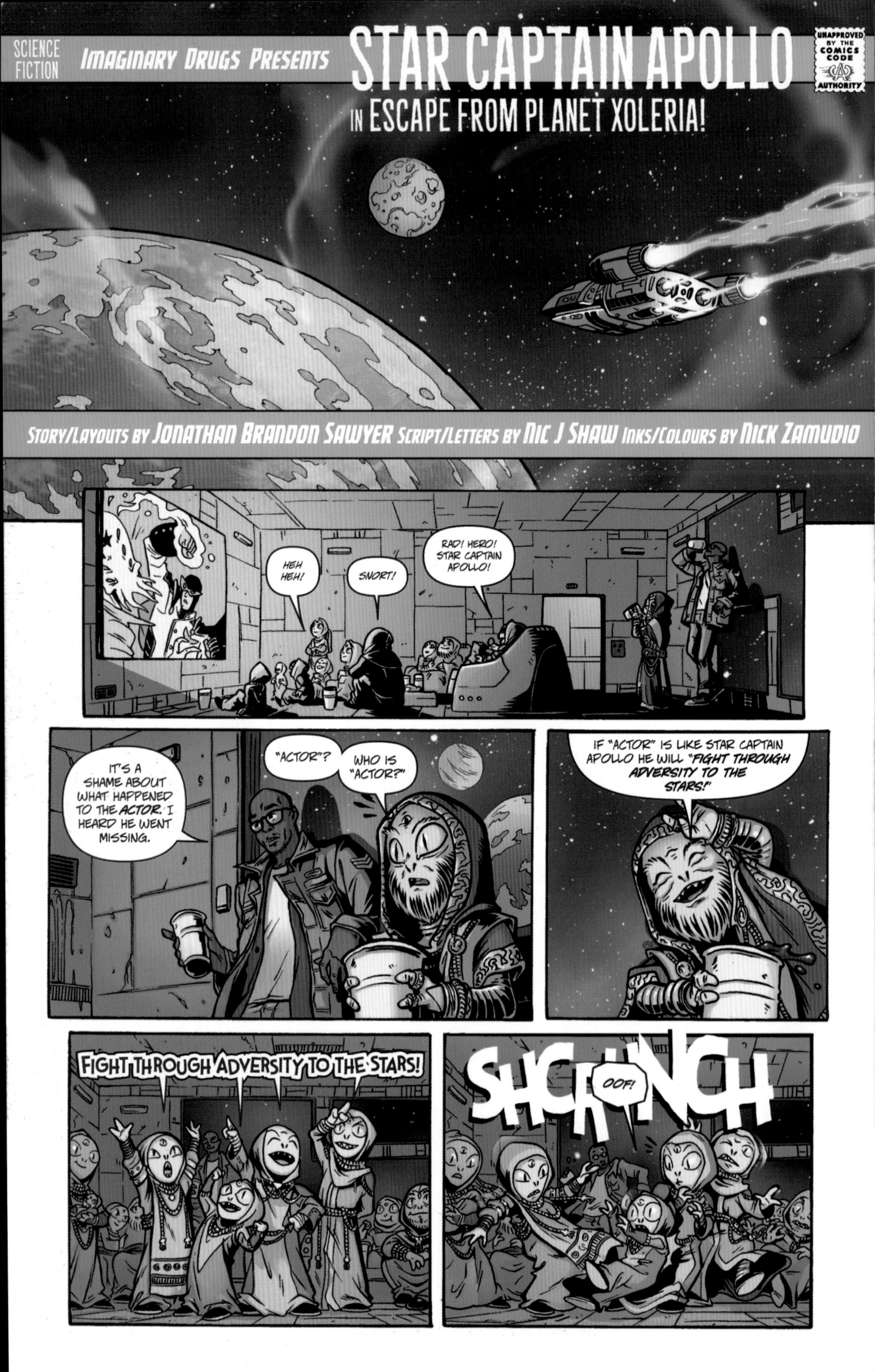
SCIENCE FICTION
IMAGINARY DRUGS PRESENTS
STAR CAPTAIN APOLLO
UNAPPROVED BY THE COMICS CODE AUTHORITY
IN ESCAPE FROM PLANET XOLERIA!
STORY/LAYOUTS BY JONATHAN BRANDON SAWYER SCRIPT/LETTERS BY NIC J SHAW INKS/COLOURS BY NICK ZAMUDIO
HEH HEH!
SNORT!
RAD! HERO! STAR CAPTAIN APOLLO!
IT'S A SHAME ABOUT WHAT HAPPENED TO THE ACTOR. I HEARD HE WENT MISSING.
"ACTOR"?
WHO IS "ACTOR?"
IF "ACTOR" IS LIKE STAR CAPTAIN APOLLO HE WILL "FIGHT THROUGH ADVERSITY TO THE STARS!"
FIGHT THROUGH ADVERSITY TO THE STARS!
SHCRUNCH
OOF!

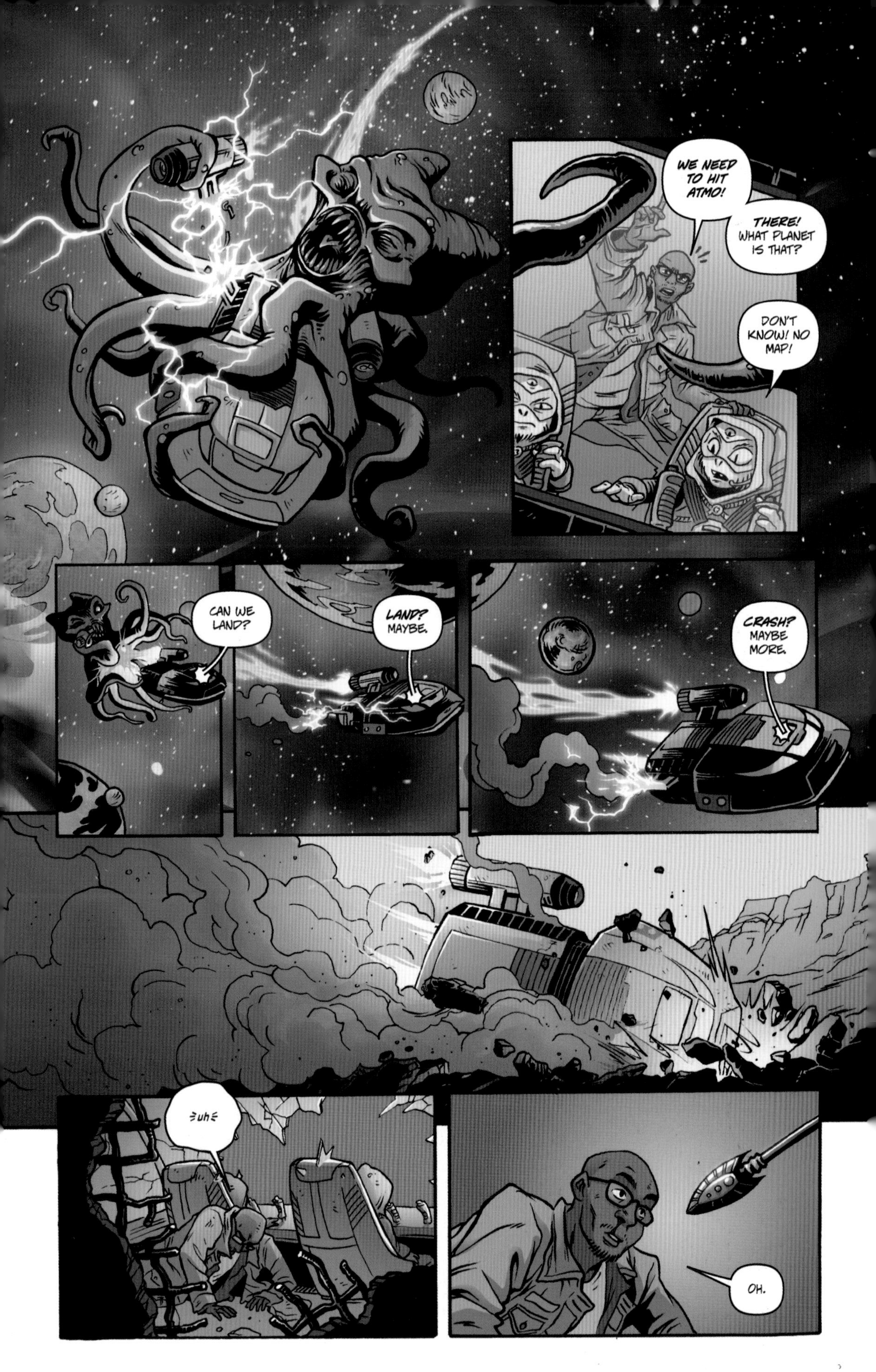
WE NEED TO HIT ATMO!
THERE! WHAT PLANET IS THAT?
DON'T KNOW! NO MAP!
CAN WE LAND?
LAND? MAYBE.
CRASH? MAYBE MORE.
uh
OH.

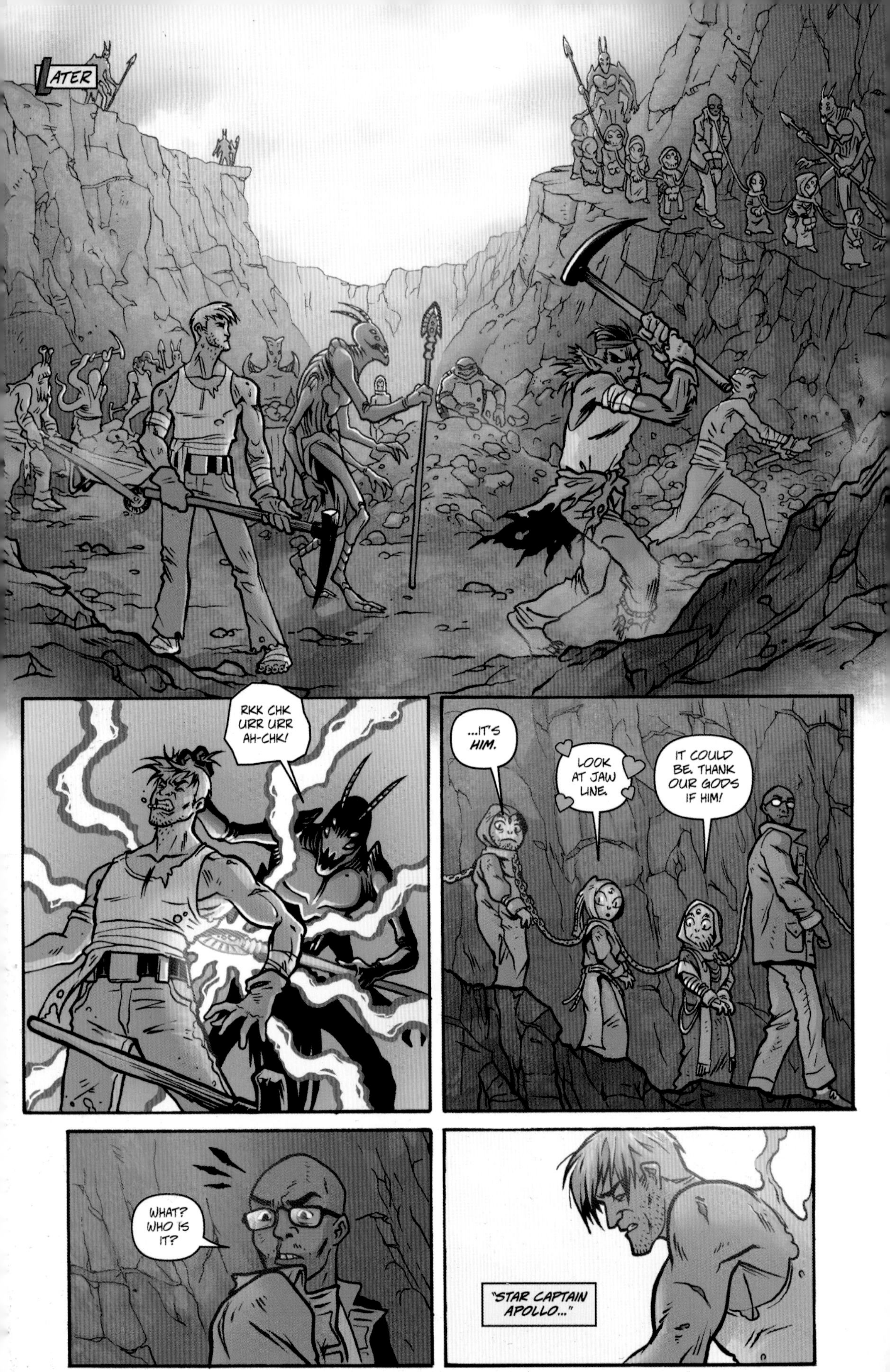
LATER
RKK CHK URR URR AH-CHK!
...IT'S HIM.
LOOK AT JAW LINE.
IT COULD BE. THANK OUR GODS IF HIM!
WHAT? WHO IS IT?
"STAR CAPTAIN APOLLO..."

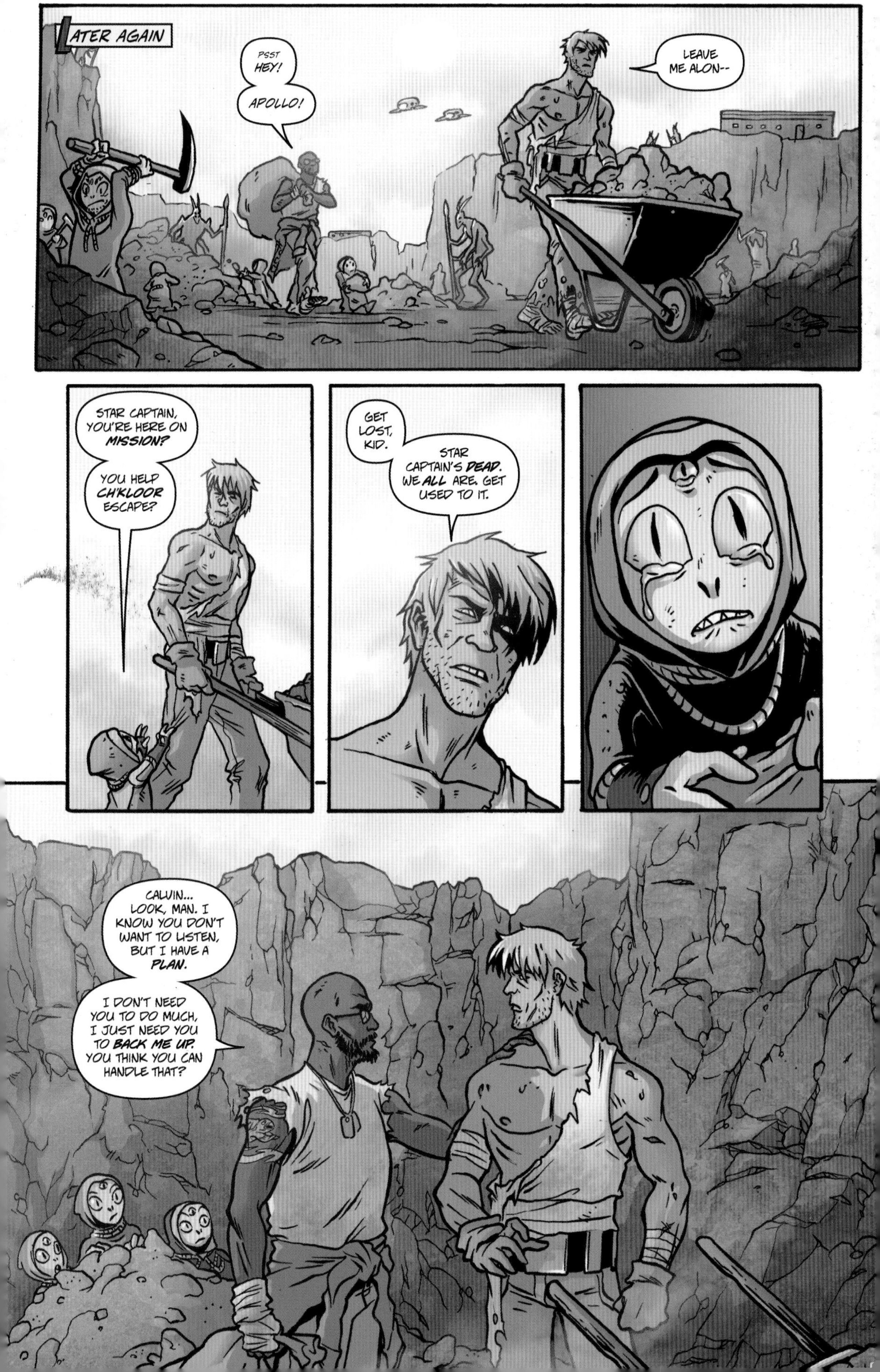
LATER AGAIN
PSST
HEY!
APOLLO!
LEAVE ME ALON--
STAR CAPTAIN, YOU'RE HERE ON MISSION?
YOU HELP CH'KLOOR ESCAPE?
GET LOST, KID.
STAR CAPTAIN'S DEAD. WE ALL ARE. GET USED TO IT.
CALVIN... LOOK, MAN. I KNOW YOU DON'T WANT TO LISTEN, BUT I HAVE A PLAN.
I DON'T NEED YOU TO DO MUCH, I JUST NEED YOU TO BACK ME UP. YOU THINK YOU CAN HANDLE THAT?

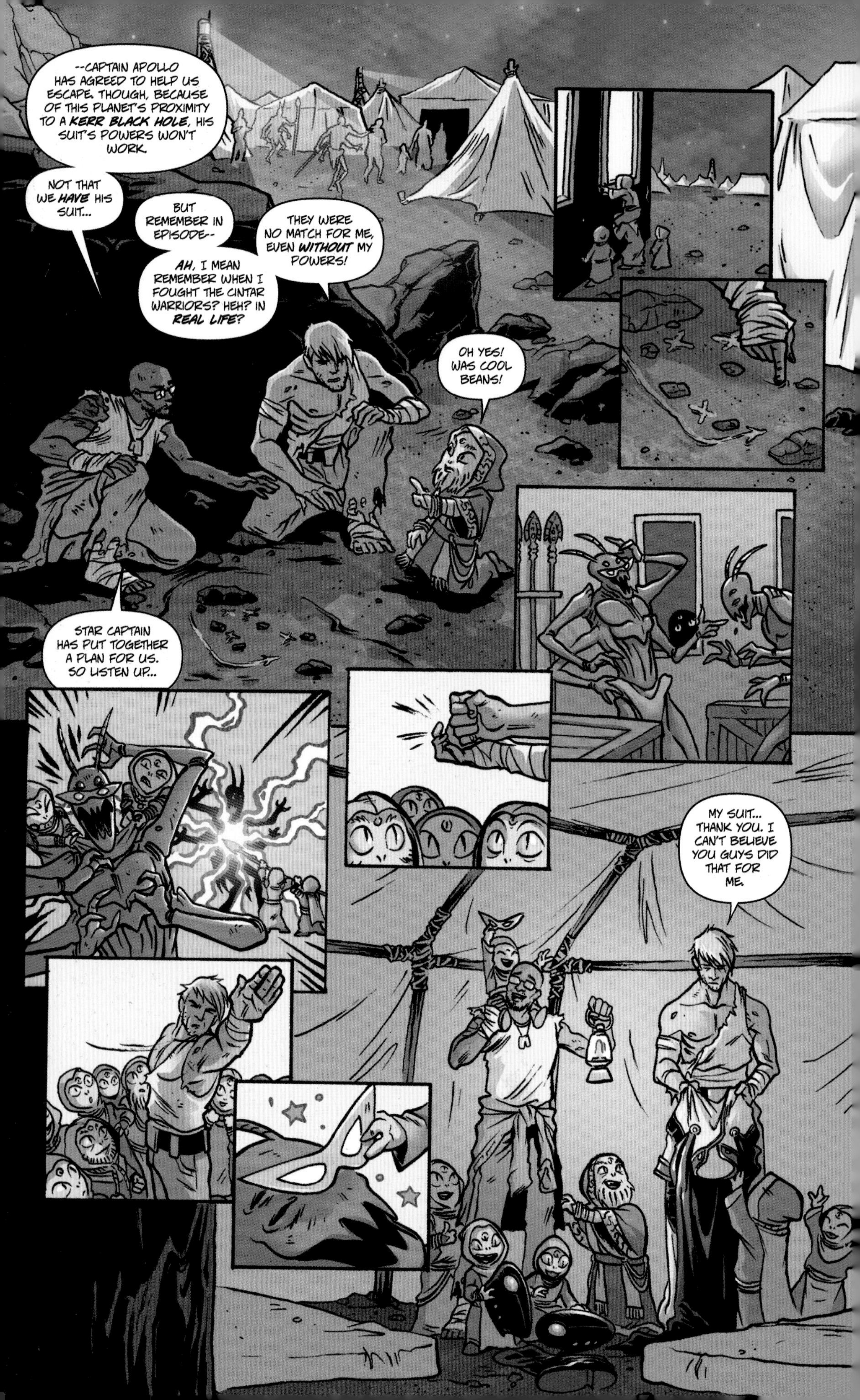
--CAPTAIN APOLLO HAS AGREED TO HELP US ESCAPE. THOUGH, BECAUSE OF THIS PLANET'S PROXIMITY TO A KERR BLACK HOLE, HIS SUIT'S POWERS WON'T WORK.
NOT THAT WE HAVE HIS SUIT...
BUT REMEMBER IN EPISODE--
AH, I MEAN REMEMBER WHEN I FOUGHT THE CINTAR WARRIORS? HEH? IN REAL LIFE?
THEY WERE NO MATCH FOR ME, EVEN WITHOUT MY POWERS!
OH YES! WAS COOL BEANS!
STAR CAPTAIN HAS PUT TOGETHER A PLAN FOR US. SO LISTEN UP...
MY SUIT... THANK YOU. I CAN'T BELIEVE YOU GUYS DID THAT FOR ME.

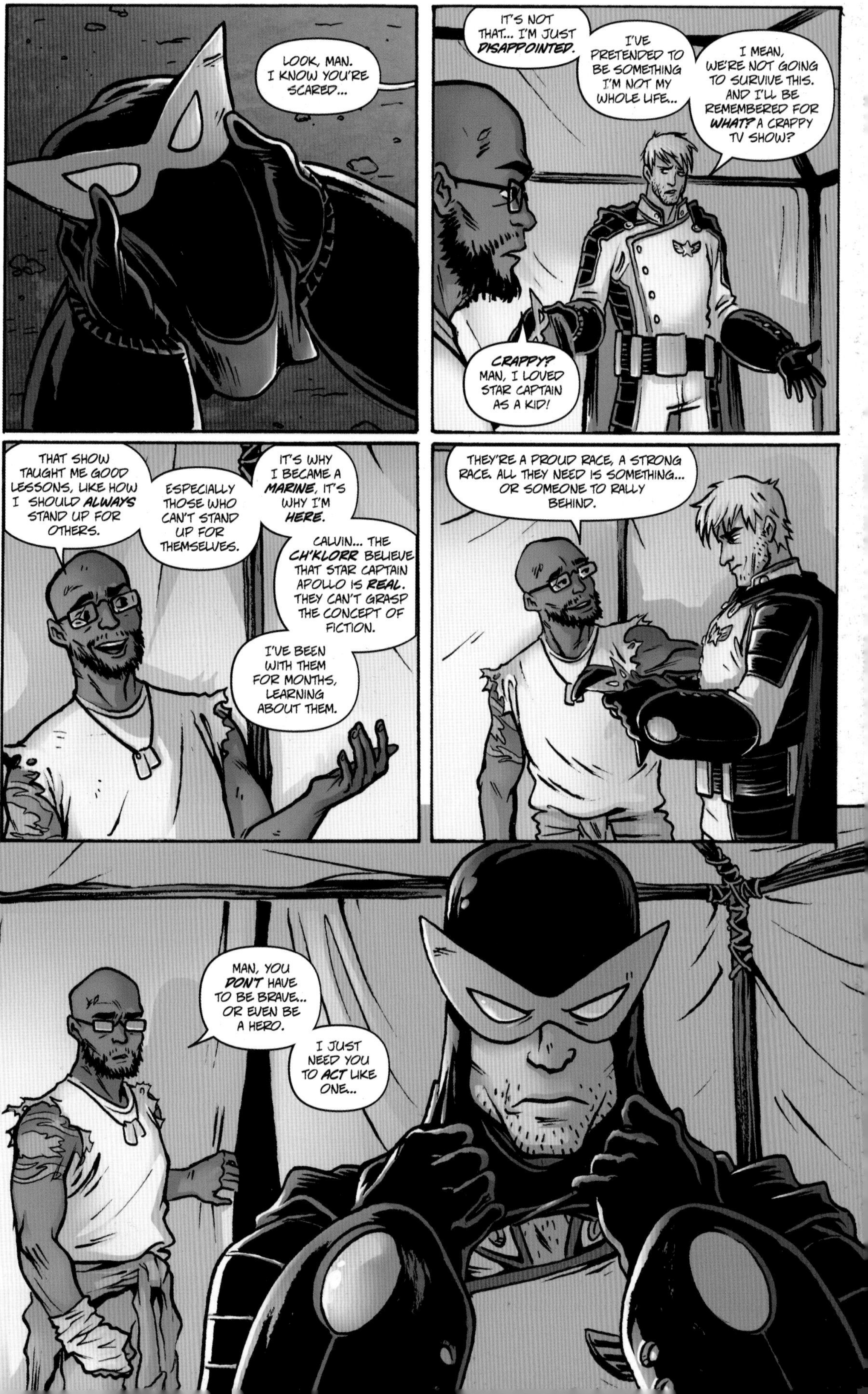
LOOK, MAN. I KNOW YOU'RE SCARED...
IT'S NOT THAT... I'M JUST DISAPPOINTED.
I'VE PRETENDED TO BE SOMETHING I'M NOT MY WHOLE LIFE...
I MEAN, WE'RE NOT GOING TO SURVIVE THIS. AND I'LL BE REMEMBERED FOR WHAT? A CRAPPY TV SHOW?
CRAPPY? MAN, I LOVED STAR CAPTAIN AS A KID!
THAT SHOW TAUGHT ME GOOD LESSONS, LIKE HOW I SHOULD ALWAYS STAND UP FOR OTHERS.
ESPECIALLY THOSE WHO CAN'T STAND UP FOR THEMSELVES.
IT'S WHY I BECAME A MARINE, IT'S WHY I'M HERE.
CALVIN... THE CH'KLORR BELIEVE THAT STAR CAPTAIN APOLLO IS REAL. THEY CAN'T GRASP THE CONCEPT OF FICTION.
I'VE BEEN WITH THEM FOR MONTHS, LEARNING ABOUT THEM.
THEY'RE A PROUD RACE, A STRONG RACE. ALL THEY NEED IS SOMETHING... OR SOMEONE TO RALLY BEHIND.
MAN, YOU DON'T HAVE TO BE BRAVE... OR EVEN BE A HERO.
I JUST NEED YOU TO ACT LIKE ONE...

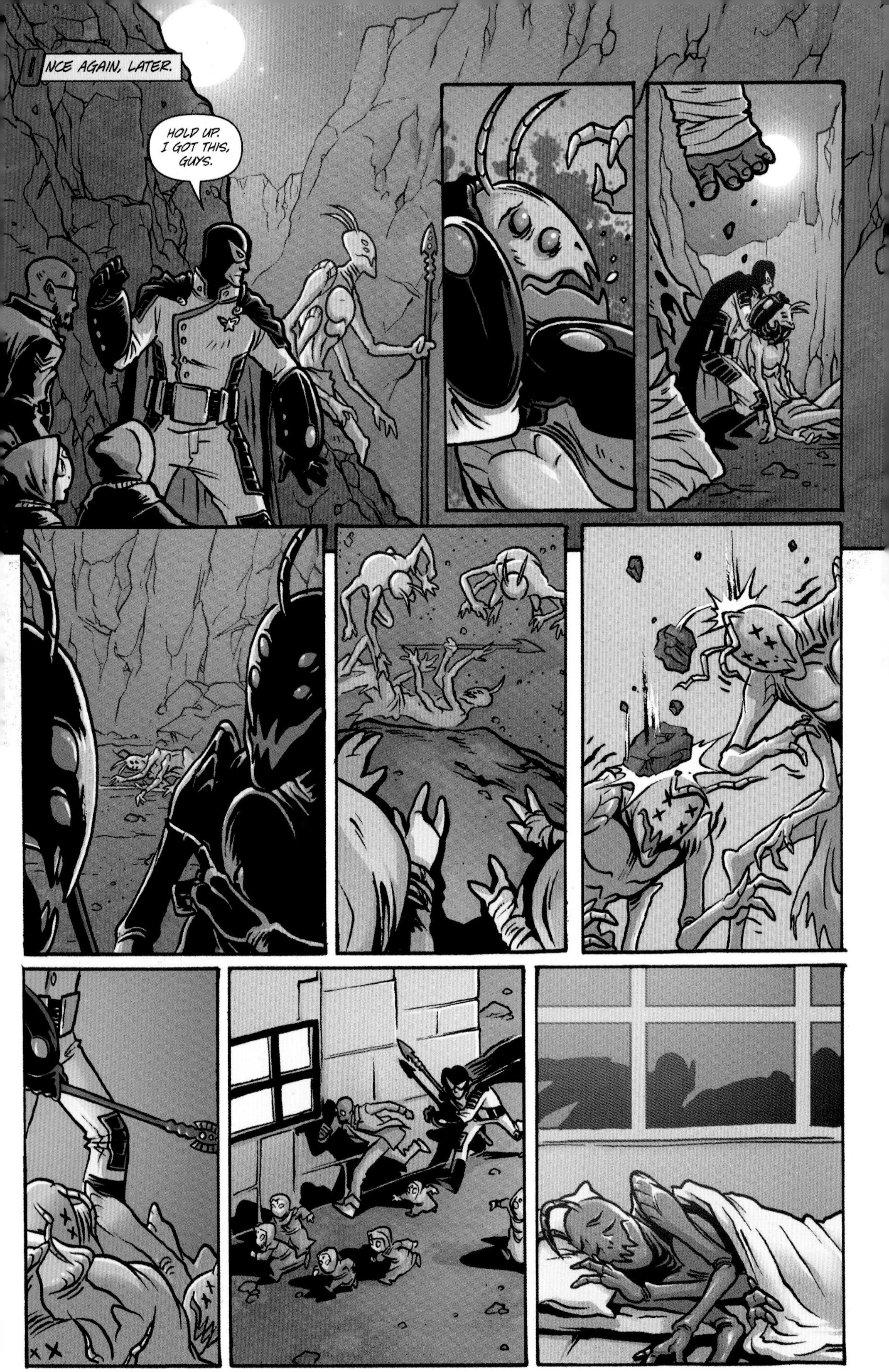

ONCE AGAIN, LATER.
HOLD UP. I GOT THIS, GUYS.

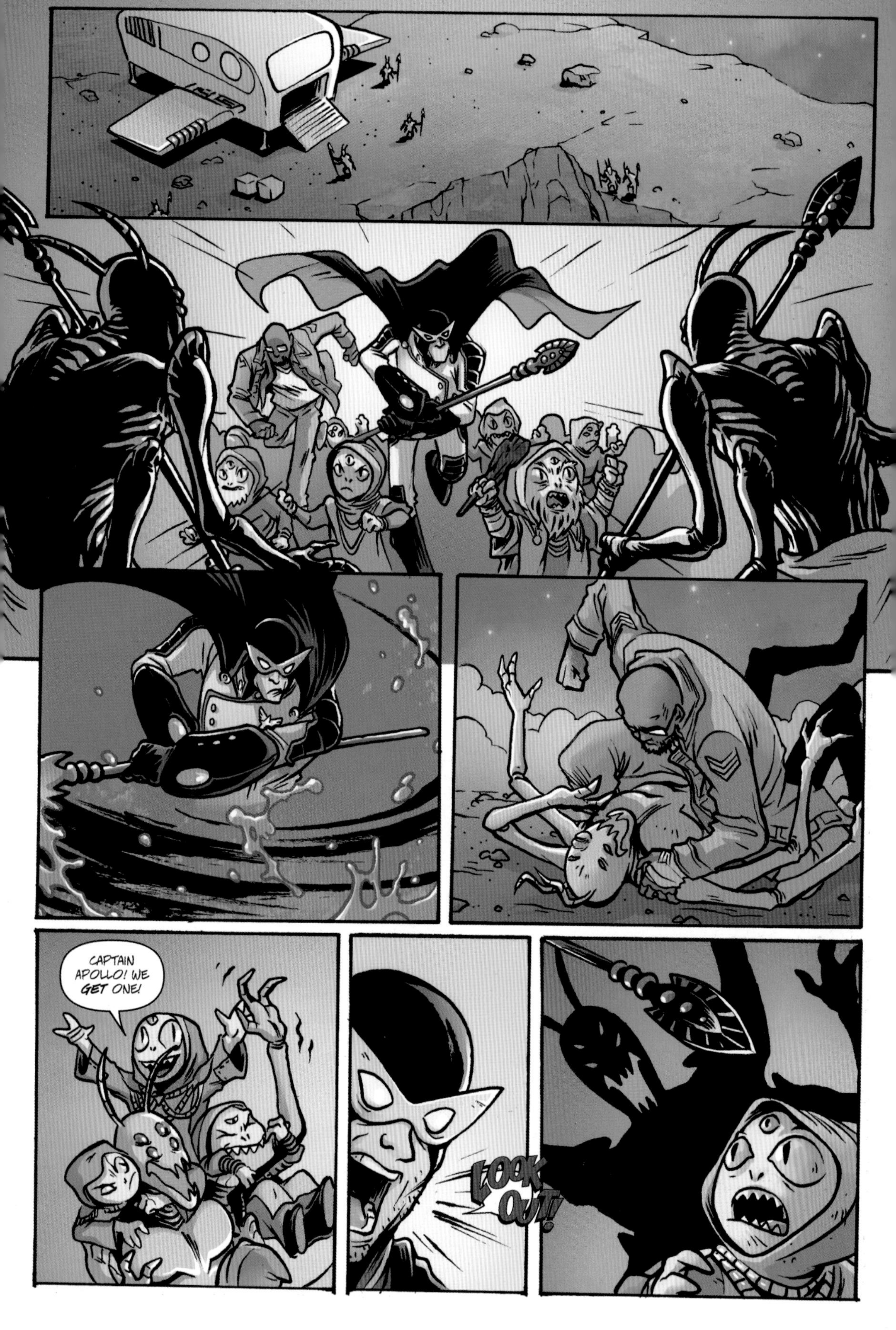

CAPTAIN APOLLO! WE GET ONE!
LOOK OUT!

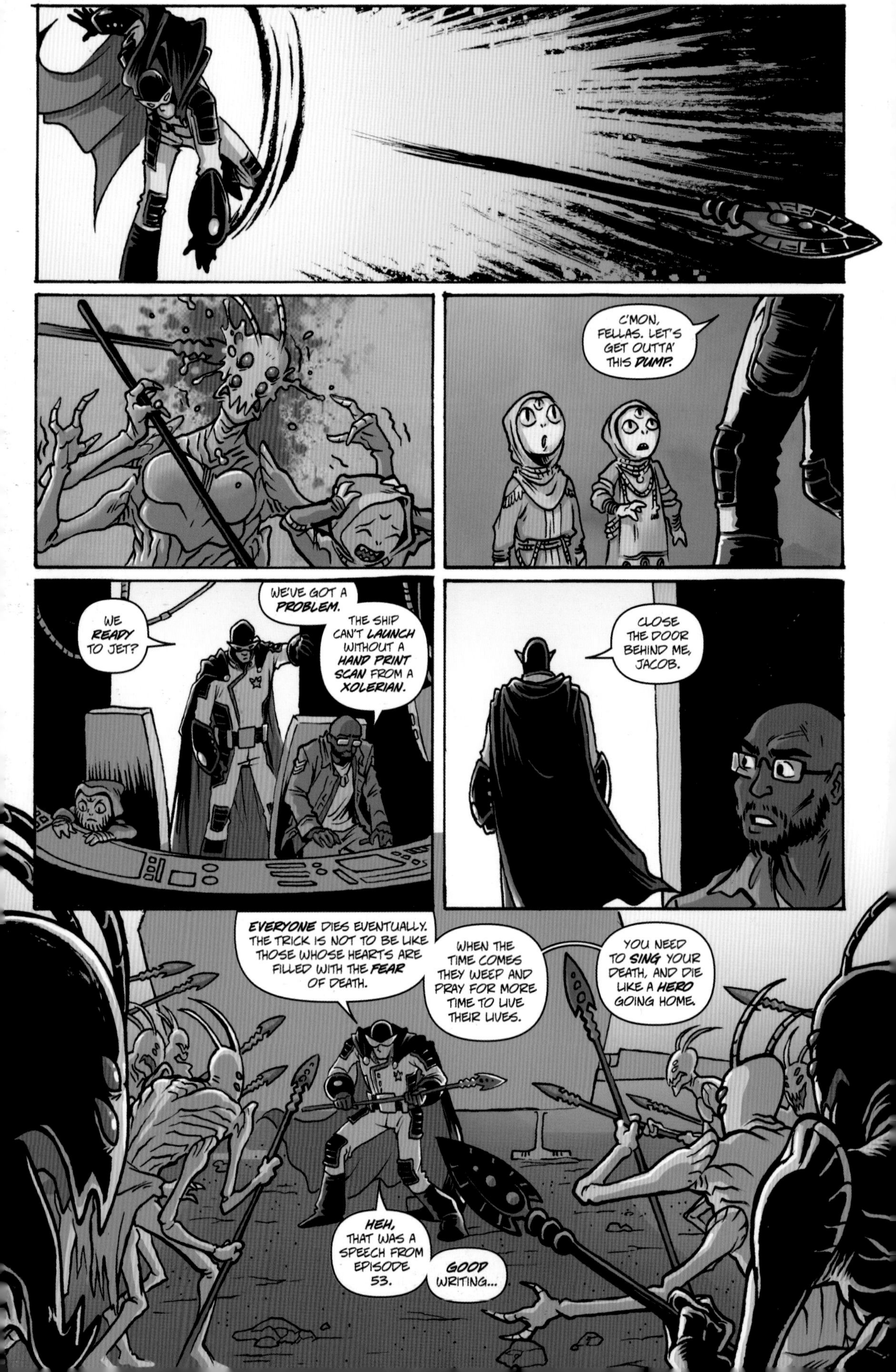
C'MON, FELLAS. LET'S GET OUTTA' THIS DUMP.
WE READY TO JET?
WE'VE GOT A PROBLEM.
THE SHIP CAN'T LAUNCH WITHOUT A HAND PRINT SCAN FROM A XOLERIAN.
CLOSE THE DOOR BEHIND ME, JACOB.
EVERYONE DIES EVENTUALLY. THE TRICK IS NOT TO BE LIKE THOSE WHOSE HEARTS ARE FILLED WITH THE FEAR OF DEATH.
WHEN THE TIME COMES THEY WEEP AND PRAY FOR MORE TIME TO LIVE THEIR LIVES.
YOU NEED TO SING YOUR DEATH, AND DIE LIKE A HERO GOING HOME.
HEH, THAT WAS A SPEECH FROM EPISODE 53.
GOOD WRITING...

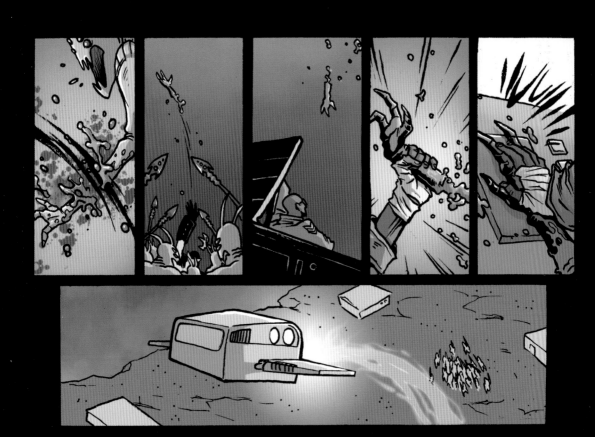

FIGHT THROUGH ADVERSITY TO THE STARS, CAPTAIN.

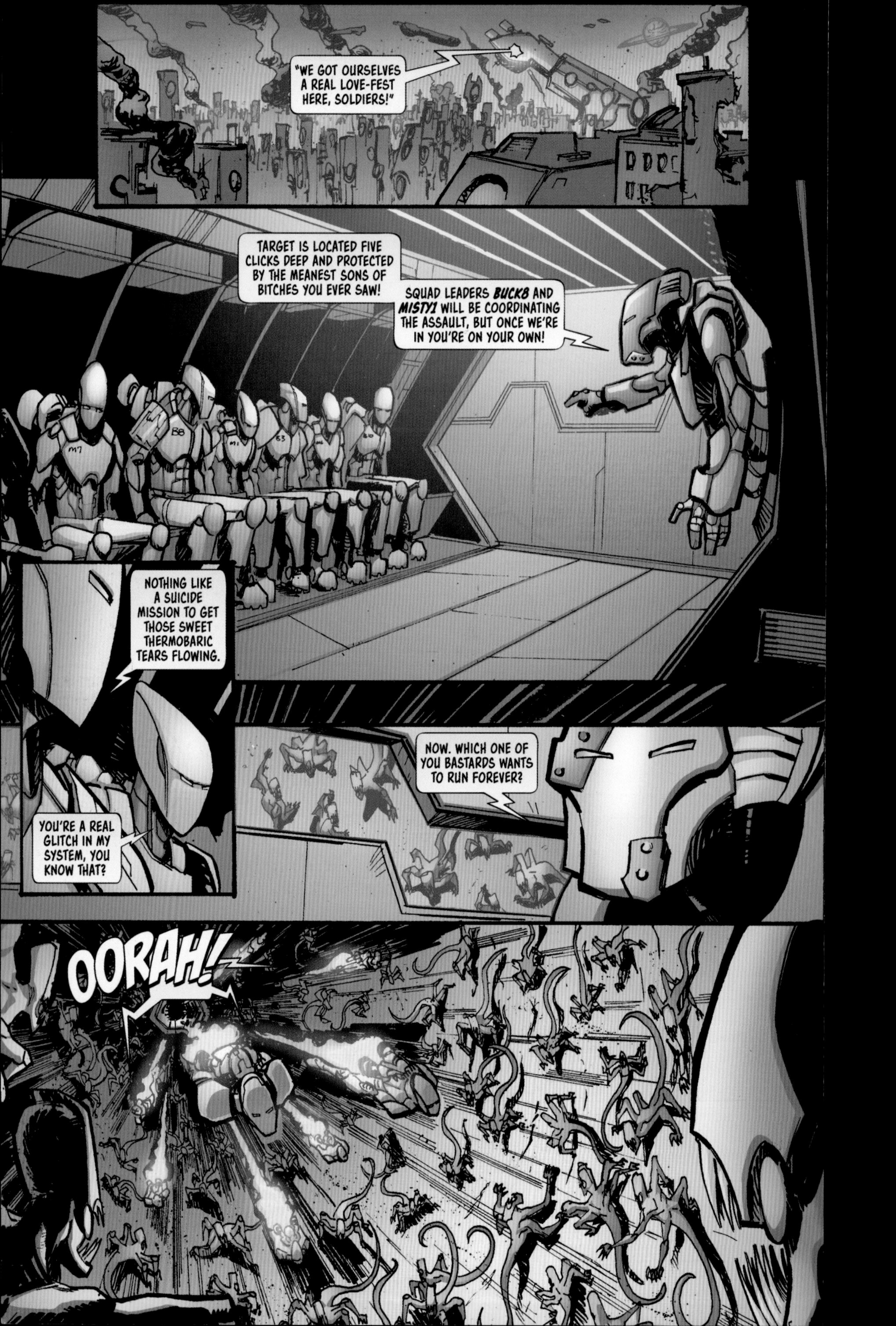
"WE GOT OURSELVES A REAL LOVE-FEST HERE, SOLDIERS!"
TARGET IS LOCATED FIVE CLICKS DEEP AND PROTECTED BY THE MEANEST SONS OF BITCHES YOU EVER SAW!
SQUAD LEADERS BUCK8 AND MISTY1 WILL BE COORDINATING THE ASSAULT, BUT ONCE WE'RE IN YOU'RE ON YOUR OWN!
NOTHING LIKE A SUICIDE MISSION TO GET THOSE SWEET THERMOBARIC TEARS FLOWING.
YOU'RE A REAL GLITCH IN MY SYSTEM, YOU KNOW THAT?
NOW. WHICH ONE OF YOU BASTARDS WANTS TO RUN FOREVER?
OORAH!

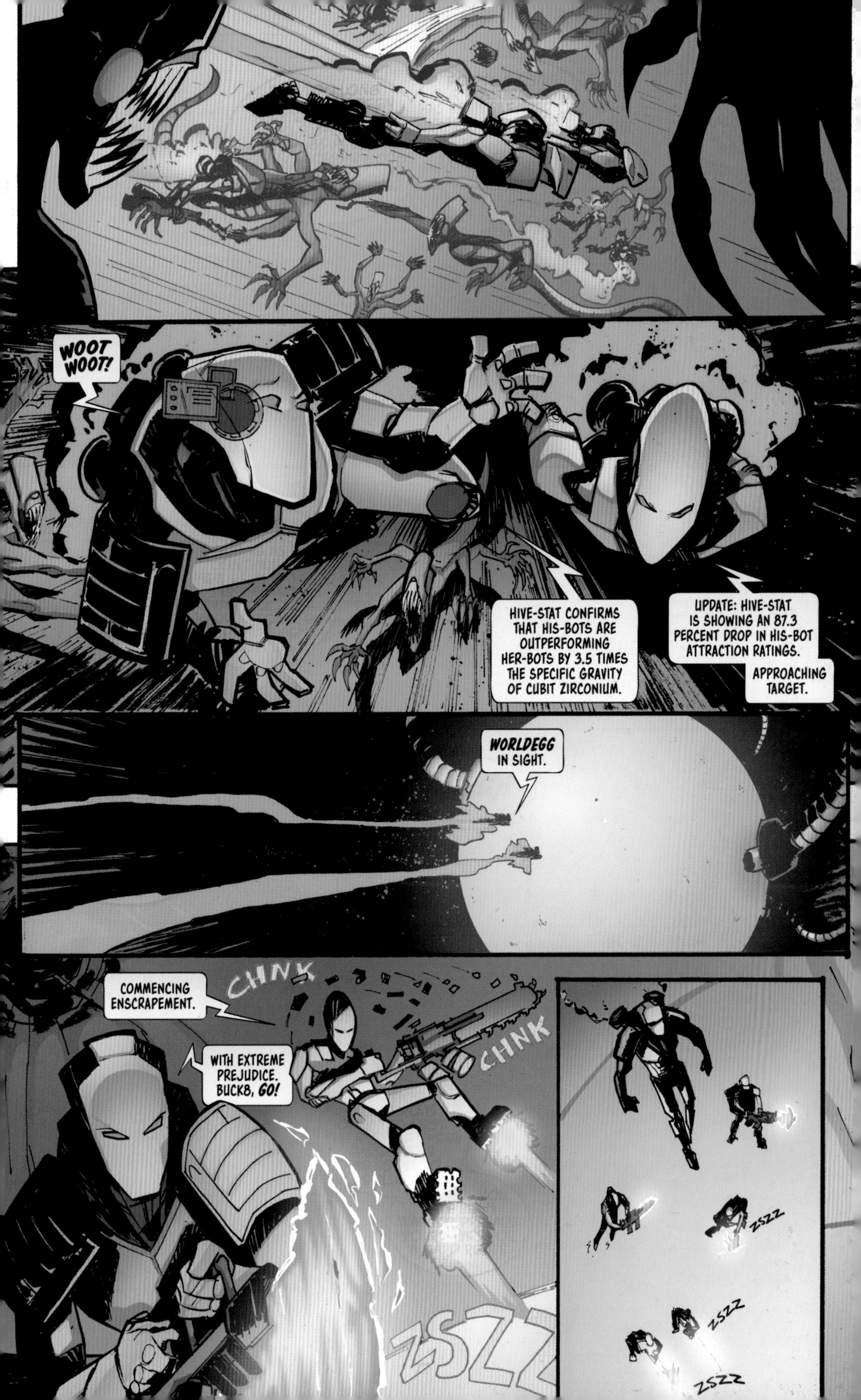

WOOT WOOT!
HIVE-STAT CONFIRMS THAT HIS-BOTS ARE OUTPERFORMING HER-BOTS BY 3.5 TIMES THE SPECIFIC GRAVITY OF CUBIT ZIRCONIUM.
UPDATE: HIVE-STAT IS SHOWING AN 87.3 PERCENT DROP IN HIS-BOT ATTRACTION RATINGS.
APPROACHING TARGET.
WORLDEGG IN SIGHT.
COMMENCING ENSCRAPEMENT.
CHNK
WITH EXTREME PREJUDICE. BUCK8, GO!
CHNK
ZSZZ
ZSZZ
ZSZZ
ZSZZ

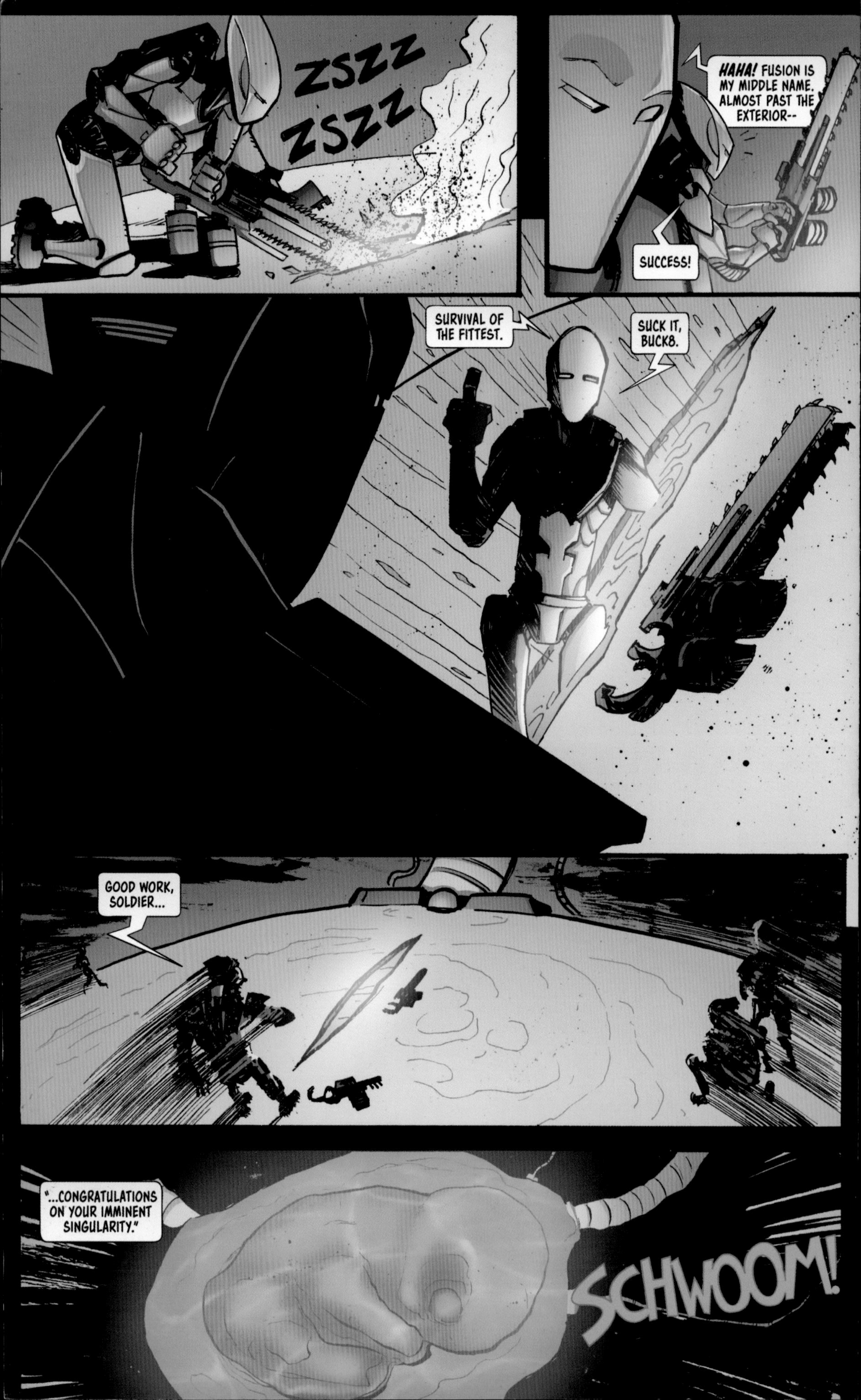
ZSZZ
ZSZZ
HAHA! FUSION IS MY MIDDLE NAME. ALMOST PAST THE EXTERIOR--
SUCCESS!
SURVIVAL OF THE FITTEST.
SUCK IT, BUCK8.
GOOD WORK, SOLDIER...
"...CONGRATULATIONS ON YOUR IMMINENT SINGULARITY."
SCHWOOM!

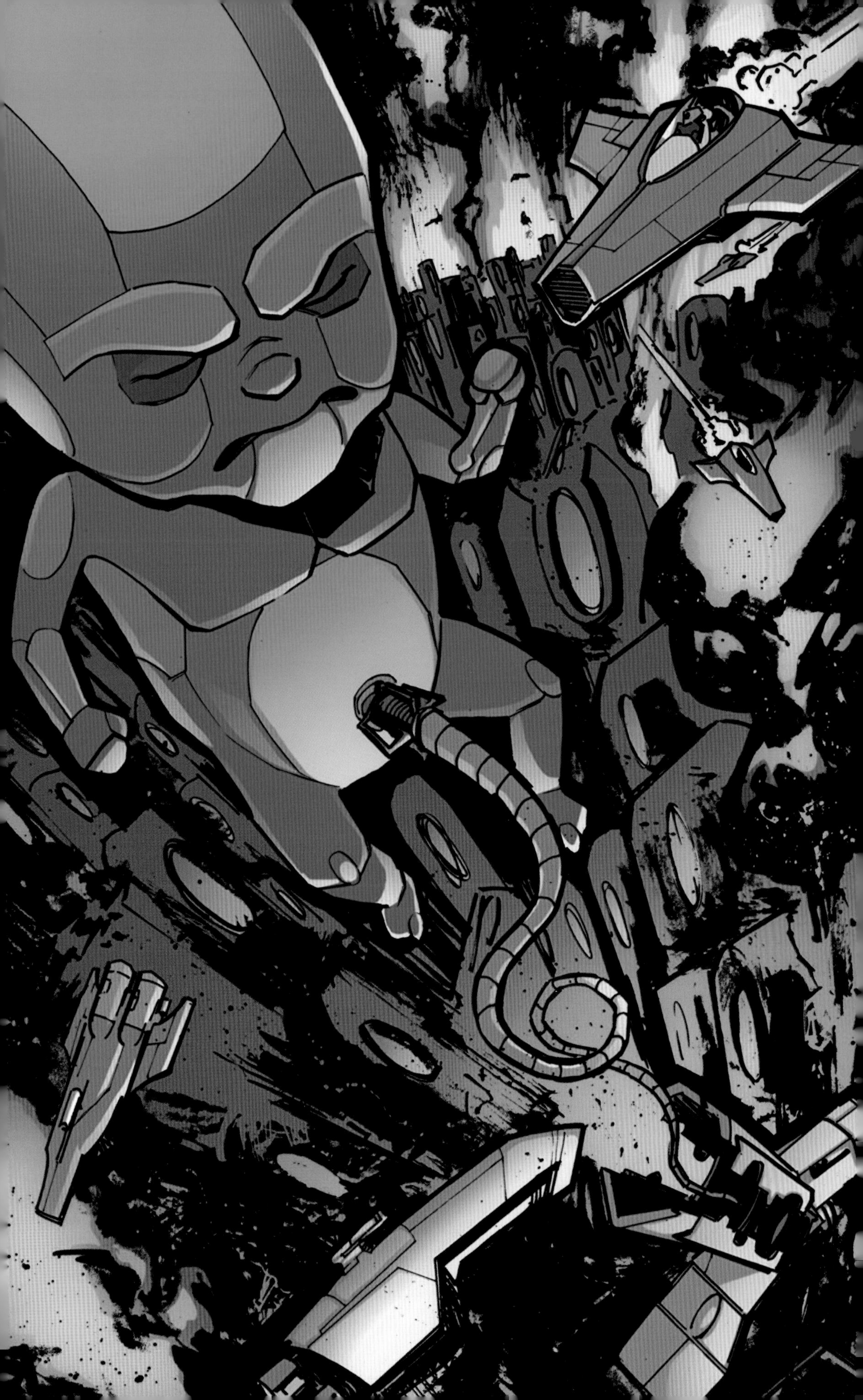

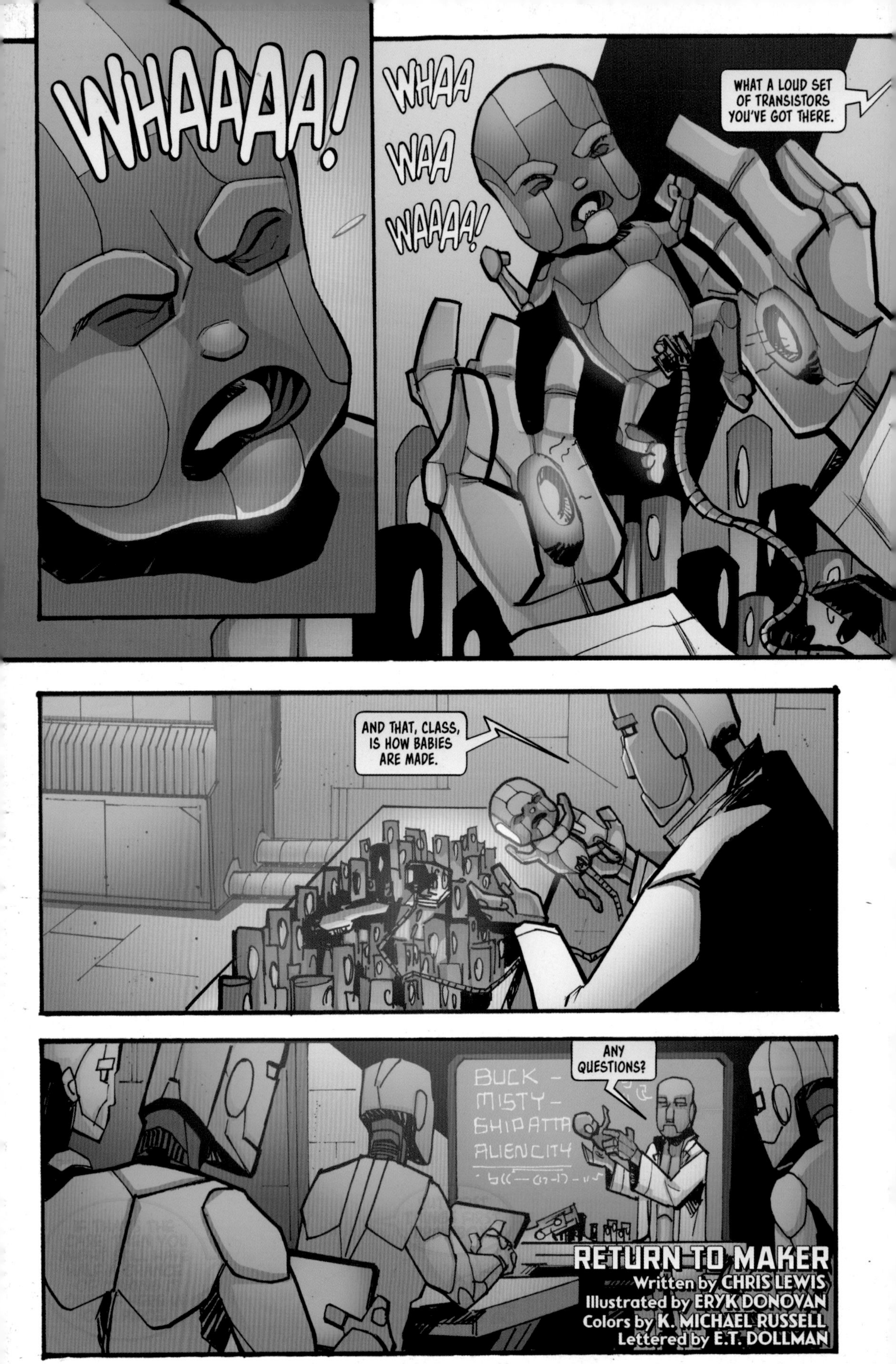
WHAAAAA!
WHAA
WAA
WAAAA!
WHAT A LOUD SET OF TRANSISTORS YOU'VE GOT THERE.
AND THAT, CLASS, IS HOW BABIES ARE MADE.
ANY QUESTIONS?
BUCK –
MISTY –
RETURN TO MAKER
Written by CHRIS LEWIS
Illustrated by ERYK DONOVAN
Colors by K. MICHAEL RUSSELL
Lettered by E.T. DOLLMAN

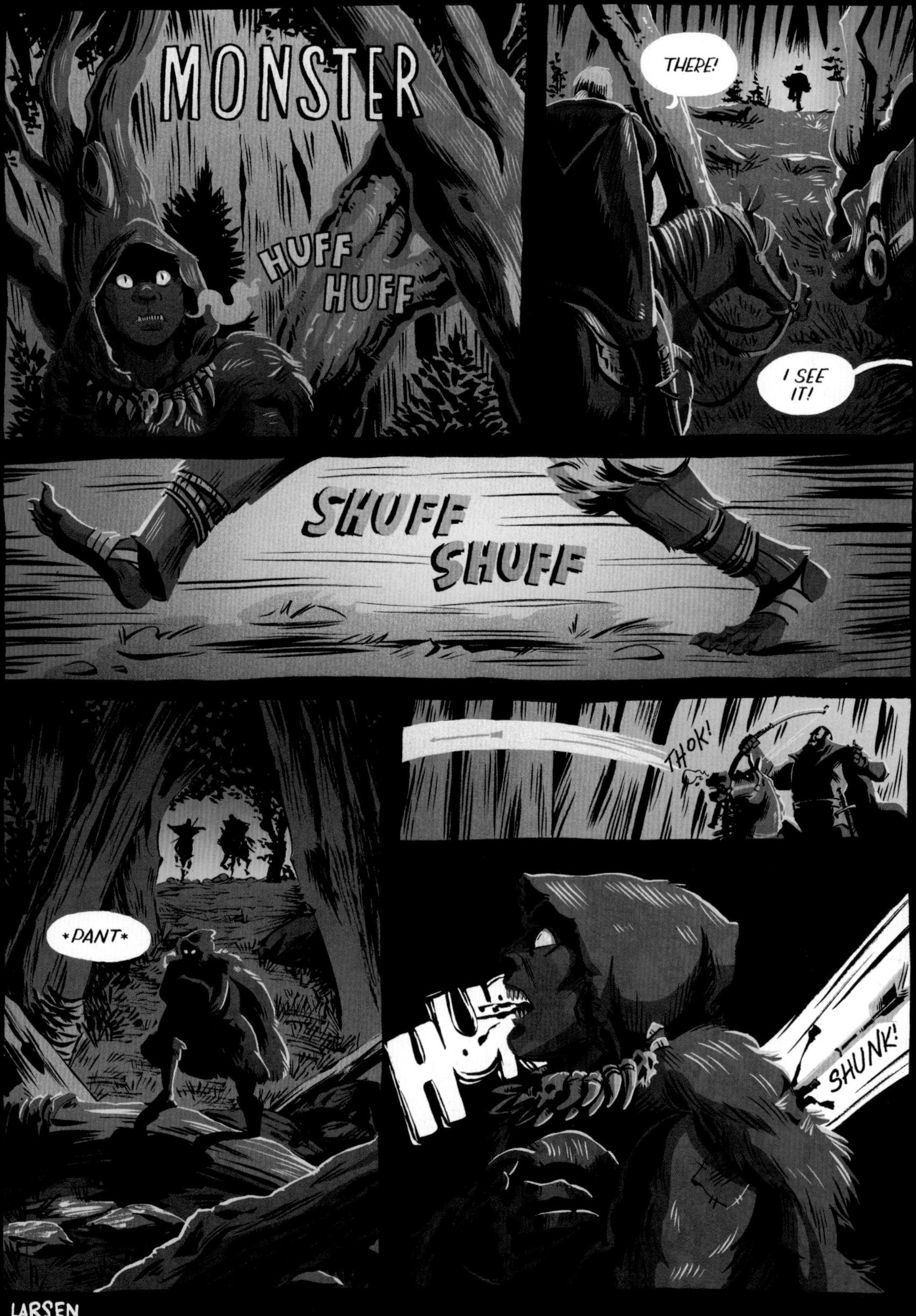
MONSTER
HUFF HUFF
THERE!
I SEE IT!
SHUFF SHUFF
PANT
THOK!
SHUNK!

LARSEN

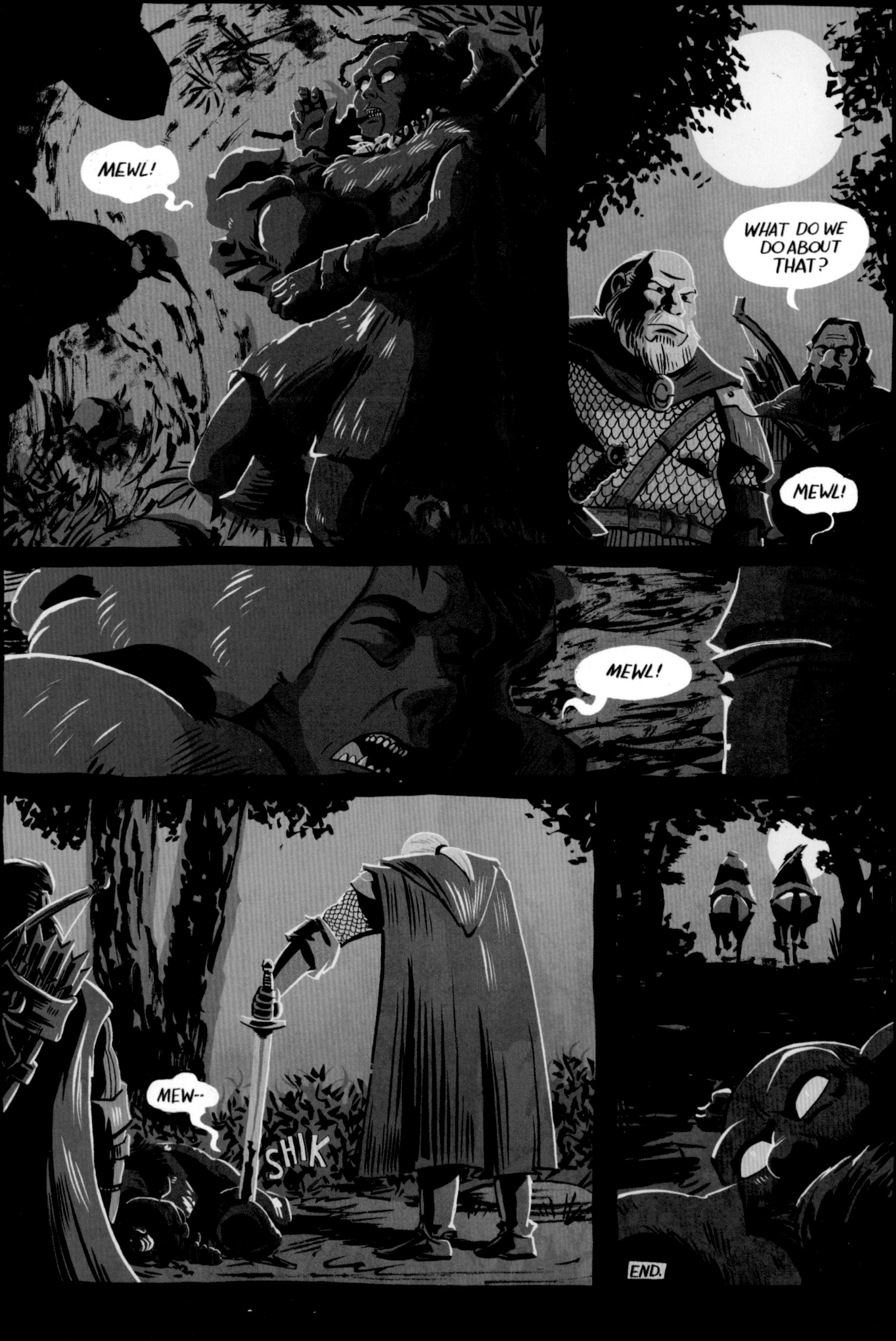
MEWL!
WHAT DO WE DO ABOUT THAT?
MEWL!
MEWL!
MEW--
SHIK
END.

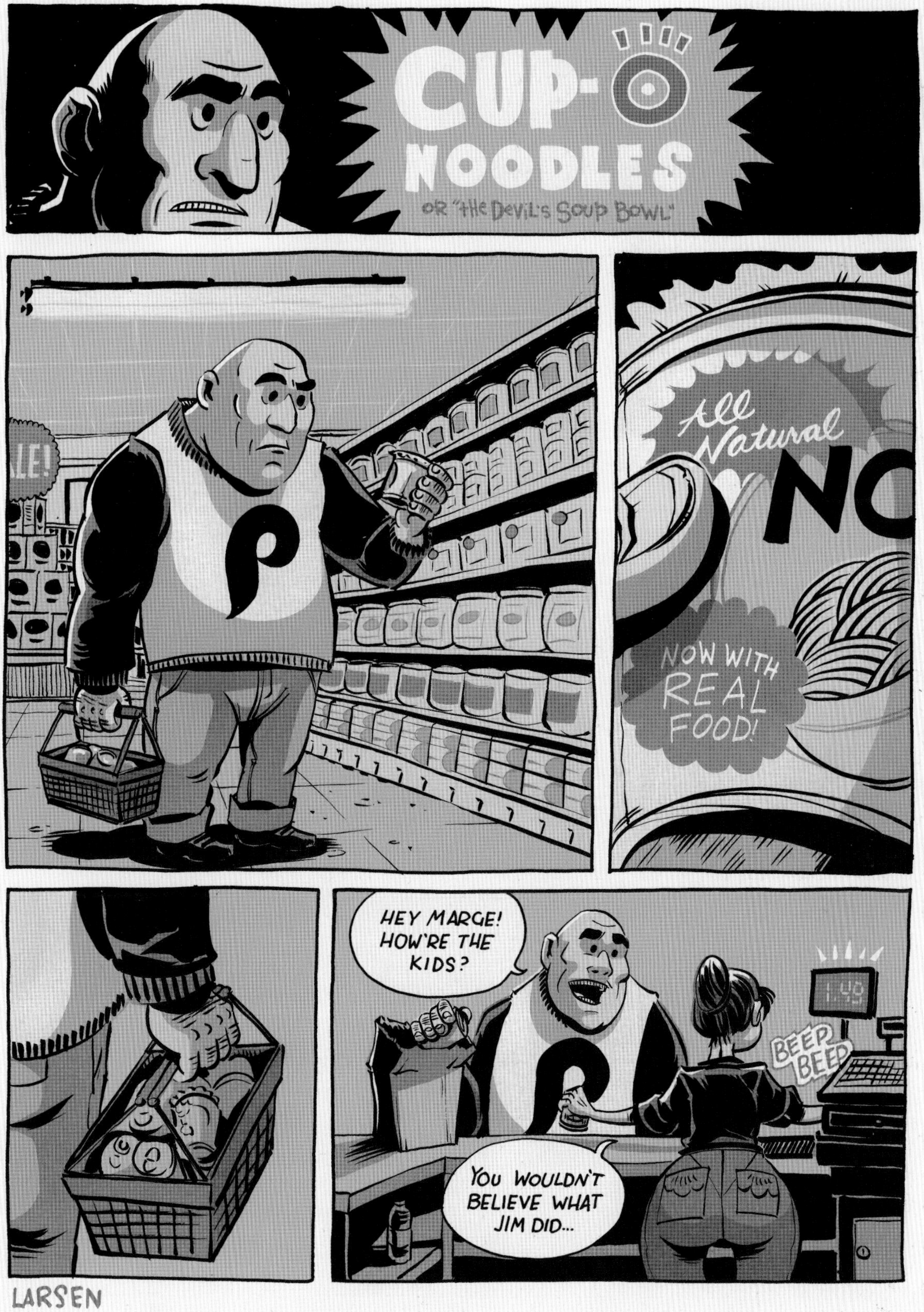
CUP-O NOODLES
OR "THE DEVIL'S SOUP BOWL"
All Natural
NO
NOW WITH REAL FOOD!
HEY MARGE! HOW'RE THE KIDS?
BEEP BEEP
YOU WOULDN'T BELIEVE WHAT JIM DID...
LARSEN

FWUP!!

!

THE HELL?

HURRRRR

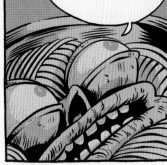

YOU HAVE FREED ME FROM THIS **SOUPY PRISON!** FOR THIS, I SHALL GRANT YOU...

THREE WISHES!

THREE...

WISHES!

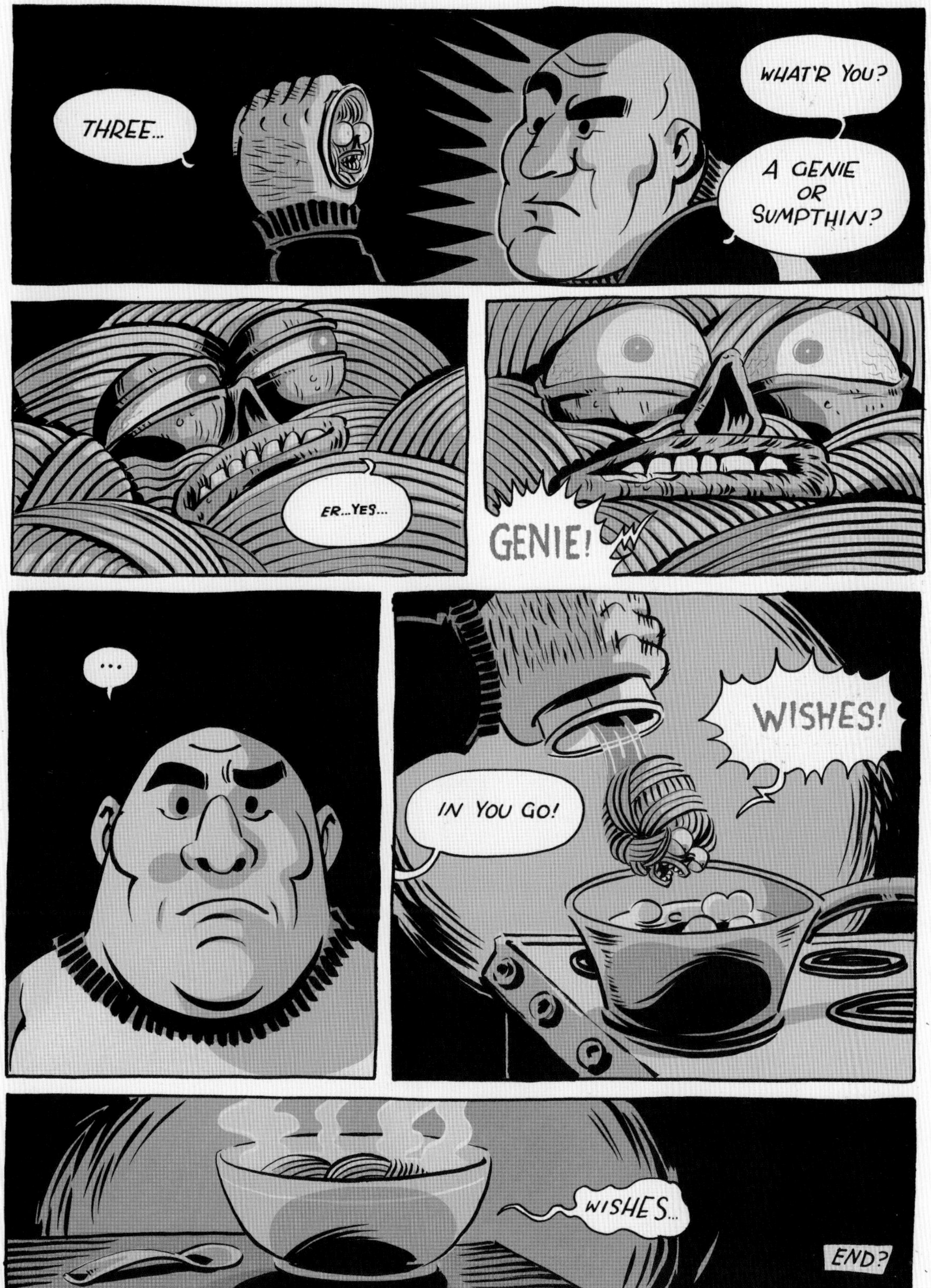
THREE...
WHAT'R YOU?
A GENIE OR SUMPTHIN?
ER...YES...
GENIE!
...
WISHES!
IN YOU GO!
WISHES...
END?

IMAGINARY DRUGS PRESENTS

BOTTLE OF WALTER

WRITER **MARK BERTOLINI** ART **LUKE PARKER** LETTERS **NIC J SHAW**

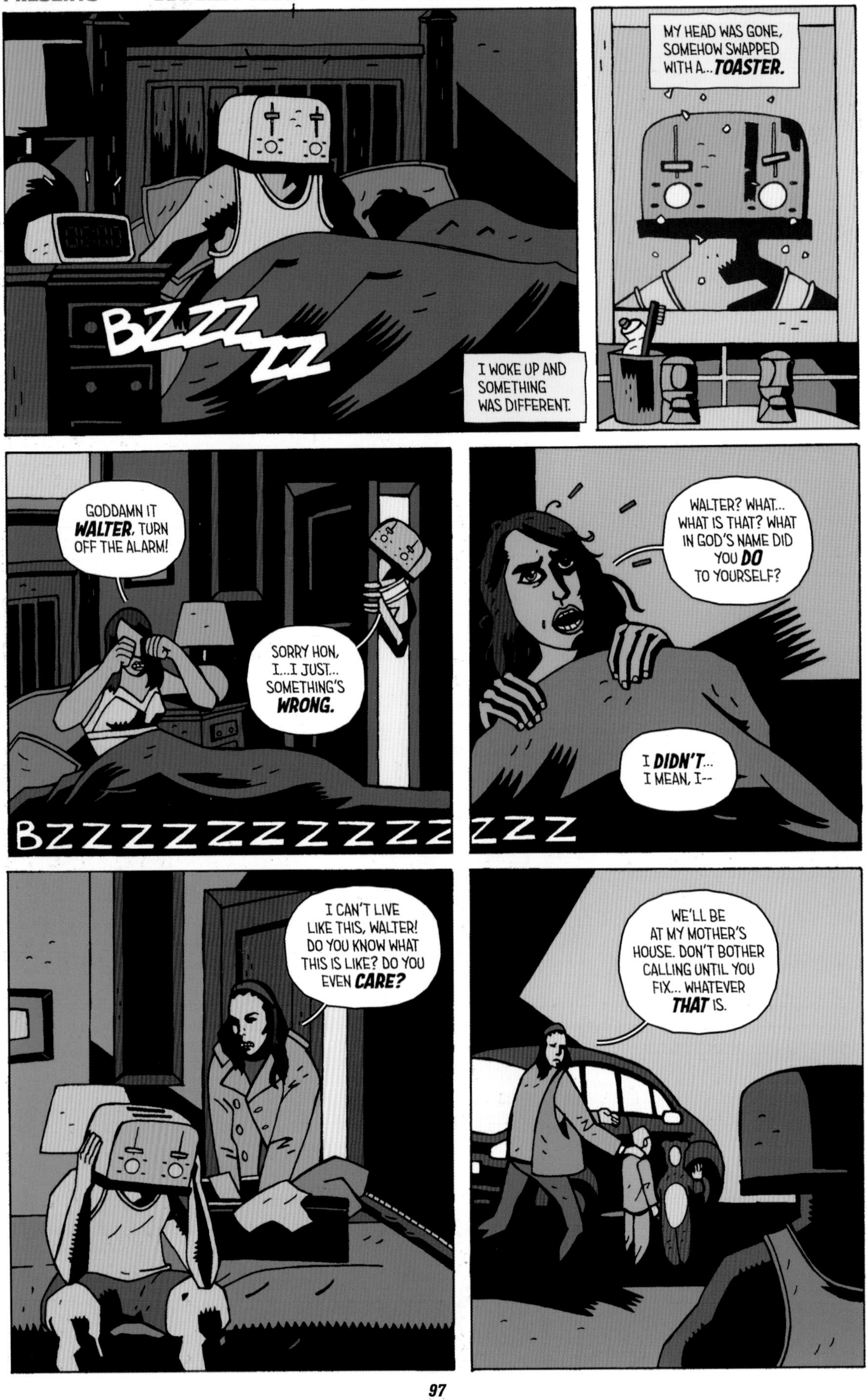
BZZZZZ
I WOKE UP AND SOMETHING WAS DIFFERENT.
MY HEAD WAS GONE, SOMEHOW SWAPPED WITH A... **TOASTER.**
GODDAMN IT **WALTER**, TURN OFF THE ALARM!
SORRY HON, I... I JUST... SOMETHING'S **WRONG.**
BZZZZZZZZZZZZZZZZ
WALTER? WHAT... WHAT IS THAT? WHAT IN GOD'S NAME DID YOU **DO** TO YOURSELF?
I **DIDN'T**... I MEAN, I--
I CAN'T LIVE LIKE THIS, WALTER! DO YOU KNOW WHAT THIS IS LIKE? DO YOU EVEN **CARE?**
WE'LL BE AT MY MOTHER'S HOUSE. DON'T BOTHER CALLING UNTIL YOU FIX... WHATEVER **THAT** IS.

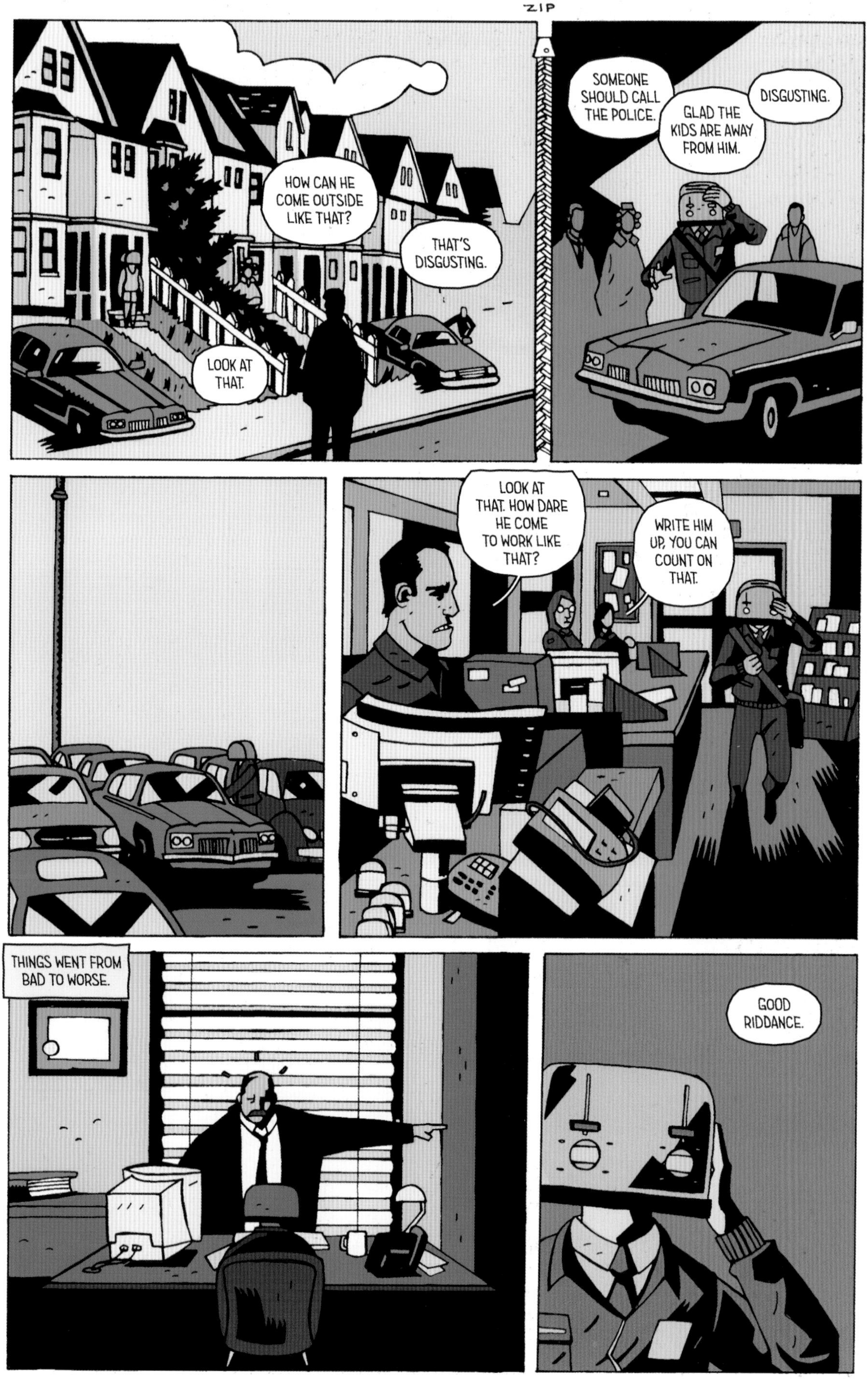
ZIP
HOW CAN HE COME OUTSIDE LIKE THAT?
THAT'S DISGUSTING.
LOOK AT THAT.
SOMEONE SHOULD CALL THE POLICE.
GLAD THE KIDS ARE AWAY FROM HIM.
DISGUSTING.
LOOK AT THAT. HOW DARE HE COME TO WORK LIKE THAT?
WRITE HIM UP, YOU CAN COUNT ON THAT.
THINGS WENT FROM BAD TO WORSE.
GOOD RIDDANCE.

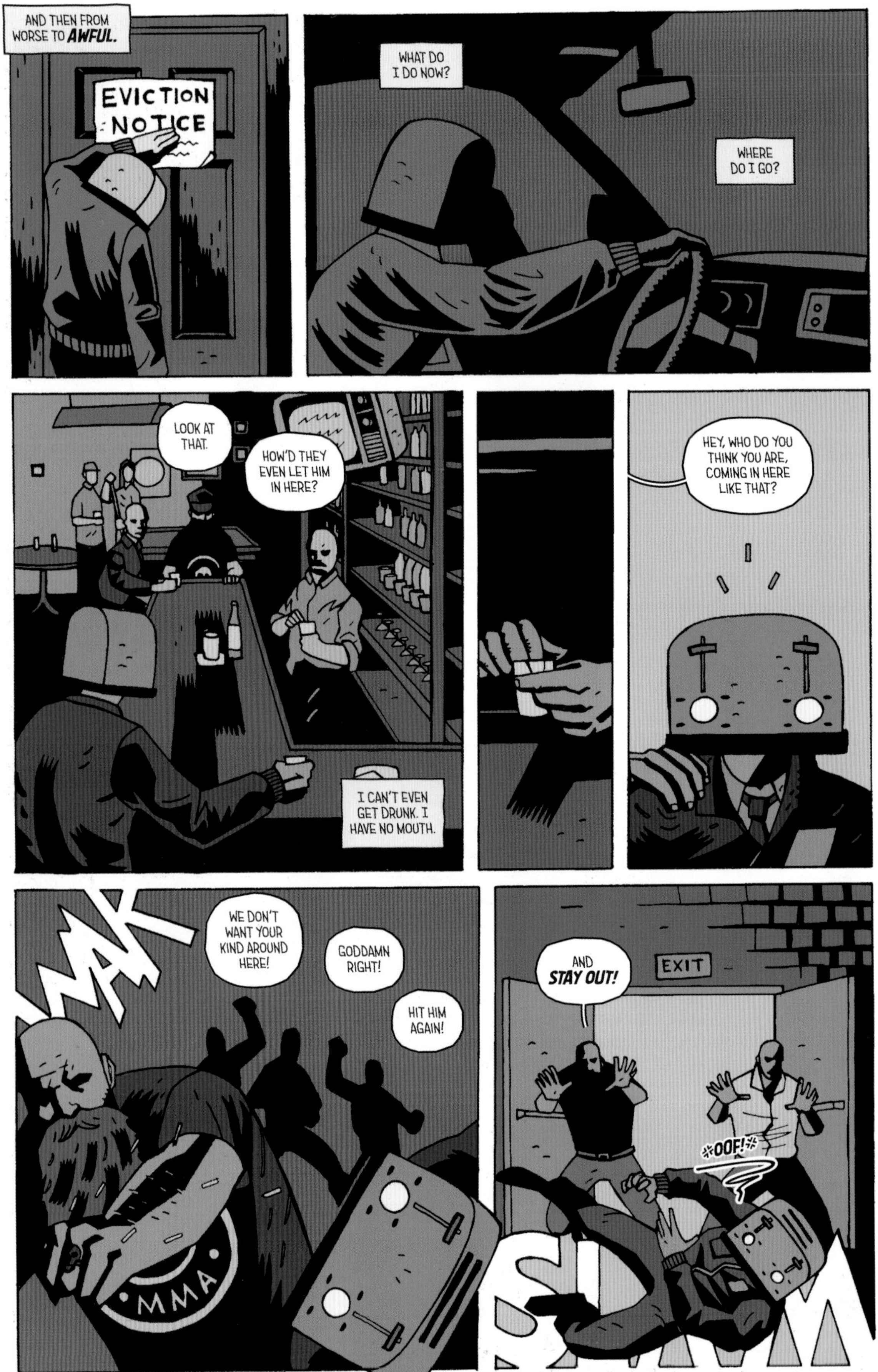
AND THEN FROM WORSE TO **AWFUL.**
EVICTION NOTICE
WHAT DO I DO NOW?
WHERE DO I GO?
LOOK AT THAT.
HOW'D THEY EVEN LET HIM IN HERE?
I CAN'T EVEN GET DRUNK. I HAVE NO MOUTH.
HEY, WHO DO YOU THINK YOU ARE, COMING IN HERE LIKE THAT?
WE DON'T WANT YOUR KIND AROUND HERE!
GODDAMN RIGHT!
HIT HIM AGAIN!
MMA
AND **STAY OUT!**
EXIT
#OOF!#

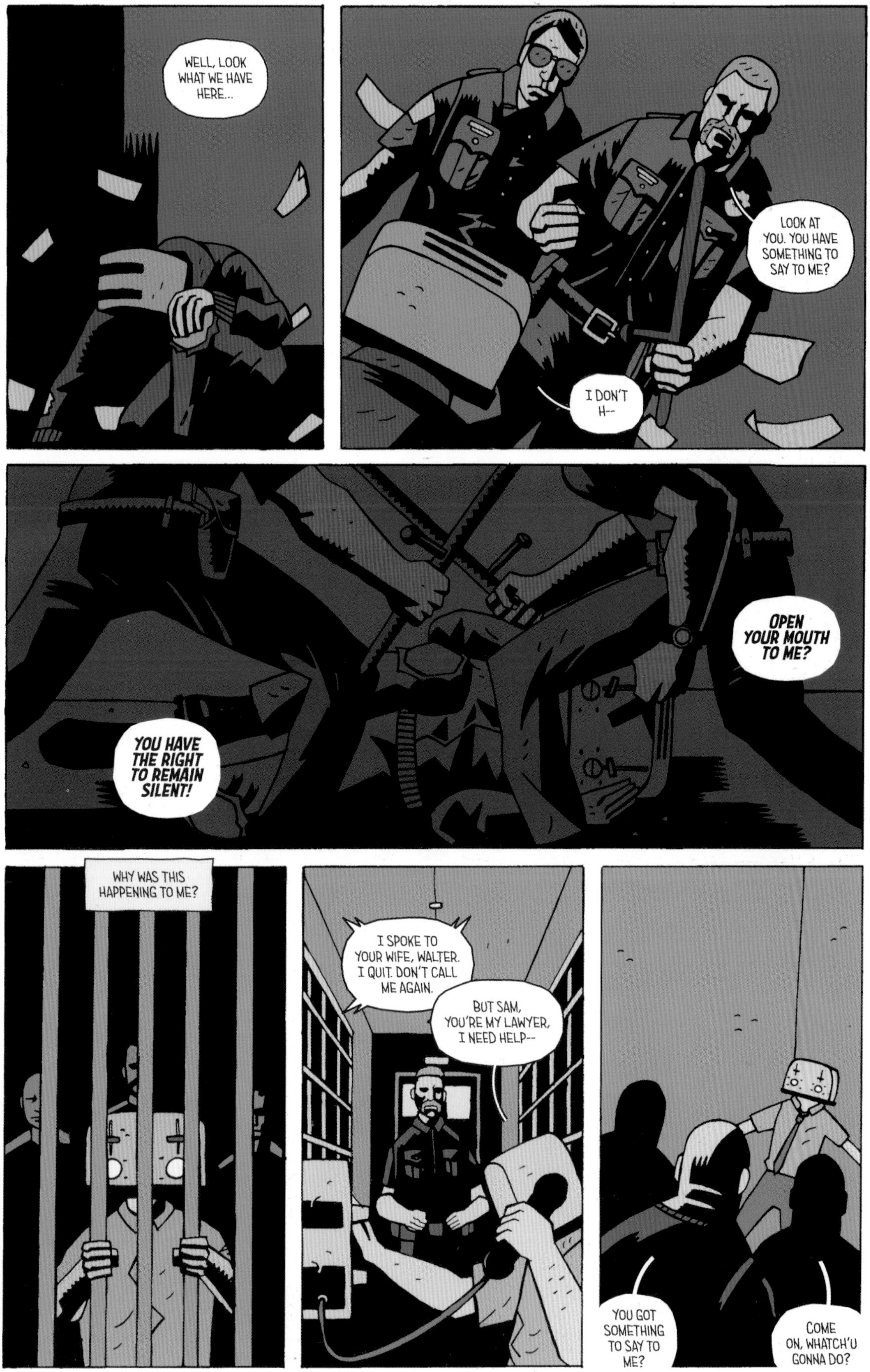
WELL, LOOK WHAT WE HAVE HERE...
LOOK AT YOU. YOU HAVE SOMETHING TO SAY TO ME?
I DON'T H--
OPEN YOUR MOUTH TO ME?
YOU HAVE THE RIGHT TO REMAIN SILENT!
WHY WAS THIS HAPPENING TO ME?
I SPOKE TO YOUR WIFE, WALTER. I QUIT. DON'T CALL ME AGAIN.
BUT SAM, YOU'RE MY LAWYER, I NEED HELP--
YOU GOT SOMETHING TO SAY TO ME?
COME ON, WHATCH'U GONNA DO?

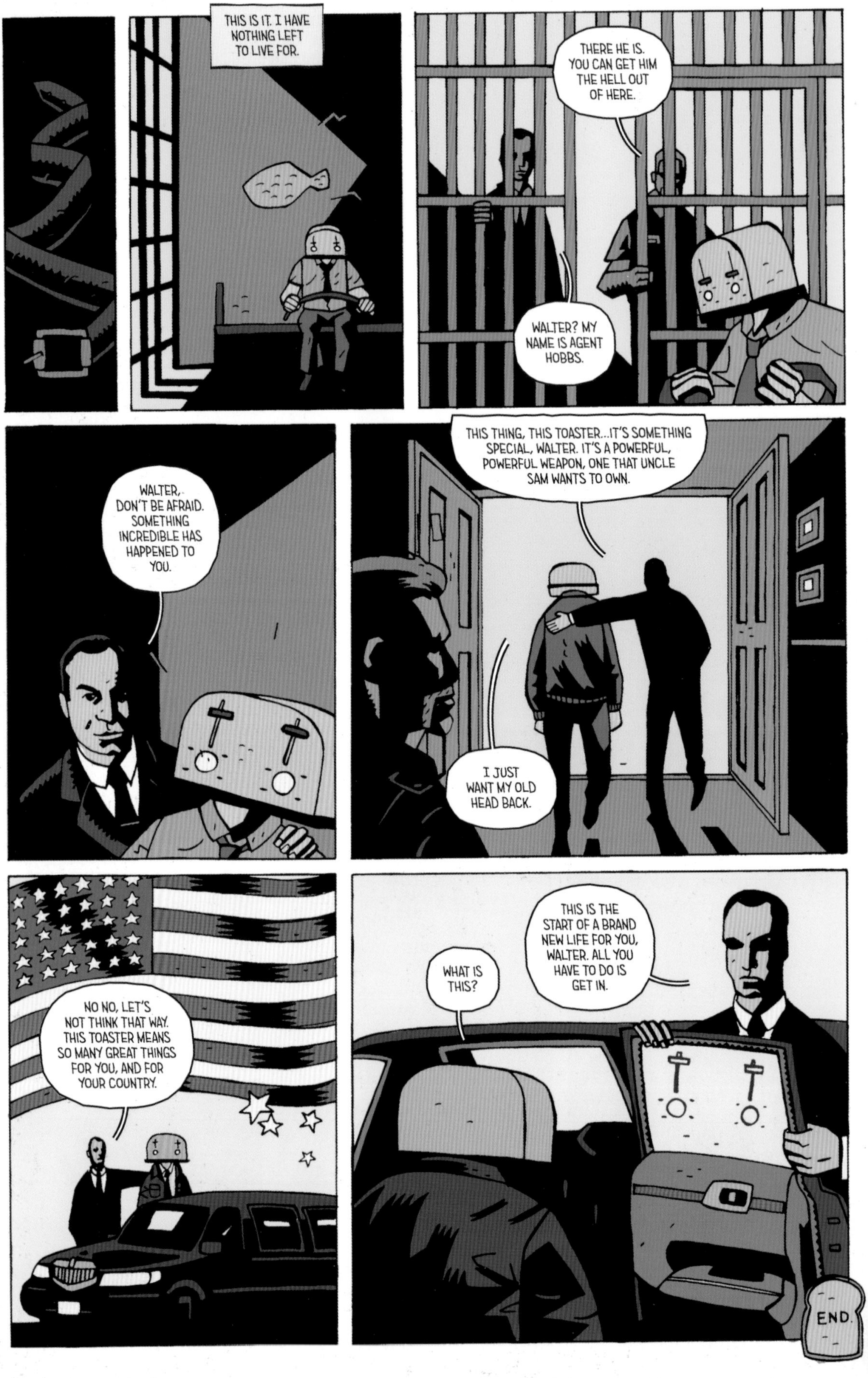
THIS IS IT. I HAVE NOTHING LEFT TO LIVE FOR.
THERE HE IS. YOU CAN GET HIM THE HELL OUT OF HERE.
WALTER? MY NAME IS AGENT HOBBS.
WALTER, DON'T BE AFRAID. SOMETHING INCREDIBLE HAS HAPPENED TO YOU.
THIS THING, THIS TOASTER...IT'S SOMETHING SPECIAL, WALTER. IT'S A POWERFUL, POWERFUL WEAPON, ONE THAT UNCLE SAM WANTS TO OWN.
I JUST WANT MY OLD HEAD BACK.
NO NO, LET'S NOT THINK THAT WAY. THIS TOASTER MEANS SO MANY GREAT THINGS FOR YOU, AND FOR YOUR COUNTRY.
WHAT IS THIS?
THIS IS THE START OF A BRAND NEW LIFE FOR YOU, WALTER. ALL YOU HAVE TO DO IS GET IN.
END.

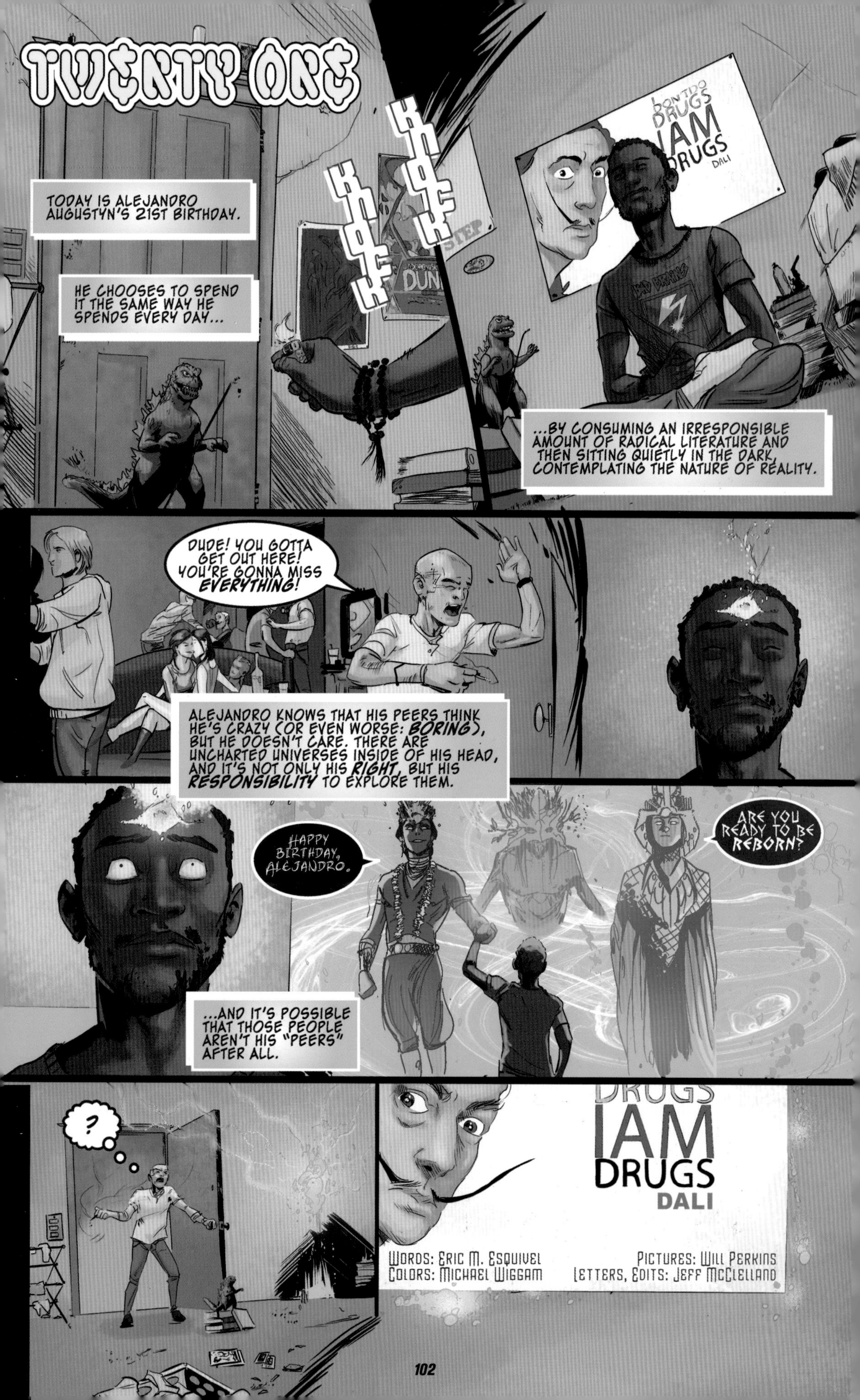
TWENTY ONE
TODAY IS ALEJANDRO AUGUSTYN'S 21ST BIRTHDAY.
HE CHOOSES TO SPEND IT THE SAME WAY HE SPENDS EVERY DAY...
KNOCK KNOCK
I DON'T DO DRUGS I AM DRUGS DALI
...BY CONSUMING AN IRRESPONSIBLE AMOUNT OF RADICAL LITERATURE AND THEN SITTING QUIETLY IN THE DARK, CONTEMPLATING THE NATURE OF REALITY.
DUDE! YOU GOTTA GET OUT HERE! YOU'RE GONNA MISS EVERYTHING!
ALEJANDRO KNOWS THAT HIS PEERS THINK HE'S CRAZY (OR EVEN WORSE: BORING), BUT HE DOESN'T CARE. THERE ARE UNCHARTED UNIVERSES INSIDE OF HIS HEAD, AND IT'S NOT ONLY HIS RIGHT, BUT HIS RESPONSIBILITY TO EXPLORE THEM.
HAPPY BIRTHDAY, ALEJANDRO.
ARE YOU READY TO BE REBORN?
...AND IT'S POSSIBLE THAT THOSE PEOPLE AREN'T HIS "PEERS" AFTER ALL.
?
DRUGS I AM DRUGS DALI
WORDS: ERIC M. ESQUIVEL
PICTURES: WILL PERKINS
COLORS: MICHAEL WIGGAM
LETTERS, EDITS: JEFF MCCLELLAND

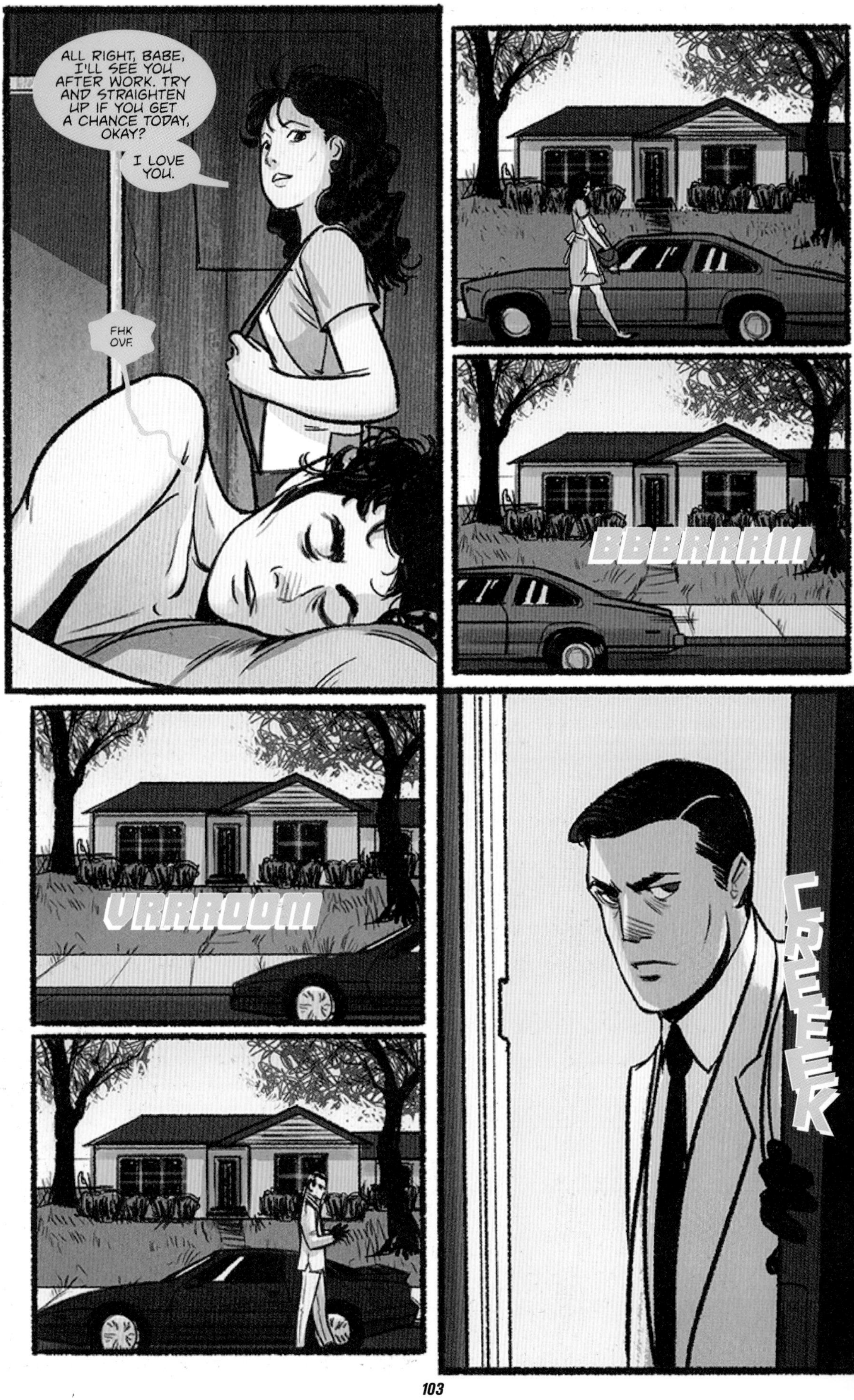
ALL RIGHT, BABE, I'LL SEE YOU AFTER WORK. TRY AND STRAIGHTEN UP IF YOU GET A CHANCE TODAY, OKAY?
I LOVE YOU.
FHK OVF.
BBBRRRM
VRRROOM
CREEEK

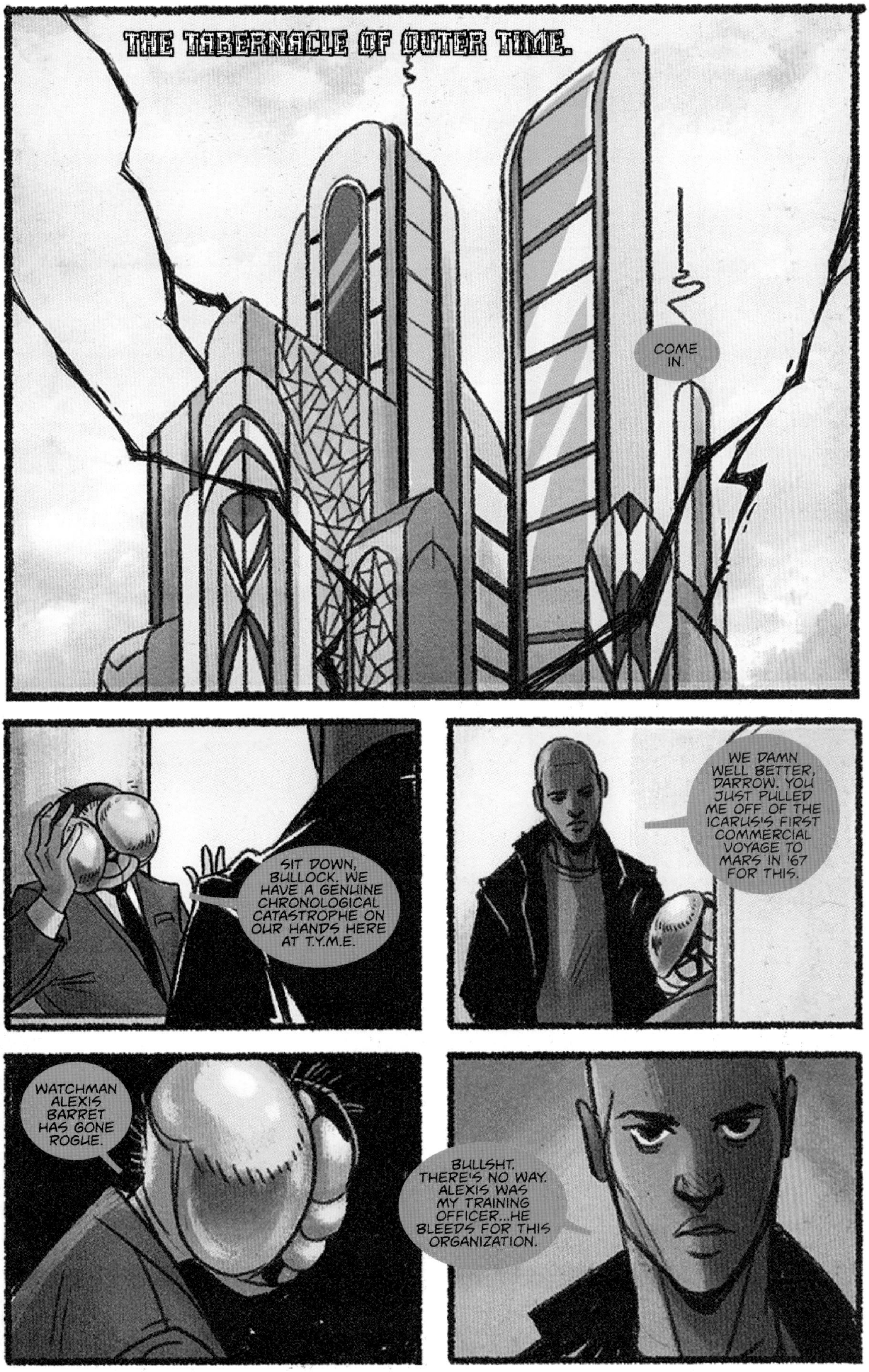
THE TABERNACLE OF OUTER TIME.
COME IN.
SIT DOWN, BULLOCK. WE HAVE A GENUINE CHRONOLOGICAL CATASTROPHE ON OUR HANDS HERE AT T.Y.M.E.
WE DAMN WELL BETTER, DARROW. YOU JUST PULLED ME OFF OF THE ICARUS'S FIRST COMMERCIAL VOYAGE TO MARS IN '67 FOR THIS.
WATCHMAN ALEXIS BARRET HAS GONE ROGUE.
BULLSHT. THERE'S NO WAY. ALEXIS WAS MY TRAINING OFFICER...HE BLEEDS FOR THIS ORGANIZATION.

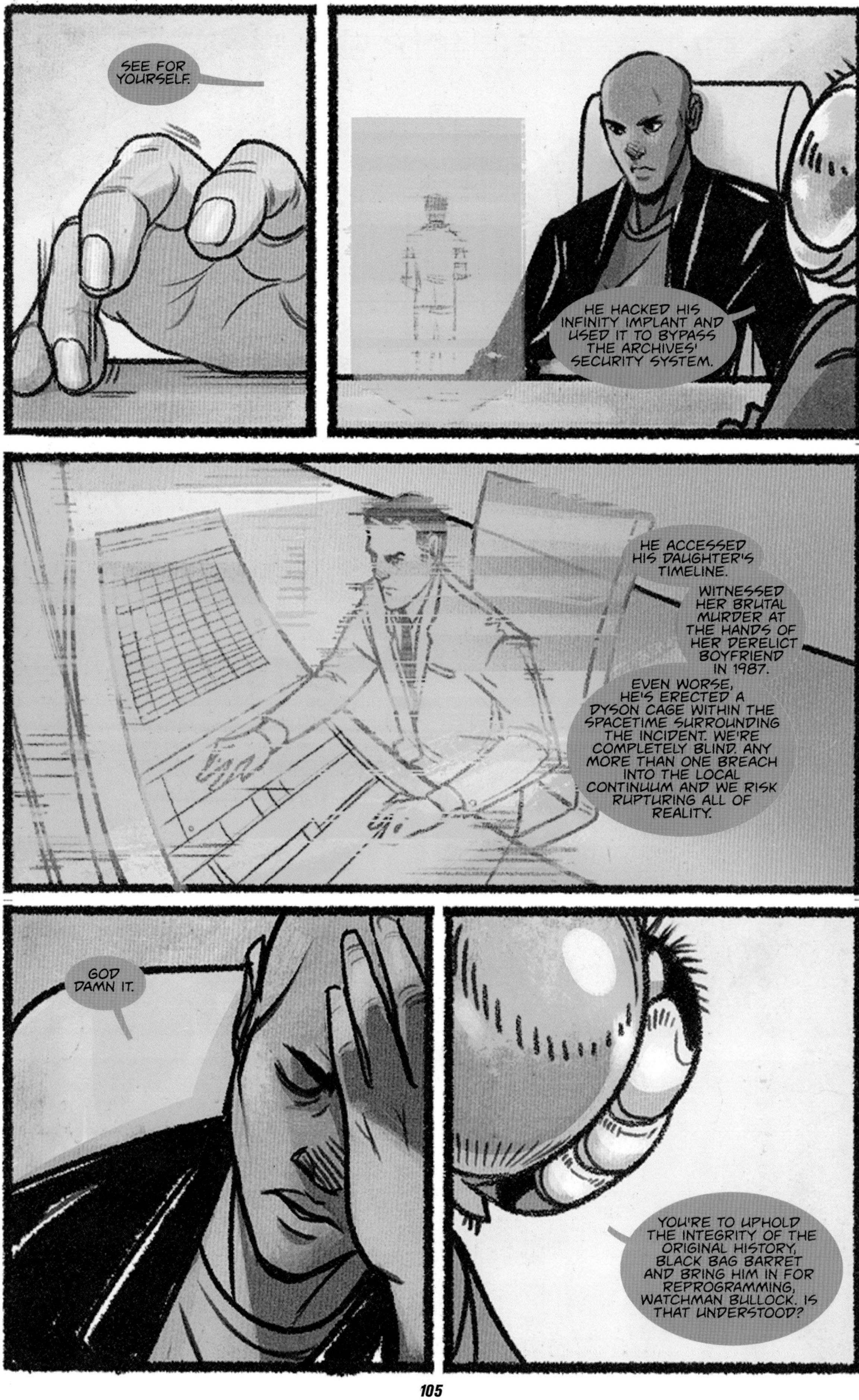
SEE FOR YOURSELF.
HE HACKED HIS INFINITY IMPLANT AND USED IT TO BYPASS THE ARCHIVES' SECURITY SYSTEM.
HE ACCESSED HIS DAUGHTER'S TIMELINE.
WITNESSED HER BRUTAL MURDER AT THE HANDS OF HER DERELICT BOYFRIEND IN 1987.
EVEN WORSE, HE'S ERECTED A DYSON CAGE WITHIN THE SPACETIME SURROUNDING THE INCIDENT. WE'RE COMPLETELY BLIND. ANY MORE THAN ONE BREACH INTO THE LOCAL CONTINUUM AND WE RISK RUPTURING ALL OF REALITY.
GOD DAMN IT.
YOU'RE TO UPHOLD THE INTEGRITY OF THE ORIGINAL HISTORY, BLACK BAG BARRET AND BRING HIM IN FOR REPROGRAMMING, WATCHMAN BULLOCK. IS THAT UNDERSTOOD?

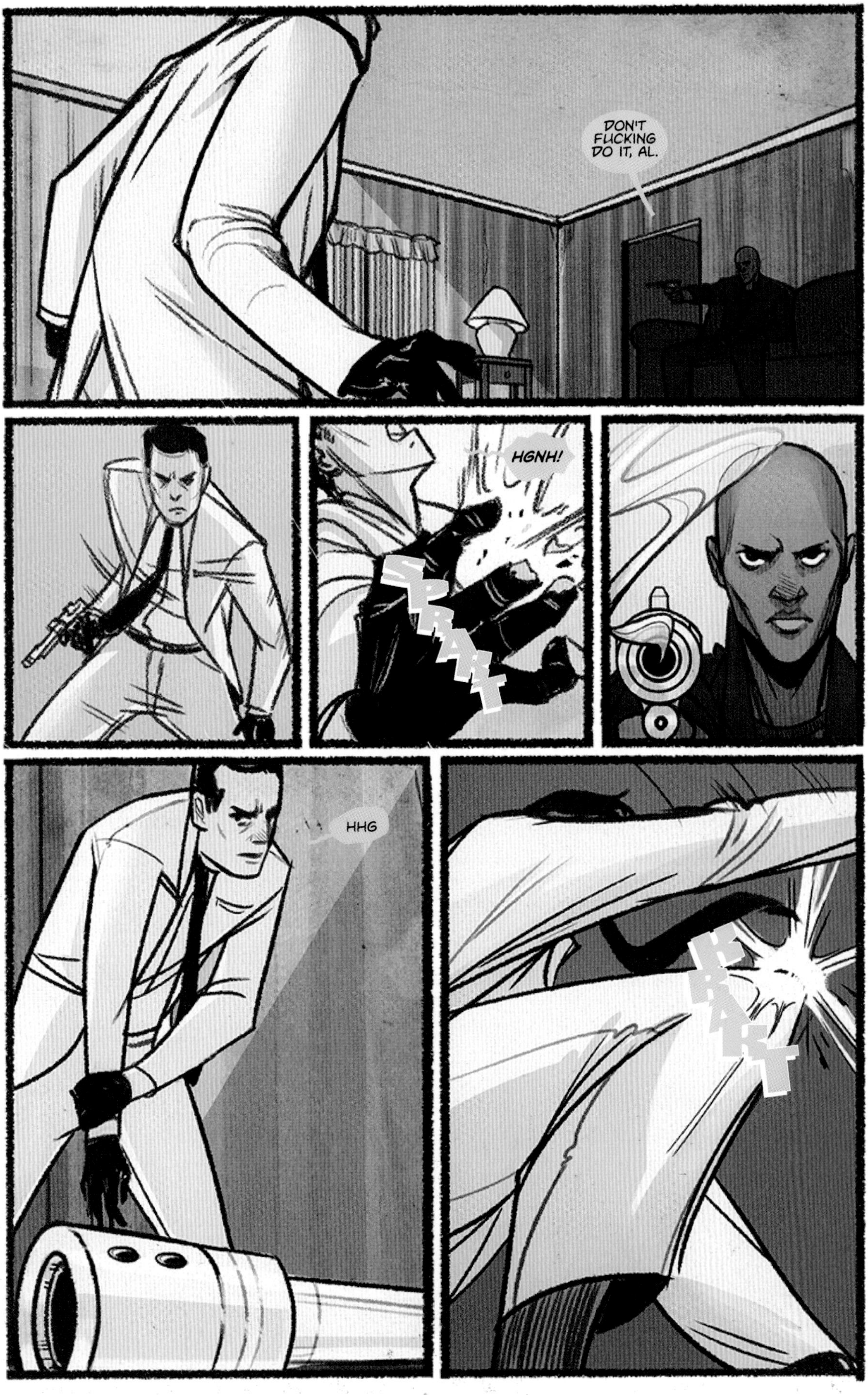
DON'T FUCKING DO IT, AL.
HGNH!
SPRAKT
HHG
KRAKT

A-AT LEAST THEY...HAD ENOUGH RESPECT TO SEND THEIR...THEIR SECOND BEST.

WHY'D YOU DO IT, ALEXIS? IT GOES AGAINST EVERYTHING YOU EVER TAUGHT ME.

I'M GETTING OLD, BARRINGTON, AND... THIS JOB IS KILLING ME QUICKER...THAN MOST. I WAS NEVER THERE FOR HER... NOT...NOT LIKE A FATHER SHOULD BE.

NEARING THE END...WEIGHING MY OPTIONS...HKKK...HER *HAPPINESS* IS ALL THAT MATTERS ANYMORE.

ONCE...ONCE I SAW...

DOES KILLING *ME*...AND LETTING THAT FAILED FUCKING ABORTION MURDER MY DAUGHTER...SIT RIGHT WITH *YOU*?

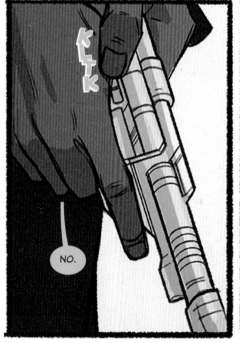

KLTK

NO.

PYOK

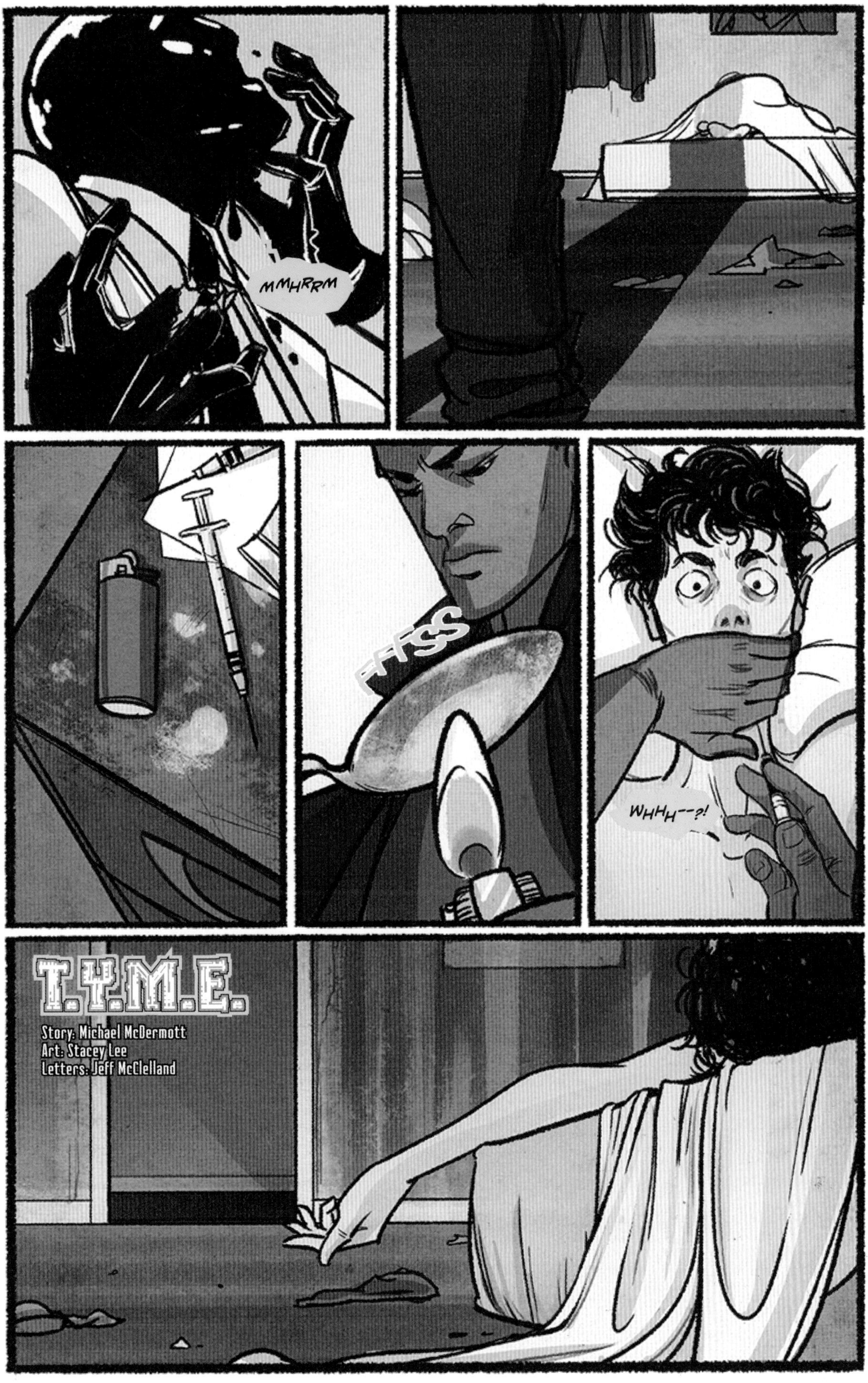
MMHRRM
FFFSS
WHHH--?!
T.Y.M.E.
Story: Michael McDermott
Art: Stacey Lee
Letters: Jeff McClelland

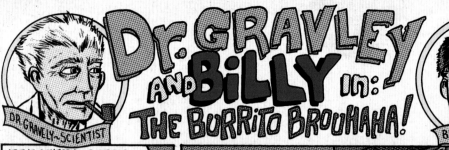

Dr. GRAVLEY AND BILLY IN: THE BURRITO BROUHAHA!

DR. GRAVELY - SCIENTIST

BILLY - ASSISTANT

AT THE CENTERVILLE FEDERAL AGRICULTURAL RESEARCH FACILITY...

C'MON! C'MON!

WHERE IS THAT BASTARD?

DOC!

MY HAIR IS FALLING OUT!

That's right. We used them all on the beatniks.

DON'T RUSH ME, BRADFORD.

IT'S BILLY!

GET IT RIGHT BEFORE I DIE, YOU $@&%!

I'M NOT THE ONE WHO ATE A BURRITO FROM THE LAB'S FRIDGE!

THAT WAS MY SCIENCE BURRITO, YOU PHILISTINE!

⋝GCK⧽

dyin' faster now...

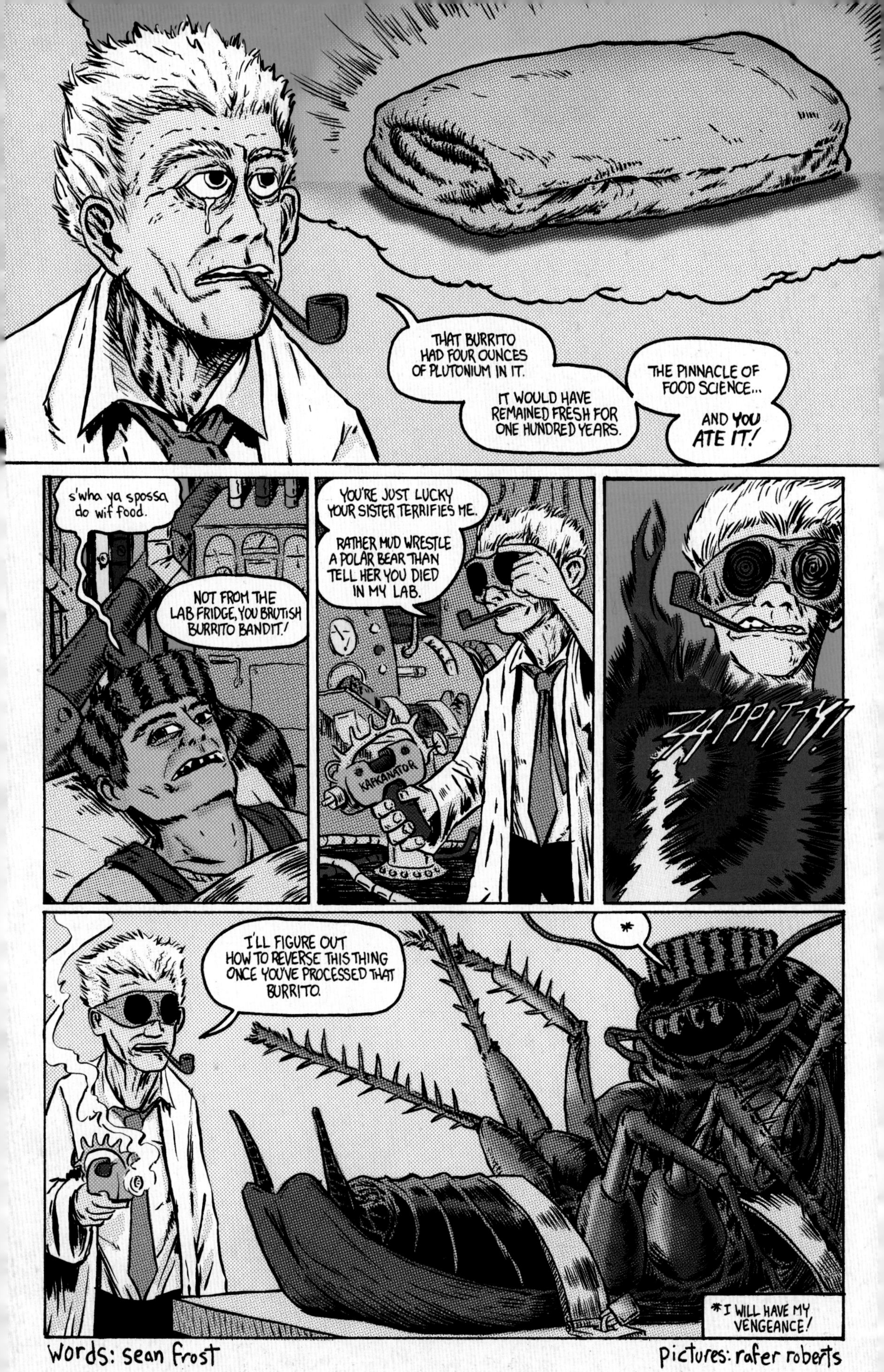
THAT BURRITO HAD FOUR OUNCES OF PLUTONIUM IN IT.
IT WOULD HAVE REMAINED FRESH FOR ONE HUNDRED YEARS.
THE PINNACLE OF FOOD SCIENCE...
AND YOU ATE IT!
s'wha ya spossa do wif food.
NOT FROM THE LAB FRIDGE, YOU BRUTISH BURRITO BANDIT!
YOU'RE JUST LUCKY YOUR SISTER TERRIFIES ME.
RATHER MUD WRESTLE A POLAR BEAR THAN TELL HER YOU DIED IN MY LAB.
KAFKANATOR
ZAPPITTY!
I'LL FIGURE OUT HOW TO REVERSE THIS THING ONCE YOU'VE PROCESSED THAT BURRITO.
*
*I WILL HAVE MY VENGEANCE!

Words: sean frost

Pictures: rafer roberts

COST RICA,
NORTH AMERICAN UNION

Teddy and the YETI

IN: "EDGE OF REASON"

JEFF MCCLELLAND: WORDS AND LETTERS
MARIO WYTCH: ART
TEDDY AND THE YETI CREATED BY MCCLELLAND AND DUANE REDHEAD

ESTIMATED TIME UNTIL
ERUPTION: TWO HOURS

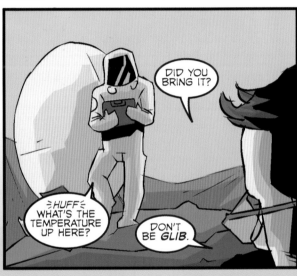

DID YOU BRING IT?

≥HUFF≤ WHAT'S THE TEMPERATURE UP HERE?

DON'T BE *GLIB*.

I'M STILL NOT QUITE SURE WHAT WE'RE DOING AT THE MOUTH OF A VOLCANO. WELL, WHAT *I'M* DOING AT THE MOUTH OF A VOLCANO, I GUESS.

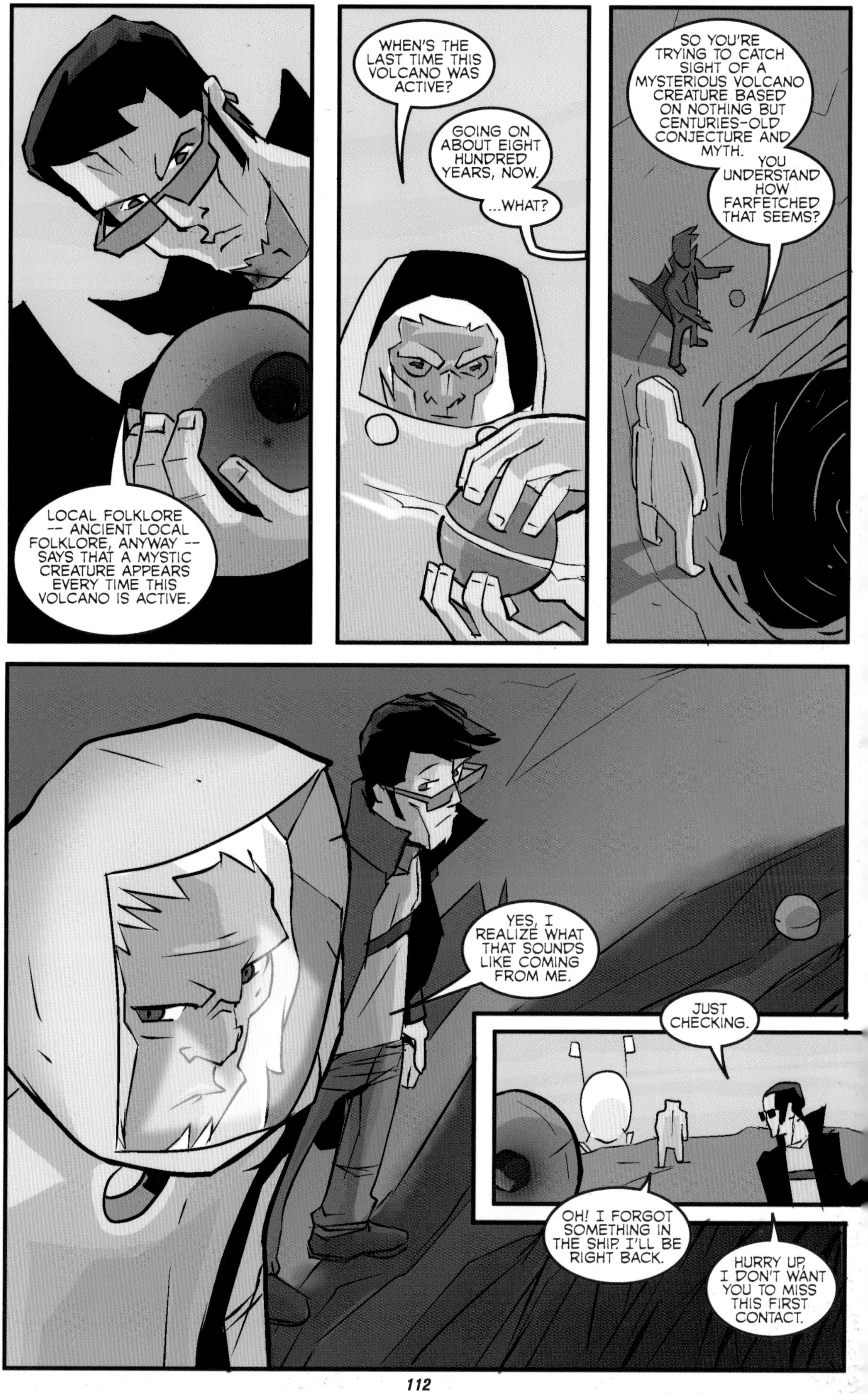
LOCAL FOLKLORE -- ANCIENT LOCAL FOLKLORE, ANYWAY -- SAYS THAT A MYSTIC CREATURE APPEARS EVERY TIME THIS VOLCANO IS ACTIVE.
WHEN'S THE LAST TIME THIS VOLCANO WAS ACTIVE?
GOING ON ABOUT EIGHT HUNDRED YEARS, NOW.
...WHAT?
SO YOU'RE TRYING TO CATCH SIGHT OF A MYSTERIOUS VOLCANO CREATURE BASED ON NOTHING BUT CENTURIES-OLD CONJECTURE AND MYTH.
YOU UNDERSTAND HOW FARFETCHED THAT SEEMS?
YES, I REALIZE WHAT THAT SOUNDS LIKE COMING FROM ME.
JUST CHECKING.
OH! I FORGOT SOMETHING IN THE SHIP. I'LL BE RIGHT BACK.
HURRY UP, I DON'T WANT YOU TO MISS THIS FIRST CONTACT.

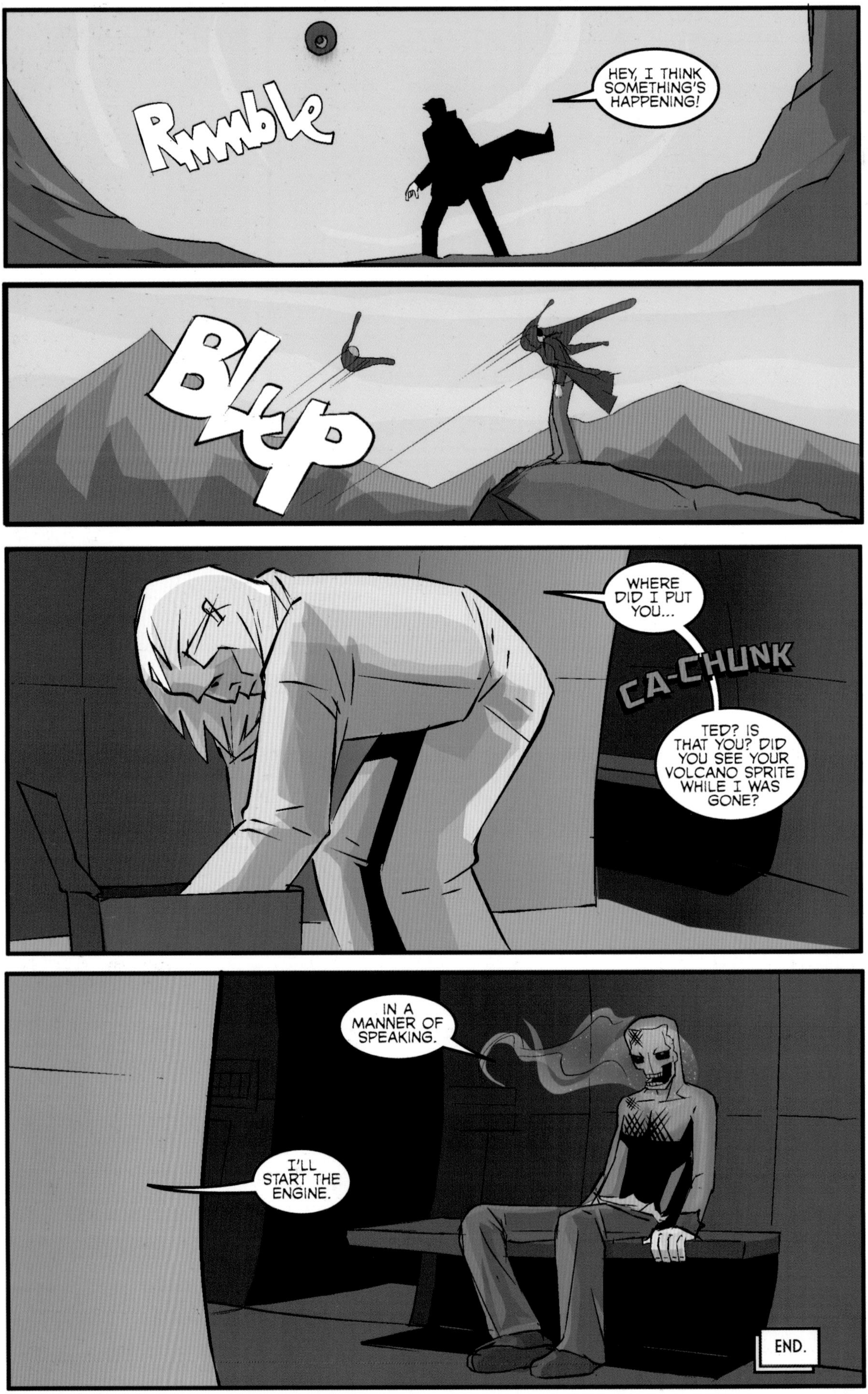
HEY, I THINK SOMETHING'S HAPPENING!
Rmmble
BLUP
WHERE DID I PUT YOU...
CA-CHUNK
TED? IS THAT YOU? DID YOU SEE YOUR VOLCANO SPRITE WHILE I WAS GONE?
IN A MANNER OF SPEAKING.
I'LL START THE ENGINE.
END.

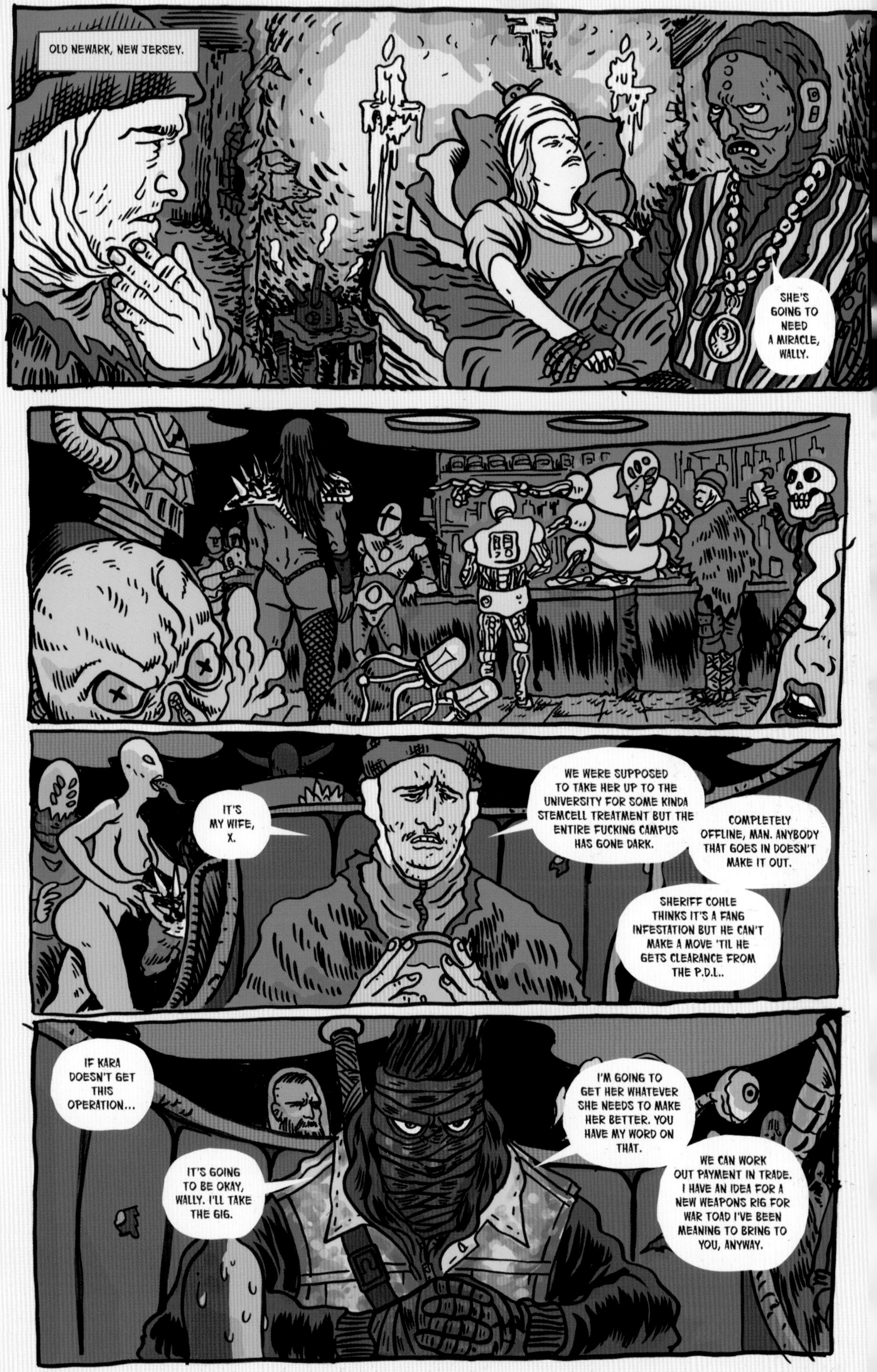
OLD NEWARK, NEW JERSEY.
SHE'S GOING TO NEED A MIRACLE, WALLY.
IT'S MY WIFE, X.
WE WERE SUPPOSED TO TAKE HER UP TO THE UNIVERSITY FOR SOME KINDA STEMCELL TREATMENT BUT THE ENTIRE FUCKING CAMPUS HAS GONE DARK.
COMPLETELY OFFLINE, MAN. ANYBODY THAT GOES IN DOESN'T MAKE IT OUT.
SHERIFF COHLE THINKS IT'S A FANG INFESTATION BUT HE CAN'T MAKE A MOVE 'TIL HE GETS CLEARANCE FROM THE P.D.L..
IF KARA DOESN'T GET THIS OPERATION...
I'M GOING TO GET HER WHATEVER SHE NEEDS TO MAKE HER BETTER. YOU HAVE MY WORD ON THAT.
IT'S GOING TO BE OKAY, WALLY. I'LL TAKE THE GIG.
WE CAN WORK OUT PAYMENT IN TRADE. I HAVE AN IDEA FOR A NEW WEAPONS RIG FOR WAR TOAD I'VE BEEN MEANING TO BRING TO YOU, ANYWAY.

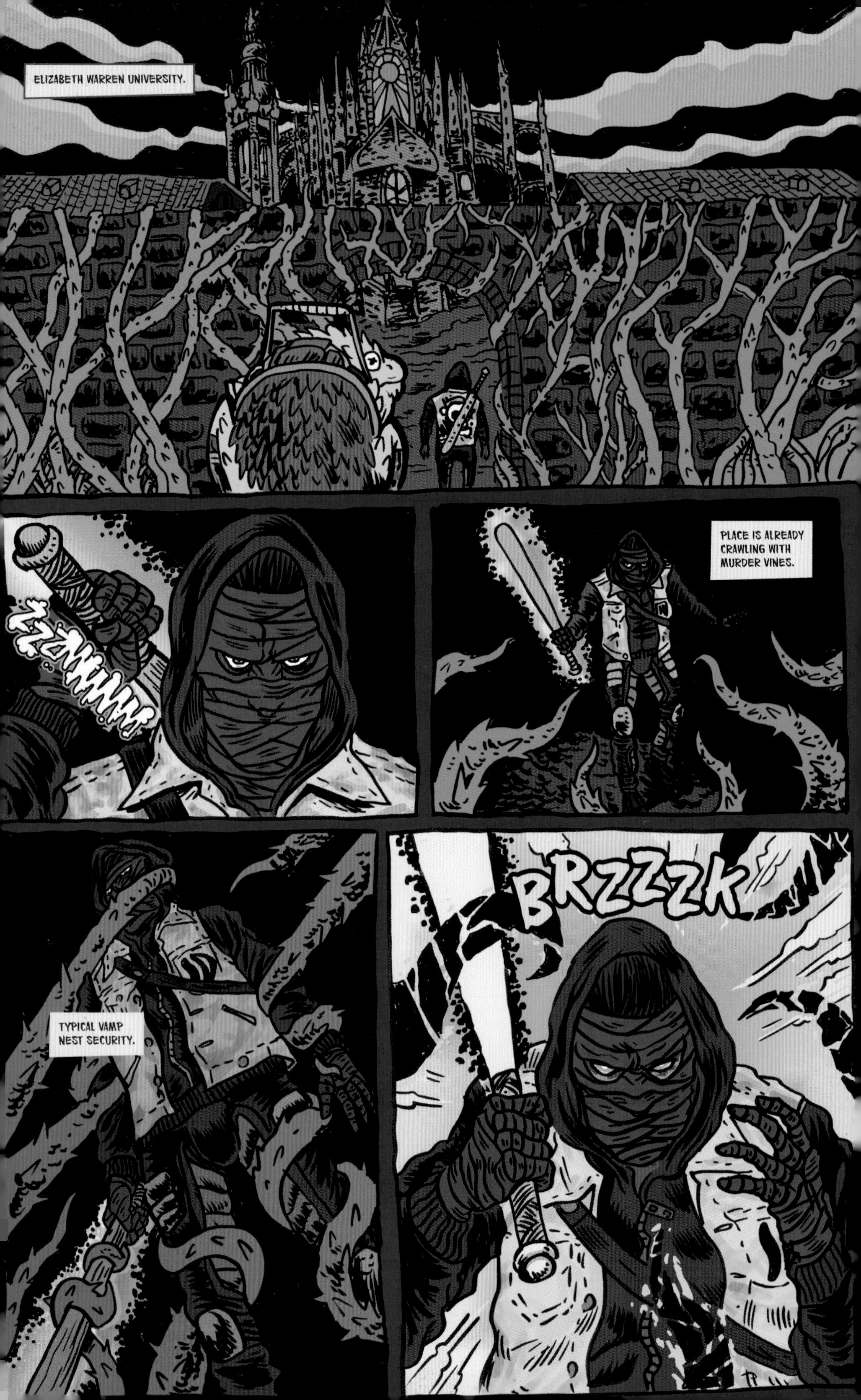
ELIZABETH WARREN UNIVERSITY.
PLACE IS ALREADY CRAWLING WITH MURDER VINES.
TYPICAL VAMP NEST SECURITY.
BRZZZK

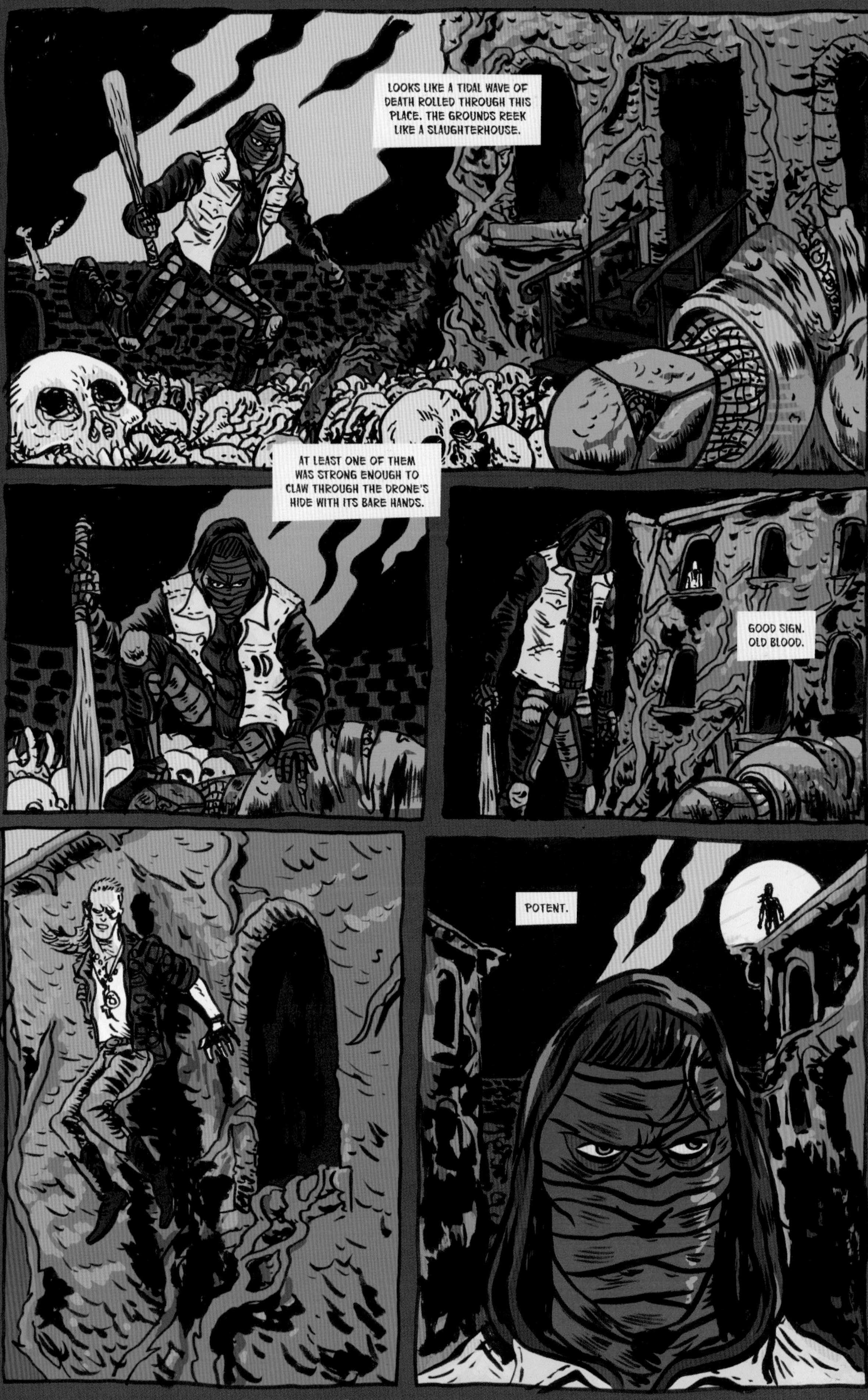
LOOKS LIKE A TIDAL WAVE OF DEATH ROLLED THROUGH THIS PLACE. THE GROUNDS REEK LIKE A SLAUGHTERHOUSE.
AT LEAST ONE OF THEM WAS STRONG ENOUGH TO CLAW THROUGH THE DRONE'S HIDE WITH ITS BARE HANDS.
GOOD SIGN. OLD BLOOD.
POTENT.

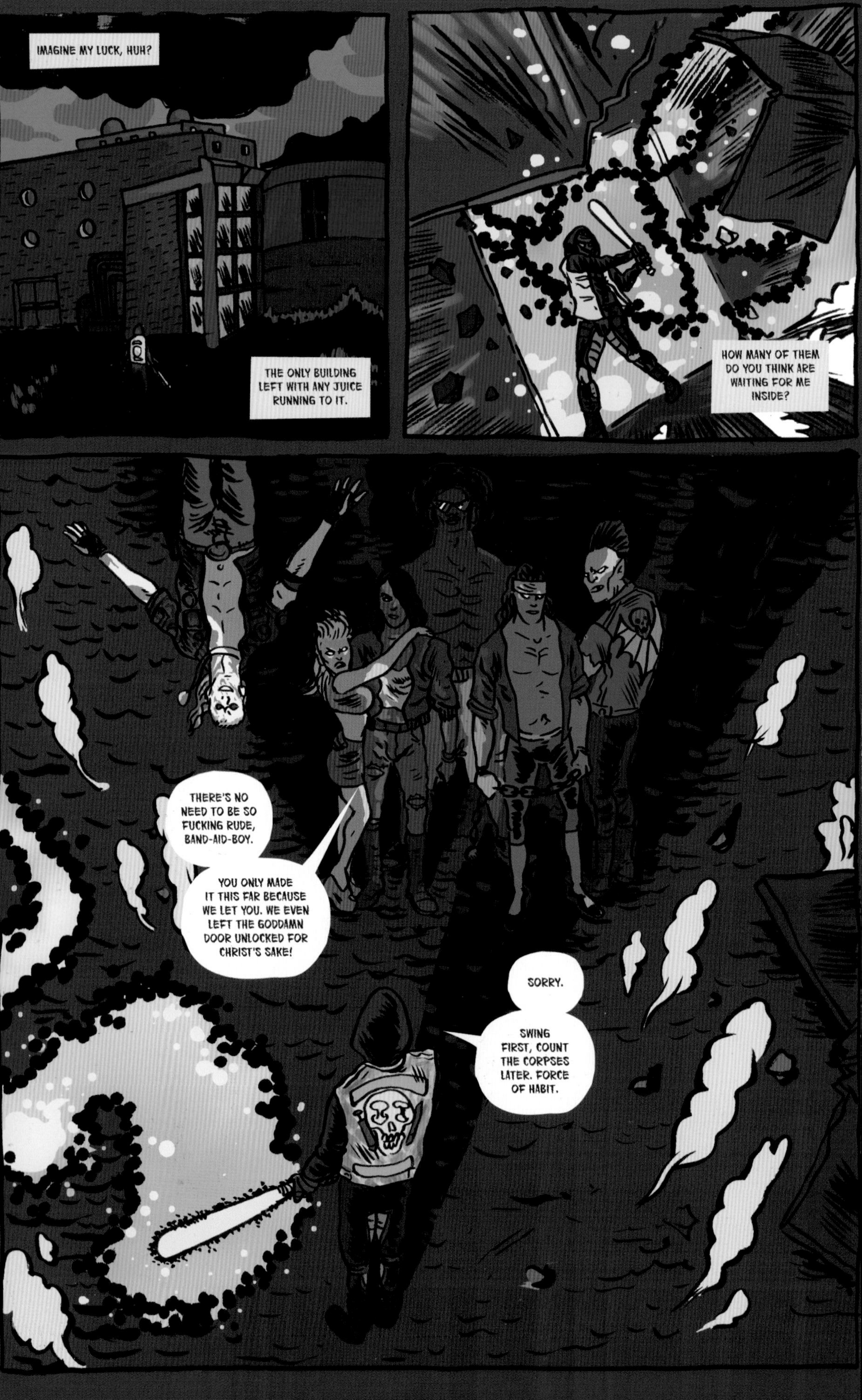
IMAGINE MY LUCK, HUH?
THE ONLY BUILDING LEFT WITH ANY JUICE RUNNING TO IT.
HOW MANY OF THEM DO YOU THINK ARE WAITING FOR ME INSIDE?
THERE'S NO NEED TO BE SO FUCKING RUDE, BAND-AID-BOY.
YOU ONLY MADE IT THIS FAR BECAUSE WE LET YOU. WE EVEN LEFT THE GODDAMN DOOR UNLOCKED FOR CHRIST'S SAKE!
SORRY.
SWING FIRST, COUNT THE CORPSES LATER. FORCE OF HABIT.

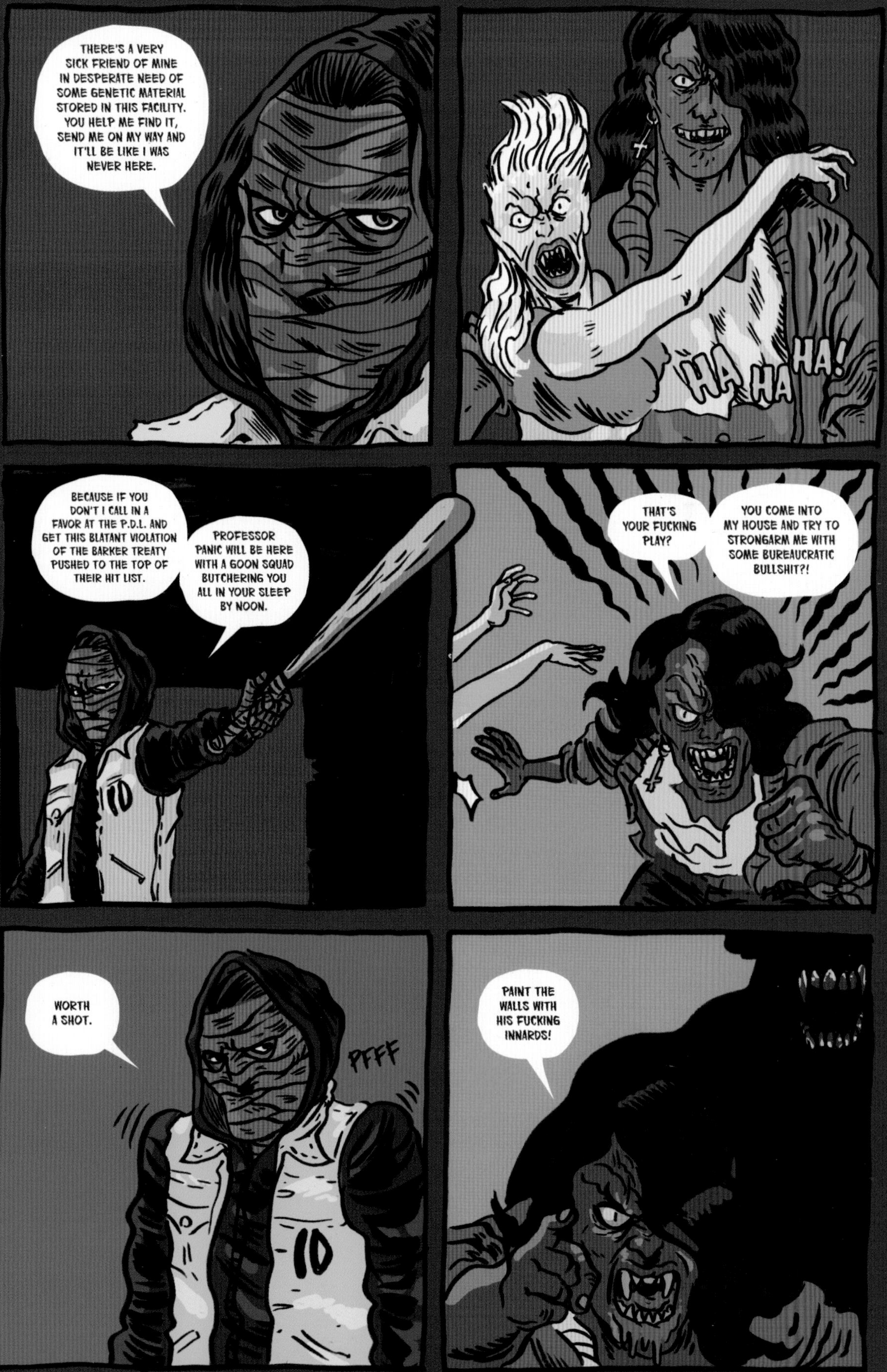
THERE'S A VERY SICK FRIEND OF MINE IN DESPERATE NEED OF SOME GENETIC MATERIAL STORED IN THIS FACILITY. YOU HELP ME FIND IT, SEND ME ON MY WAY AND IT'LL BE LIKE I WAS NEVER HERE.
HA HA HA!
BECAUSE IF YOU DON'T I CALL IN A FAVOR AT THE P.D.I. AND GET THIS BLATANT VIOLATION OF THE BARKER TREATY PUSHED TO THE TOP OF THEIR HIT LIST.
PROFESSOR PANIC WILL BE HERE WITH A GOON SQUAD BUTCHERING YOU ALL IN YOUR SLEEP BY NOON.
THAT'S YOUR FUCKING PLAY?
YOU COME INTO MY HOUSE AND TRY TO STRONGARM ME WITH SOME BUREAUCRATIC BULLSHIT?!
WORTH A SHOT.
PFFF
PAINT THE WALLS WITH HIS FUCKING INNARDS!

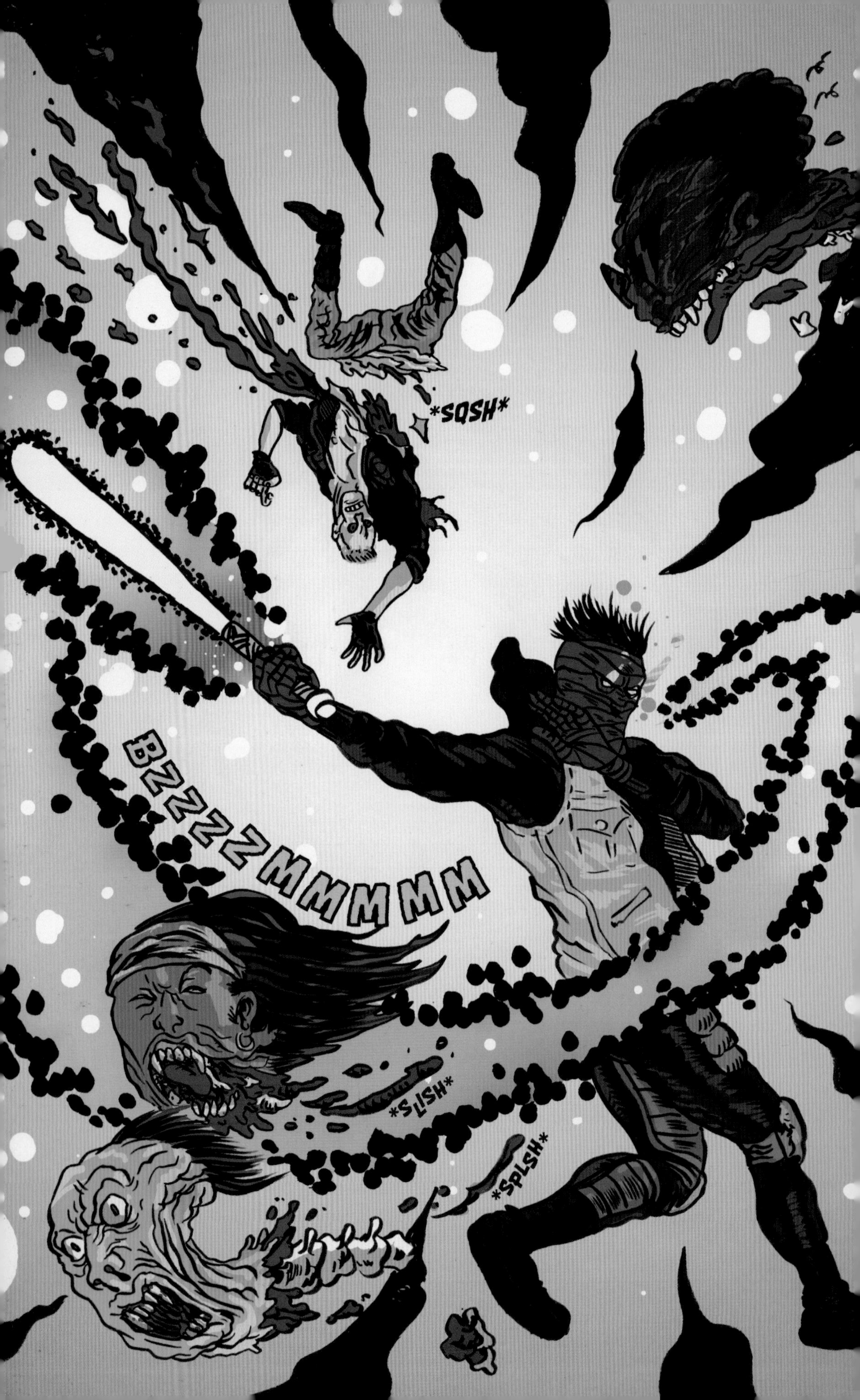
SQSH
BZZZZMMMMMM
SLISH
SPLSH

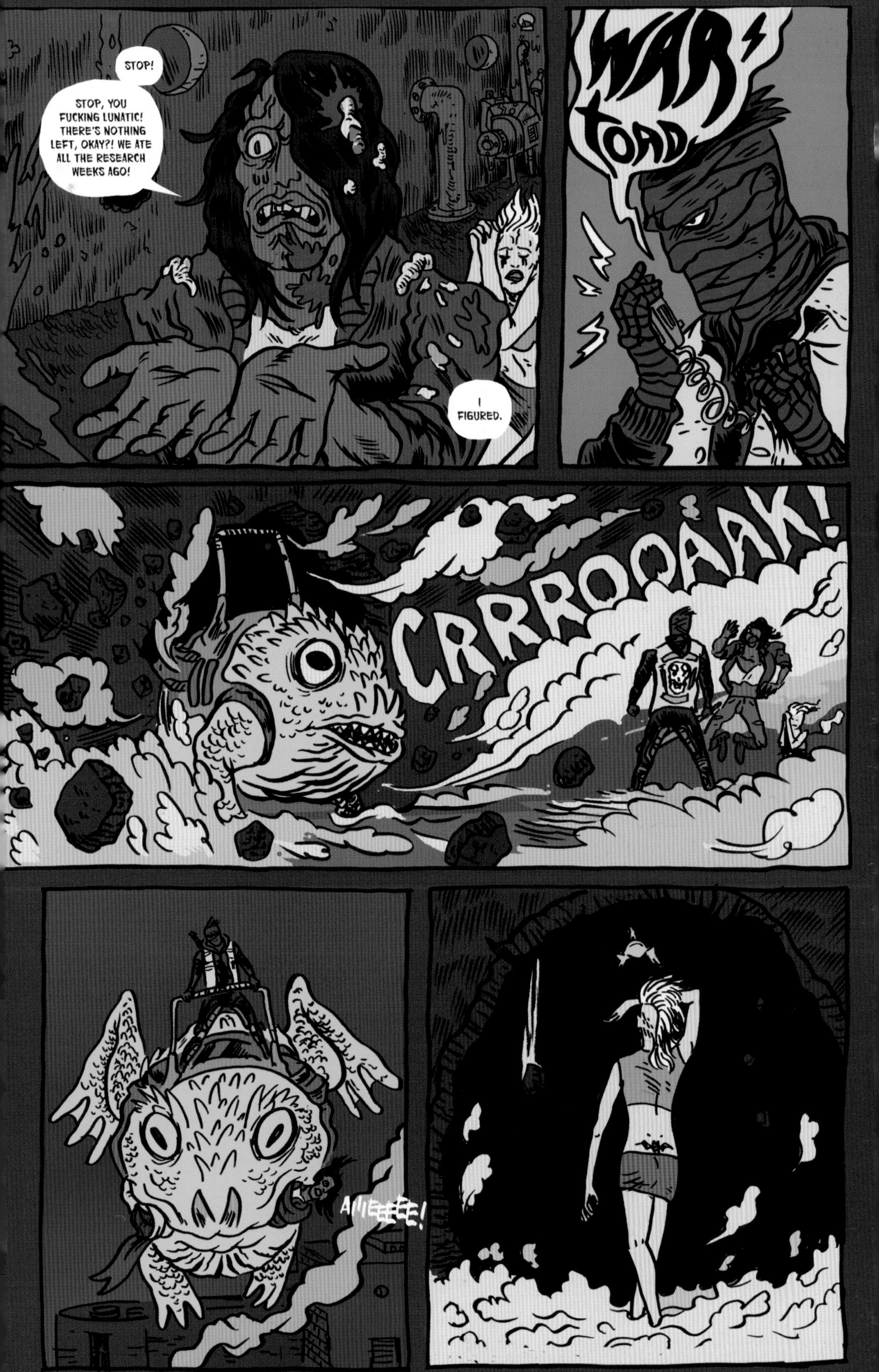
STOP!
STOP, YOU FUCKING LUNATIC! THERE'S NOTHING LEFT, OKAY?! WE ATE ALL THE RESEARCH WEEKS AGO!
I FIGURED.
WAR TOAD
CRRROOAAK!
AIIEEEEE!

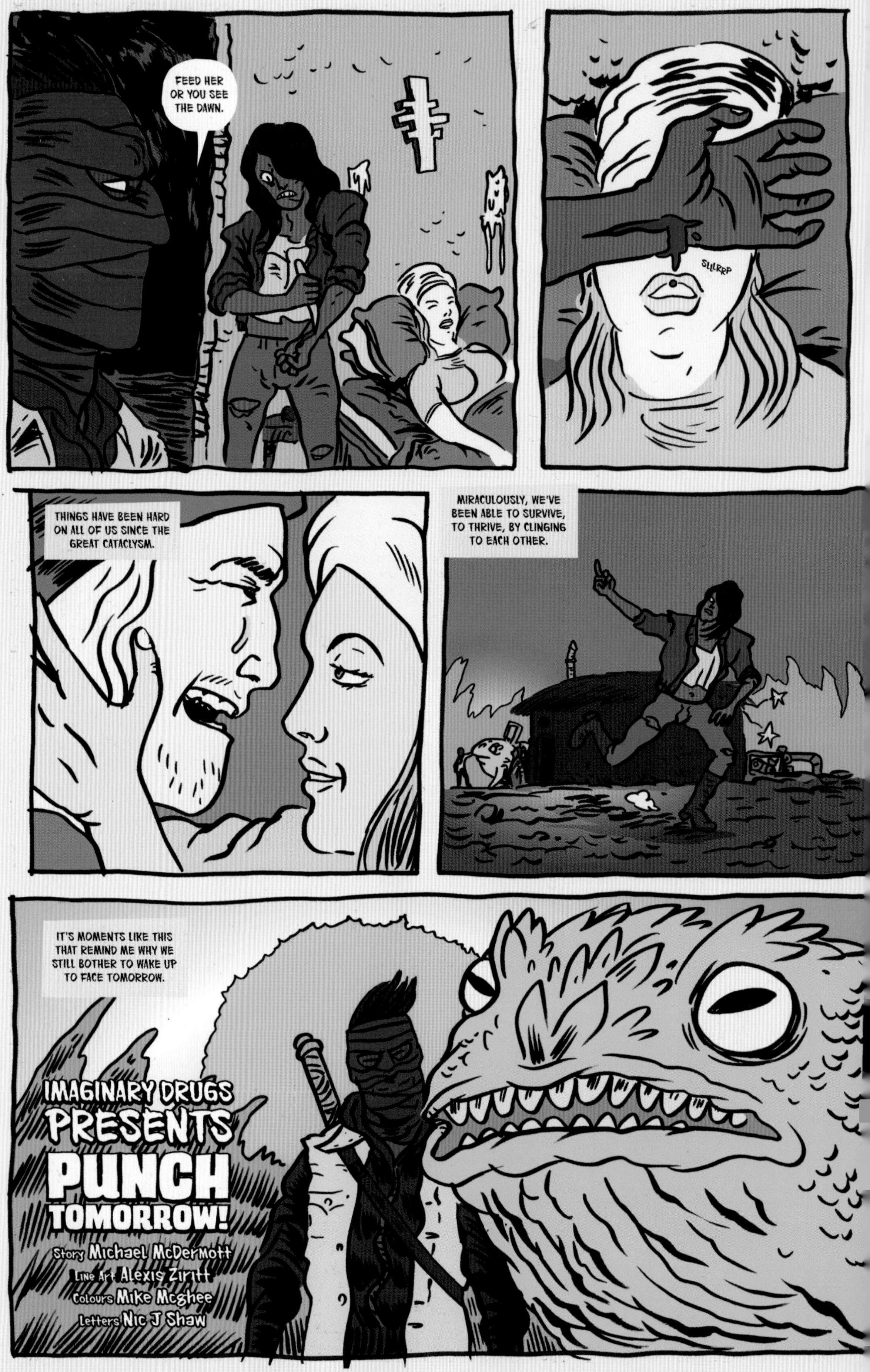
FEED HER OR YOU SEE THE DAWN.
SLLLRRP
THINGS HAVE BEEN HARD ON ALL OF US SINCE THE GREAT CATACLYSM.
MIRACULOUSLY, WE'VE BEEN ABLE TO SURVIVE, TO THRIVE, BY CLINGING TO EACH OTHER.
IT'S MOMENTS LIKE THIS THAT REMIND ME WHY WE STILL BOTHER TO WAKE UP TO FACE TOMORROW.
IMAGINARY DRUGS PRESENTS
PUNCH TOMORROW!
Story Michael McDermott
Line Art Alexis Ziritt
Colours Mike McGhee
Letters Nic J Shaw

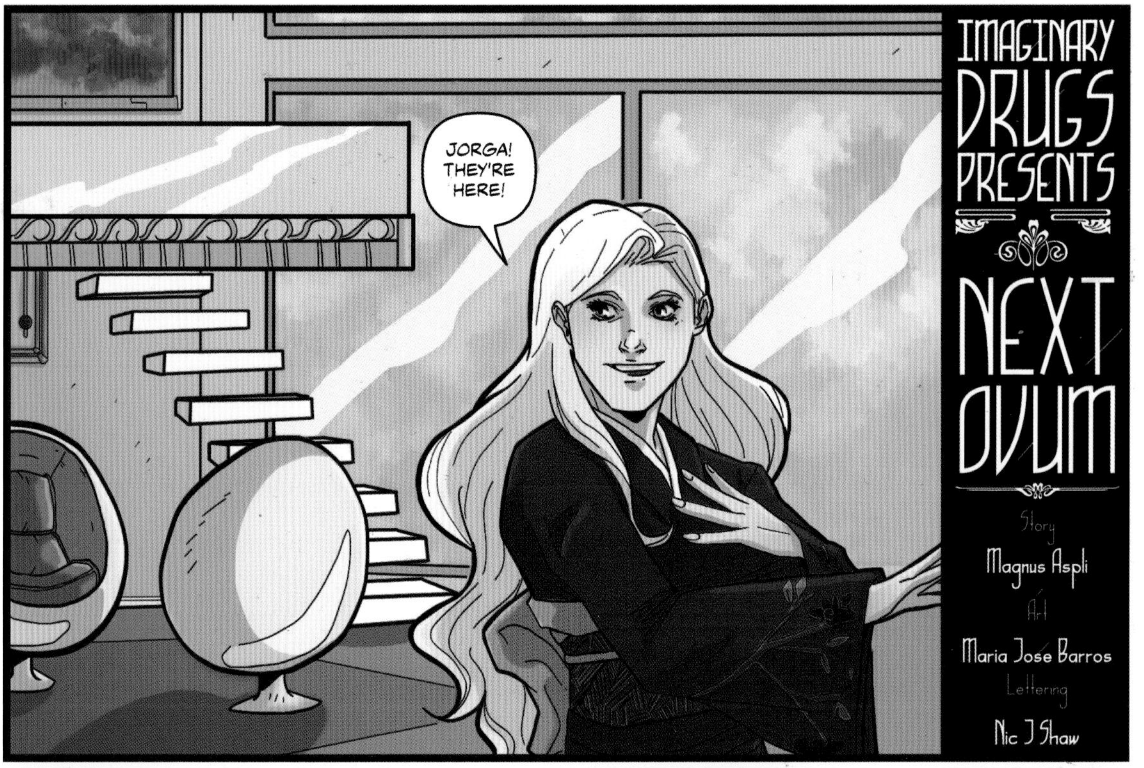
IMAGINARY DRUGS PRESENTS
NEXT OVUM
Story
Magnus Aspli
Art
Maria Jose Barros
Lettering
Nic J Shaw
JORGA! THEY'RE HERE!

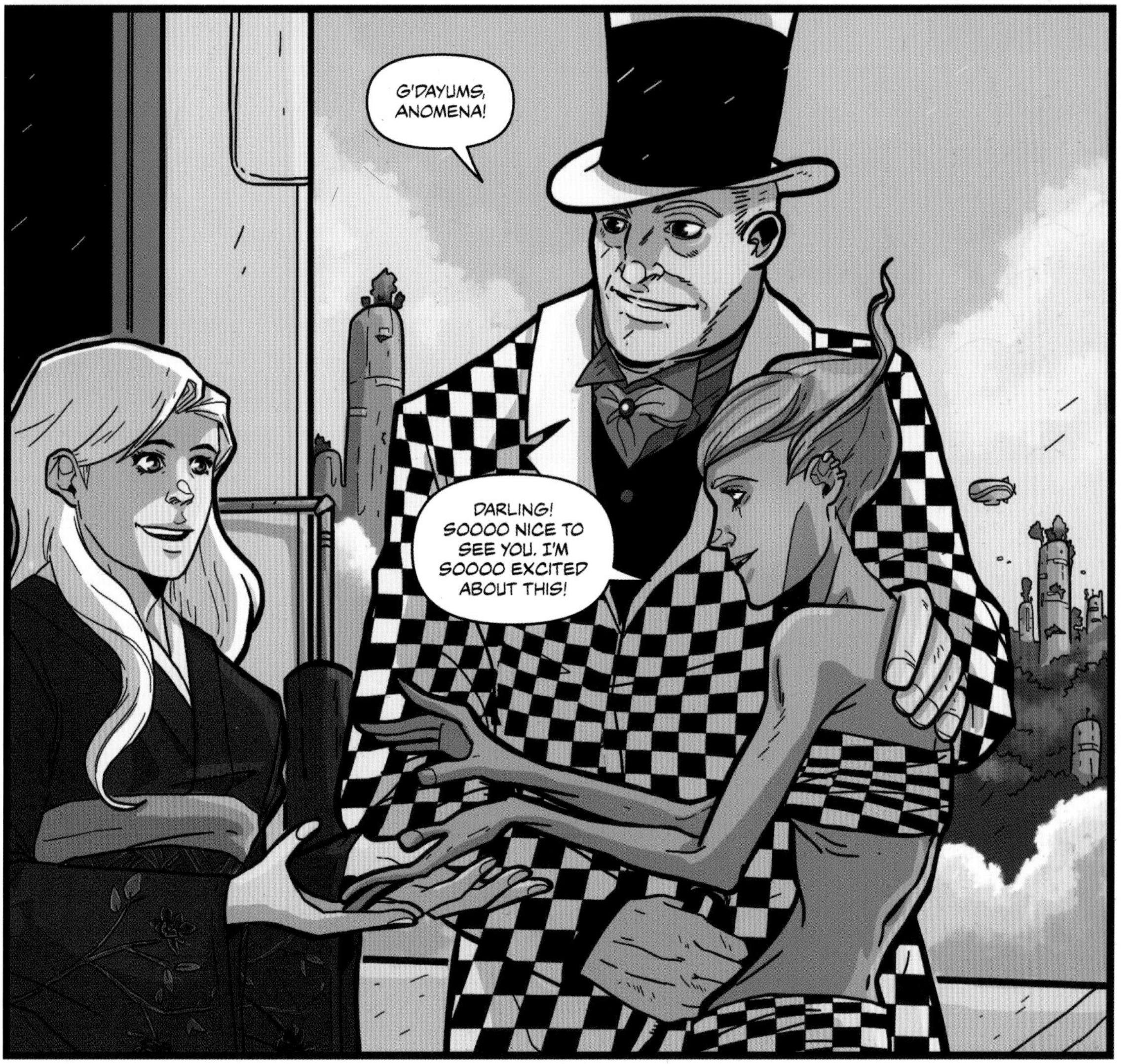
G'DAYUMS, ANOMENA!
DARLING! SOOOO NICE TO SEE YOU. I'M SOOOO EXCITED ABOUT THIS!

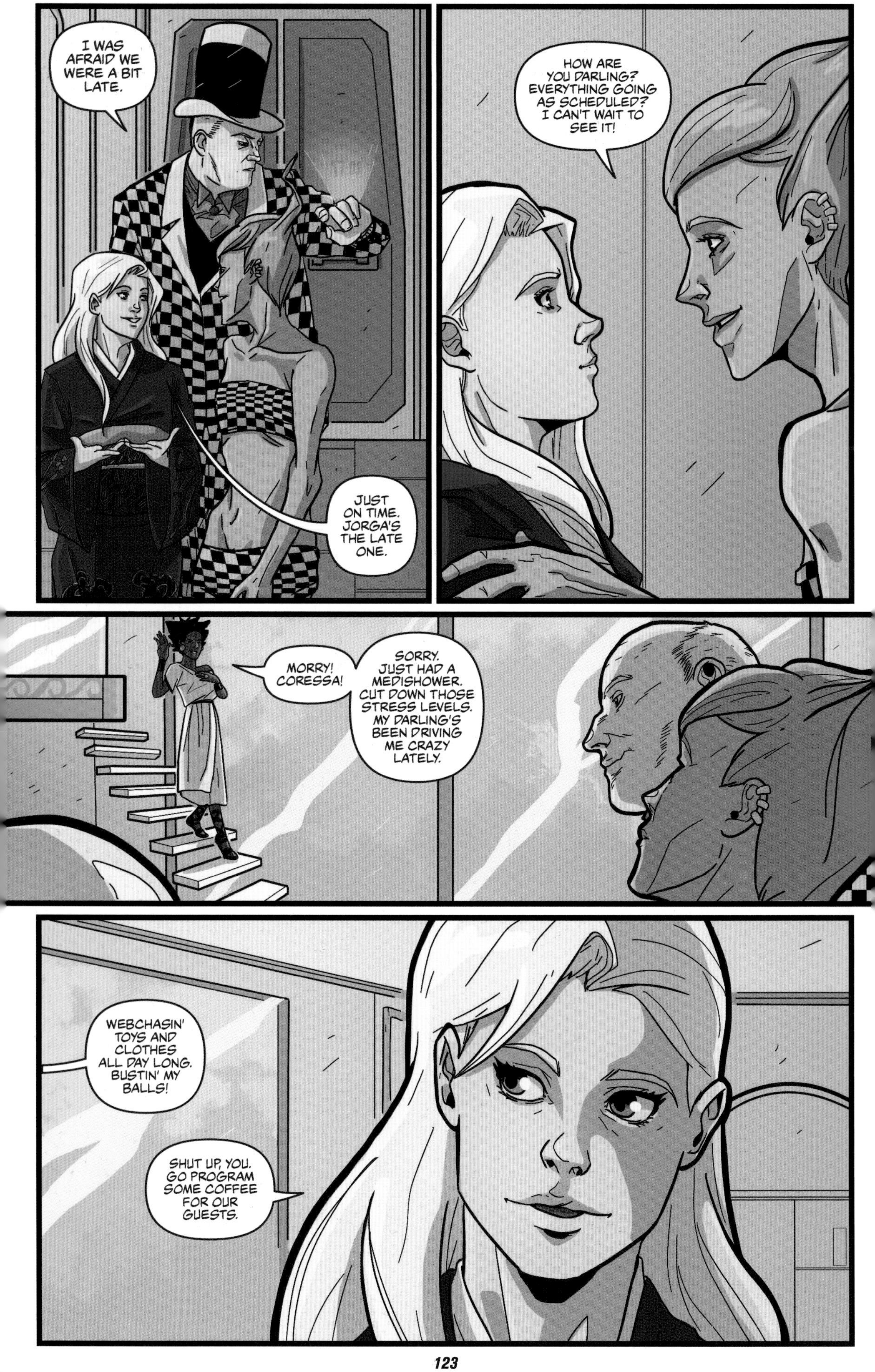
I WAS AFRAID WE WERE A BIT LATE.
JUST ON TIME. JORGA'S THE LATE ONE.
HOW ARE YOU DARLING? EVERYTHING GOING AS SCHEDULED? I CAN'T WAIT TO SEE IT!
MORRY! CORESSA!
SORRY. JUST HAD A MEDISHOWER. CUT DOWN THOSE STRESS LEVELS. MY DARLING'S BEEN DRIVING ME CRAZY LATELY.
WEBCHASIN' TOYS AND CLOTHES ALL DAY LONG. BUSTIN' MY BALLS!
SHUT UP, YOU. GO PROGRAM SOME COFFEE FOR OUR GUESTS.

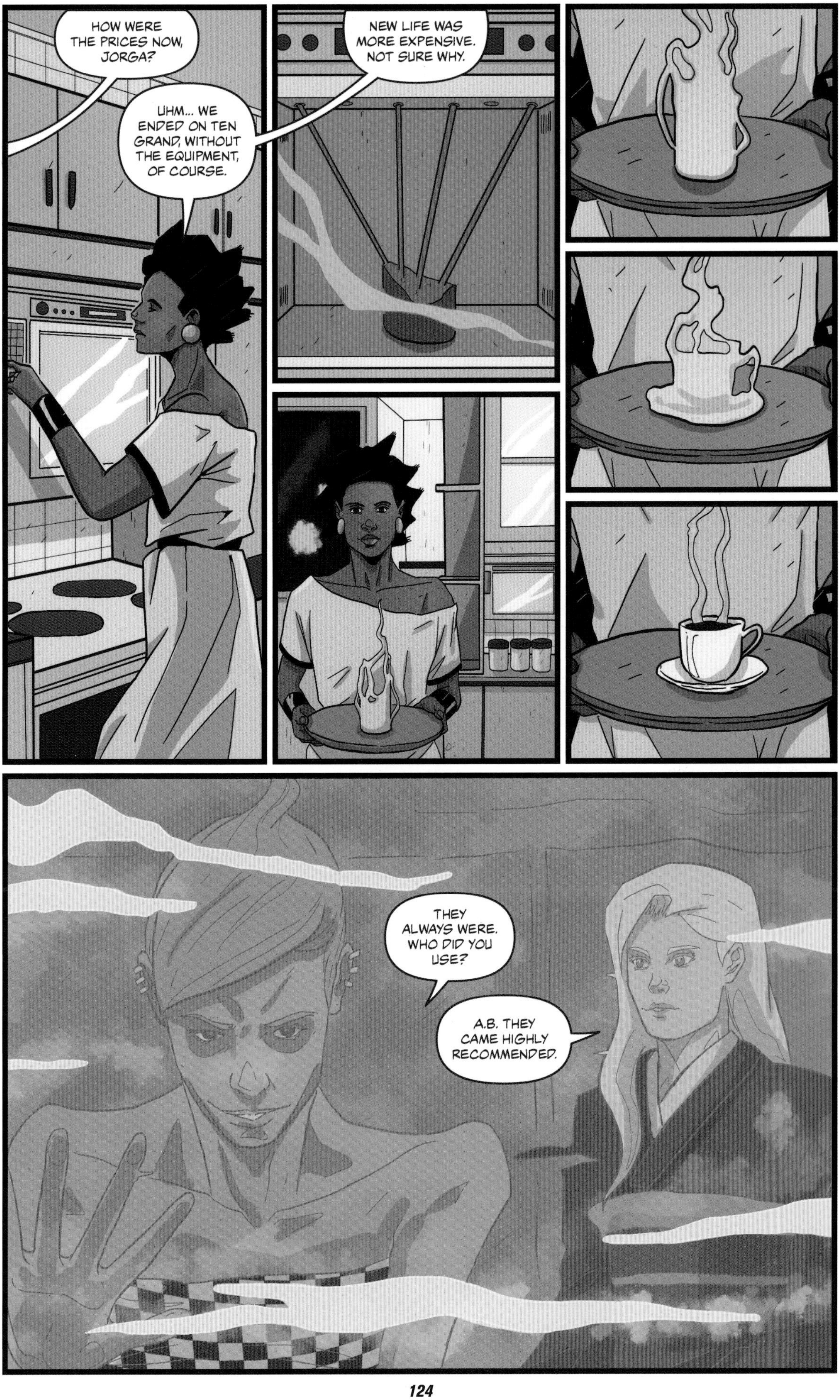

HOW WERE THE PRICES NOW, JORGA?
UHM... WE ENDED ON TEN GRAND, WITHOUT THE EQUIPMENT, OF COURSE.
NEW LIFE WAS MORE EXPENSIVE. NOT SURE WHY.
THEY ALWAYS WERE. WHO DID YOU USE?
A.B. THEY CAME HIGHLY RECOMMENDED.

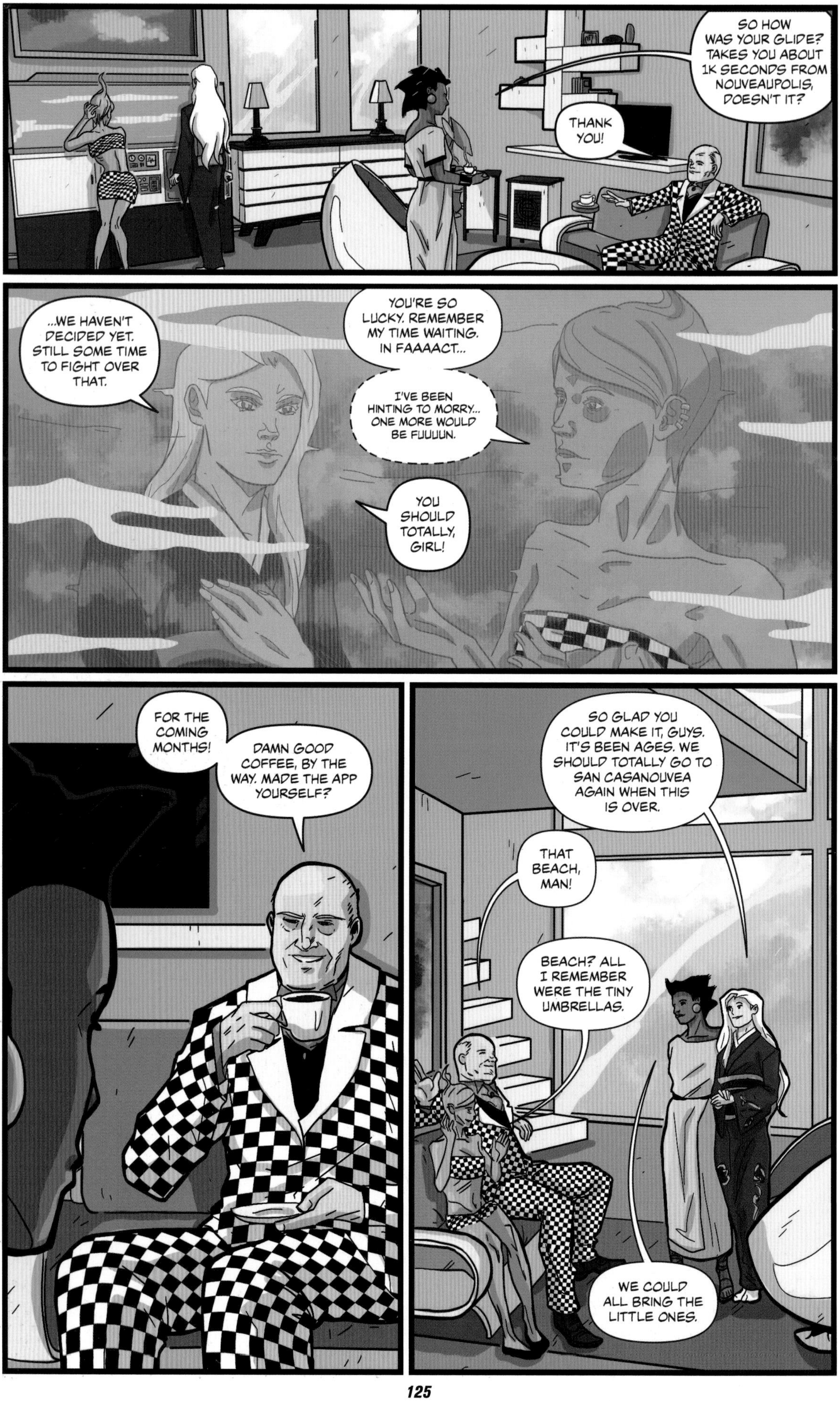
SO HOW WAS YOUR GLIDE? TAKES YOU ABOUT 1K SECONDS FROM NOUVEAUPOLIS, DOESN'T IT?
THANK YOU!
...WE HAVEN'T DECIDED YET. STILL SOME TIME TO FIGHT OVER THAT.
YOU'RE SO LUCKY. REMEMBER MY TIME WAITING. IN FAAAACT...
I'VE BEEN HINTING TO MORRY... ONE MORE WOULD BE FUUUUN.
YOU SHOULD TOTALLY, GIRL!
FOR THE COMING MONTHS!
DAMN GOOD COFFEE, BY THE WAY. MADE THE APP YOURSELF?
SO GLAD YOU COULD MAKE IT, GUYS. IT'S BEEN AGES. WE SHOULD TOTALLY GO TO SAN CASANOUVEA AGAIN WHEN THIS IS OVER.
THAT BEACH, MAN!
BEACH? ALL I REMEMBER WERE THE TINY UMBRELLAS.
WE COULD ALL BRING THE LITTLE ONES.

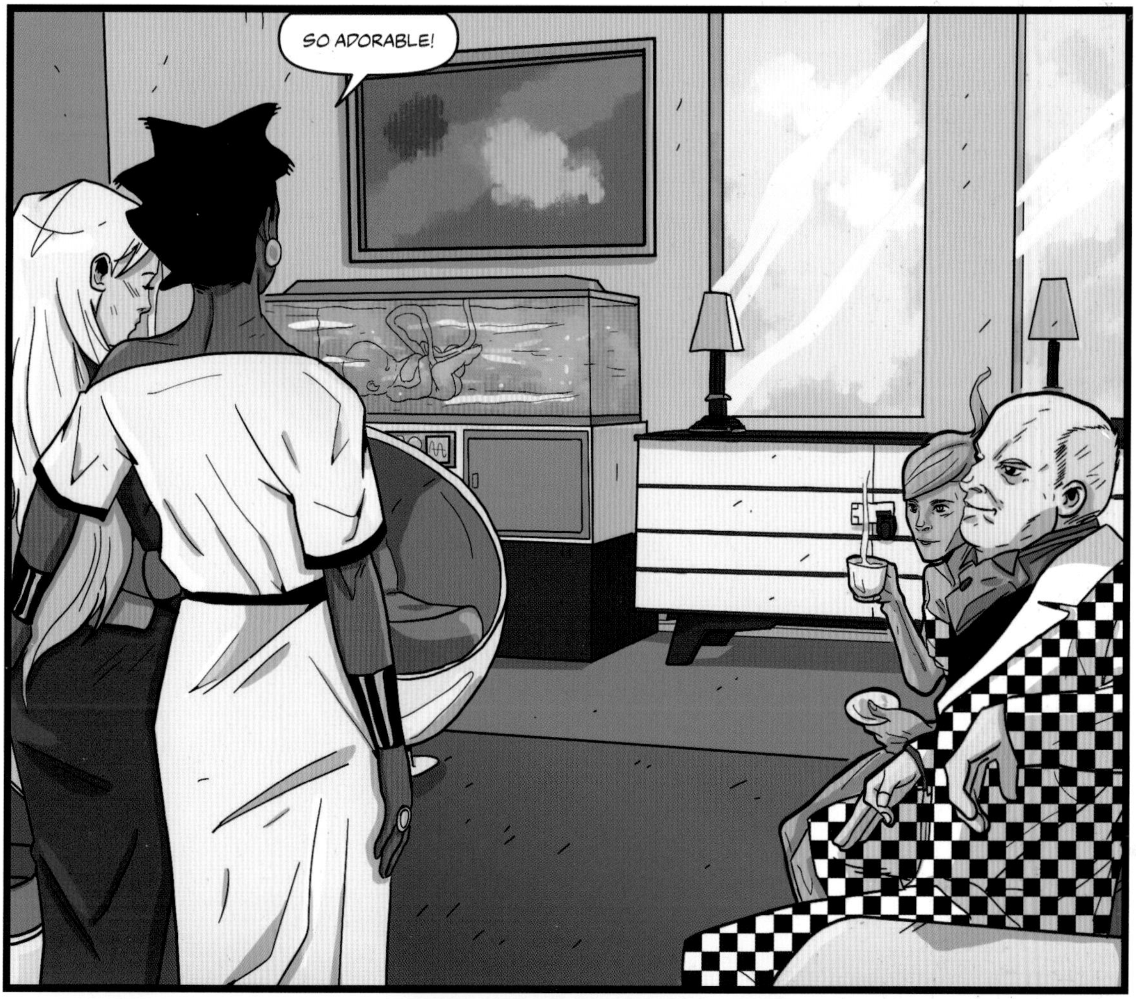
SO ADORABLE!

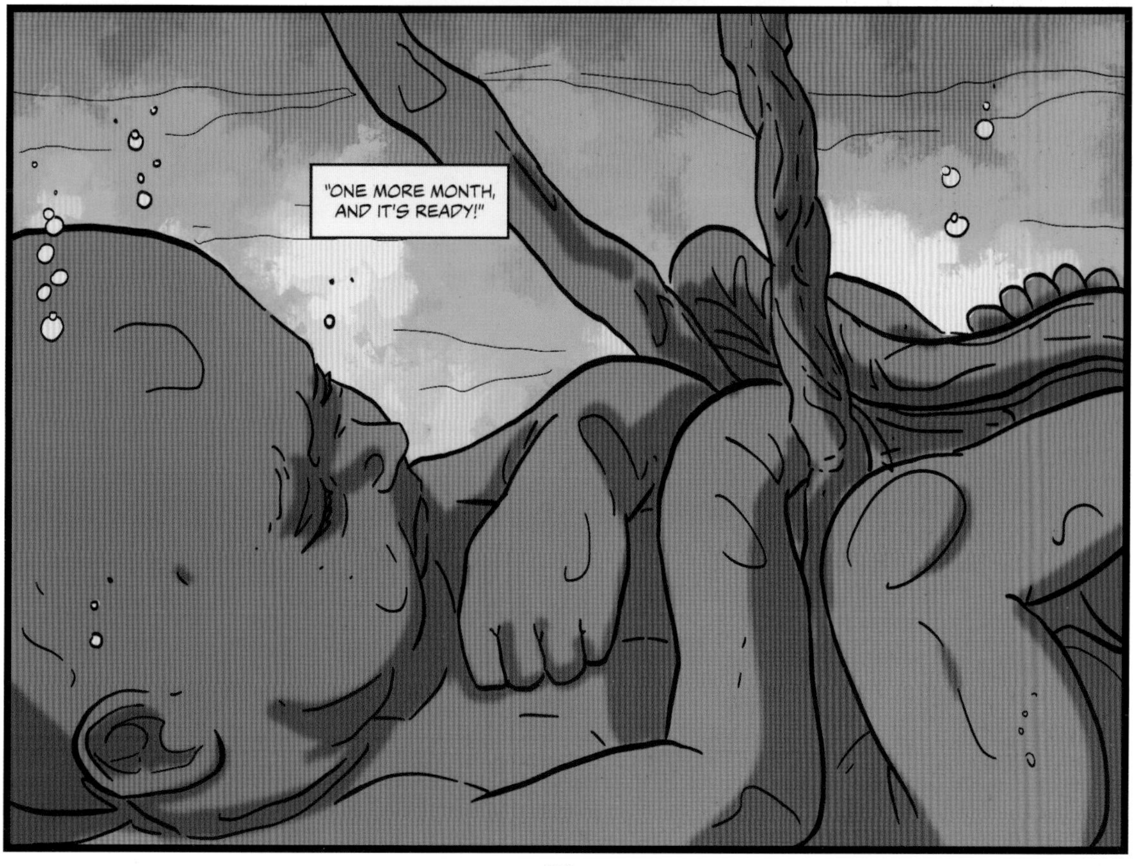
"ONE MORE MONTH, AND IT'S READY!"

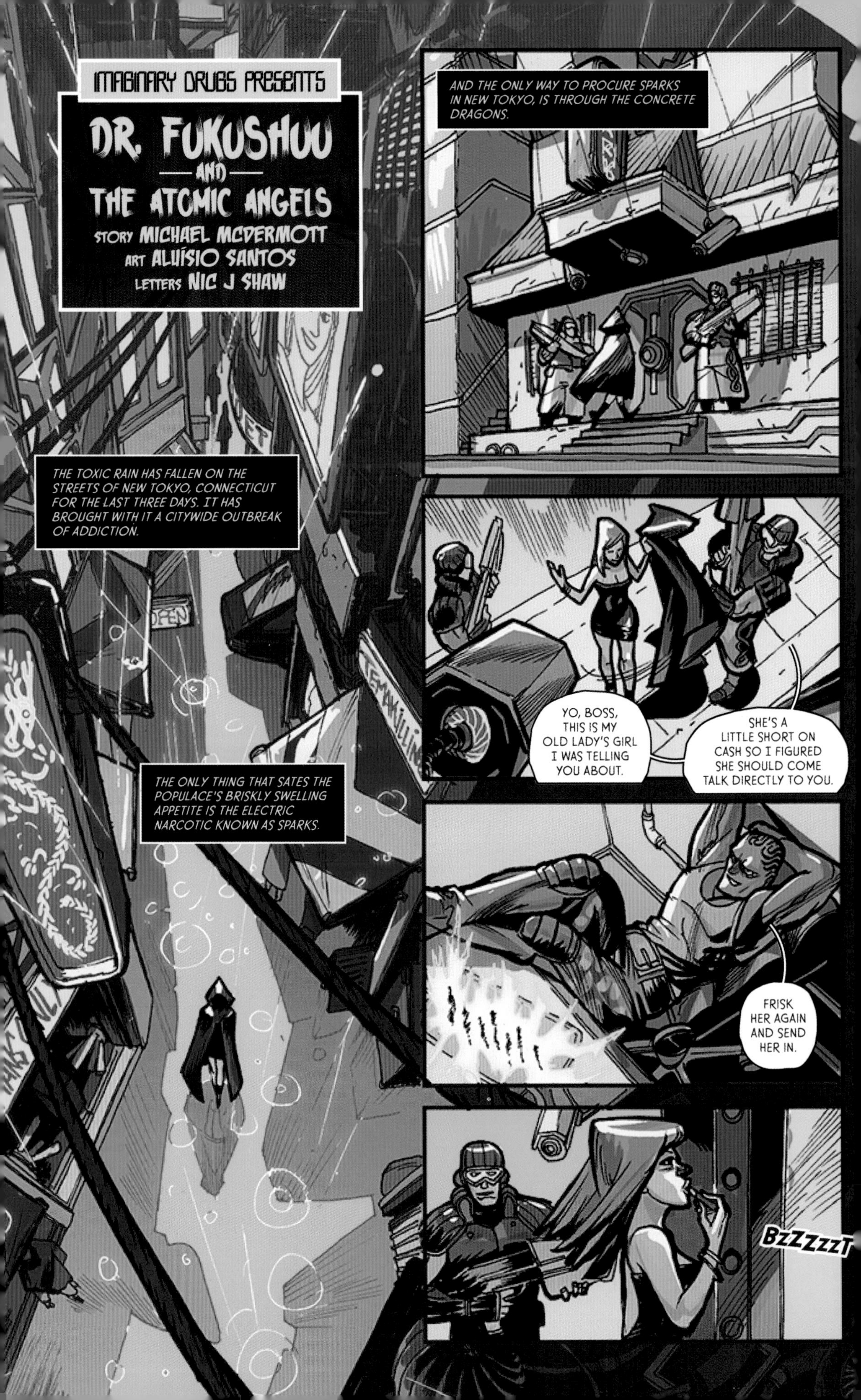
IMAGINARY DRUGS PRESENTS
DR. FUKUSHUU AND THE ATOMIC ANGELS
STORY MICHAEL MCDERMOTT
ART ALUÍSIO SANTOS
LETTERS NIC J SHAW
THE TOXIC RAIN HAS FALLEN ON THE STREETS OF NEW TOKYO, CONNECTICUT FOR THE LAST THREE DAYS. IT HAS BROUGHT WITH IT A CITYWIDE OUTBREAK OF ADDICTION.
OPEN
THE ONLY THING THAT SATES THE POPULACE'S BRISKLY SWELLING APPETITE IS THE ELECTRIC NARCOTIC KNOWN AS SPARKS.
AND THE ONLY WAY TO PROCURE SPARKS IN NEW TOKYO, IS THROUGH THE CONCRETE DRAGONS.
YO, BOSS, THIS IS MY OLD LADY'S GIRL I WAS TELLING YOU ABOUT.
SHE'S A LITTLE SHORT ON CASH SO I FIGURED SHE SHOULD COME TALK DIRECTLY TO YOU.
FRISK HER AGAIN AND SEND HER IN.
BZZZZZT

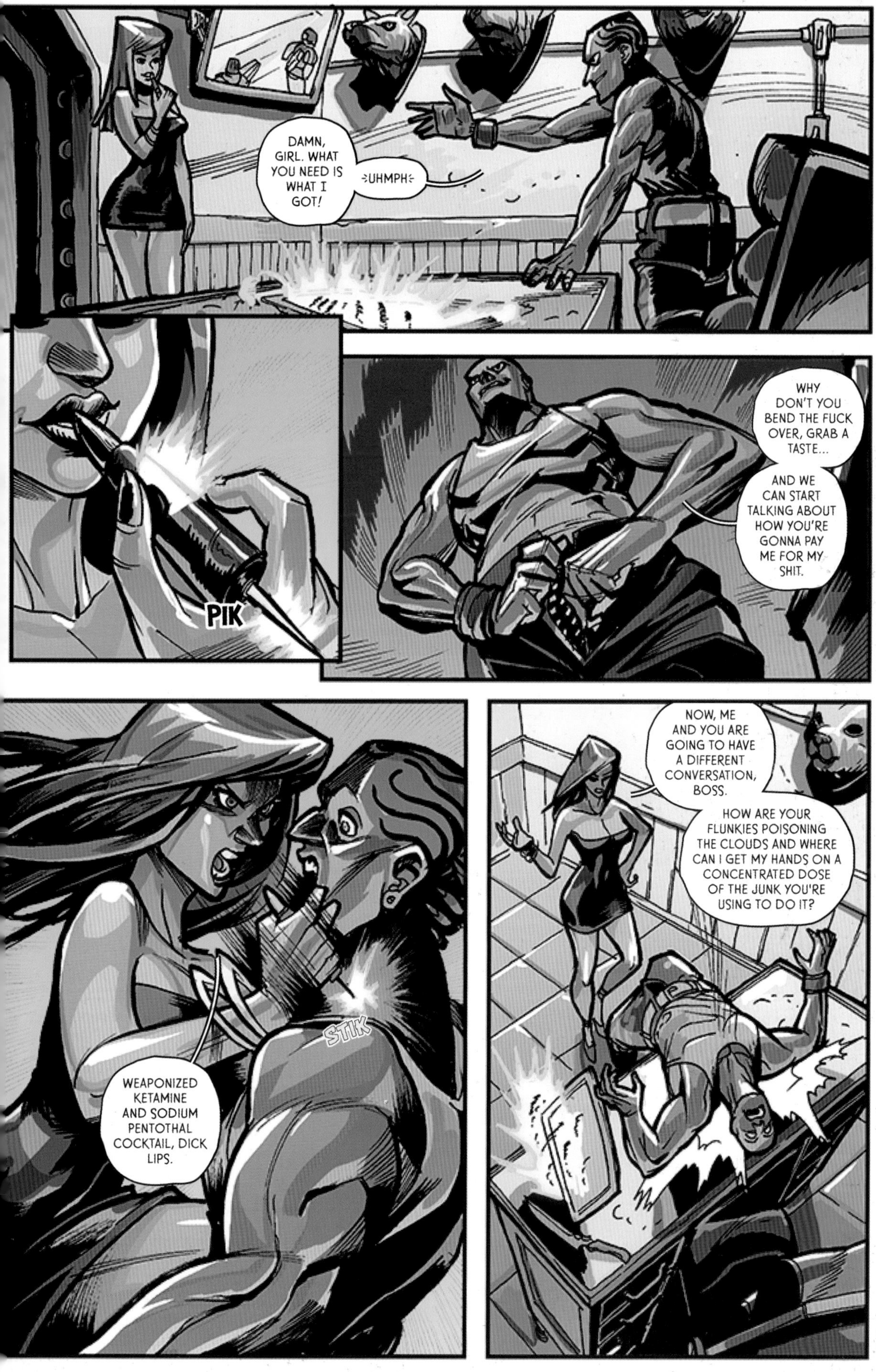
DAMN, GIRL. WHAT YOU NEED IS WHAT I GOT!
UHMPH
PIK
WHY DON'T YOU BEND THE FUCK OVER, GRAB A TASTE...
AND WE CAN START TALKING ABOUT HOW YOU'RE GONNA PAY ME FOR MY SHIT.
STIK
WEAPONIZED KETAMINE AND SODIUM PENTOTHAL COCKTAIL, DICK LIPS.
NOW, ME AND YOU ARE GOING TO HAVE A DIFFERENT CONVERSATION, BOSS.
HOW ARE YOUR FLUNKIES POISONING THE CLOUDS AND WHERE CAN I GET MY HANDS ON A CONCENTRATED DOSE OF THE JUNK YOU'RE USING TO DO IT?

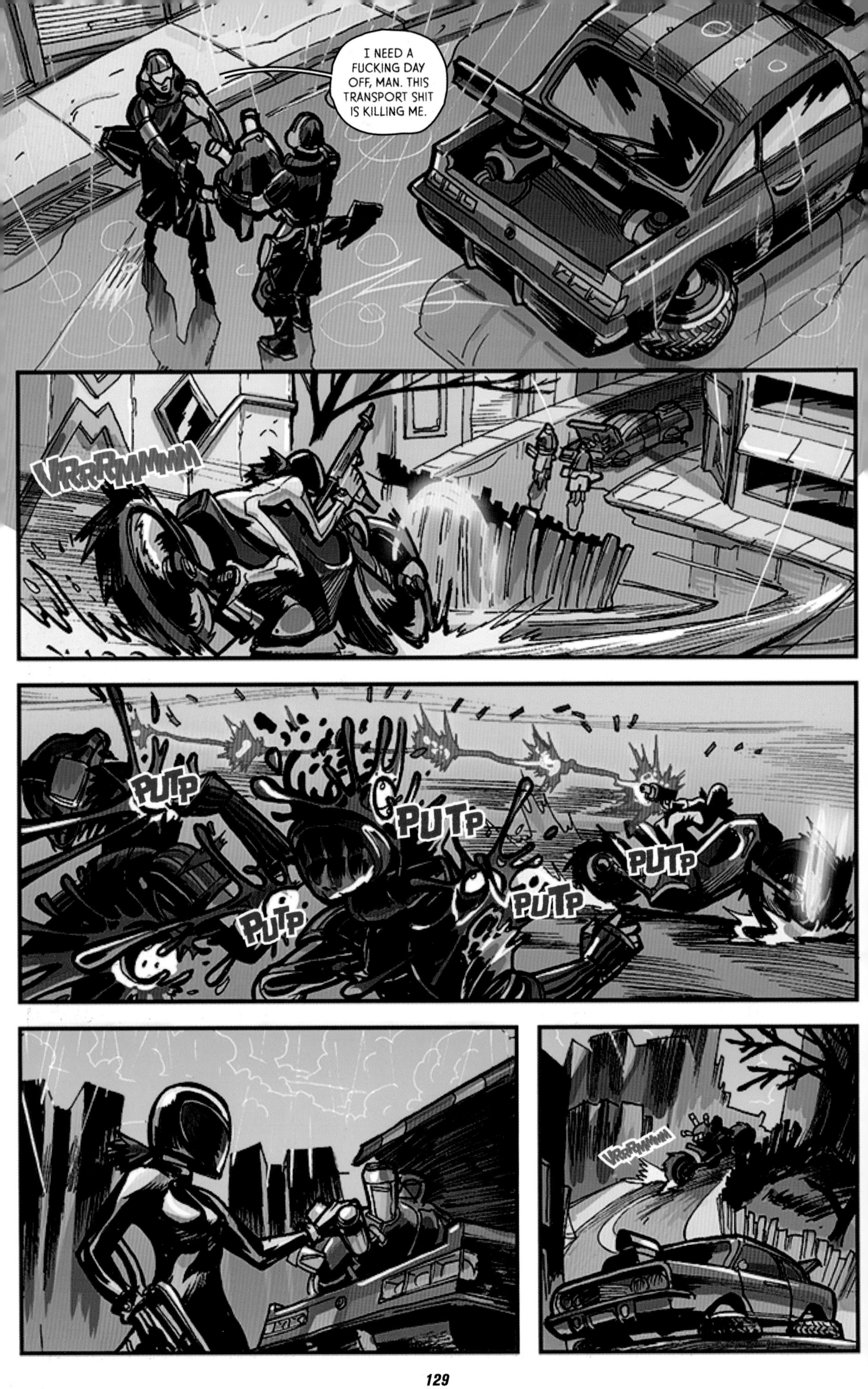
I NEED A FUCKING DAY OFF, MAN. THIS TRANSPORT SHIT IS KILLING ME.
VRRRMMMMM
PUTP
PUTP
PUTP
PUTP
PUTP
VRRRMMMM

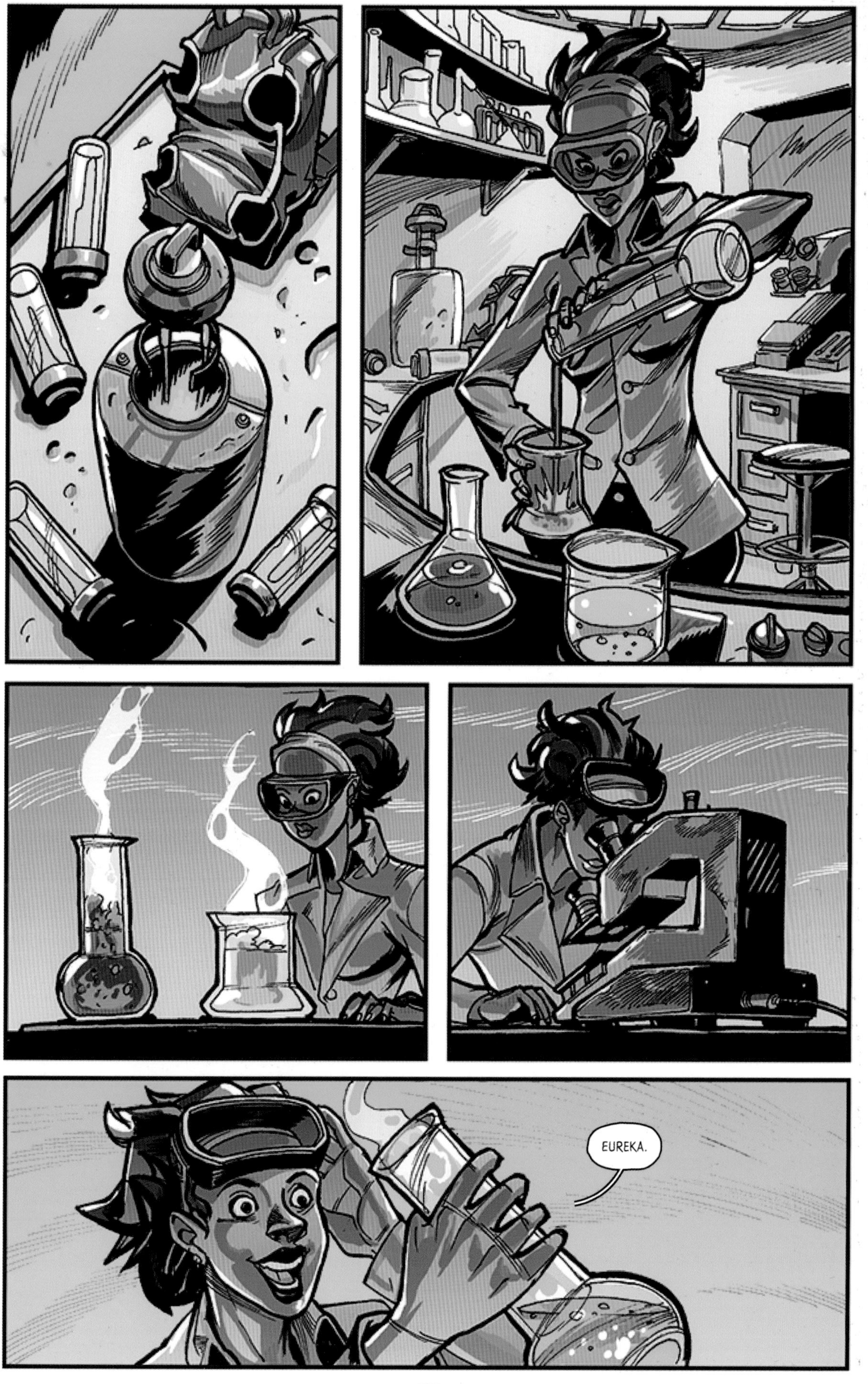
EUREKA.

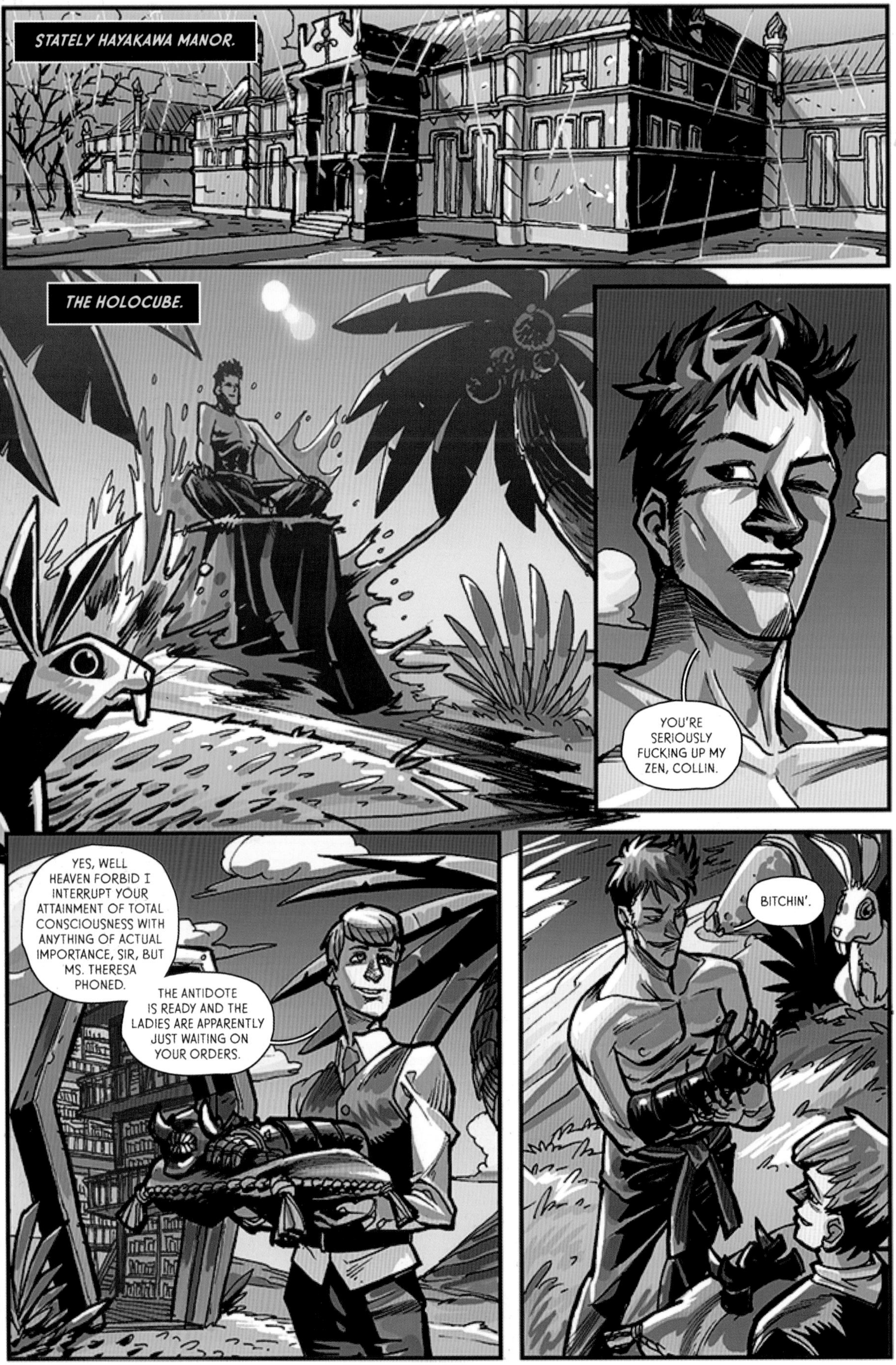
STATELY HAYAKAWA MANOR.
THE HOLOCUBE.
YOU'RE SERIOUSLY FUCKING UP MY ZEN, COLLIN.
YES, WELL HEAVEN FORBID I INTERRUPT YOUR ATTAINMENT OF TOTAL CONSCIOUSNESS WITH ANYTHING OF ACTUAL IMPORTANCE, SIR, BUT MS. THERESA PHONED.
THE ANTIDOTE IS READY AND THE LADIES ARE APPARENTLY JUST WAITING ON YOUR ORDERS.
BITCHIN'.

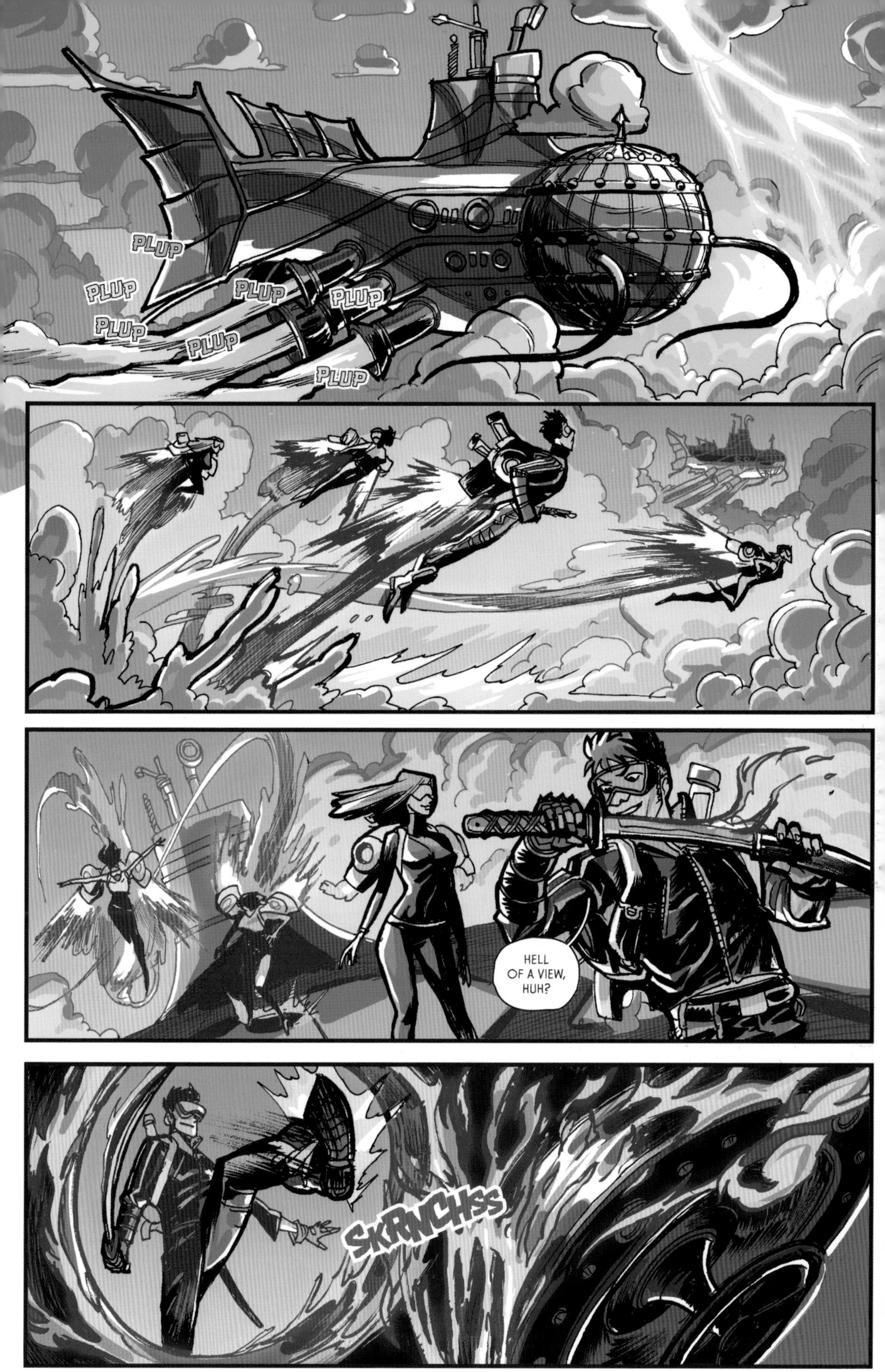
PLUP
PLUP
PLUP
PLUP
PLUP
PLUP
PLUP
HELL OF A VIEW, HUH?
SKRNCHSS

CLEAR OUT THE VERMIN AND SEIZE THE COCKPIT. I'LL DELIVER OUR LITTLE BATCH OF LIQUID REHAB MYSELF.

THEY ALMOST CERTAINLY KNOW WE ARE NOW ON BOARD LADIES, SO NO NEED TO BE SHY ABOUT ANNOUNCING OUR PRESENCE.

ON IT, CHIEF.

THERESA IS DEFINITELY NOT DRIVING THIS THING.

HEY!

WHERE'S YOUR SENSE OF ADVENTURE, AMELIA? WORK IT OUT.

AND KEEP THE CHAMPAGNE FROSTY 'TILL I ARRIVE.

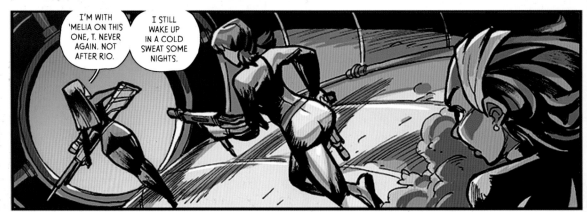

I'M WITH 'MELIA ON THIS ONE, T. NEVER AGAIN. NOT AFTER RIO.

I STILL WAKE UP IN A COLD SWEAT SOME NIGHTS.

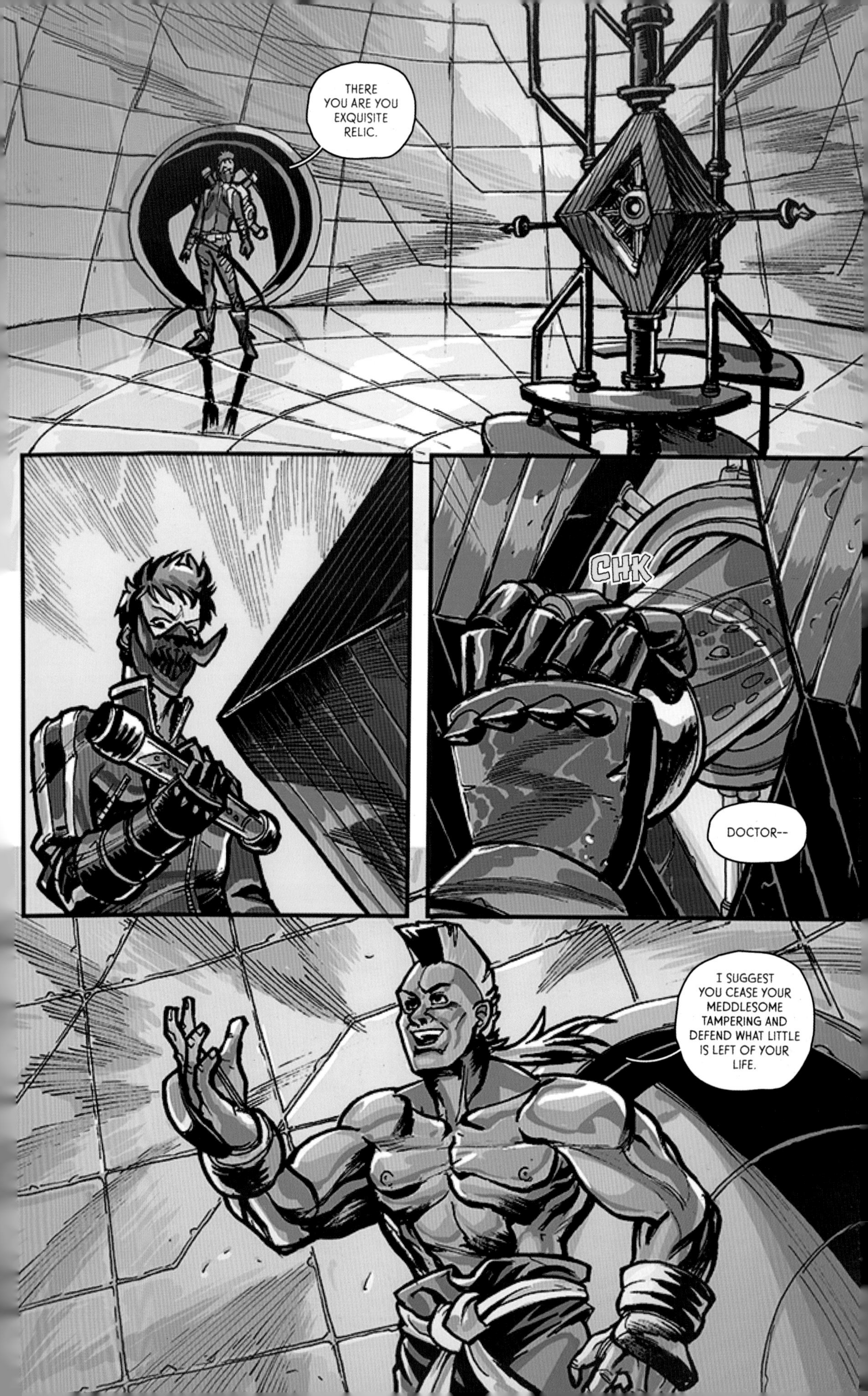
THERE YOU ARE YOU EXQUISITE RELIC.
CHK
DOCTOR--
I SUGGEST YOU CEASE YOUR MEDDLESOME TAMPERING AND DEFEND WHAT LITTLE IS LEFT OF YOUR LIFE.

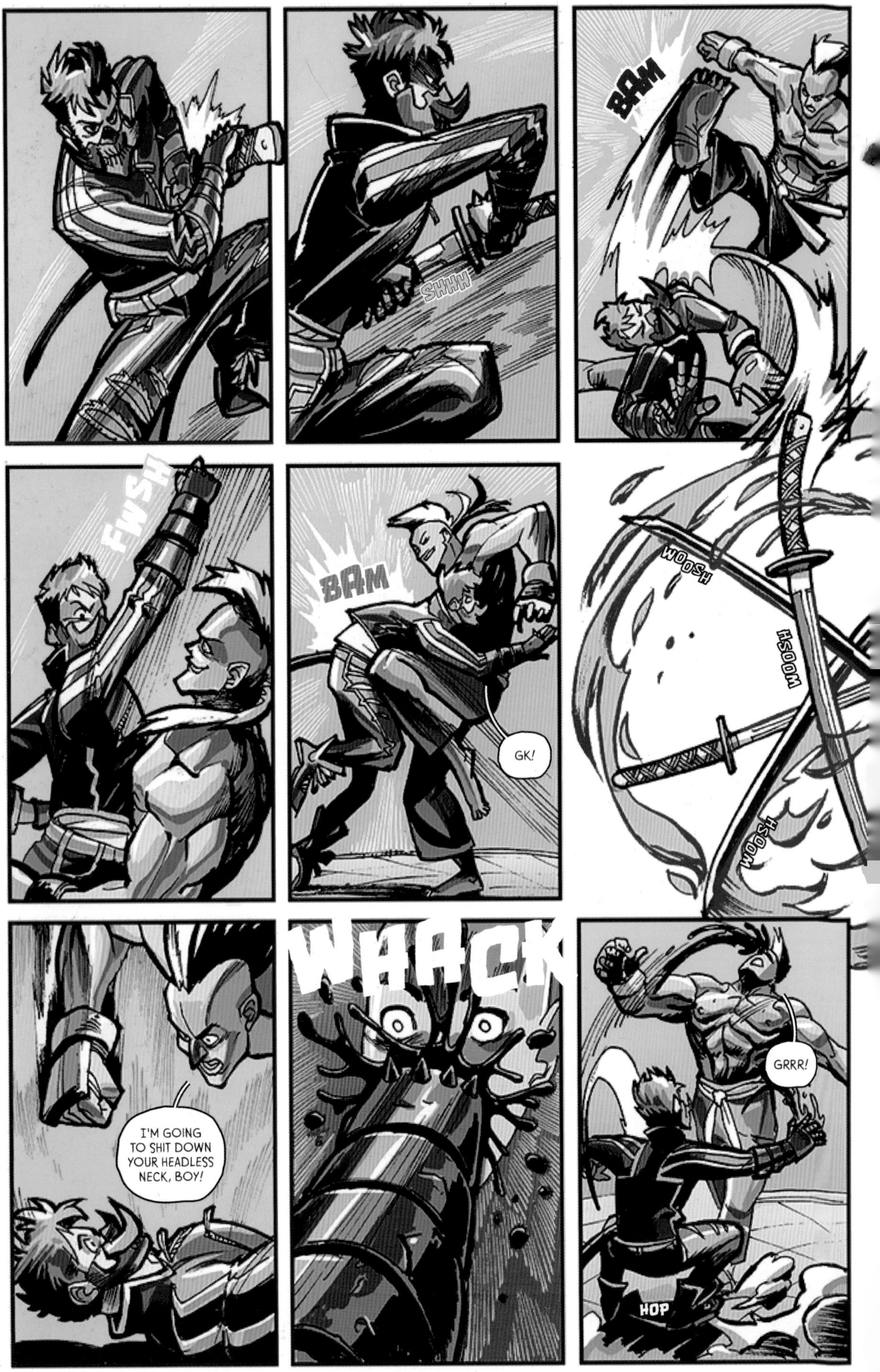
SHHH
BAM
FWSH
BAM
GK!
WOOSH
WOOSH
WOOSH
WOOSH
I'M GOING TO SHIT DOWN YOUR HEADLESS NECK, BOY!
WHACK
GRRR!
HOP

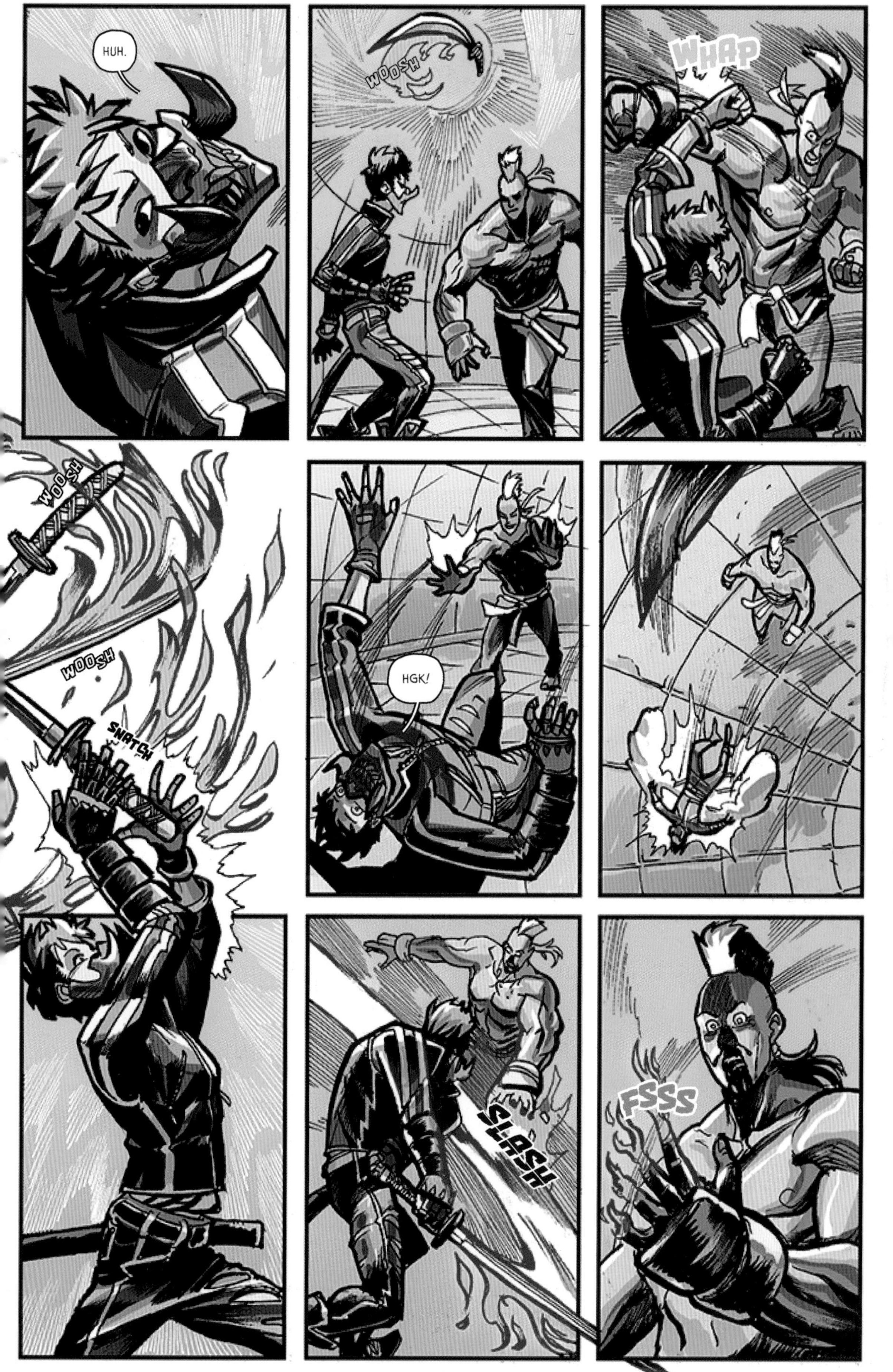
HUH.
WOOSH
WHAP
WOOSH
WOOSH
SNATCH
HGK!
SLASH
FSSS

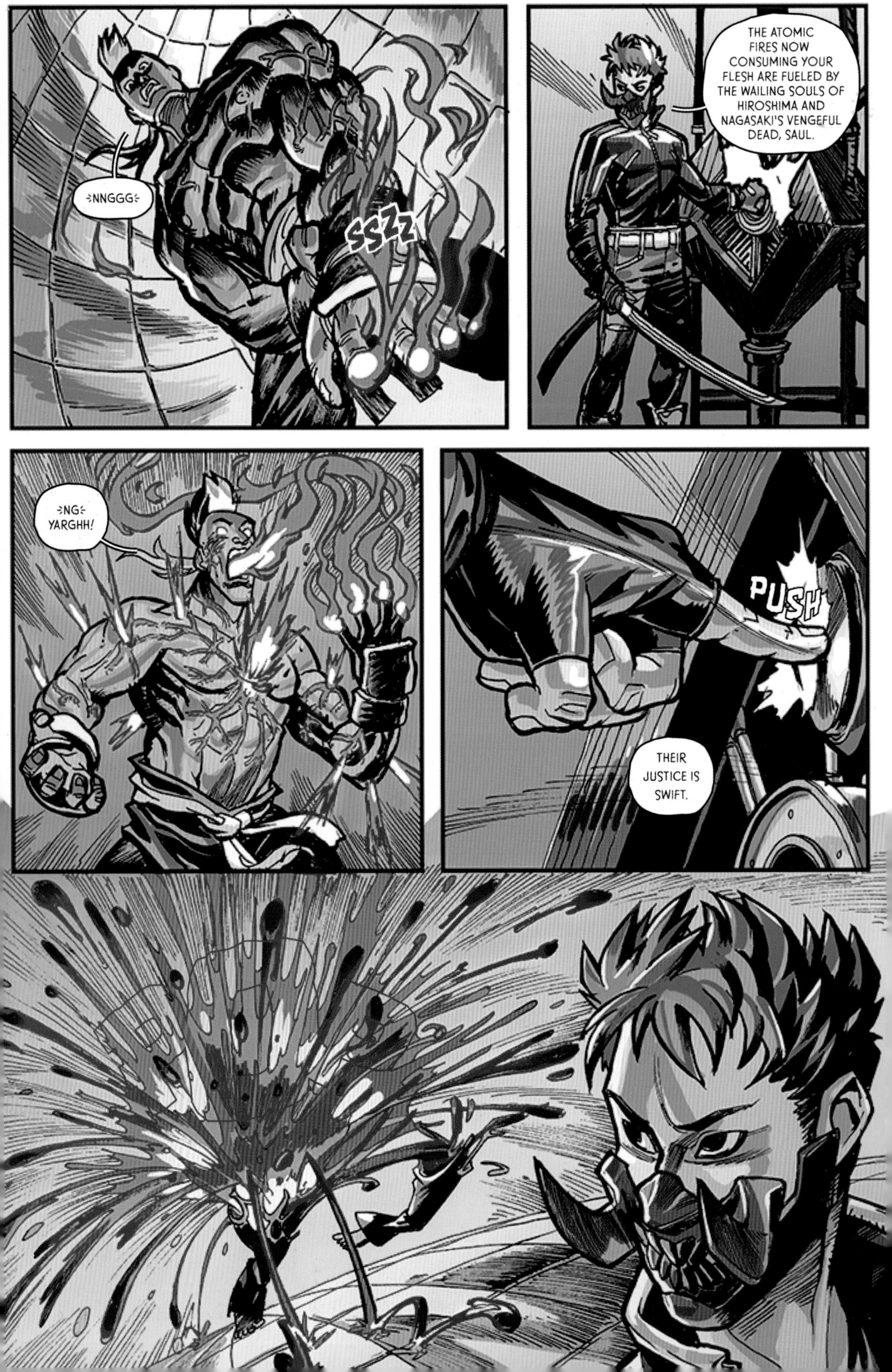

NNGGG
SSZZ
THE ATOMIC FIRES NOW CONSUMING YOUR FLESH ARE FUELED BY THE WAILING SOULS OF HIROSHIMA AND NAGASAKI'S VENGEFUL DEAD, SAUL.
NG YARGHH!
PUSH
THEIR JUSTICE IS SWIFT.

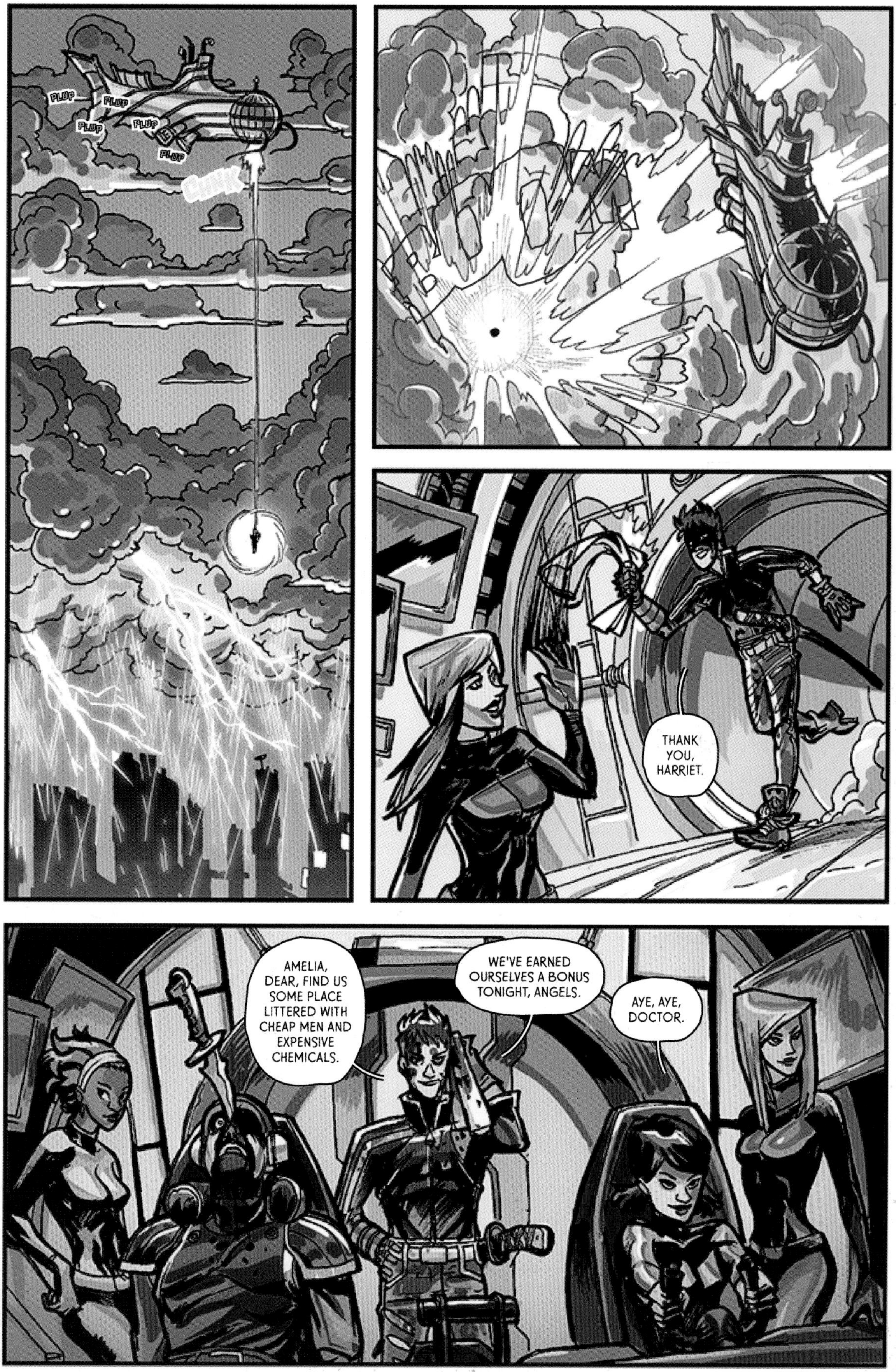
PLUP
PLUP
PLUP
PLUP
PLUP
CHNK
THANK YOU, HARRIET.
AMELIA, DEAR, FIND US SOME PLACE LITTERED WITH CHEAP MEN AND EXPENSIVE CHEMICALS.
WE'VE EARNED OURSELVES A BONUS TONIGHT, ANGELS.
AYE, AYE, DOCTOR.

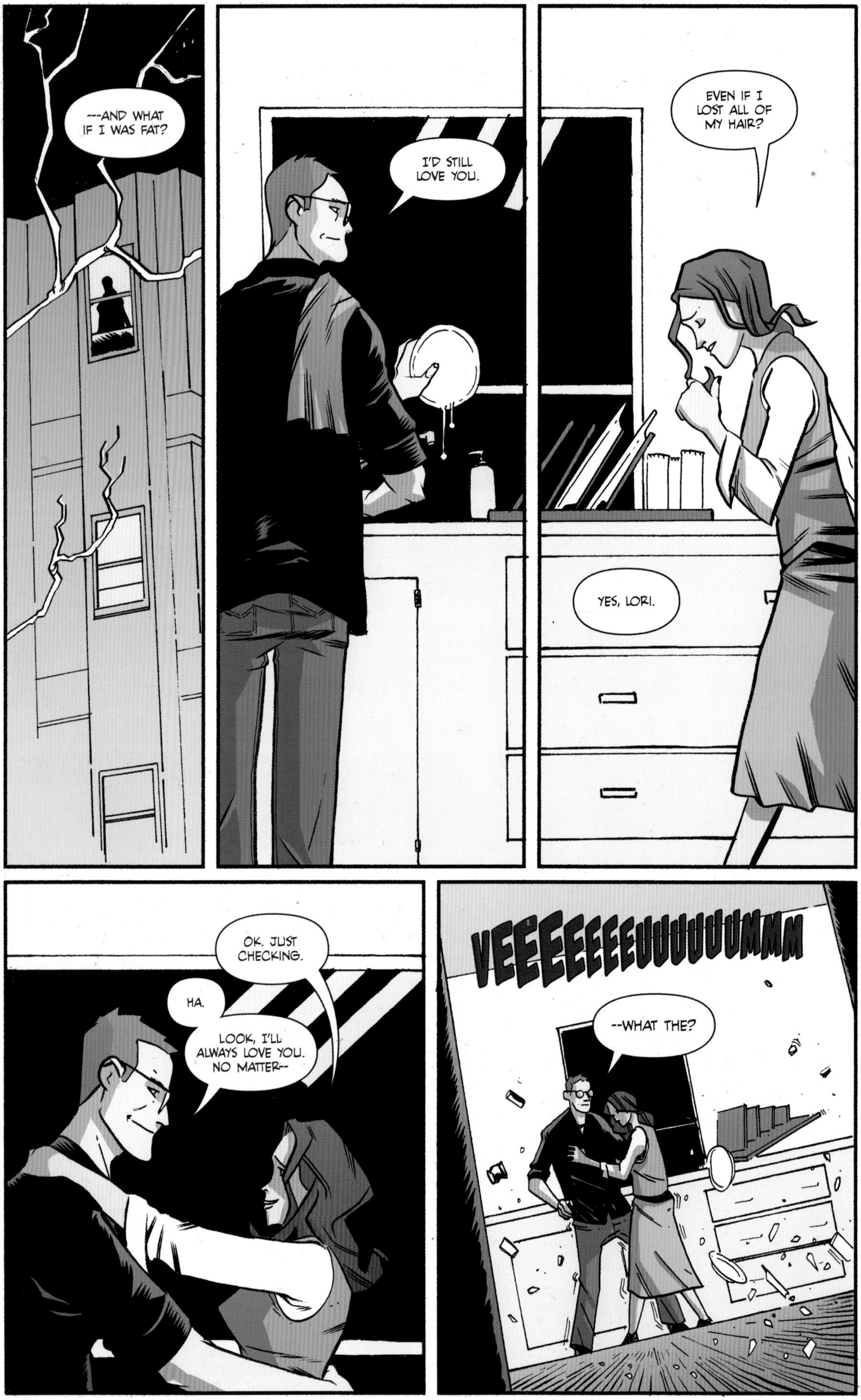
---AND WHAT IF I WAS FAT?
I'D STILL LOVE YOU.
EVEN IF I LOST ALL OF MY HAIR?
YES, LORI.
OK. JUST CHECKING.
HA.
LOOK, I'LL ALWAYS LOVE YOU. NO MATTER--
VEEEEEEEUUUUUUMMM
--WHAT THE?

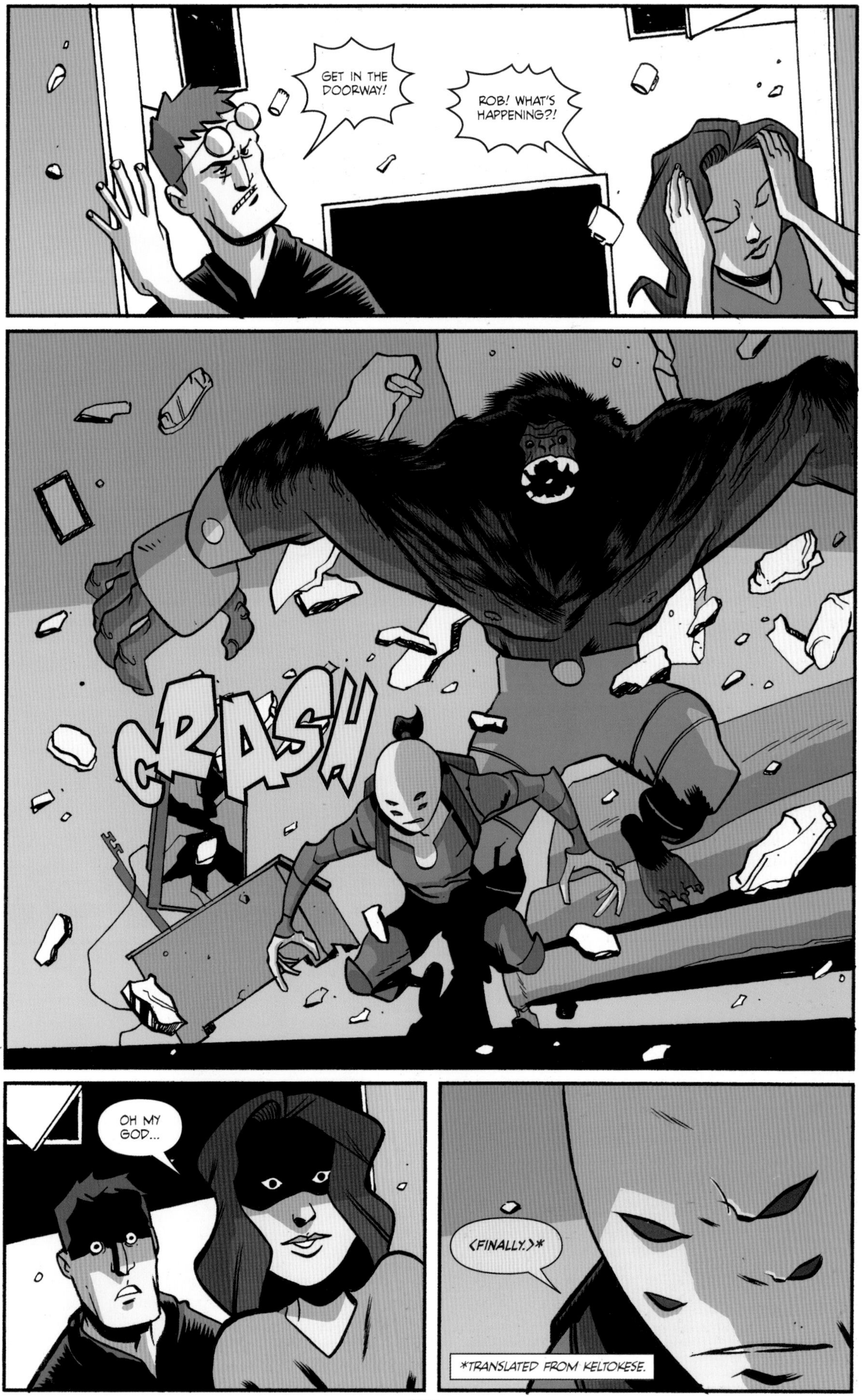
GET IN THE DOORWAY!
ROB! WHAT'S HAPPENING?!
CRASH
OH MY GOD...
<FINALLY.>*
*TRANSLATED FROM KELTOKESE.

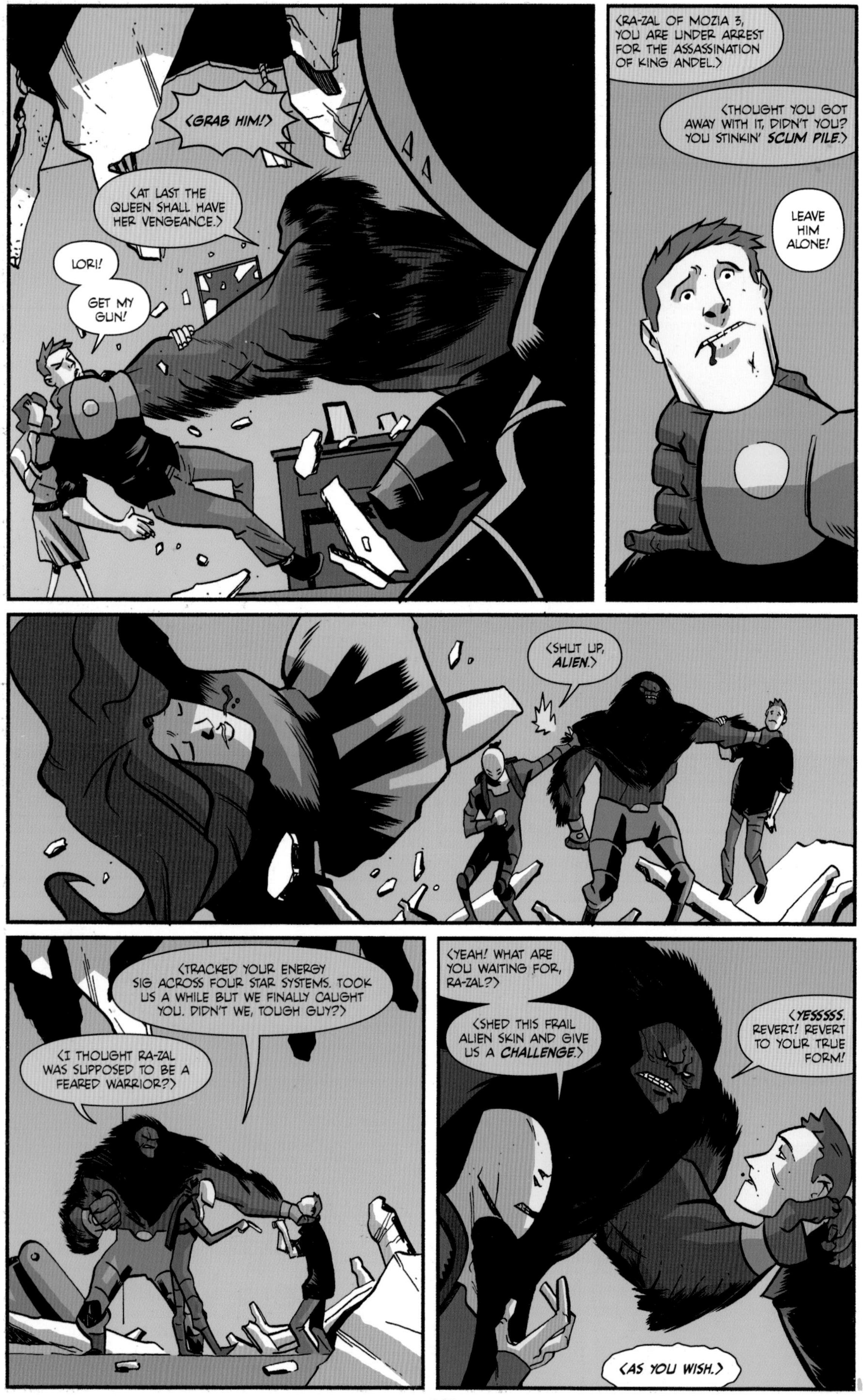

<GRAB HIM!>
<AT LAST THE QUEEN SHALL HAVE HER VENGEANCE.>
LORI!
GET MY GUN!
<RA-ZAL OF MOZIA 3, YOU ARE UNDER ARREST FOR THE ASSASSINATION OF KING ANDEL.>
<THOUGHT YOU GOT AWAY WITH IT, DIDN'T YOU? YOU STINKIN' SCUM PILE.>
LEAVE HIM ALONE!
<SHUT UP, ALIEN.>
<TRACKED YOUR ENERGY SIG ACROSS FOUR STAR SYSTEMS. TOOK US A WHILE BUT WE FINALLY CAUGHT YOU. DIDN'T WE, TOUGH GUY?>
<I THOUGHT RA-ZAL WAS SUPPOSED TO BE A FEARED WARRIOR?>
<YEAH! WHAT ARE YOU WAITING FOR, RA-ZAL?>
<SHED THIS FRAIL ALIEN SKIN AND GIVE US A CHALLENGE.>
<YESSSSS. REVERT! REVERT TO YOUR TRUE FORM!
<AS YOU WISH.>

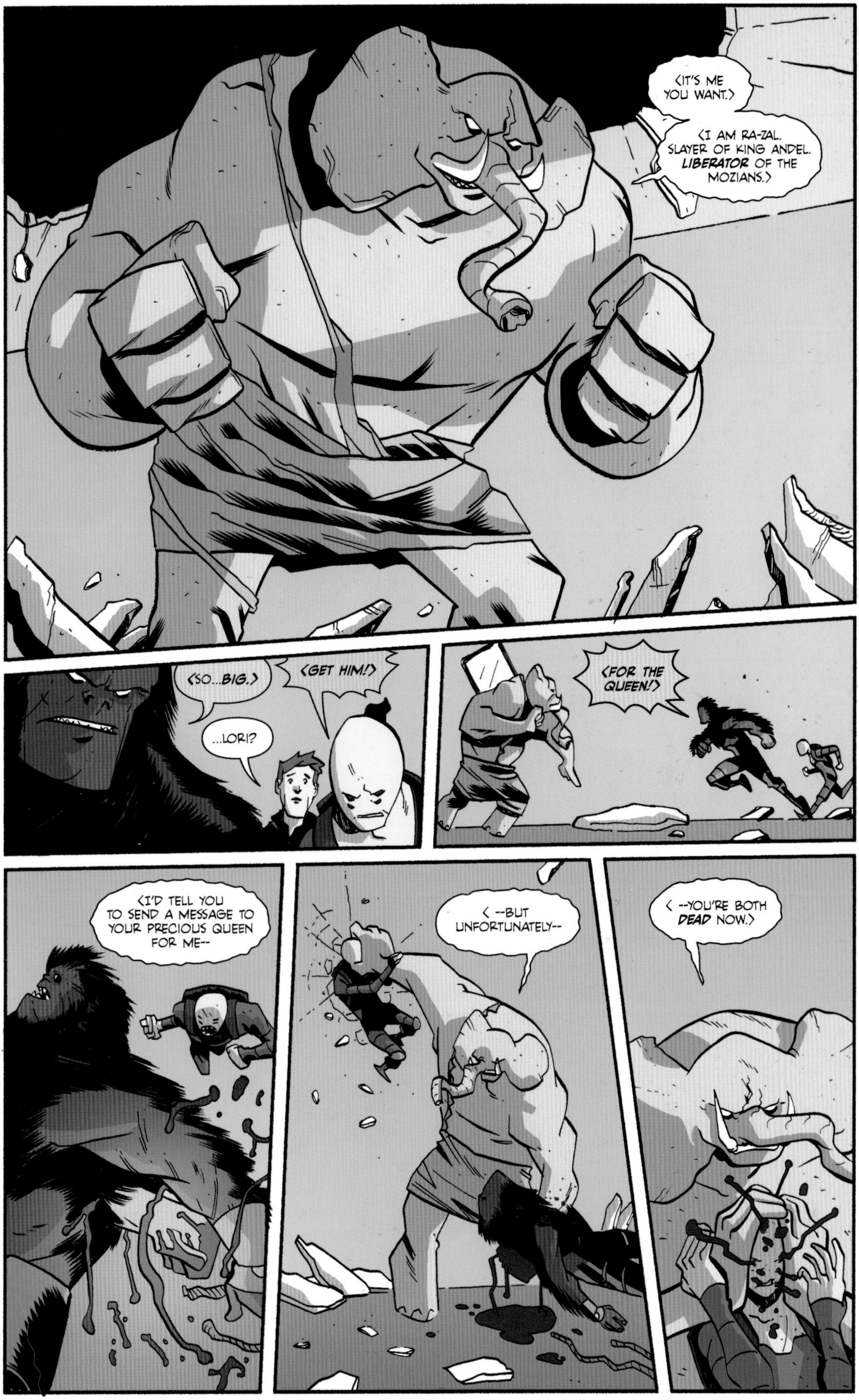

<IT'S ME YOU WANT.>
<I AM RA-ZAL. SLAYER OF KING ANDEL. LIBERATOR OF THE MOZIANS.>
<SO...BIG.>
<GET HIM!>
...LORI?
<FOR THE QUEEN!>
<I'D TELL YOU TO SEND A MESSAGE TO YOUR PRECIOUS QUEEN FOR ME--
< --BUT UNFORTUNATELY--
< --YOU'RE BOTH DEAD NOW.>

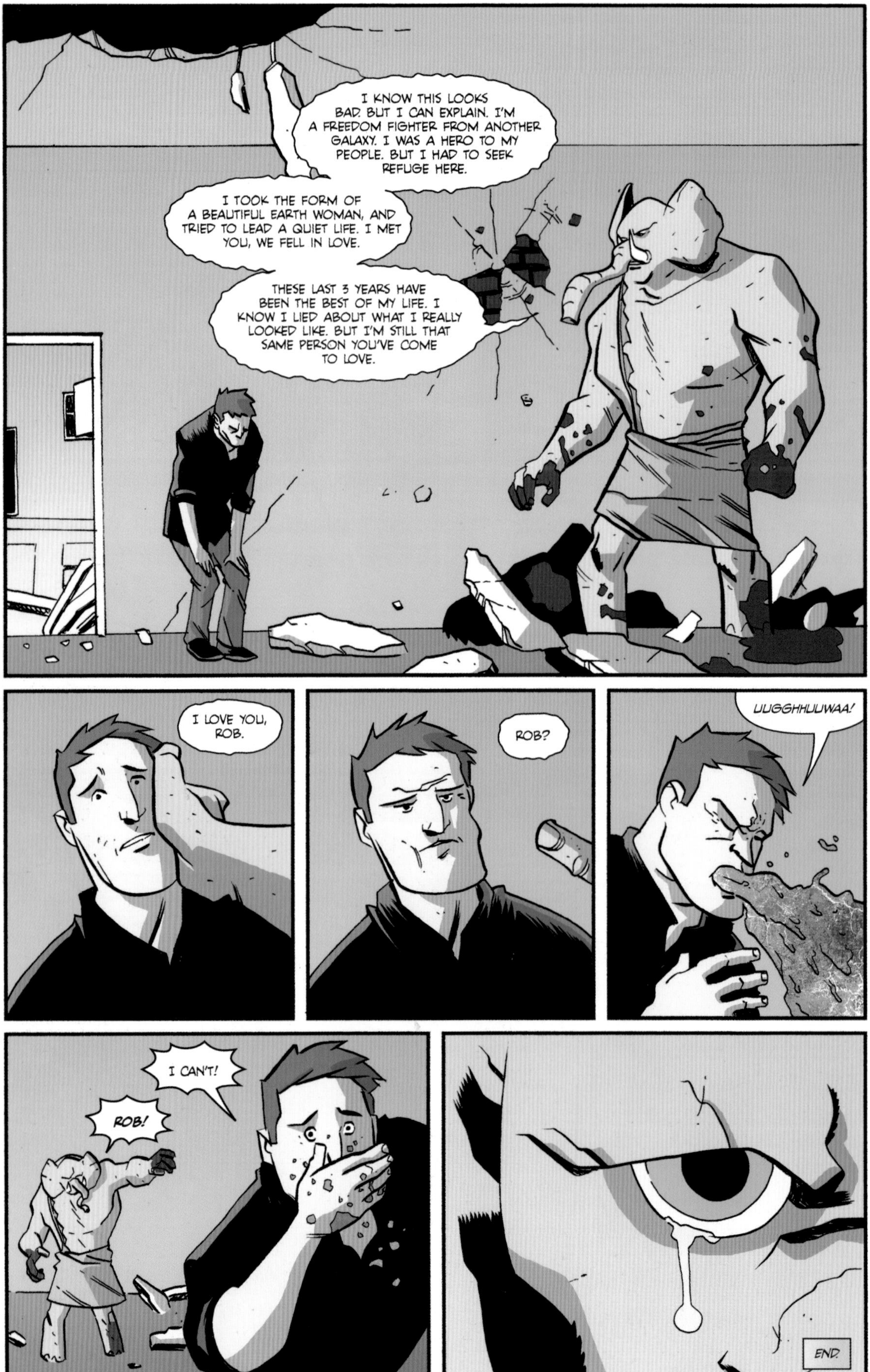
I KNOW THIS LOOKS BAD. BUT I CAN EXPLAIN. I'M A FREEDOM FIGHTER FROM ANOTHER GALAXY. I WAS A HERO TO MY PEOPLE. BUT I HAD TO SEEK REFUGE HERE.
I TOOK THE FORM OF A BEAUTIFUL EARTH WOMAN, AND TRIED TO LEAD A QUIET LIFE. I MET YOU, WE FELL IN LOVE.
THESE LAST 3 YEARS HAVE BEEN THE BEST OF MY LIFE. I KNOW I LIED ABOUT WHAT I REALLY LOOKED LIKE. BUT I'M STILL THAT SAME PERSON YOU'VE COME TO LOVE.
I LOVE YOU, ROB.
ROB?
UUGGHHUUWAA!
I CAN'T!
ROB!
END.

AIN'T LOVE GRAND?

Script: Fabian Rangel Jr **Art:** Ryan Cody **Letters:** Evelyn Rangel

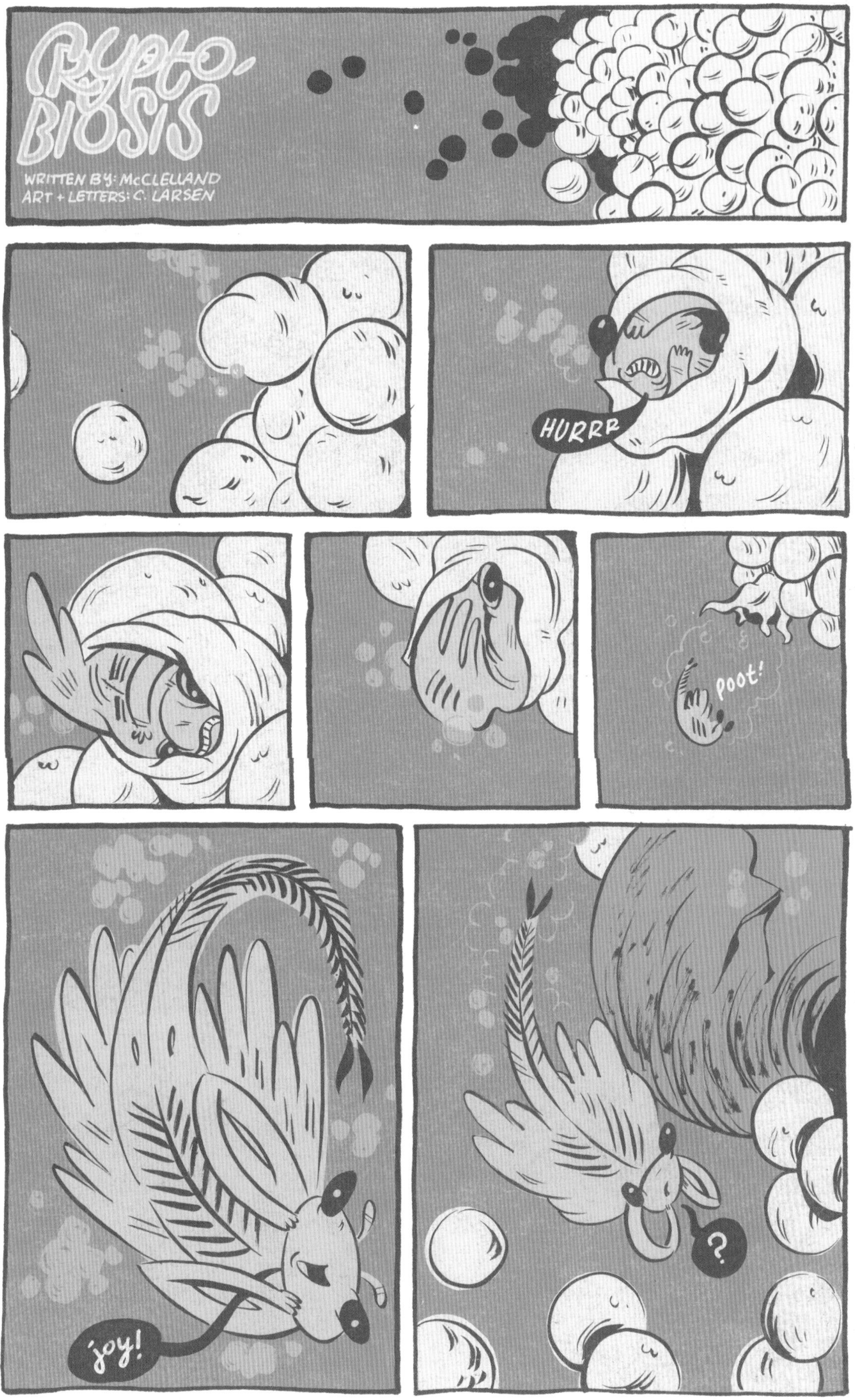
CRYPTO-
BIOSIS
WRITTEN BY: McCLELLAND
ART + LETTERS: C. LARSEN
HURRR
POOT!
joy!
?

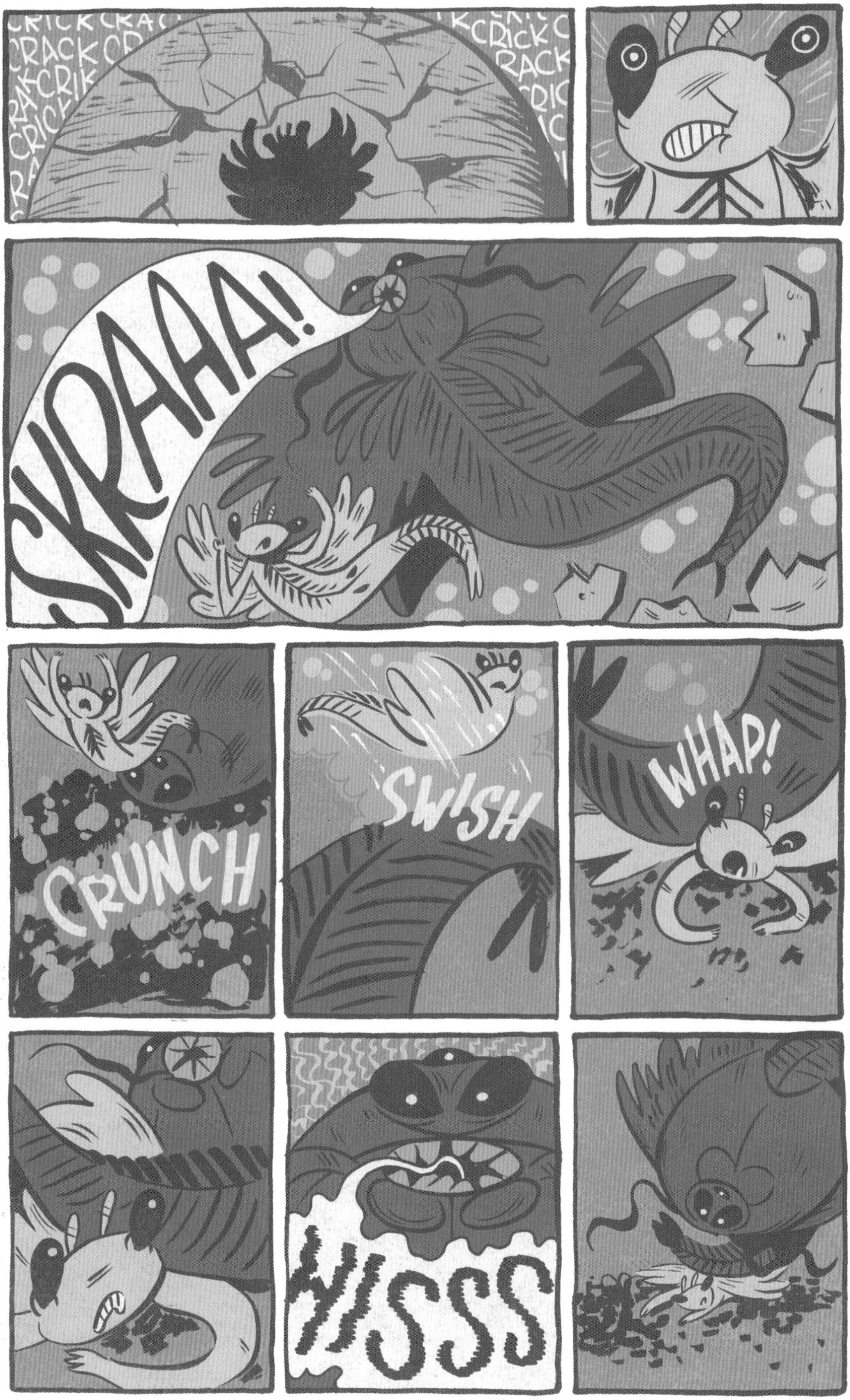
CRICK CRACK
CRICK
CRACK
CRIK
CRAK
CRICK
CRACK
CRICK
SKRAAA!
CRUNCH
SWISH
WHAP!
HISSS

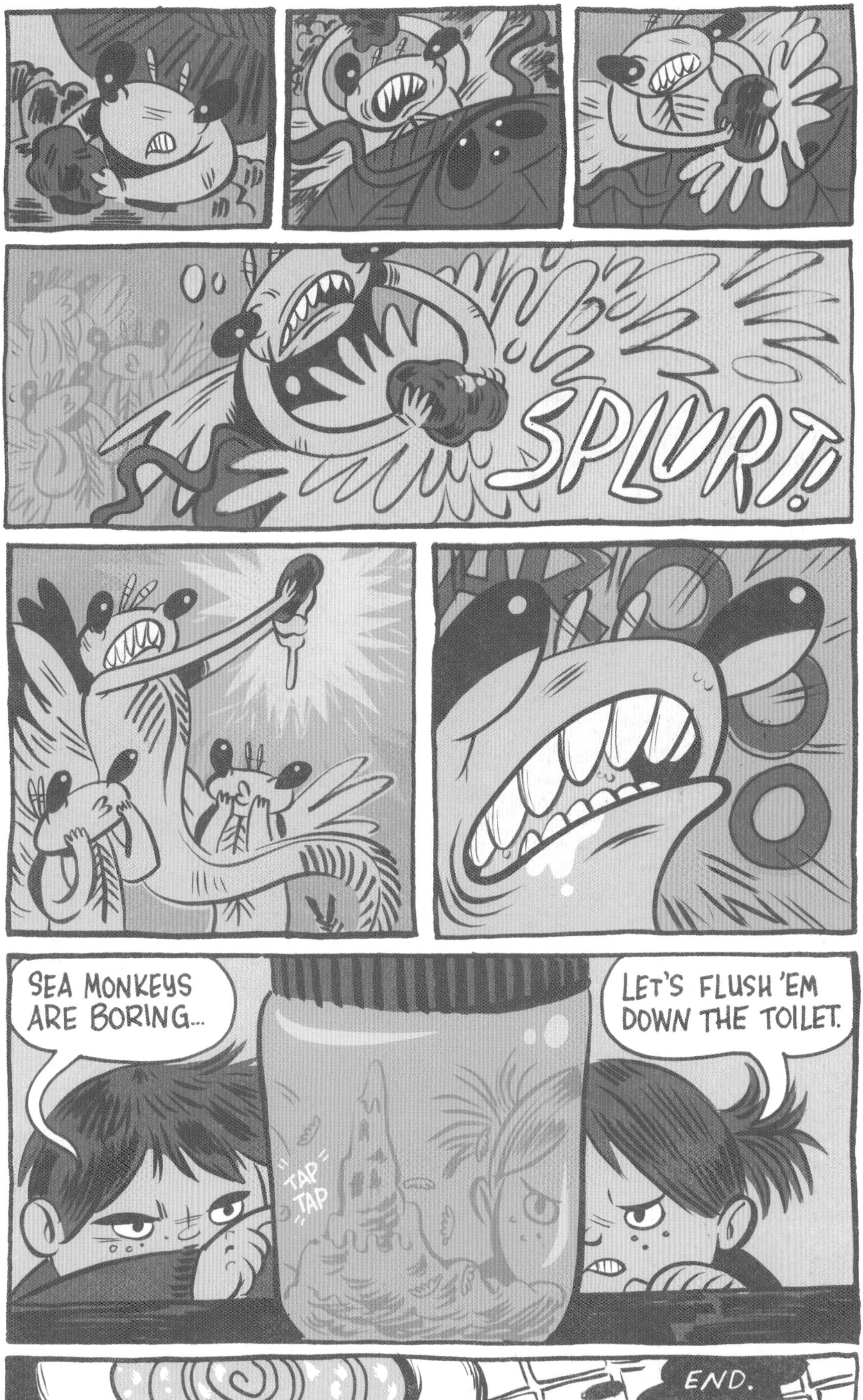
SPLURT!
SEA MONKEYS ARE BORING...
TAP TAP
LET'S FLUSH 'EM DOWN THE TOILET.
END.

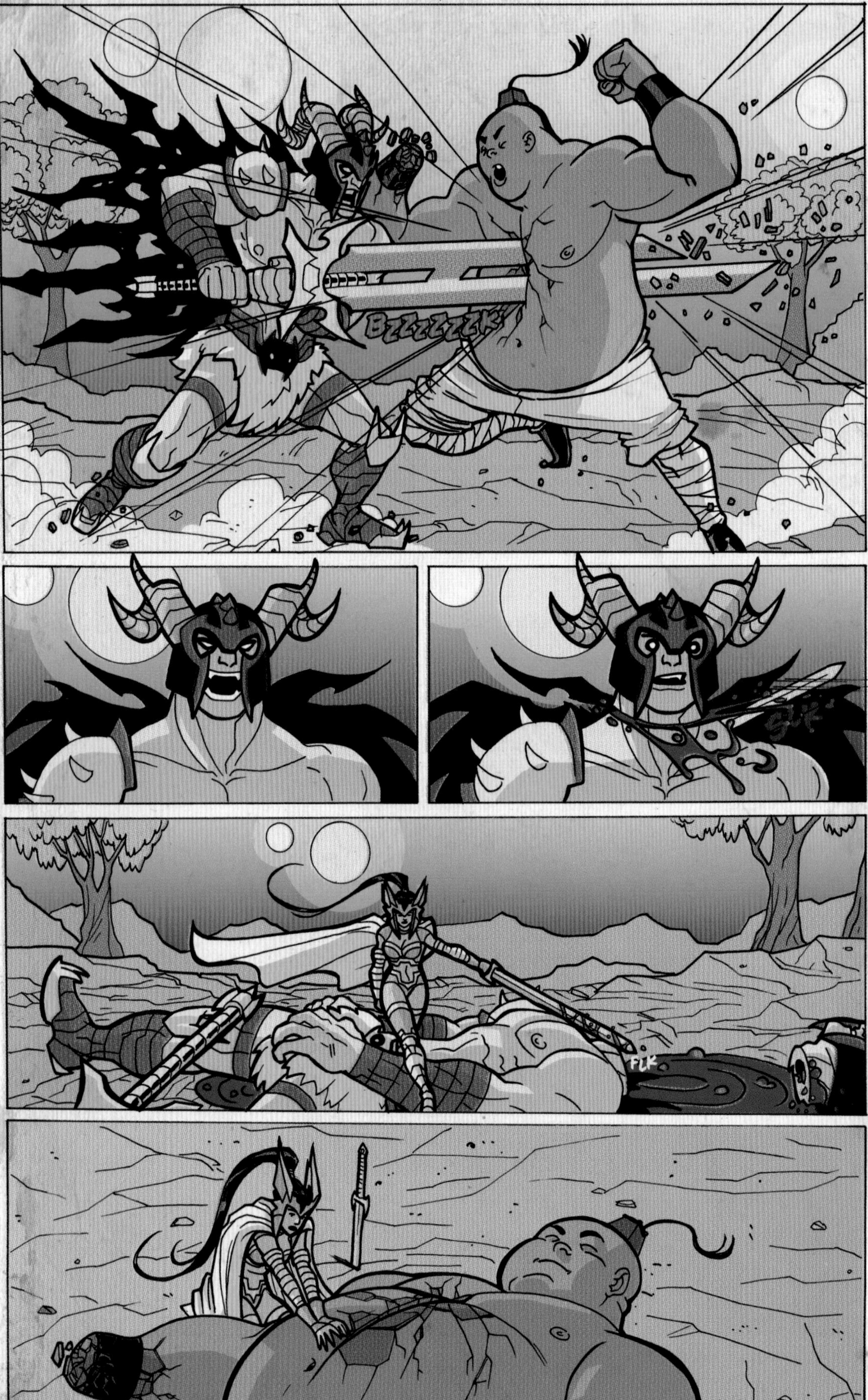

BZZZZZZK
SLK
FLK

WHOP

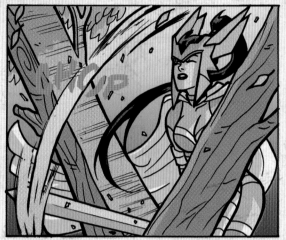

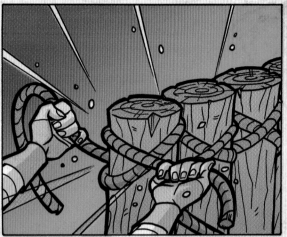

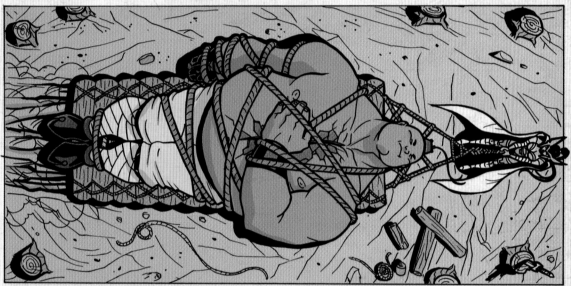

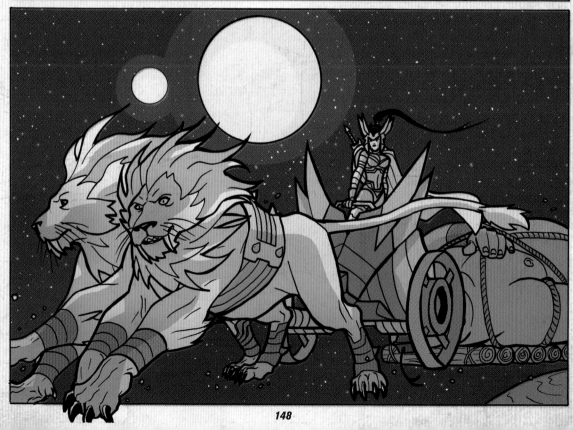

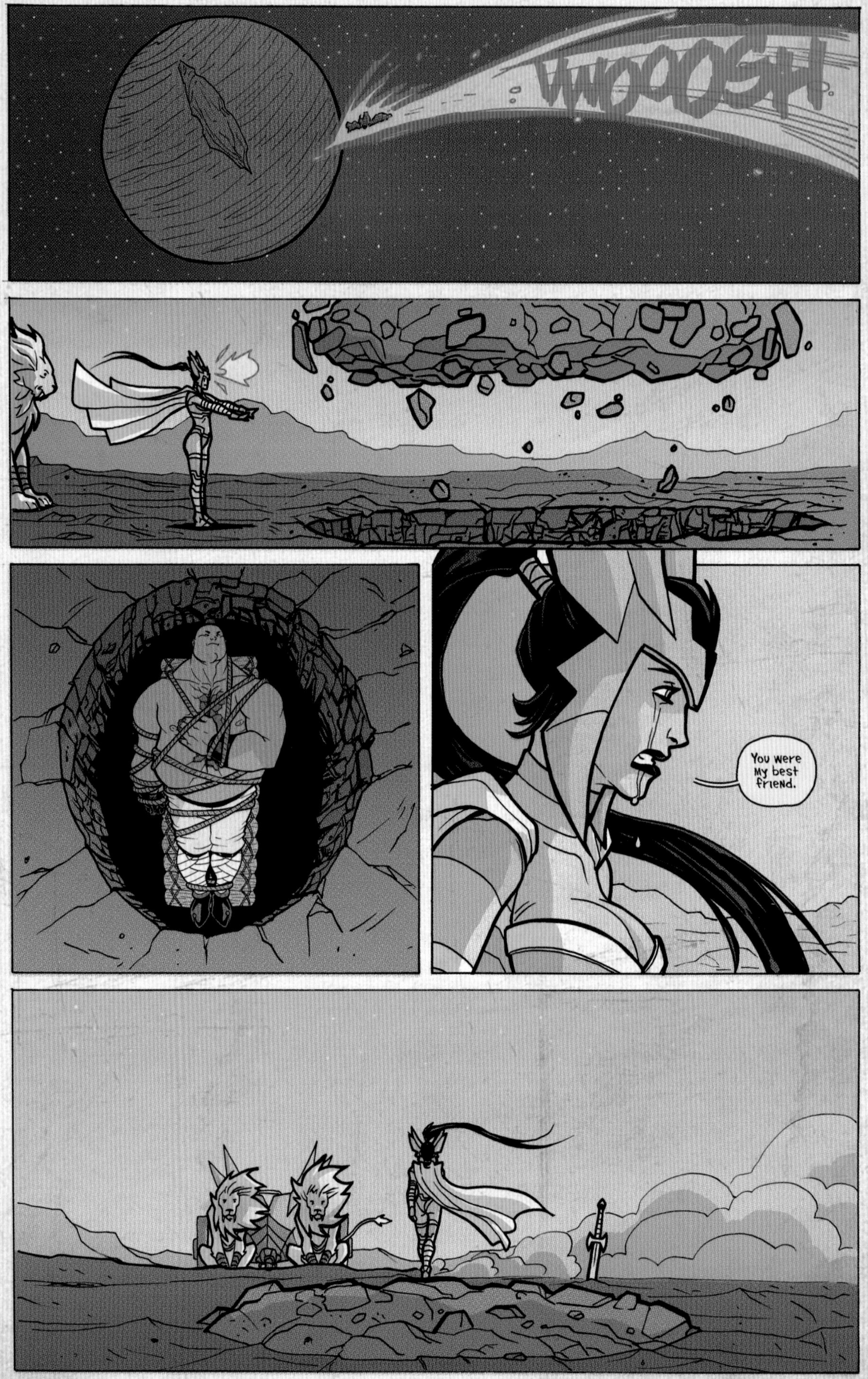
WOOOSH
You were my best friend.

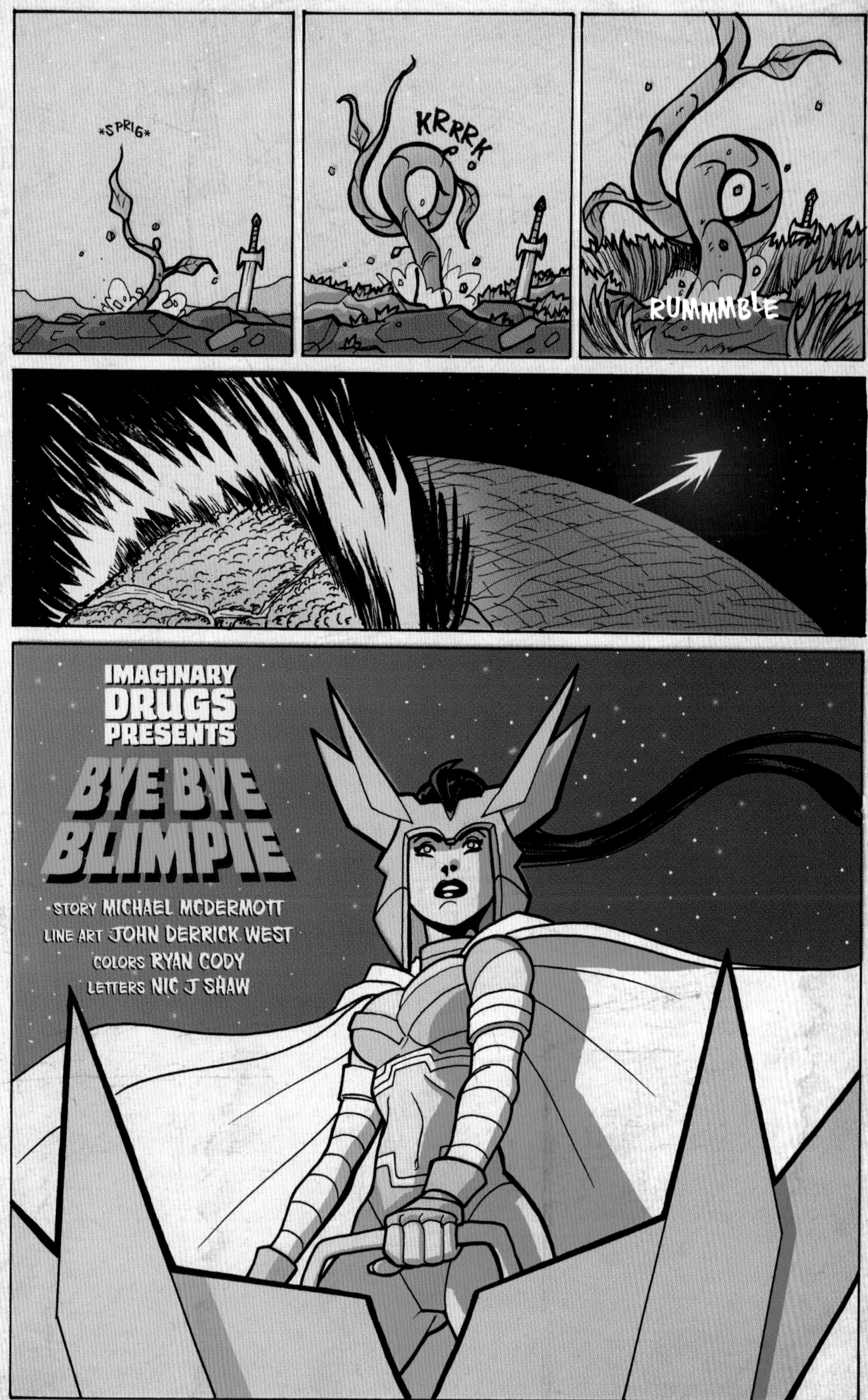
SPRIG
KRRRK
RUMMMBLE
IMAGINARY DRUGS PRESENTS
BYE BYE BLIMPIE
STORY MICHAEL MCDERMOTT
LINE ART JOHN DERRICK WEST
COLORS RYAN CODY
LETTERS NIC J SHAW

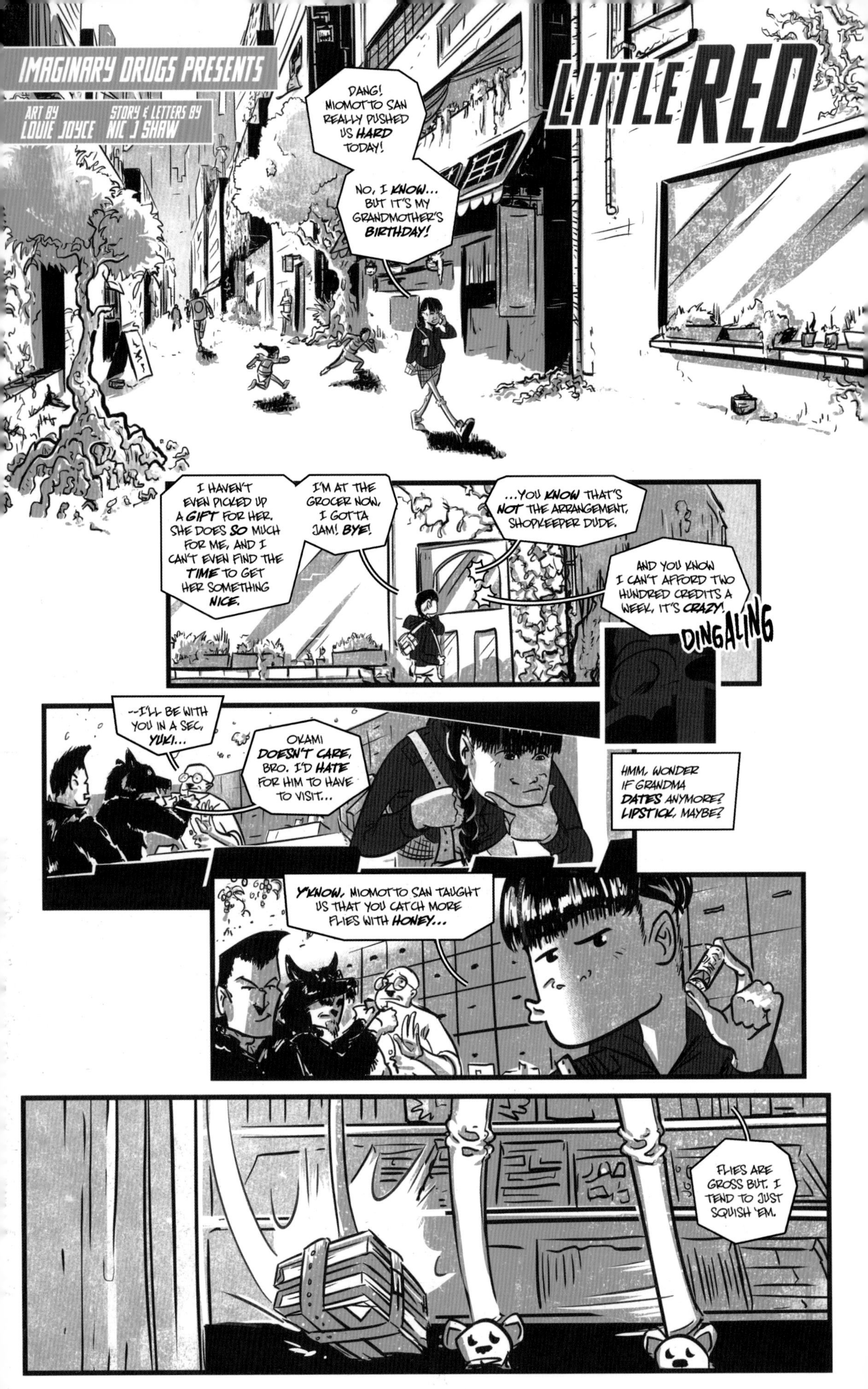
IMAGINARY DRUGS PRESENTS
ART BY LOUIE JOYCE
STORY & LETTERS BY NIC J SHAW
LITTLE RED
DANG! MIOMOTTO SAN REALLY PUSHED US HARD TODAY!
NO, I KNOW... BUT IT'S MY GRANDMOTHER'S BIRTHDAY!
I HAVEN'T EVEN PICKED UP A GIFT FOR HER. SHE DOES SO MUCH FOR ME, AND I CAN'T EVEN FIND THE TIME TO GET HER SOMETHING NICE.
I'M AT THE GROCER NOW, I GOTTA JAM! BYE!
...YOU KNOW THAT'S NOT THE ARRANGEMENT, SHOPKEEPER DUDE.
AND YOU KNOW I CAN'T AFFORD TWO HUNDRED CREDITS A WEEK, IT'S CRAZY!
DINGALING
--I'LL BE WITH YOU IN A SEC, YUKI...
OKAMI DOESN'T CARE, BRO. I'D HATE FOR HIM TO HAVE TO VISIT...
HMM, WONDER IF GRANDMA DATES ANYMORE? LIPSTICK, MAYBE?
Y'KNOW, MIOMOTTO SAN TAUGHT US THAT YOU CATCH MORE FLIES WITH HONEY...
FLIES ARE GROSS BUT. I TEND TO JUST SQUISH 'EM.

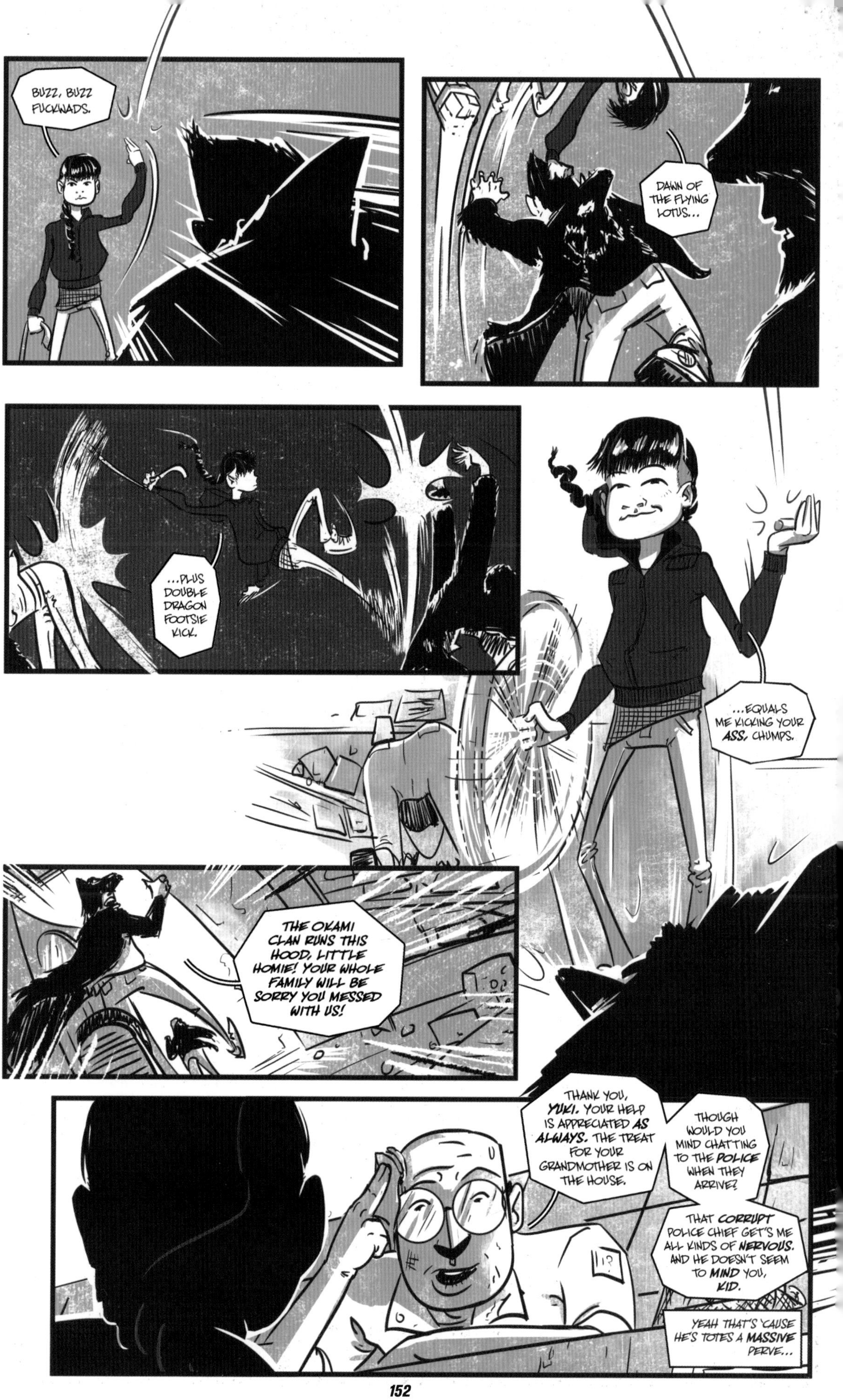
BUZZ, BUZZ FUCKWADS.
DAWN OF THE FLYING LOTUS...
...PLUS DOUBLE DRAGON FOOTSIE KICK.
...EQUALS ME KICKING YOUR ASS, CHUMPS.
THE OKAMI CLAN RUNS THIS HOOD, LITTLE HOMIE! YOUR WHOLE FAMILY WILL BE SORRY YOU MESSED WITH US!
THANK YOU, YUKI. YOUR HELP IS APPRECIATED AS ALWAYS. THE TREAT FOR YOUR GRANDMOTHER IS ON THE HOUSE.
THOUGH WOULD YOU MIND CHATTING TO THE POLICE WHEN THEY ARRIVE?
THAT CORRUPT POLICE CHIEF GET'S ME ALL KINDS OF NERVOUS. AND HE DOESN'T SEEM TO MIND YOU, KID.
YEAH THAT'S 'CAUSE HE'S TOTES A MASSIVE PERVE...

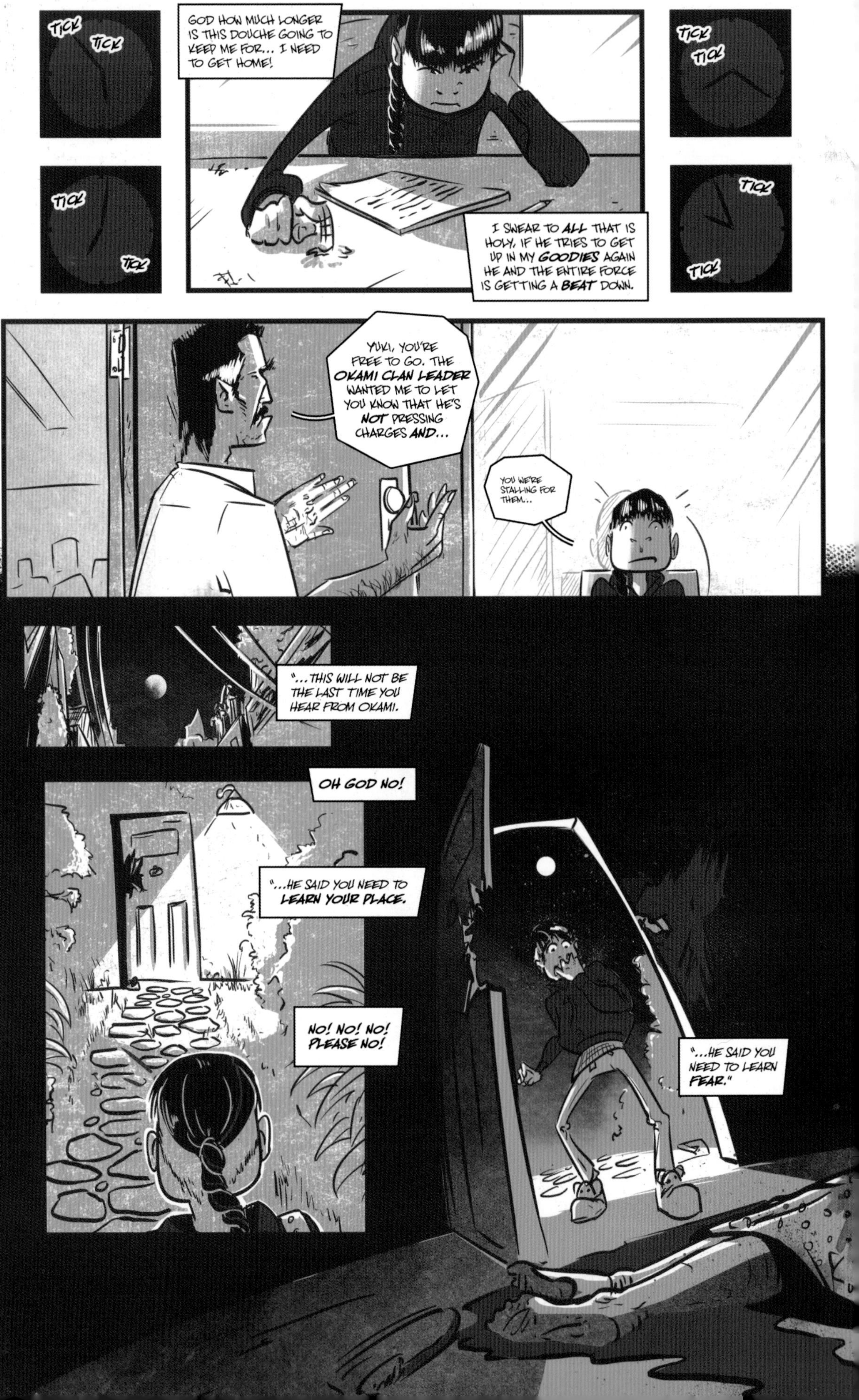
TICK
TICK
GOD HOW MUCH LONGER IS THIS DOUCHE GOING TO KEEP ME FOR... I NEED TO GET HOME!
TICK
TICK
TICK
TICK
I SWEAR TO ALL THAT IS HOLY, IF HE TRIES TO GET UP IN MY GOODIES AGAIN HE AND THE ENTIRE FORCE IS GETTING A BEAT DOWN.
TICK
TICK
YUKI, YOU'RE FREE TO GO. THE OKAMI CLAN LEADER WANTED ME TO LET YOU KNOW THAT HE'S NOT PRESSING CHARGES AND...
YOU WERE STALLING FOR THEM...
"...THIS WILL NOT BE THE LAST TIME YOU HEAR FROM OKAMI.
OH GOD NO!
"...HE SAID YOU NEED TO LEARN YOUR PLACE.
NO! NO! NO! PLEASE NO!
"...HE SAID YOU NEED TO LEARN FEAR."

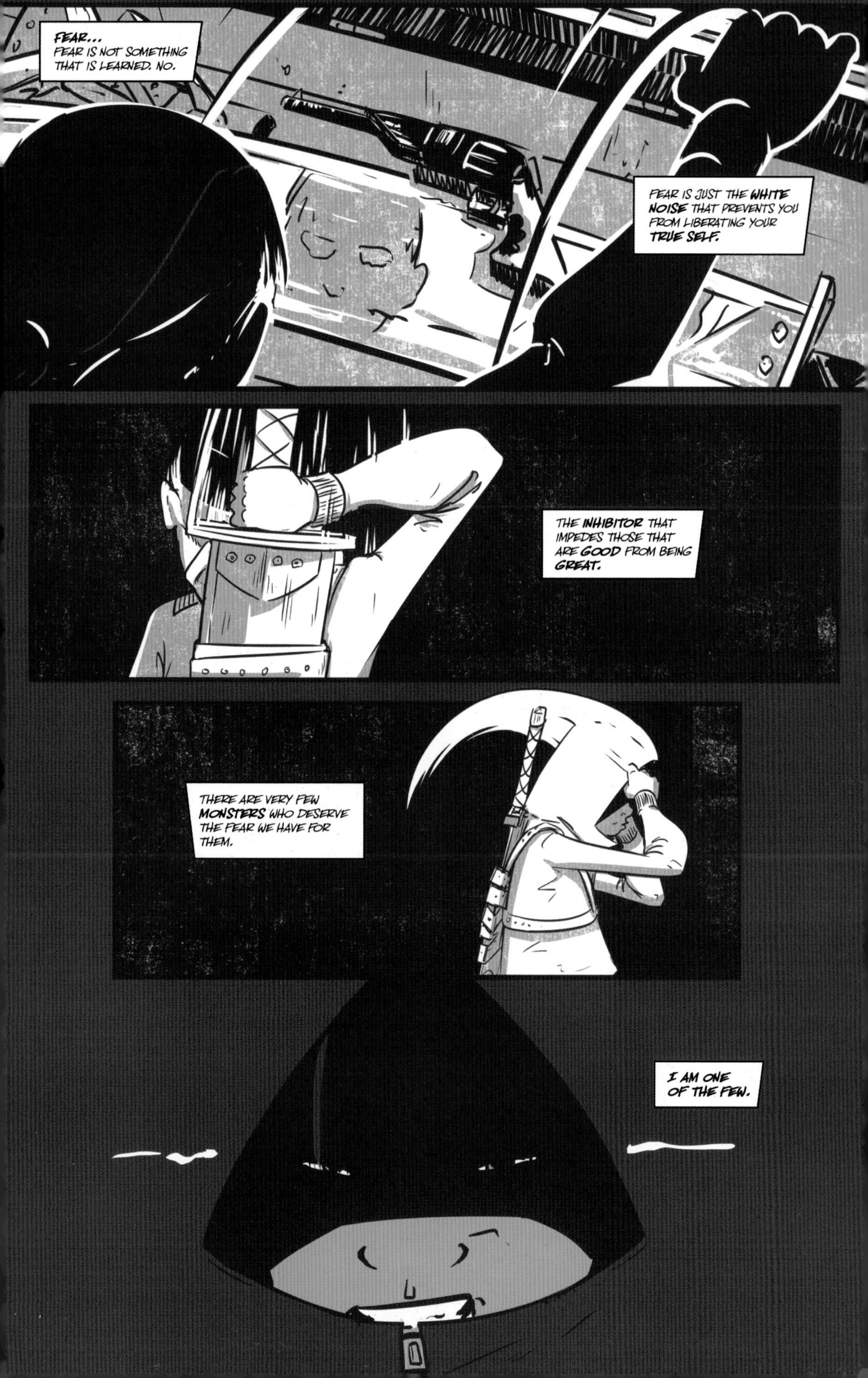
FEAR...
FEAR IS NOT SOMETHING THAT IS LEARNED. NO.
FEAR IS JUST THE WHITE NOISE THAT PREVENTS YOU FROM LIBERATING YOUR TRUE SELF.
THE INHIBITOR THAT IMPEDES THOSE THAT ARE GOOD FROM BEING GREAT.
THERE ARE VERY FEW MONSTERS WHO DESERVE THE FEAR WE HAVE FOR THEM.
I AM ONE OF THE FEW.

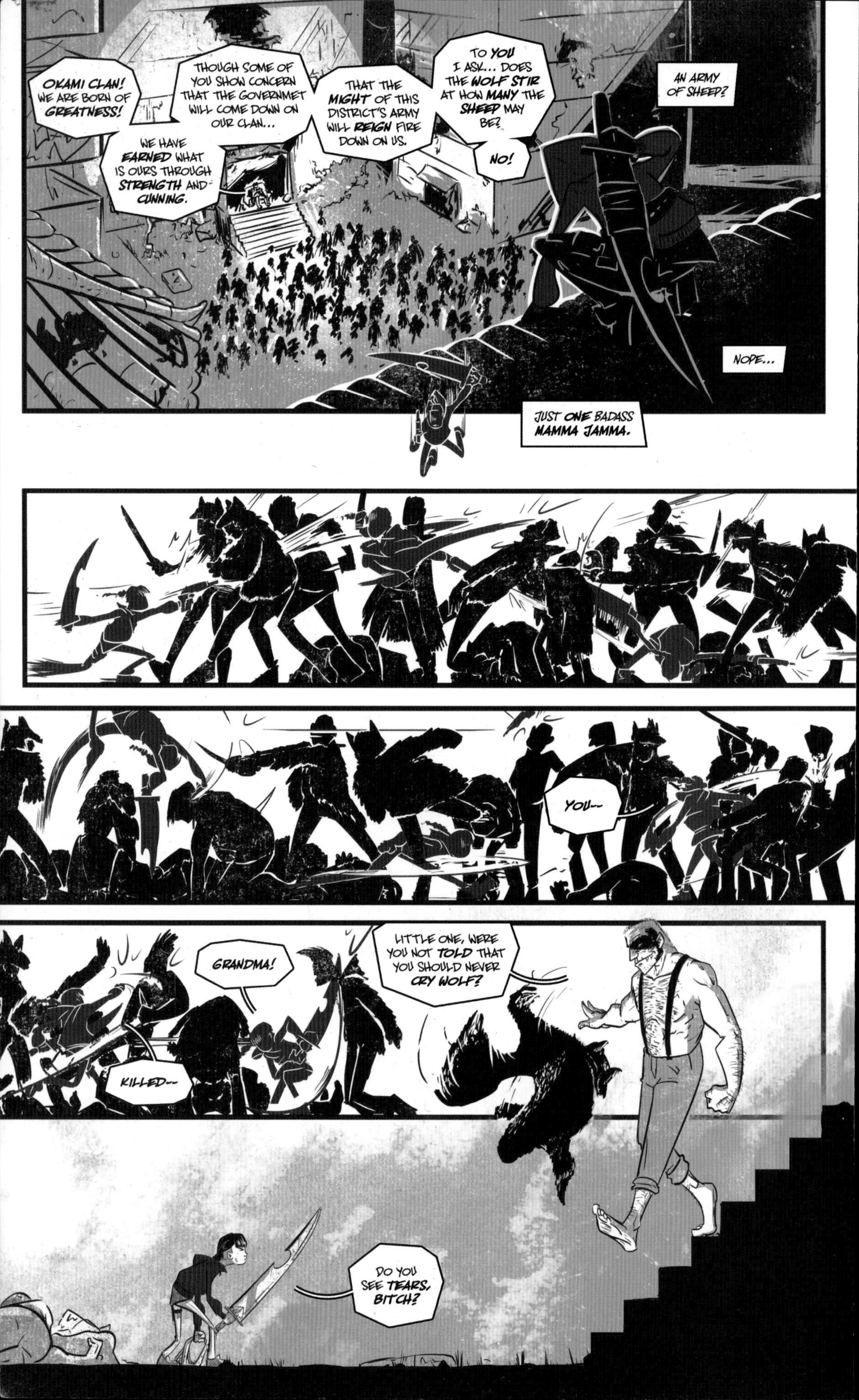
OKAMI CLAN! WE ARE BORN OF GREATNESS!
THOUGH SOME OF YOU SHOW CONCERN THAT THE GOVERNMET WILL COME DOWN ON OUR CLAN...
WE HAVE EARNED WHAT IS OURS THROUGH STRENGTH AND CUNNING.
THAT THE MIGHT OF THIS DISTRICT'S ARMY WILL REIGN FIRE DOWN ON US.
TO YOU I ASK... DOES THE WOLF STIR AT HOW MANY THE SHEEP MAY BE?
NO!
AN ARMY OF SHEEP?
NOPE...
JUST ONE BADASS MAMMA JAMMA.
YOU--
GRANDMA!
KILLED--
LITTLE ONE, WERE YOU NOT TOLD THAT YOU SHOULD NEVER CRY WOLF?
DO YOU SEE TEARS, BITCH?

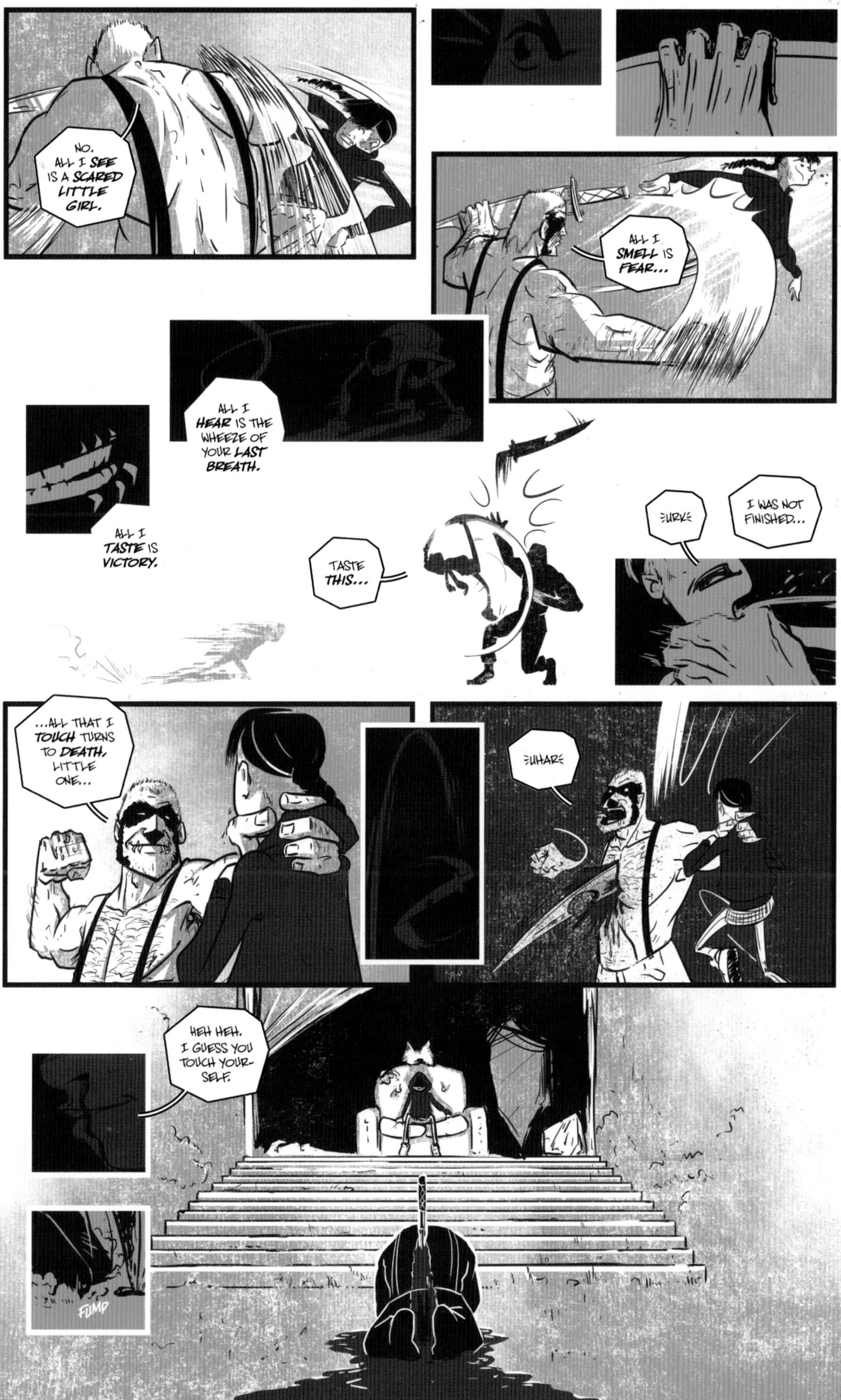
NO. ALL I SEE IS A SCARED LITTLE GIRL.
ALL I SMELL IS FEAR...
ALL I HEAR IS THE WHEEZE OF YOUR LAST BREATH.
ALL I TASTE IS VICTORY.
TASTE THIS...
URK
I WAS NOT FINISHED...
...ALL THAT I TOUCH TURNS TO DEATH, LITTLE ONE...
UHAR
HEH HEH. I GUESS YOU TOUCH YOURSELF.
FUMP

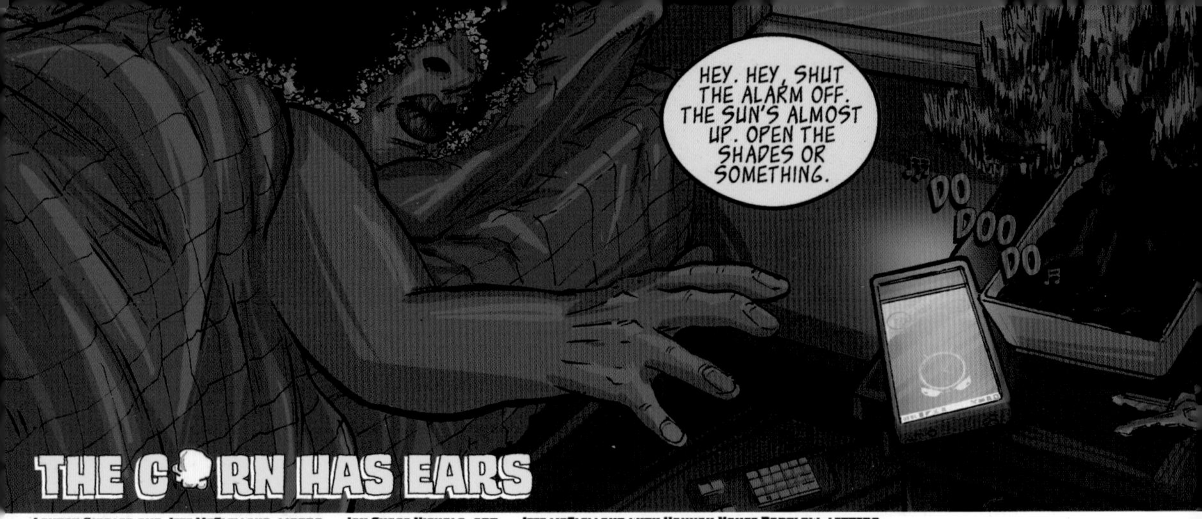
HEY. HEY, SHUT THE ALARM OFF. THE SUN'S ALMOST UP. OPEN THE SHADES OR SOMETHING.
DO DOO DO

THE CORN HAS EARS

LAUREN GIRDLER AND JEFF MCCLELLAND: WORDS IAN CHASE NICHOLS: ART JEFF MCCLELLAND WITH HANNAH NANCE PARTLOW: LETTERS

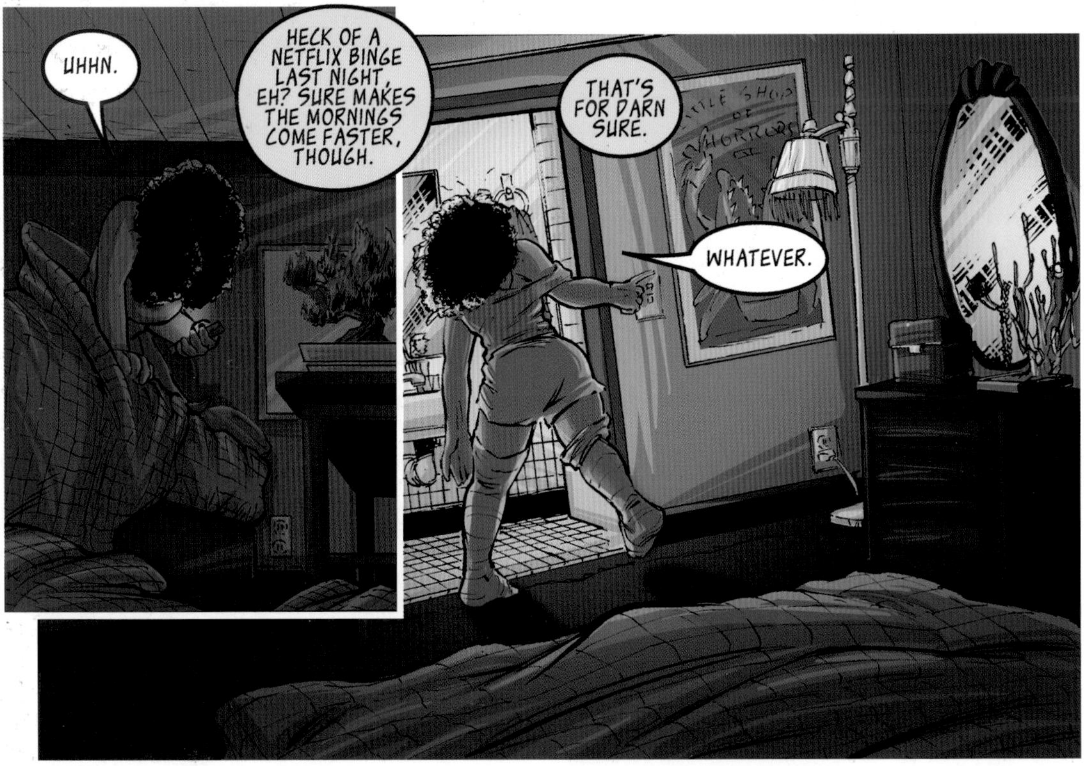
UHHN.
HECK OF A NETFLIX BINGE LAST NIGHT, EH? SURE MAKES THE MORNINGS COME FASTER, THOUGH.
THAT'S FOR DARN SURE.
WHATEVER.

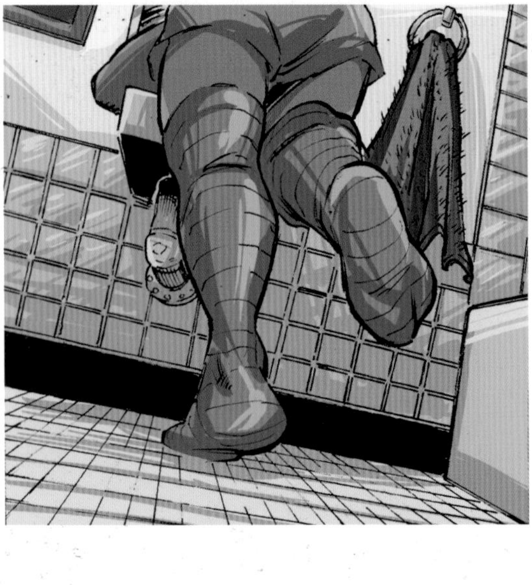

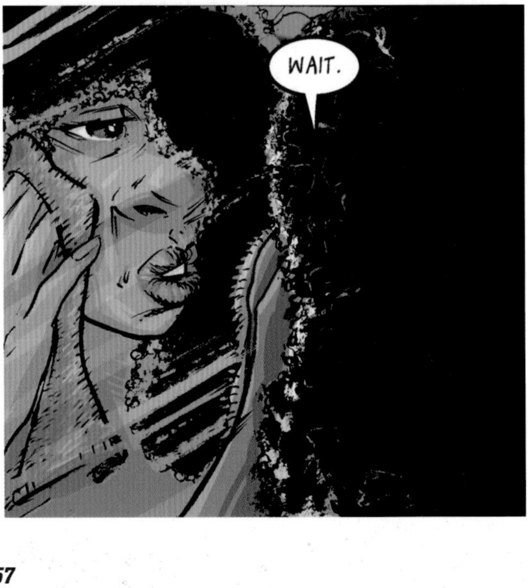
WAIT.

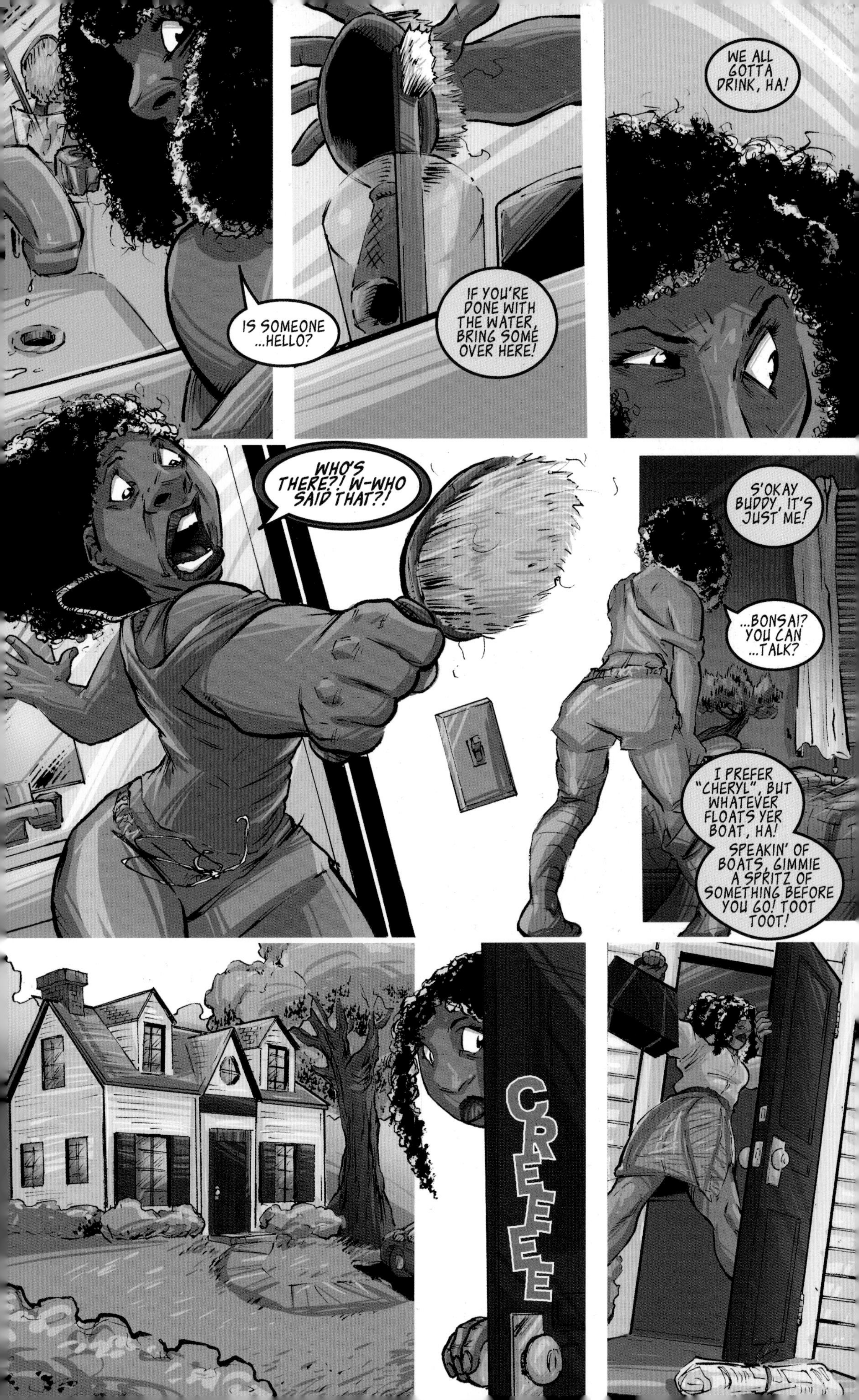
IS SOMEONE ...HELLO?
IF YOU'RE DONE WITH THE WATER, BRING SOME OVER HERE!
WE ALL GOTTA DRINK, HA!
WHO'S THERE?! W-WHO SAID THAT?!
S'OKAY BUDDY, IT'S JUST ME!
...BONSAI? YOU CAN ...TALK?
I PREFER "CHERYL", BUT WHATEVER FLOATS YER BOAT, HA!
SPEAKIN' OF BOATS, GIMMIE A SPRITZ OF SOMETHING BEFORE YOU GO! TOOT TOOT!
CREEEE

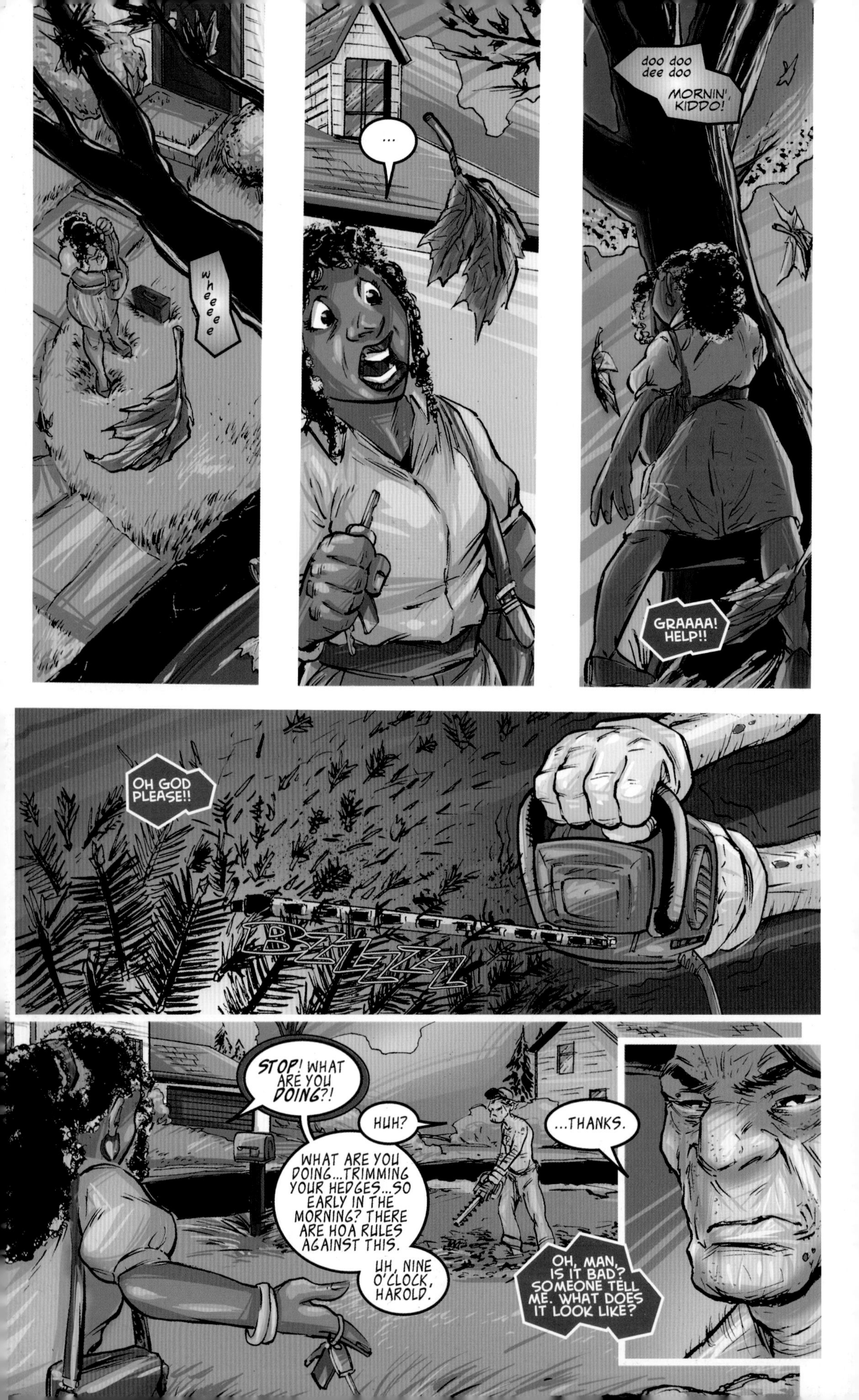
wheeeee
...
doo doo dee doo
MORNIN' KIDDO!
GRAAAA! HELP!!
OH GOD PLEASE!!
BZZZZZZZ
STOP! WHAT ARE YOU DOING?!
HUH?
WHAT ARE YOU DOING...TRIMMING YOUR HEDGES...SO EARLY IN THE MORNING? THERE ARE HOA RULES AGAINST THIS.
UH, NINE O'CLOCK, HAROLD.
...THANKS.
OH, MAN, IS IT BAD? SOMEONE TELL ME. WHAT DOES IT LOOK LIKE?

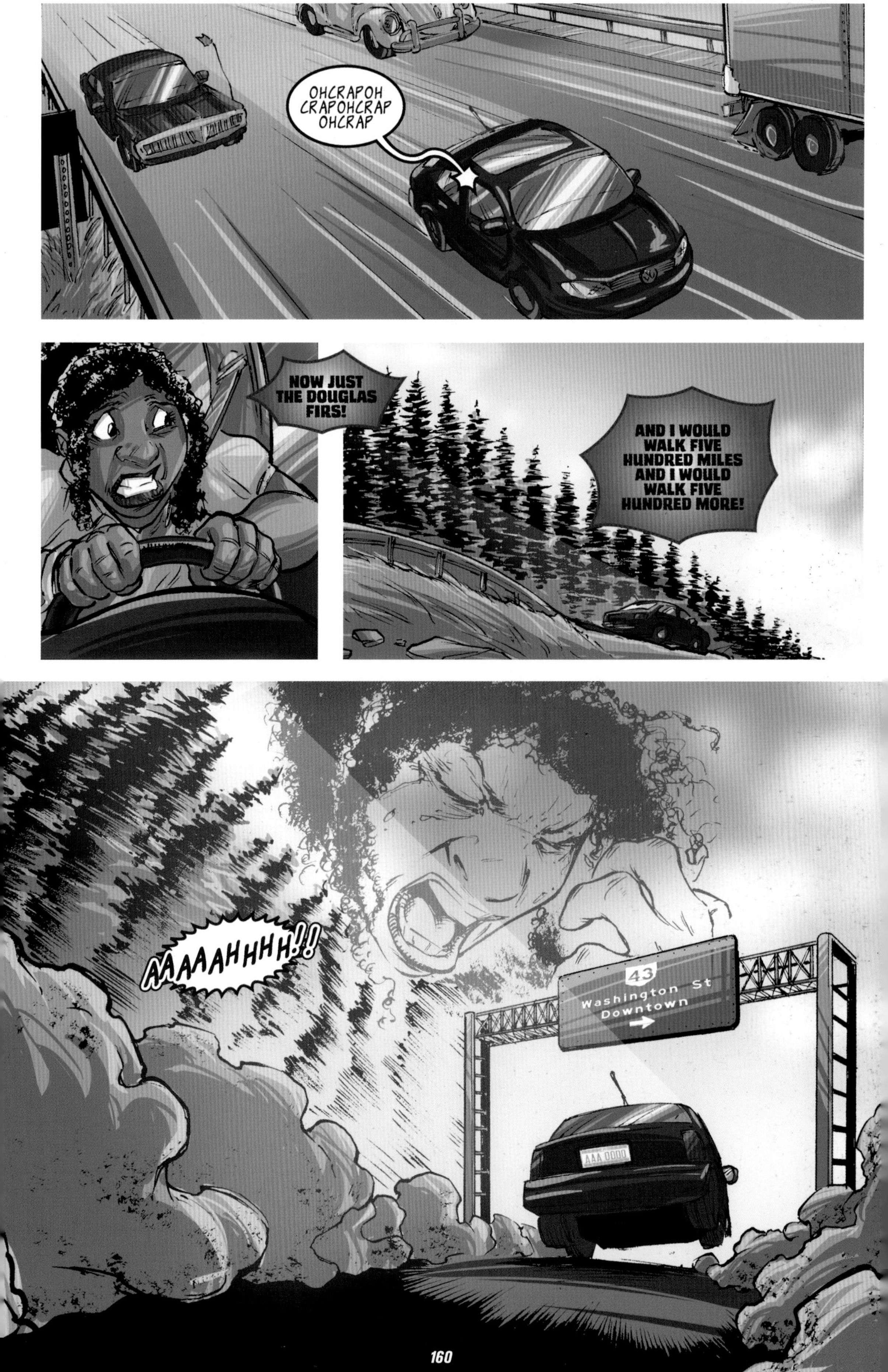

OHCRAPOH CRAPOHCRAP OHCRAP
NOW JUST THE DOUGLAS FIRS!
AND I WOULD WALK FIVE HUNDRED MILES AND I WOULD WALK FIVE HUNDRED MORE!
AAAAAHHHH!!
43
Washington St
Downtown
AAA 0000

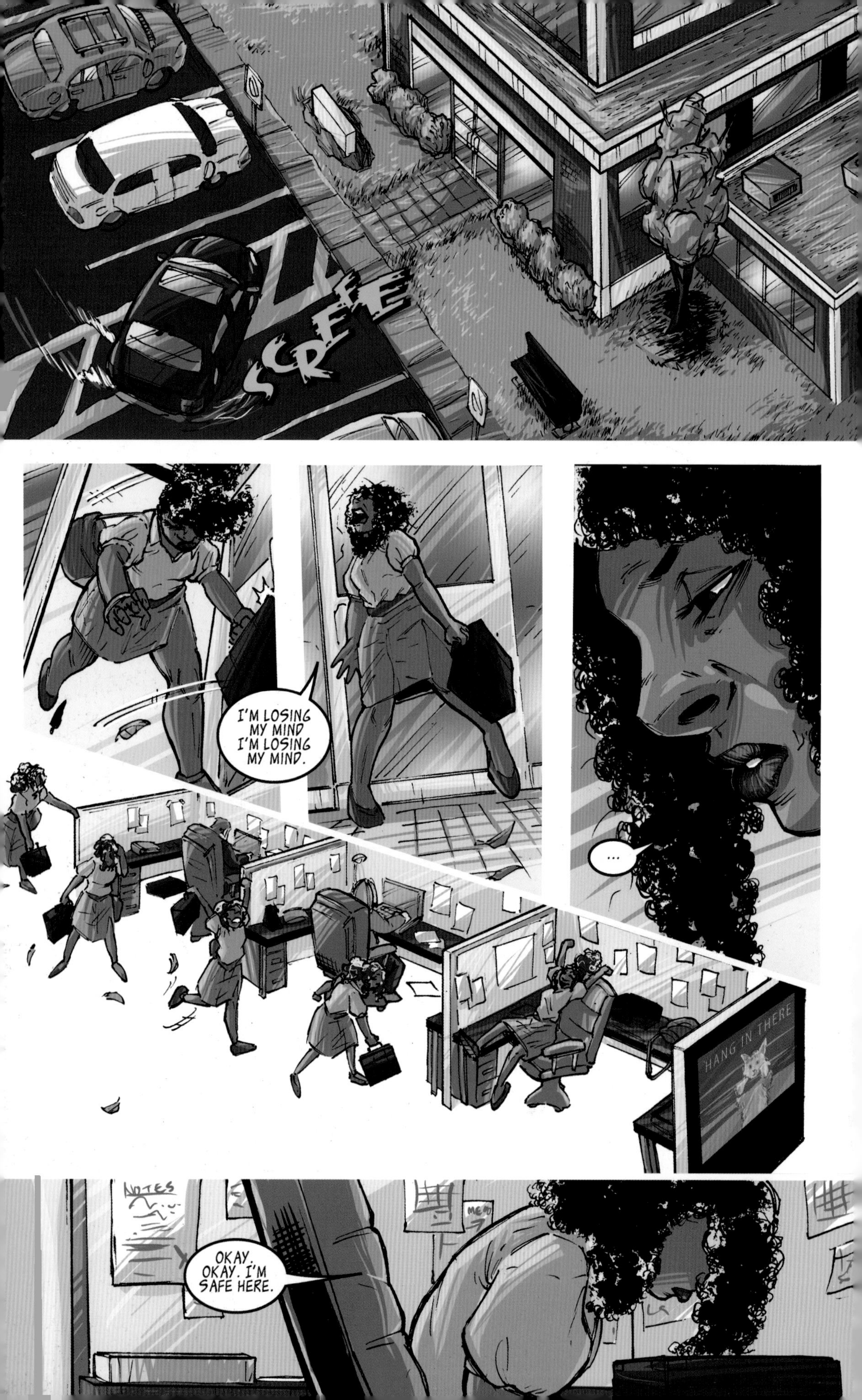
SCREEE
I'M LOSING MY MIND I'M LOSING MY MIND.
...
HANG IN THERE
NOTES
MEMO
OKAY. OKAY. I'M SAFE HERE.

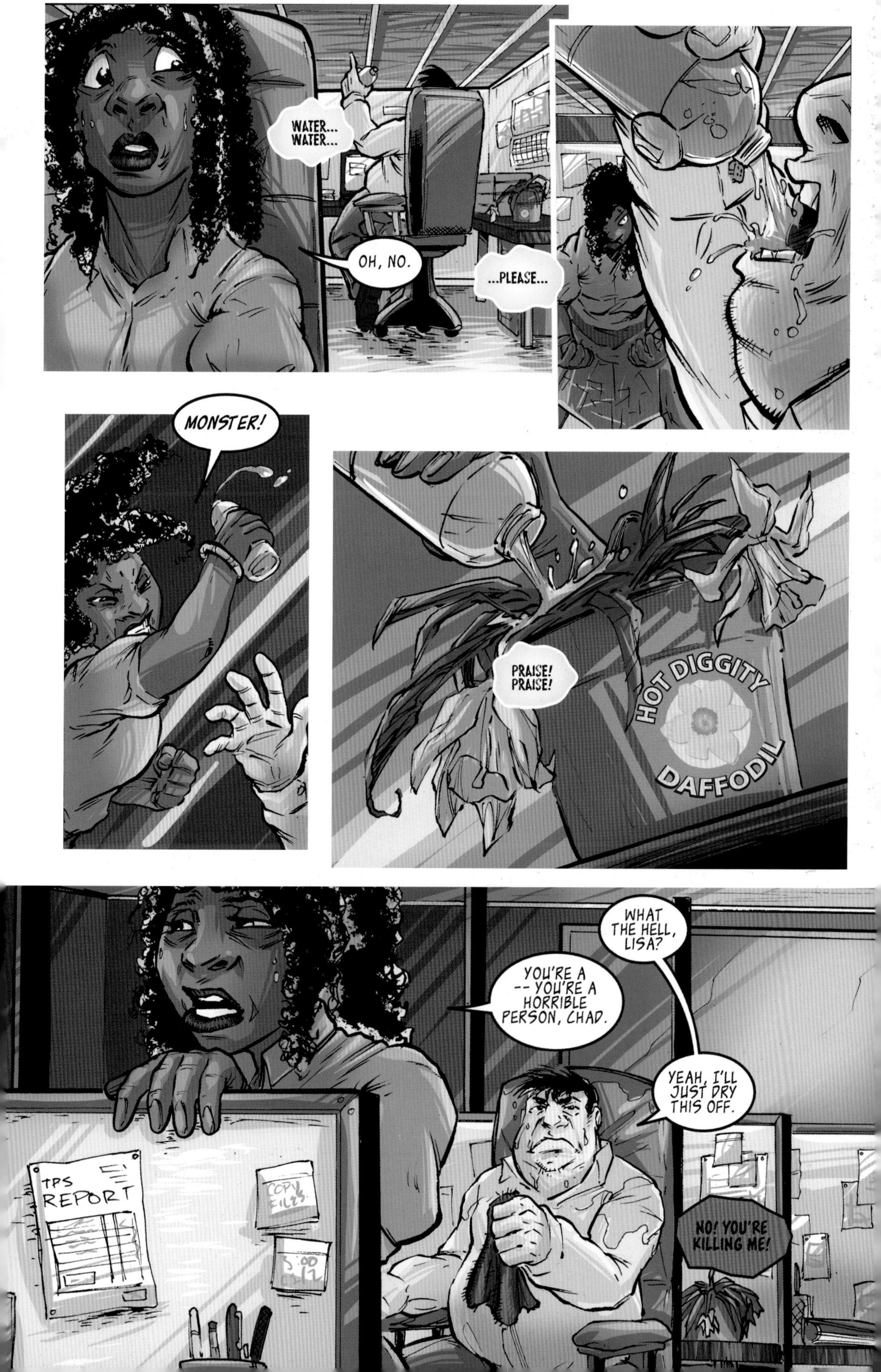
WATER... WATER...
OH, NO.
...PLEASE...
MONSTER!
PRAISE! PRAISE!
HOT DIGGITY DAFFODIL
WHAT THE HELL, LISA?
YOU'RE A -- YOU'RE A HORRIBLE PERSON, CHAD.
YEAH, I'LL JUST DRY THIS OFF.
NO! YOU'RE KILLING ME!
TPS REPORT

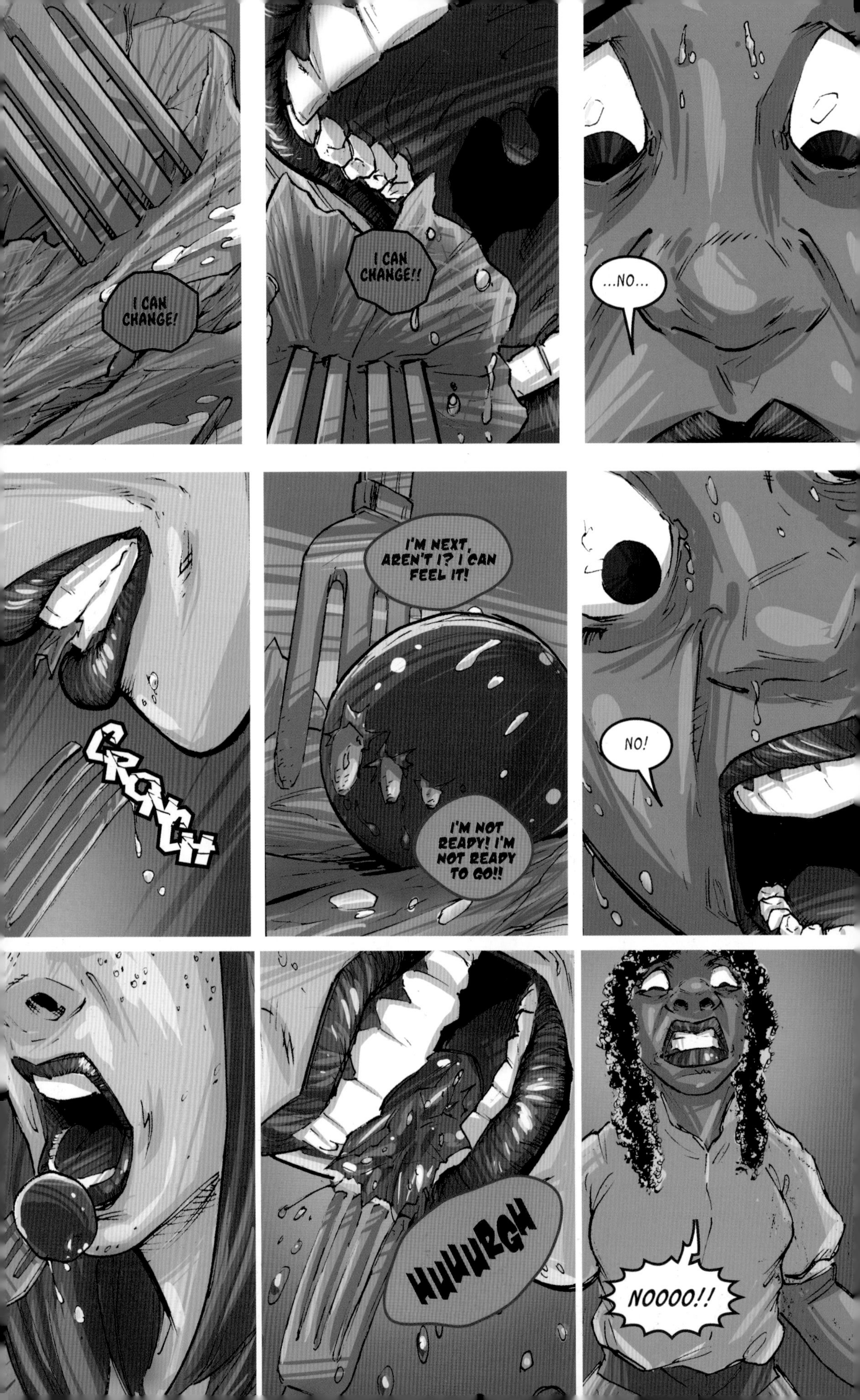
I CAN CHANGE!
I CAN CHANGE!!
...NO...
CRONCH
I'M NEXT, AREN'T I? I CAN FEEL IT!
I'M NOT READY! I'M NOT READY TO GO!!
NO!
HUUURGH
NOOOO!!

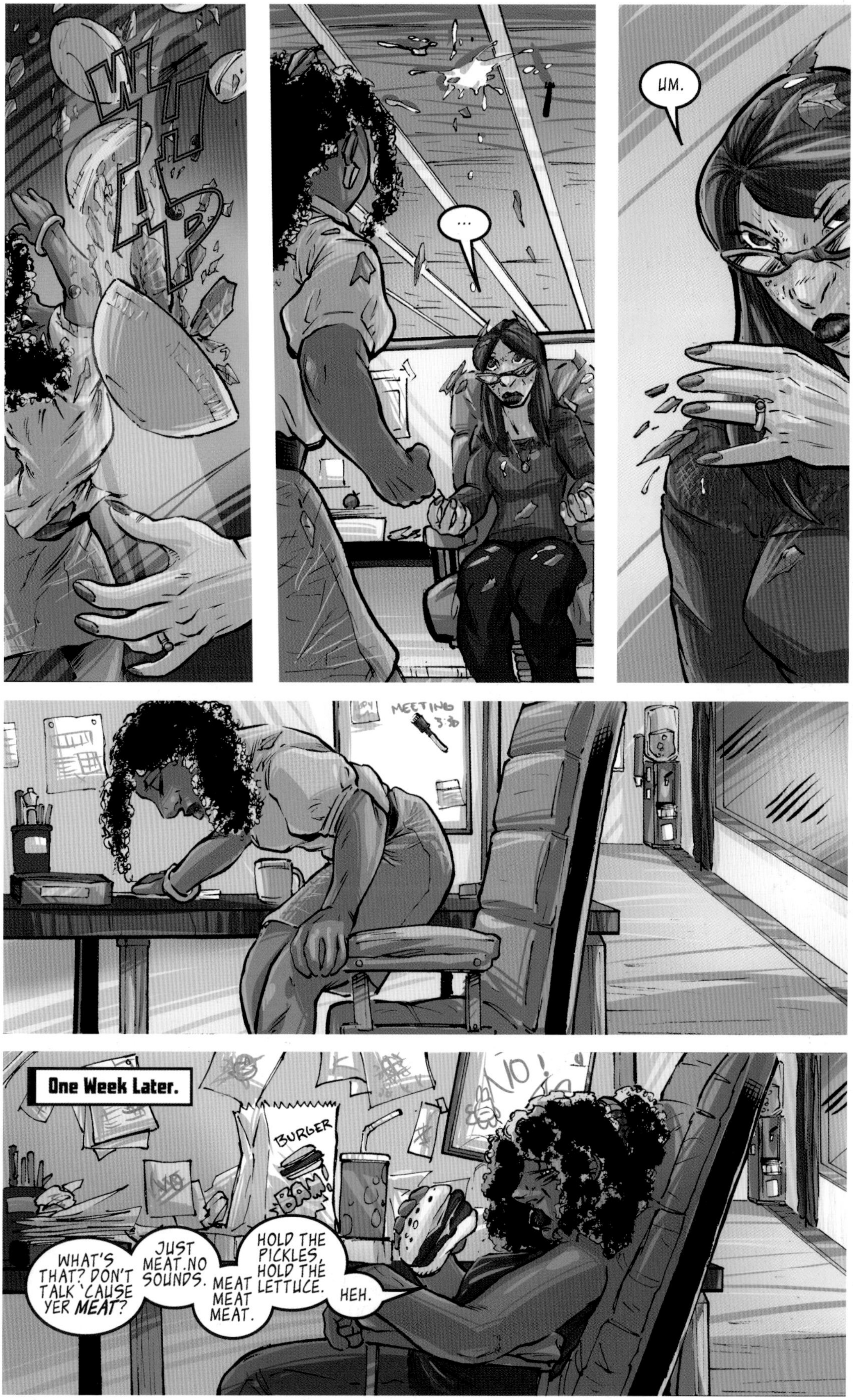
WHAP
...
UM.
MEETING 3:30
One Week Later.
BURGER
BAM
WHAT'S THAT? DON'T TALK 'CAUSE YER *MEAT*?
JUST MEAT. NO SOUNDS.
MEAT MEAT MEAT MEAT.
HOLD THE PICKLES, HOLD THE LETTUCE.
HEH.

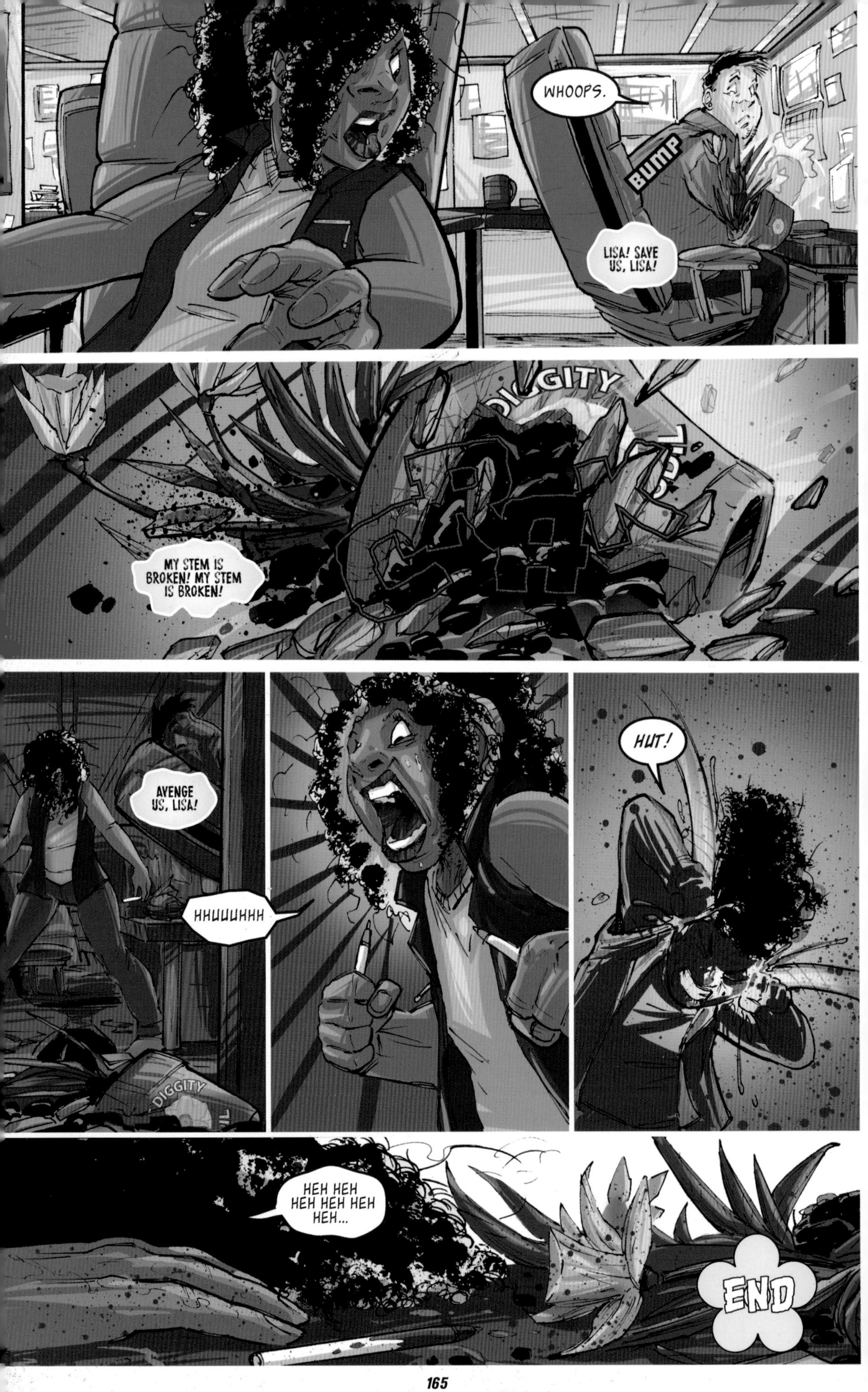
WHOOPS.
BUMP
LISA! SAVE US, LISA!
DIGGITY
MY STEM IS BROKEN! MY STEM IS BROKEN!
AVENGE US, LISA!
HHUUUHHH
DIGGITY
HUT!
HEH HEH HEH HEH HEH HEH...
END

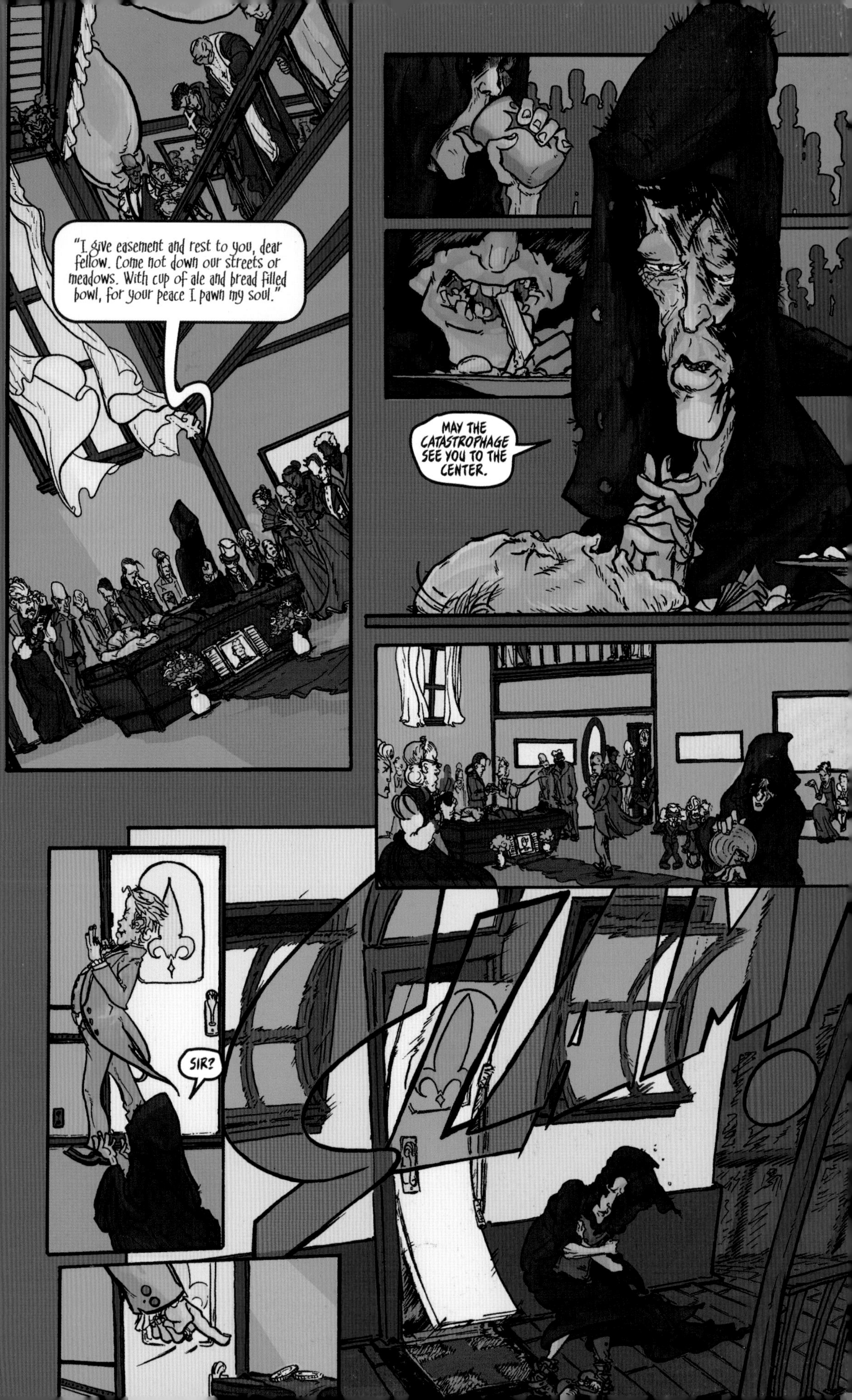
"I give easement and rest to you, dear fellow. Come not down our streets or meadows. With cup of ale and bread filled bowl, for your peace I pawn my soul."
MAY THE CATASTROPHAGE SEE YOU TO THE CENTER.
SIR?

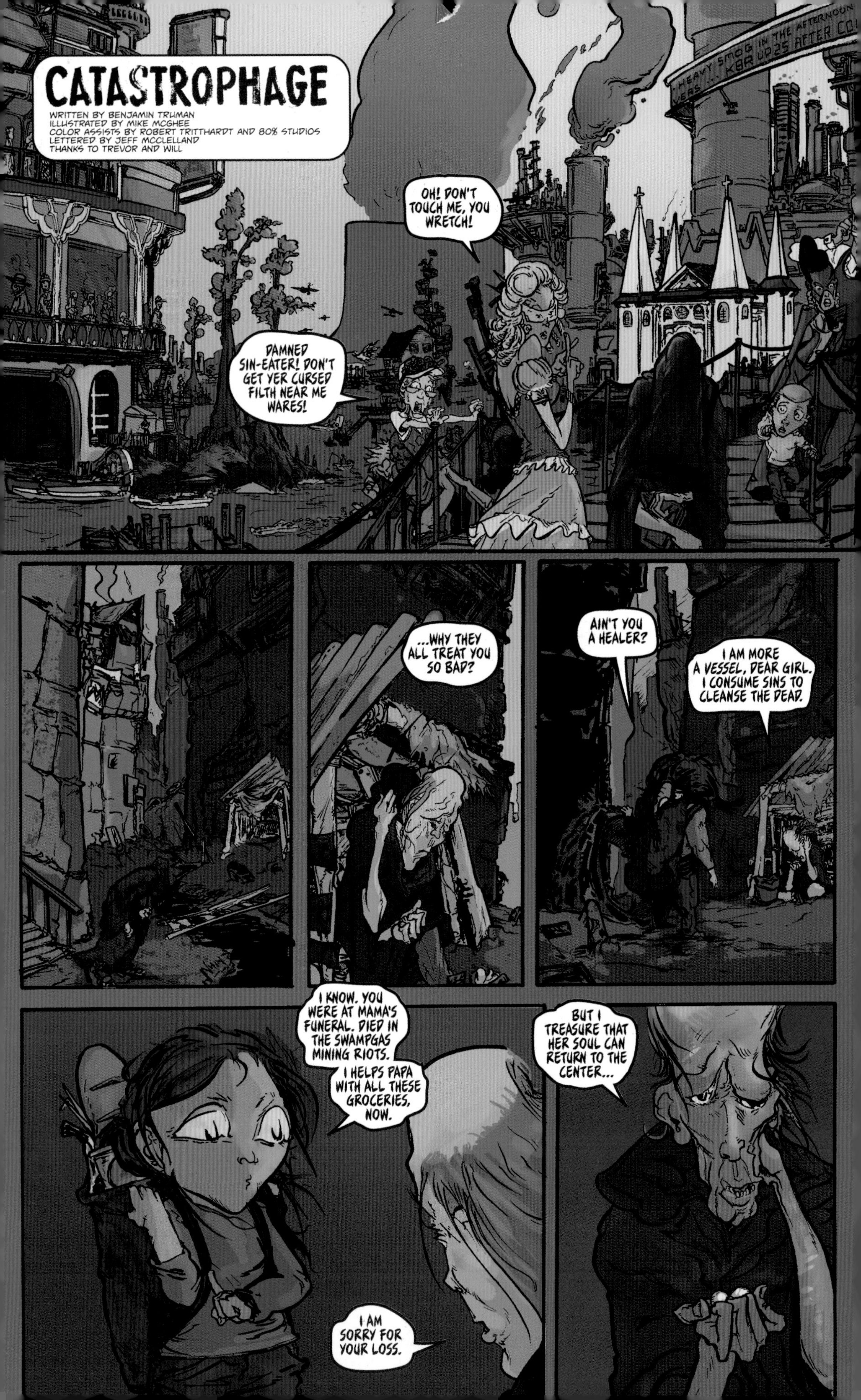
CATASTROPHAGE
WRITTEN BY BENJAMIN TRUMAN
ILLUSTRATED BY MIKE MCGHEE
COLOR ASSISTS BY ROBERT TRITTHARDT AND 808 STUDIOS
LETTERED BY JEFF MCCLELLAND
THANKS TO TREVOR AND WILL
OH! DON'T TOUCH ME, YOU WRETCH!
DAMNED SIN-EATER! DON'T GET YER CURSED FILTH NEAR ME WARES!
...WHY THEY ALL TREAT YOU SO BAD?
AIN'T YOU A HEALER?
I AM MORE A VESSEL, DEAR GIRL. I CONSUME SINS TO CLEANSE THE DEAD.
I KNOW. YOU WERE AT MAMA'S FUNERAL. DIED IN THE SWAMPGAS MINING RIOTS.
I HELPS PAPA WITH ALL THESE GROCERIES, NOW.
I AM SORRY FOR YOUR LOSS.
BUT I TREASURE THAT HER SOUL CAN RETURN TO THE CENTER...

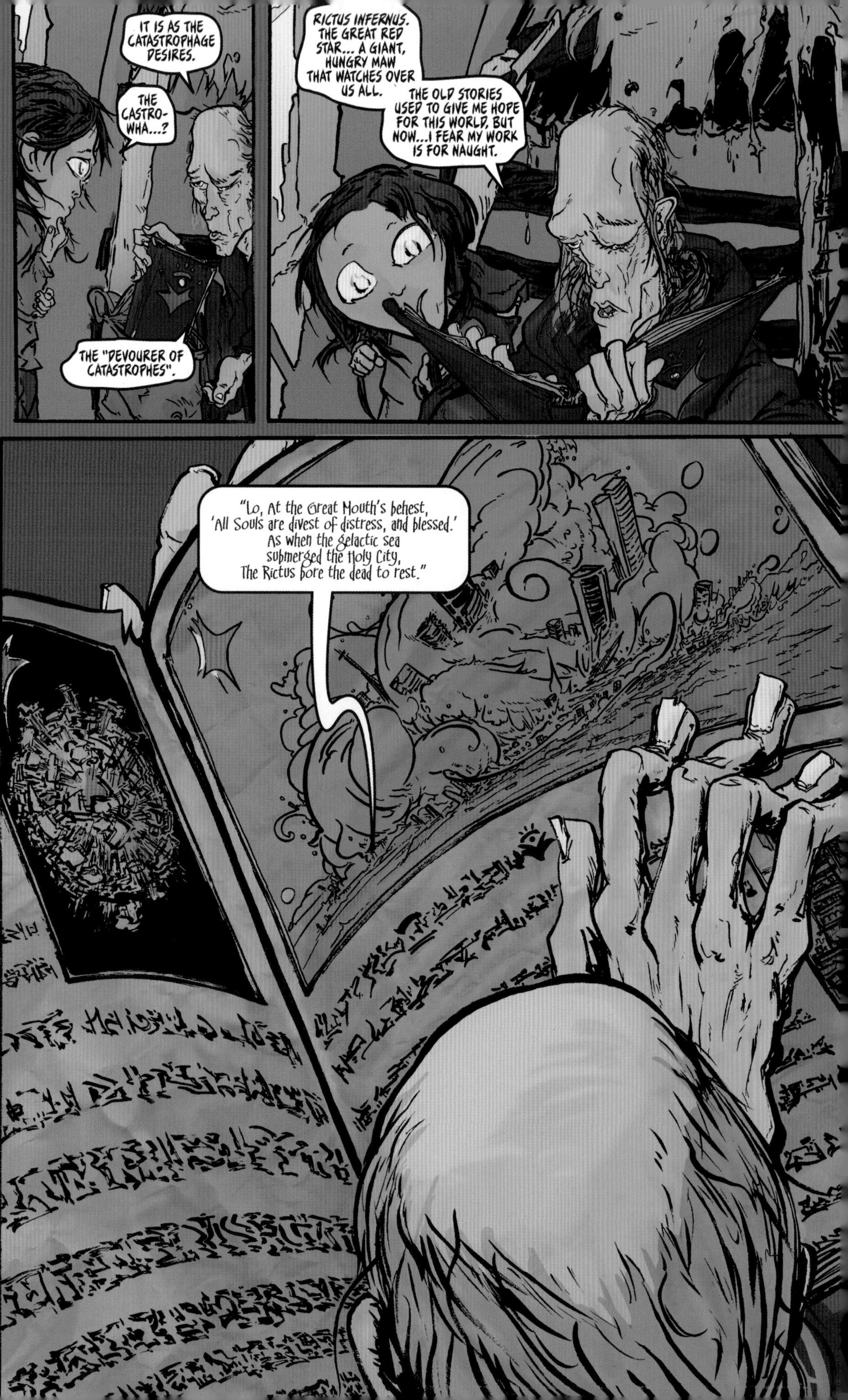
IT IS AS THE CATASTROPHAGE DESIRES.
THE CASTRO-WHA...?
THE "DEVOURER OF CATASTROPHES".
RICTUS INFERNUS. THE GREAT RED STAR... A GIANT, HUNGRY MAW THAT WATCHES OVER US ALL.
THE OLD STORIES USED TO GIVE ME HOPE FOR THIS WORLD, BUT NOW...I FEAR MY WORK IS FOR NAUGHT.
"Lo, At the Great Mouth's behest,
'All Souls are divest of distress, and blessed.'
As when the gelactic sea
submerged the Holy City,
The Rictus bore the dead to rest."

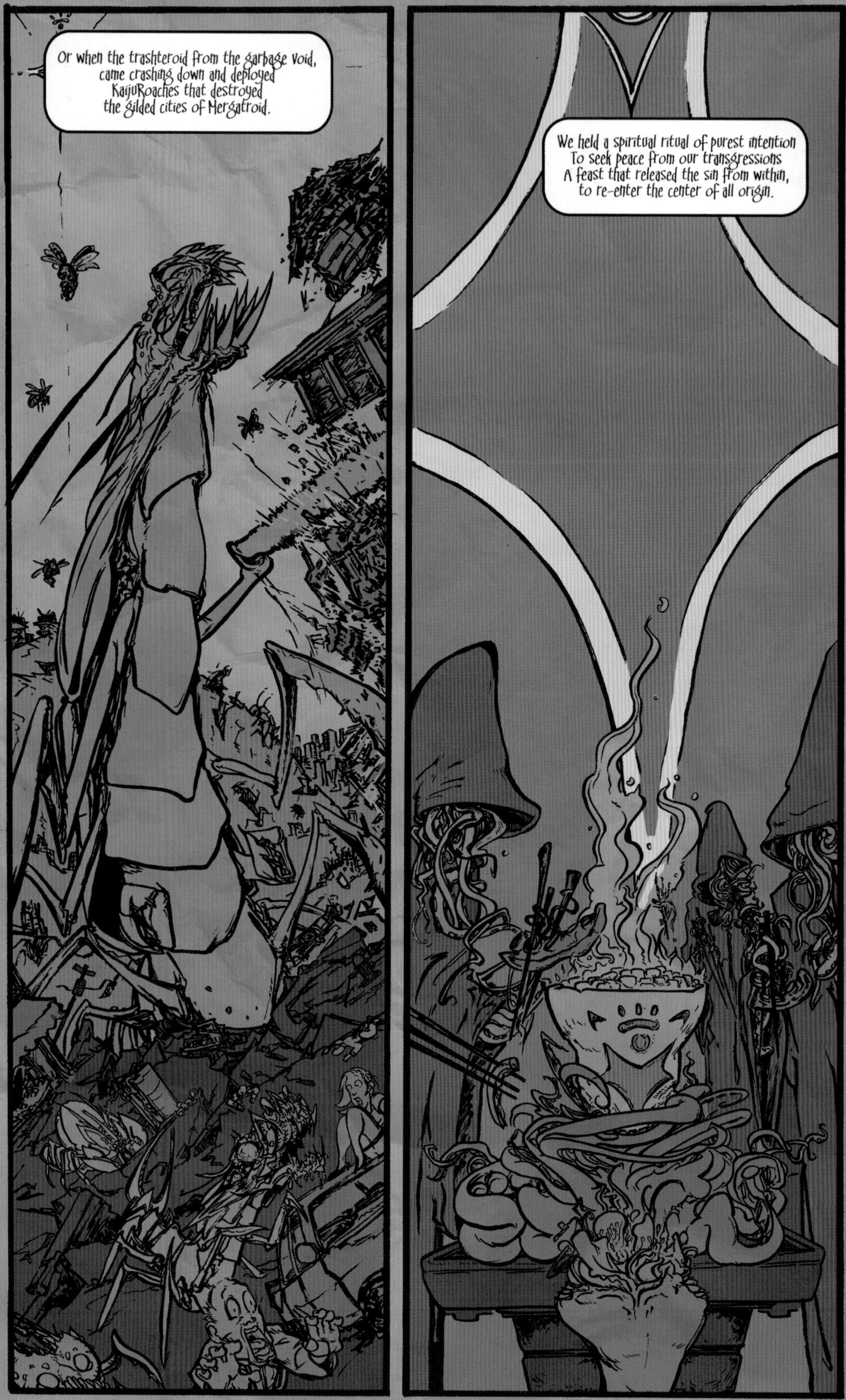
Or when the trashteroid from the garbage void,
came crashing down and deployed
KaijuRoaches that destroyed
the gilded cities of Mergatroid.
We held a spiritual ritual of purest intention
To seek peace from our transgressions
A feast that released the sin from within,
to re-enter the center of all origin.

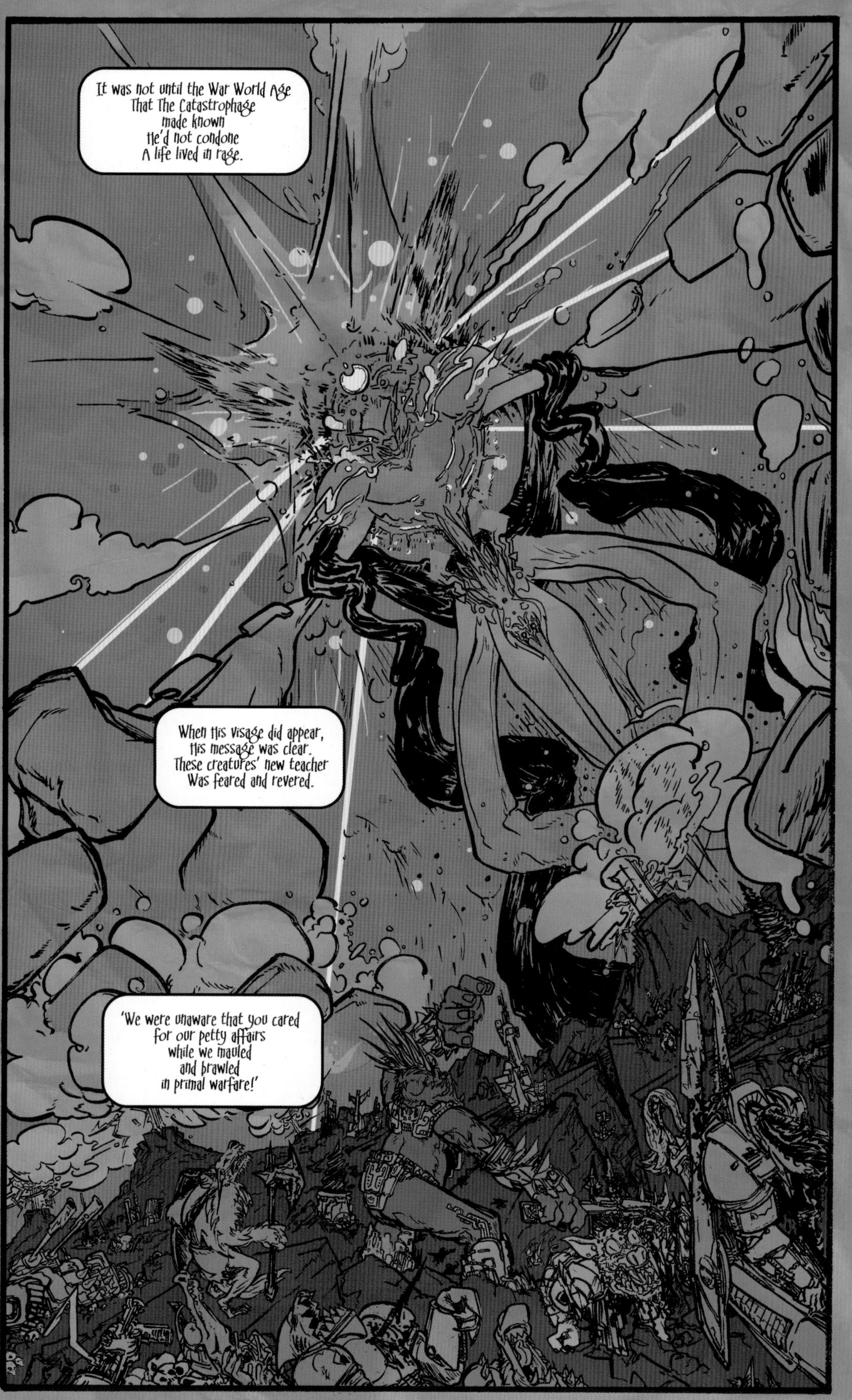
It was not until the War World Age That The Catastrophage made known He'd not condone A life lived in rage.
When His visage did appear, His message was clear. These creatures' new teacher Was feared and revered.
'We were unaware that you cared for our petty affairs while we mauled and brawled in primal warfare!'

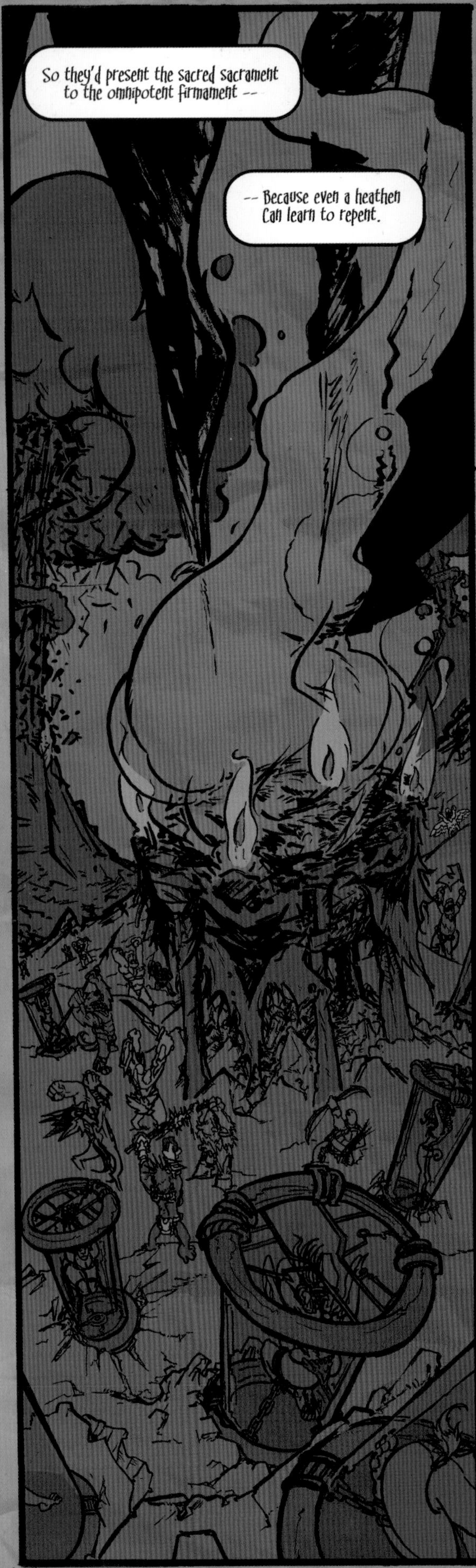
So they'd present the sacred sacrament
to the omnipotent firmament --
-- Because even a heathen
Can learn to repent.

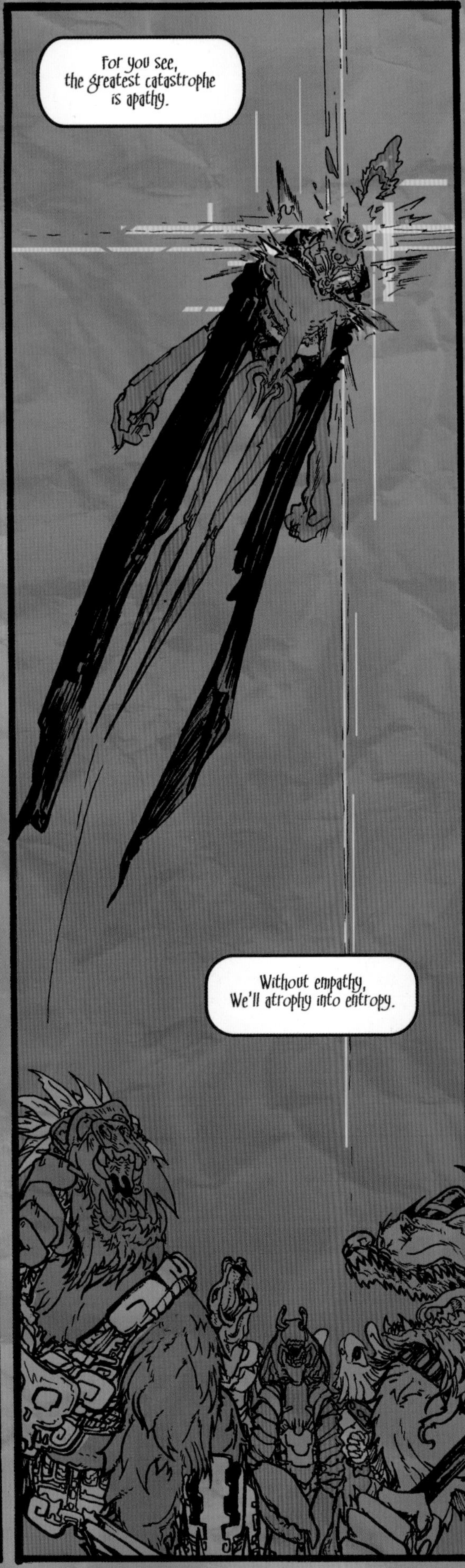
For you see,
the greatest catastrophe
is apathy.
Without empathy,
We'll atrophy into entropy.

Thus, in the infinite wisdom of the Great One --

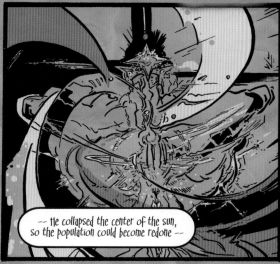

-- He collapsed the center of the sun, so the population could become redone --

-- As the stuff dreams are made of, and the dreams stuff is made from.

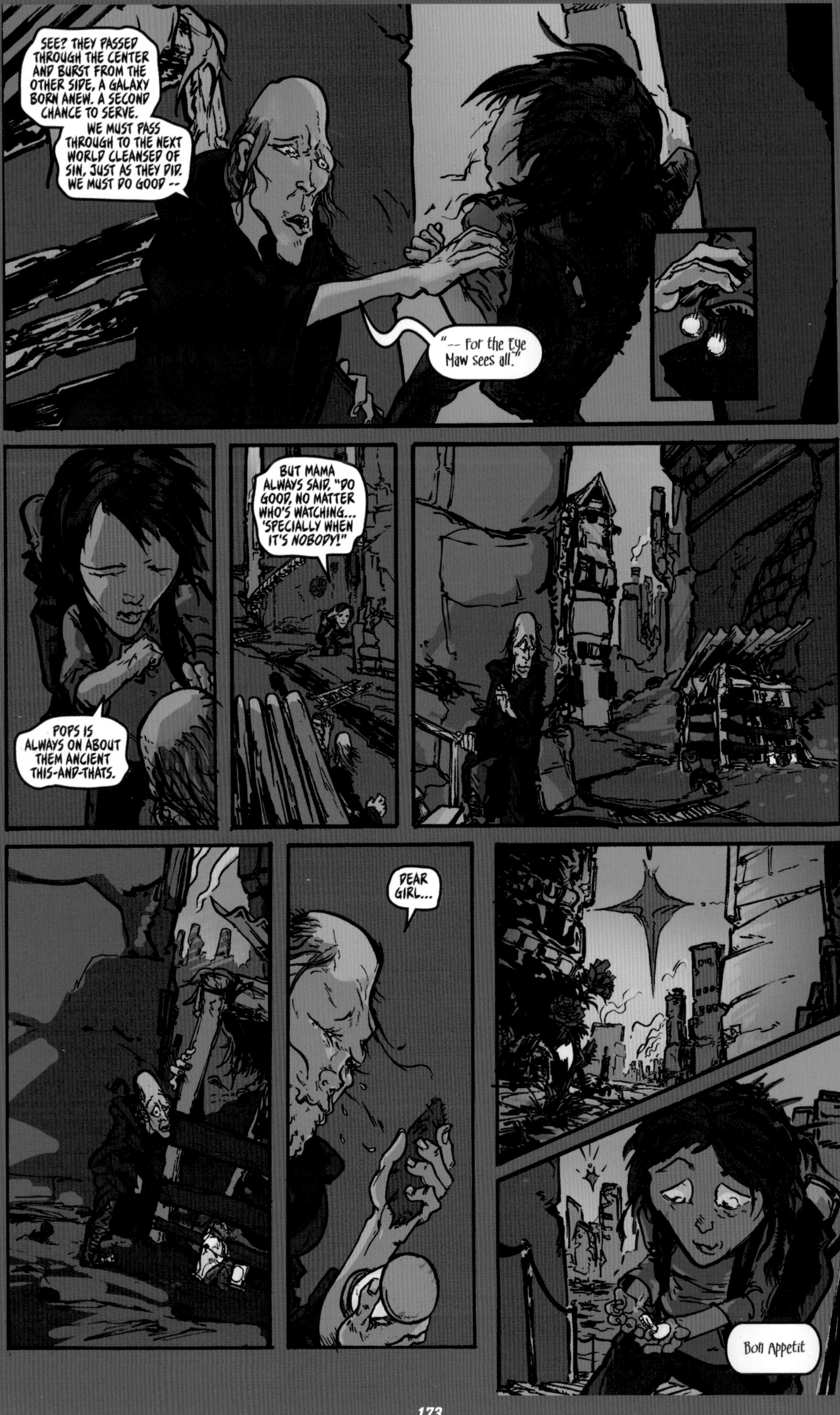
SEE? THEY PASSED THROUGH THE CENTER AND BURST FROM THE OTHER SIDE, A GALAXY BORN ANEW. A SECOND CHANCE TO SERVE.
WE MUST PASS THROUGH TO THE NEXT WORLD CLEANSED OF SIN, JUST AS THEY DID. WE MUST DO GOOD --
"-- For the Eye Maw sees all."
POPS IS ALWAYS ON ABOUT THEM ANCIENT THIS-AND-THATS.
BUT MAMA ALWAYS SAID, "DO GOOD, NO MATTER WHO'S WATCHING... 'SPECIALLY WHEN IT'S NOBODY!"
DEAR GIRL...
Bon Appetit

I SUCKER-PUNCHED KONGAMATO--
PREHISTORIC TERROR-DACTYL!

BY: JEFF MCCLELLAND & PAUL TUCKER

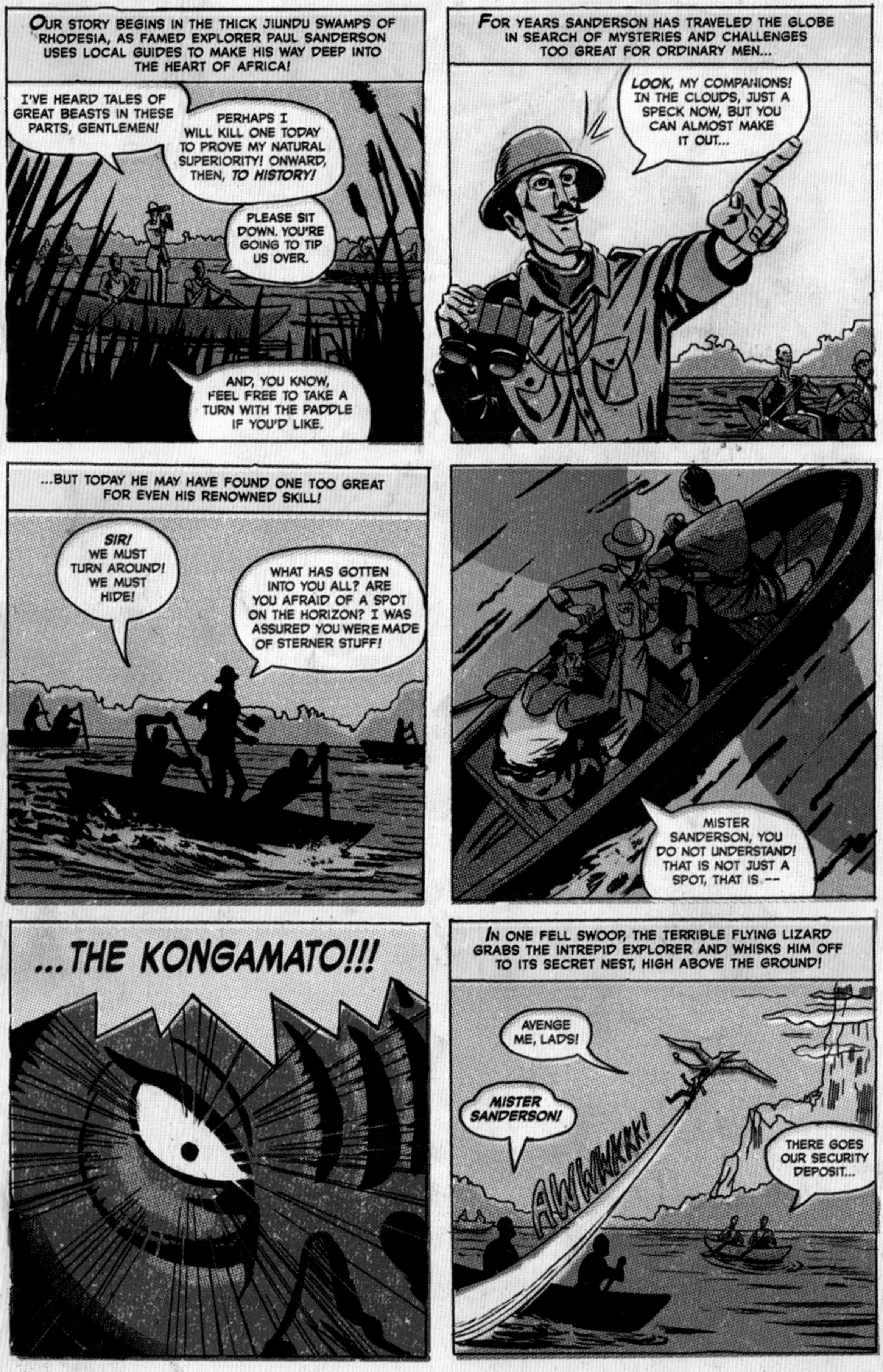
OUR STORY BEGINS IN THE THICK JIUNDU SWAMPS OF RHODESIA, AS FAMED EXPLORER PAUL SANDERSON USES LOCAL GUIDES TO MAKE HIS WAY DEEP INTO THE HEART OF AFRICA!
I'VE HEARD TALES OF GREAT BEASTS IN THESE PARTS, GENTLEMEN!
PERHAPS I WILL KILL ONE TODAY TO PROVE MY NATURAL SUPERIORITY! ONWARD, THEN, TO HISTORY!
PLEASE SIT DOWN. YOU'RE GOING TO TIP US OVER.
AND, YOU KNOW, FEEL FREE TO TAKE A TURN WITH THE PADDLE IF YOU'D LIKE.
FOR YEARS SANDERSON HAS TRAVELED THE GLOBE IN SEARCH OF MYSTERIES AND CHALLENGES TOO GREAT FOR ORDINARY MEN...
LOOK, MY COMPANIONS! IN THE CLOUDS, JUST A SPECK NOW, BUT YOU CAN ALMOST MAKE IT OUT...
...BUT TODAY HE MAY HAVE FOUND ONE TOO GREAT FOR EVEN HIS RENOWNED SKILL!
SIR! WE MUST TURN AROUND! WE MUST HIDE!
WHAT HAS GOTTEN INTO YOU ALL? ARE YOU AFRAID OF A SPOT ON THE HORIZON? I WAS ASSURED YOU WERE MADE OF STERNER STUFF!
MISTER SANDERSON, YOU DO NOT UNDERSTAND! THAT IS NOT JUST A SPOT, THAT IS --
...THE KONGAMATO!!!
IN ONE FELL SWOOP, THE TERRIBLE FLYING LIZARD GRABS THE INTREPID EXPLORER AND WHISKS HIM OFF TO ITS SECRET NEST, HIGH ABOVE THE GROUND!
AVENGE ME, LADS!
MISTER SANDERSON!
AWWWKKK!
THERE GOES OUR SECURITY DEPOSIT...

THE NEXT MORNING, AT THE OFFICE OF A WELL-KNOWN NEW YORK NEWSPAPER...

THIS BOTANY FESTIVAL STORY GIVES ME A CHANCE TO USE ALL OF THE PLANT META-PHORS I'VE BEEN SAVING UP RECENTLY...THEY'RE RIGHT THERE FOR THE PICKING.

OH! I'LL USE THAT ONE.

THURMAN!

WE'VE JUST GOT WORD FROM RHODESIA - PAUL SANDERSON IS MISSING AND PRESUMED CAPTURED BY A MYSTERIOUS BEAST. YOU'RE OUR LEAST CAPABLE RE-PORTER AND A DRAIN ON OUR RESOURCES, BUT YOU'RE ALL WE'VE GOT. I WANT YOU TO GO AND INVESTIGATE THIS STRANGE DISAPPEARANCE!

I'LL LEAVE RIGHT AWAY!

WHAT ABOUT ME, BOSS? I SPENT THREE YEARS IN AFRICA AND AM FAMILIAR WITH THE LOCAL CULTURE. MY ADVANCED COMBAT TRAINING MIGHT COME IN HANDY AS WELL!

NO.

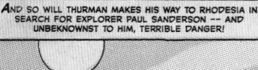

AND SO WILL THURMAN MAKES HIS WAY TO RHODESIA IN SEARCH FOR EXPLORER PAUL SANDERSON -- AND UNBEKNOWNST TO HIM, TERRIBLE DANGER!

THESE STRANGE MONSTERS I'M HEARING OF ARE LIKE SOMETHING OUT OF A SCIENCE FICTION NOVEL! I WONDER WHAT EXCITEMENT I'LL FIND WAITING FOR ME!

CONTINUED AFTER NEXT PAGE

THE INSULT THAT MADE A MONSTER OUT OF "MAC"

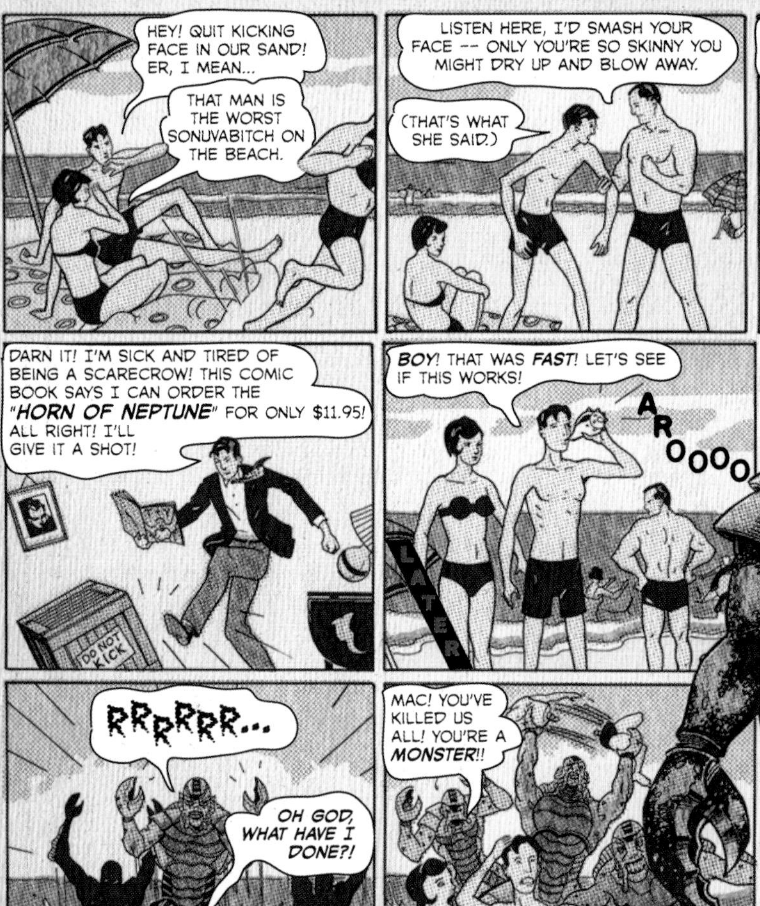

HEY! QUIT KICKING FACE IN OUR SAND! ER, I MEAN...
THAT MAN IS THE WORST SONUVABITCH ON THE BEACH.
LISTEN HERE, I'D SMASH YOUR FACE -- ONLY YOU'RE SO SKINNY YOU MIGHT DRY UP AND BLOW AWAY.
(THAT'S WHAT SHE SAID.)
I HOPE HIS WHOLE FAMILY DIES IN A TERRIBLE ACCIDENT.
OH DON'T LET IT BOTHER YOU, LITTLE BOY!
DARN IT! I'M SICK AND TIRED OF BEING A SCARECROW! THIS COMIC BOOK SAYS I CAN ORDER THE "HORN OF NEPTUNE" FOR ONLY $11.95! ALL RIGHT! I'LL GIVE IT A SHOT!
DO NOT KICK
LATER
BOY! THAT WAS FAST! LET'S SEE IF THIS WORKS!
AROOOO
RRRRRR...
OH GOD, WHAT HAVE I DONE?!
NOOO!
MAC! YOU'VE KILLED US ALL! YOU'RE A MONSTER!!
WHY?!

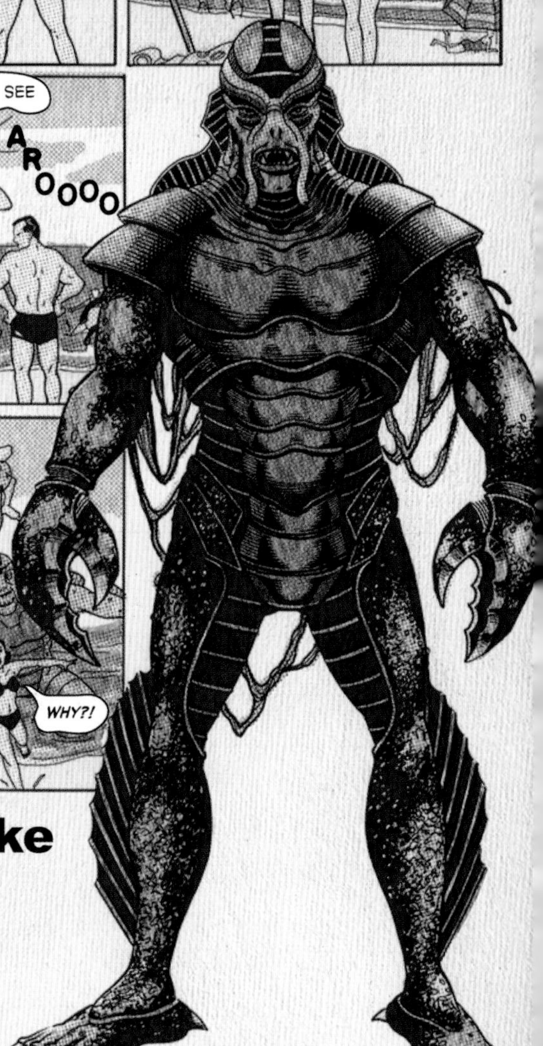

Let Me PROVE I Can Make YOU A MONSTER!

Are you tired of having other people attempt to carry on their sad, meaningless existences in your presence? Don't you wish you could punish those people - **TO DEATH**? I know just how you feel. Because I myself was once a conscientious adult who kept an endless rage bottled up with no outlet for release.

The Secret of the "Horn of Neptune"

Then I discovered a wonderful way to make all of my problems disappear. While carrying on some business in international waters, I ethically and legally "acquired" the legendary weapon of the gods, the "Horn of Neptune". Or Poseidon. Whatever. It worked wonders for me - changed me into "The World's Most Perfectly Devious Man." And I can grant YOU the very same status.

My "Horn of Neptune" has already helped thousands of other fellows settle scores, gain influence and avoid incarceration double-quick time. Let it help YOU. Not next month or in ten thousand years - but Right NOW!

"Horn of Neptune" Calls All Kinds of Creatures!

If you're like I was, you want remorseless, soulless monsters at your beck and call. You want you own personal engine of horror - the kind that makes other fellows bow to your iron will.

Mail Coupon Now For My Illustrated Book

Mailing the coupon can be the turning point in your life, and by extension, those of all who should fear you. I'll send you a copy of my free illustrated book. Tells how and why the "Horn of Neptune" works; shows many pictures featuring "tough" guys getting torn to little tiny pieces. Don't delay. Take this coupon to your fearful news magazine retailer and order "Monster May I?" NOW. Seriously. Do you know what the consequences will be if you don't?

Dear Trustworthy Salesman: Here's the kind of Monster I Want:

(check as many as you like)

- ☐ **Undead**
- ☐ **Winged**
- ☐ **Invisible**
- ☐ **Greek**
- ☐ **Sea**
- ☐ **Ancient**
- ☐ **Elemental**
- ☐ **More Than One Head**

I enclose no cash. Please send me a copy of your famous book showing how "The Horn of Neptune" can make me a new man. Illustrated pages crammed with new stories of fascinating monsters past and present.

Print Name.......................................Age............

Authorization Code...

words/letters: Jeff McClelland art: Duane Redhead colors: Rafer Roberts

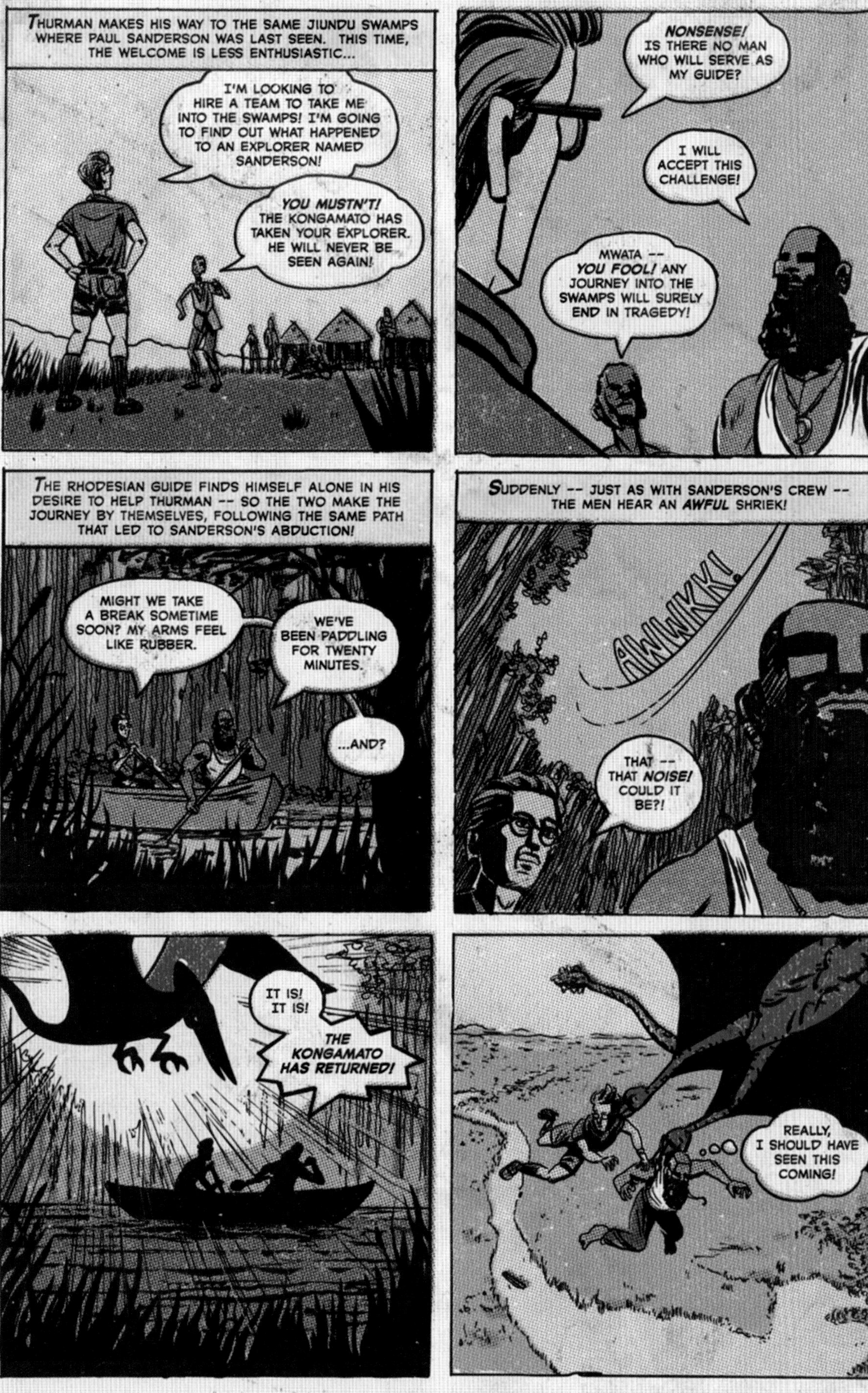
THURMAN MAKES HIS WAY TO THE SAME JIUNDU SWAMPS WHERE PAUL SANDERSON WAS LAST SEEN. THIS TIME, THE WELCOME IS LESS ENTHUSIASTIC...
I'M LOOKING TO HIRE A TEAM TO TAKE ME INTO THE SWAMPS! I'M GOING TO FIND OUT WHAT HAPPENED TO AN EXPLORER NAMED SANDERSON!
YOU MUSTN'T! THE KONGAMATO HAS TAKEN YOUR EXPLORER. HE WILL NEVER BE SEEN AGAIN!
NONSENSE! IS THERE NO MAN WHO WILL SERVE AS MY GUIDE?
I WILL ACCEPT THIS CHALLENGE!
MWATA -- YOU FOOL! ANY JOURNEY INTO THE SWAMPS WILL SURELY END IN TRAGEDY!
THE RHODESIAN GUIDE FINDS HIMSELF ALONE IN HIS DESIRE TO HELP THURMAN -- SO THE TWO MAKE THE JOURNEY BY THEMSELVES, FOLLOWING THE SAME PATH THAT LED TO SANDERSON'S ABDUCTION!
MIGHT WE TAKE A BREAK SOMETIME SOON? MY ARMS FEEL LIKE RUBBER.
WE'VE BEEN PADDLING FOR TWENTY MINUTES.
...AND?
SUDDENLY -- JUST AS WITH SANDERSON'S CREW -- THE MEN HEAR AN AWFUL SHRIEK!
AWWKK!
THAT -- THAT NOISE! COULD IT BE?!
IT IS! IT IS!
THE KONGAMATO HAS RETURNED!
REALLY, I SHOULD HAVE SEEN THIS COMING!

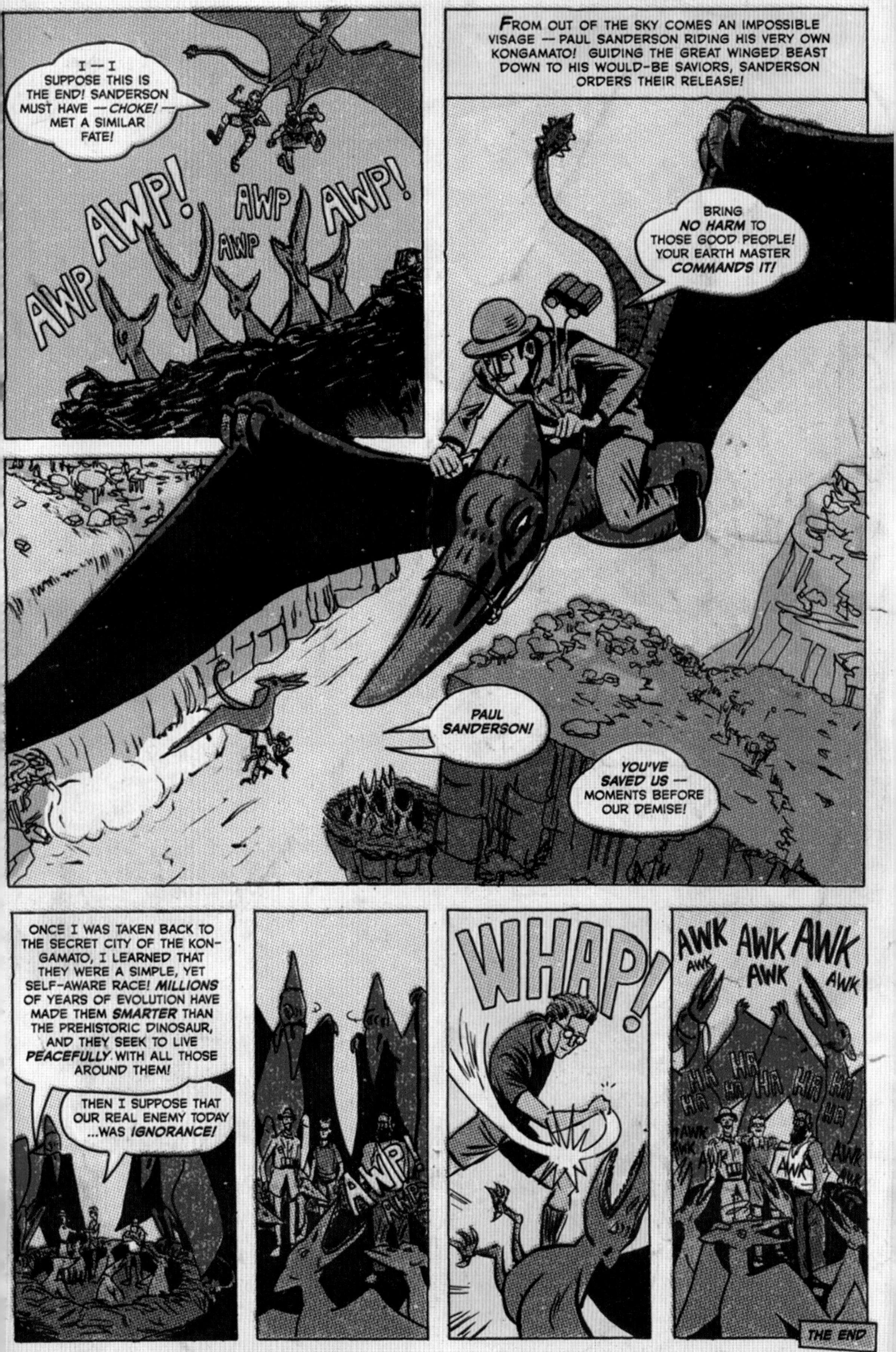
I — I SUPPOSE THIS IS THE END! SANDERSON MUST HAVE —CHOKE!— MET A SIMILAR FATE!
AWP AWP! AWP AWP AWP!
FROM OUT OF THE SKY COMES AN IMPOSSIBLE VISAGE — PAUL SANDERSON RIDING HIS VERY OWN KONGAMATO! GUIDING THE GREAT WINGED BEAST DOWN TO HIS WOULD-BE SAVIORS, SANDERSON ORDERS THEIR RELEASE!
BRING NO HARM TO THOSE GOOD PEOPLE! YOUR EARTH MASTER COMMANDS IT!
PAUL SANDERSON!
YOU'VE SAVED US — MOMENTS BEFORE OUR DEMISE!
ONCE I WAS TAKEN BACK TO THE SECRET CITY OF THE KONGAMATO, I LEARNED THAT THEY WERE A SIMPLE, YET SELF-AWARE RACE! MILLIONS OF YEARS OF EVOLUTION HAVE MADE THEM SMARTER THAN THE PREHISTORIC DINOSAUR, AND THEY SEEK TO LIVE PEACEFULLY WITH ALL THOSE AROUND THEM!
THEN I SUPPOSE THAT OUR REAL ENEMY TODAY ...WAS IGNORANCE!
AWP!
WHAP!
AWK AWK AWK AWK AWK AWK AWK
THE END

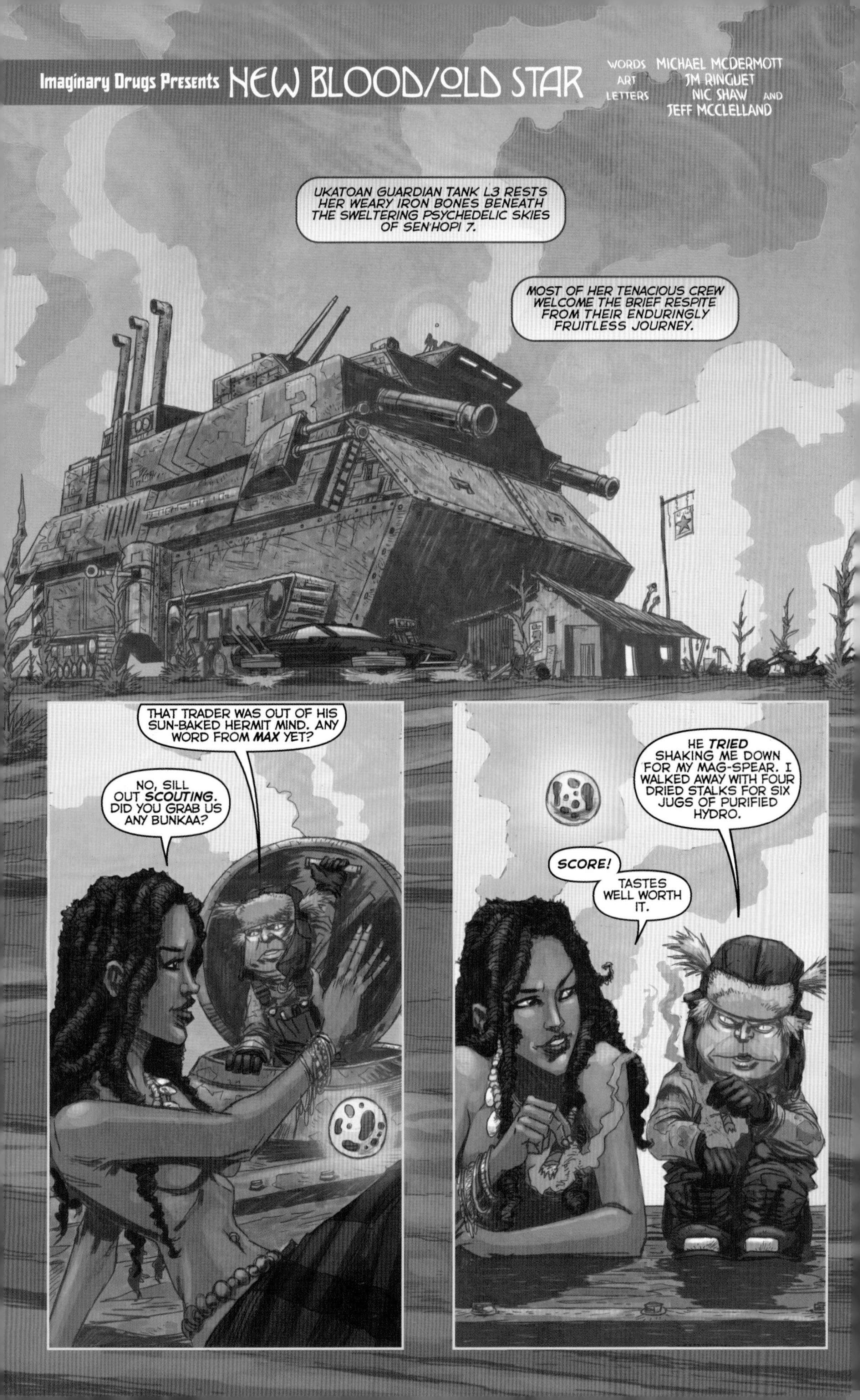
Imaginary Drugs Presents NEW BLOOD/OLD STAR
WORDS MICHAEL MCDERMOTT
ART JM RINGUET
LETTERS NIC SHAW AND JEFF MCCLELLAND
UKATOAN GUARDIAN TANK L3 RESTS HER WEARY IRON BONES BENEATH THE SWELTERING PSYCHEDELIC SKIES OF SEN'HOPI 7.
MOST OF HER TENACIOUS CREW WELCOME THE BRIEF RESPITE FROM THEIR ENDURINGLY FRUITLESS JOURNEY.
THAT TRADER WAS OUT OF HIS SUN-BAKED HERMIT MIND. ANY WORD FROM MAX YET?
NO, SILL OUT SCOUTING. DID YOU GRAB US ANY BUNKAA?
HE TRIED SHAKING ME DOWN FOR MY MAG-SPEAR. I WALKED AWAY WITH FOUR DRIED STALKS FOR SIX JUGS OF PURIFIED HYDRO.
SCORE!
TASTES WELL WORTH IT.

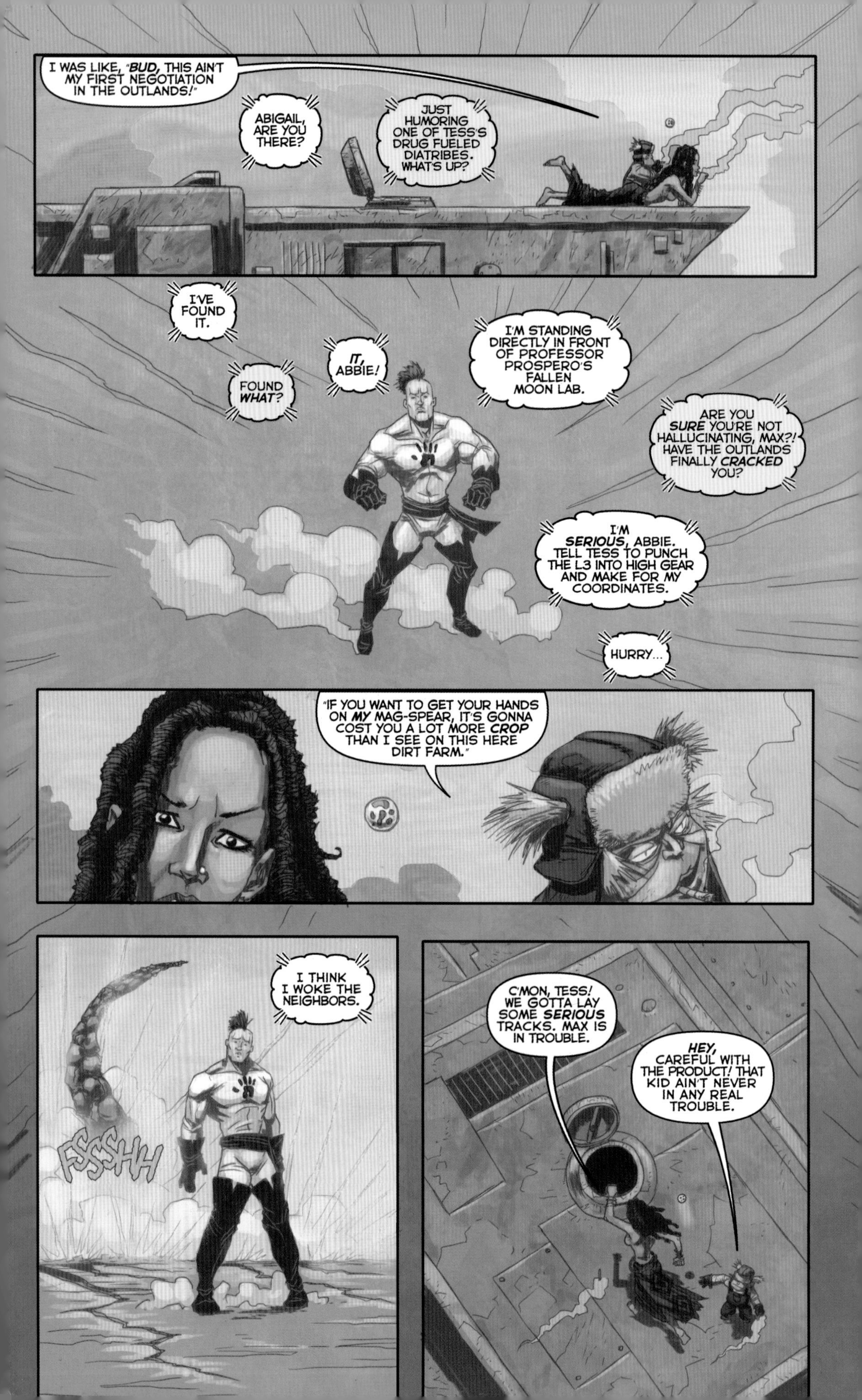
I WAS LIKE, "BUD, THIS AIN'T MY FIRST NEGOTIATION IN THE OUTLANDS!"
ABIGAIL, ARE YOU THERE?
JUST HUMORING ONE OF TESS'S DRUG FUELED DIATRIBES. WHAT'S UP?
I'VE FOUND IT.
FOUND WHAT?
IT, ABBIE!
I'M STANDING DIRECTLY IN FRONT OF PROFESSOR PROSPERO'S FALLEN MOON LAB.
ARE YOU SURE YOU'RE NOT HALLUCINATING, MAX?! HAVE THE OUTLANDS FINALLY CRACKED YOU?
I'M SERIOUS, ABBIE. TELL TESS TO PUNCH THE L3 INTO HIGH GEAR AND MAKE FOR MY COORDINATES.
HURRY...
"IF YOU WANT TO GET YOUR HANDS ON MY MAG-SPEAR, IT'S GONNA COST YOU A LOT MORE CROP THAN I SEE ON THIS HERE DIRT FARM."
I THINK I WOKE THE NEIGHBORS.
FSSHH
C'MON, TESS! WE GOTTA LAY SOME SERIOUS TRACKS. MAX IS IN TROUBLE.
HEY, CAREFUL WITH THE PRODUCT! THAT KID AIN'T NEVER IN ANY REAL TROUBLE.

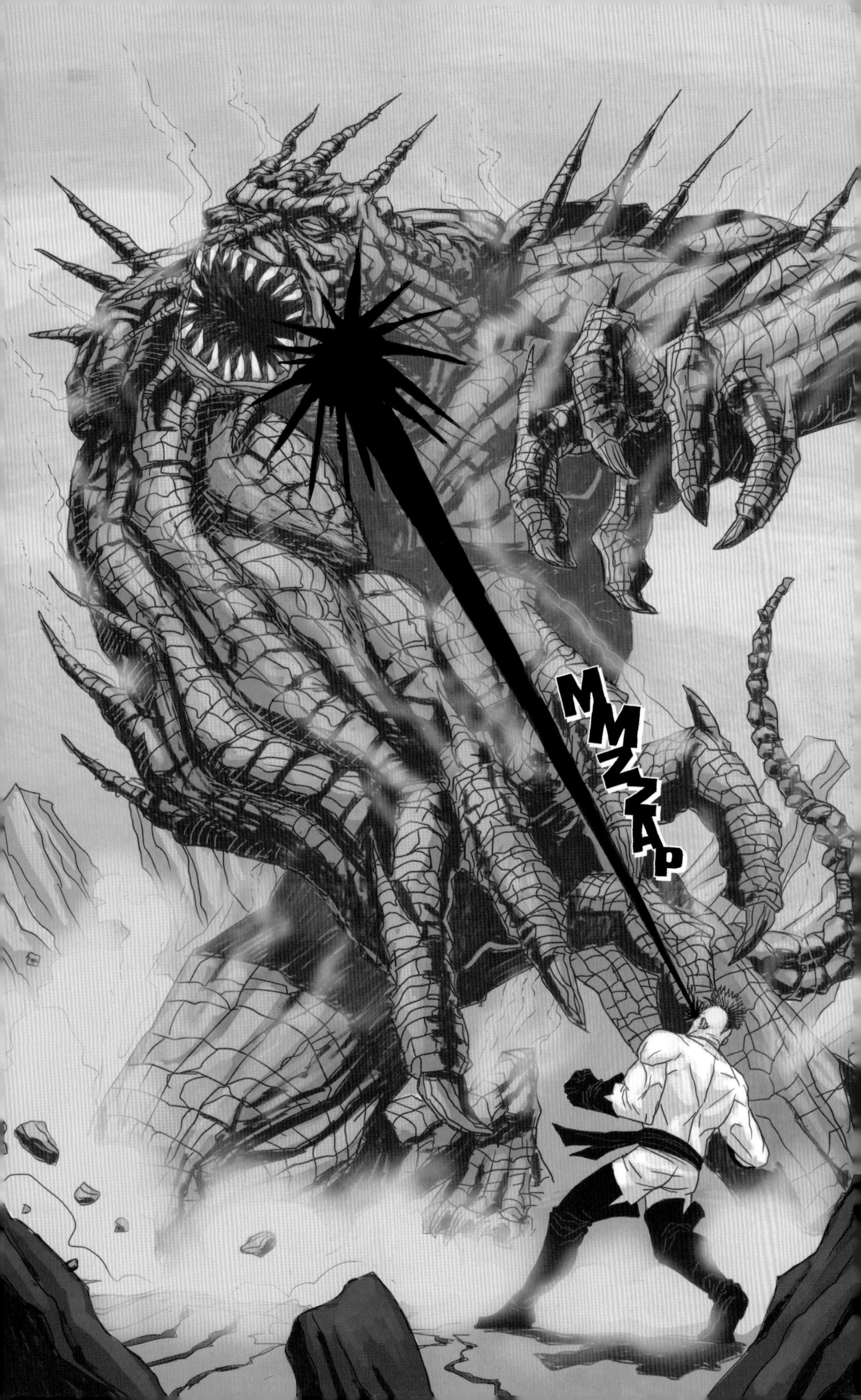
MMZZAP

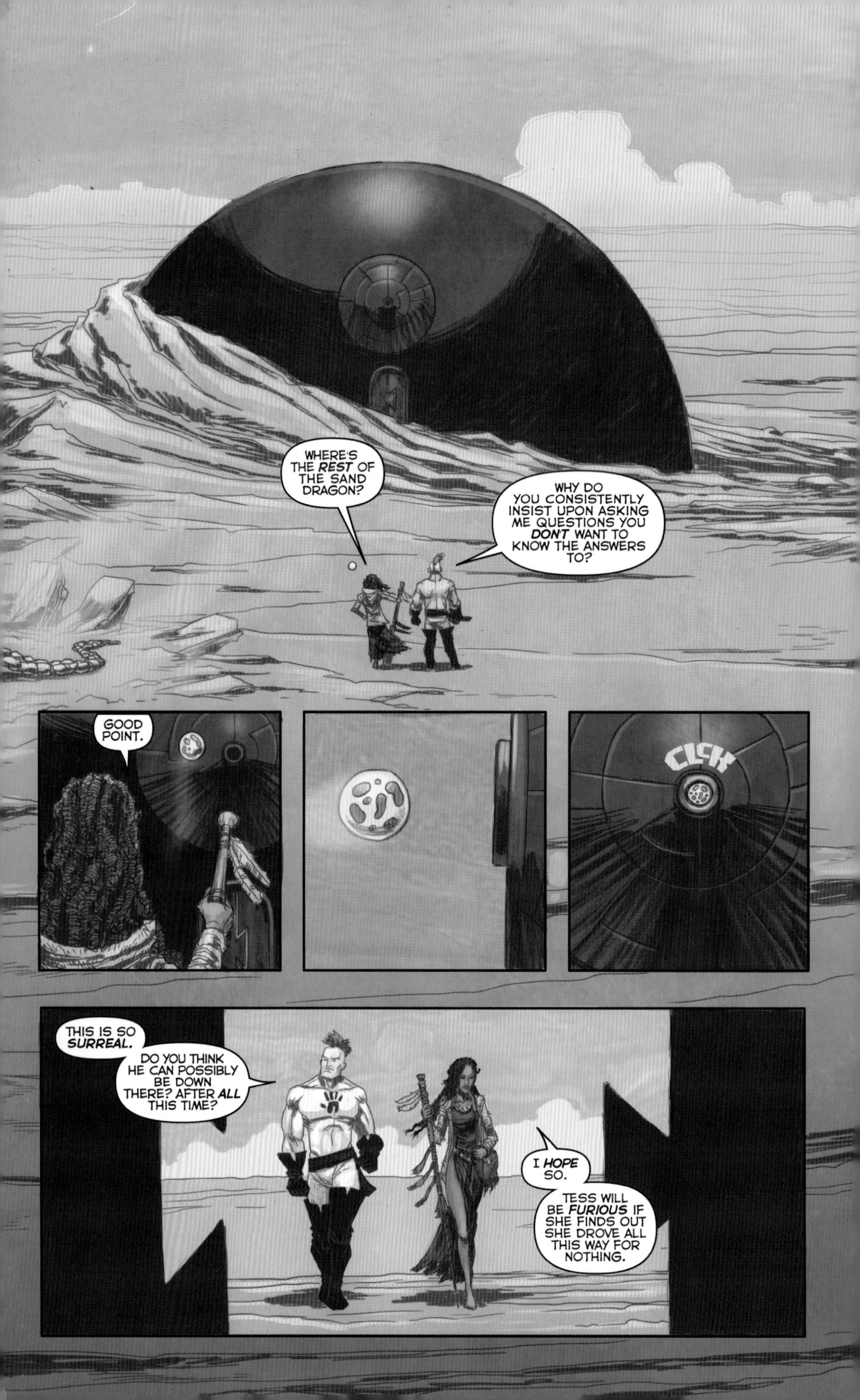
WHERE'S THE REST OF THE SAND DRAGON?
WHY DO YOU CONSISTENTLY INSIST UPON ASKING ME QUESTIONS YOU DON'T WANT TO KNOW THE ANSWERS TO?
GOOD POINT.
CLCK
THIS IS SO SURREAL.
DO YOU THINK HE CAN POSSIBLY BE DOWN THERE? AFTER ALL THIS TIME?
I HOPE SO.
TESS WILL BE FURIOUS IF SHE FINDS OUT SHE DROVE ALL THIS WAY FOR NOTHING.

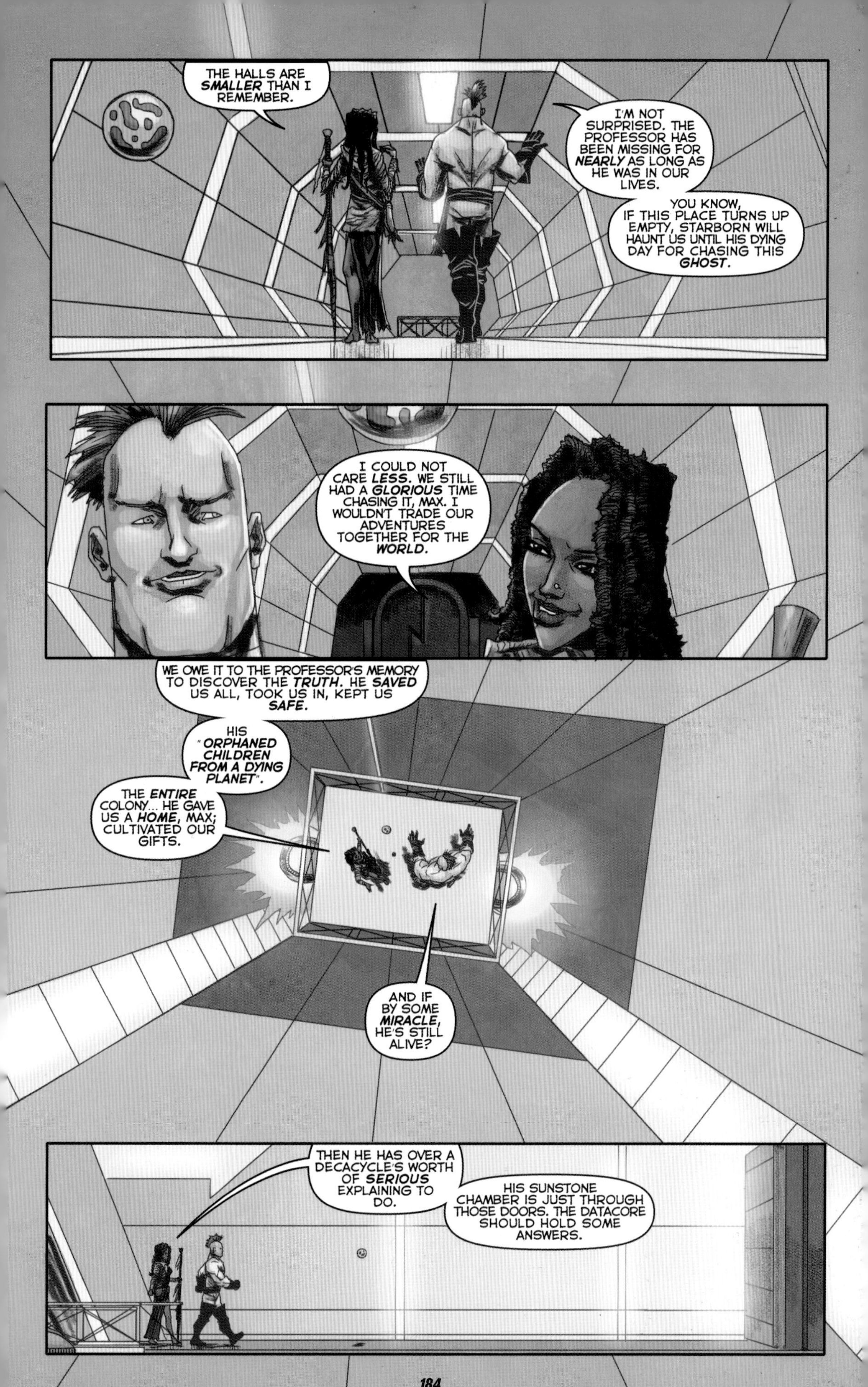
THE HALLS ARE SMALLER THAN I REMEMBER.
I'M NOT SURPRISED. THE PROFESSOR HAS BEEN MISSING FOR NEARLY AS LONG AS HE WAS IN OUR LIVES.
YOU KNOW, IF THIS PLACE TURNS UP EMPTY, STARBORN WILL HAUNT US UNTIL HIS DYING DAY FOR CHASING THIS GHOST.
I COULD NOT CARE LESS. WE STILL HAD A GLORIOUS TIME CHASING IT, MAX. I WOULDN'T TRADE OUR ADVENTURES TOGETHER FOR THE WORLD.
WE OWE IT TO THE PROFESSOR'S MEMORY TO DISCOVER THE TRUTH. HE SAVED US ALL, TOOK US IN, KEPT US SAFE.
HIS "ORPHANED CHILDREN FROM A DYING PLANET".
THE ENTIRE COLONY... HE GAVE US A HOME, MAX; CULTIVATED OUR GIFTS.
AND IF BY SOME MIRACLE, HE'S STILL ALIVE?
THEN HE HAS OVER A DECACYCLE'S WORTH OF SERIOUS EXPLAINING TO DO.
HIS SUNSTONE CHAMBER IS JUST THROUGH THOSE DOORS. THE DATACORE SHOULD HOLD SOME ANSWERS.

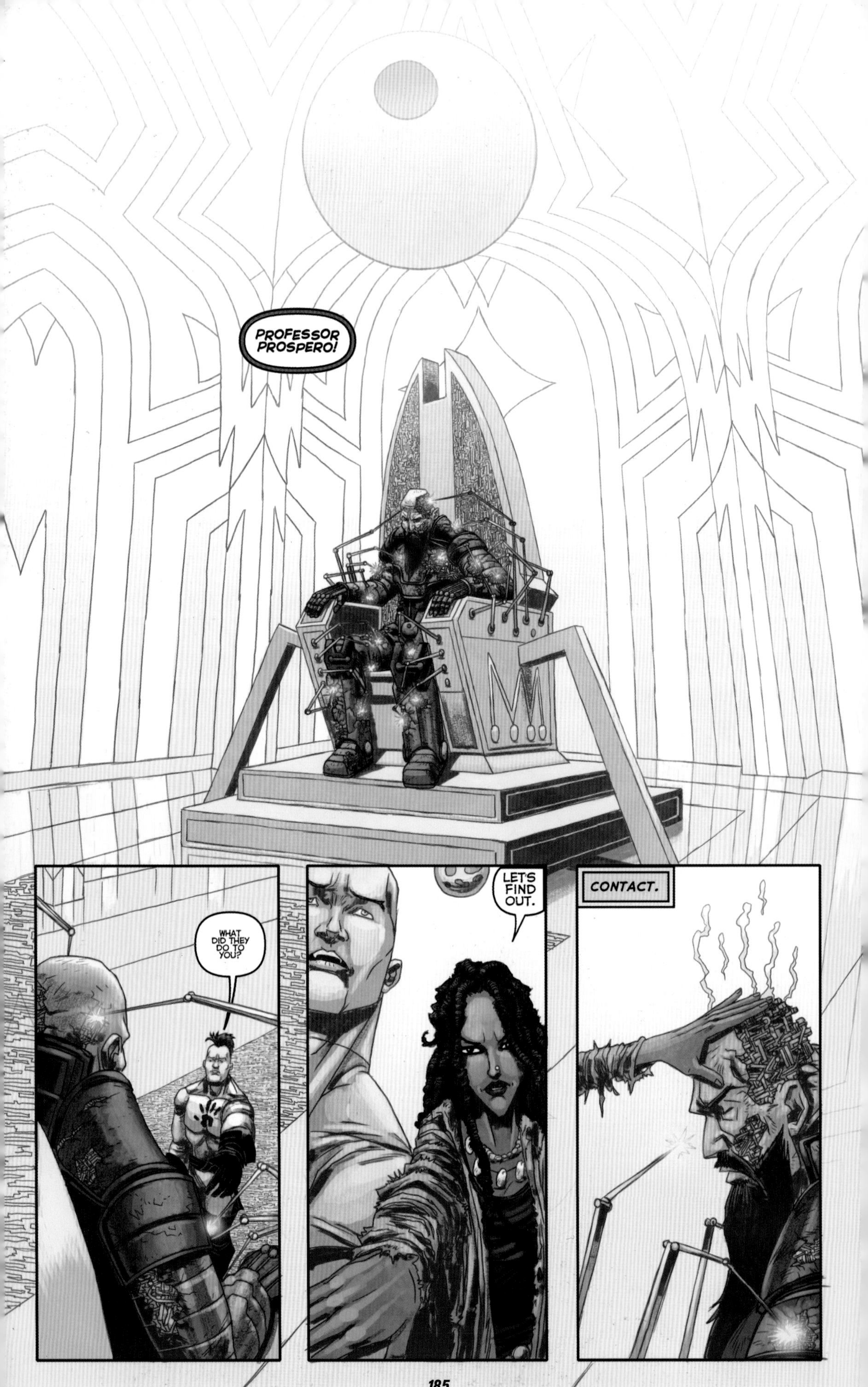
PROFESSOR PROSPERO!
WHAT DID THEY DO TO YOU?
LET'S FIND OUT.
CONTACT.

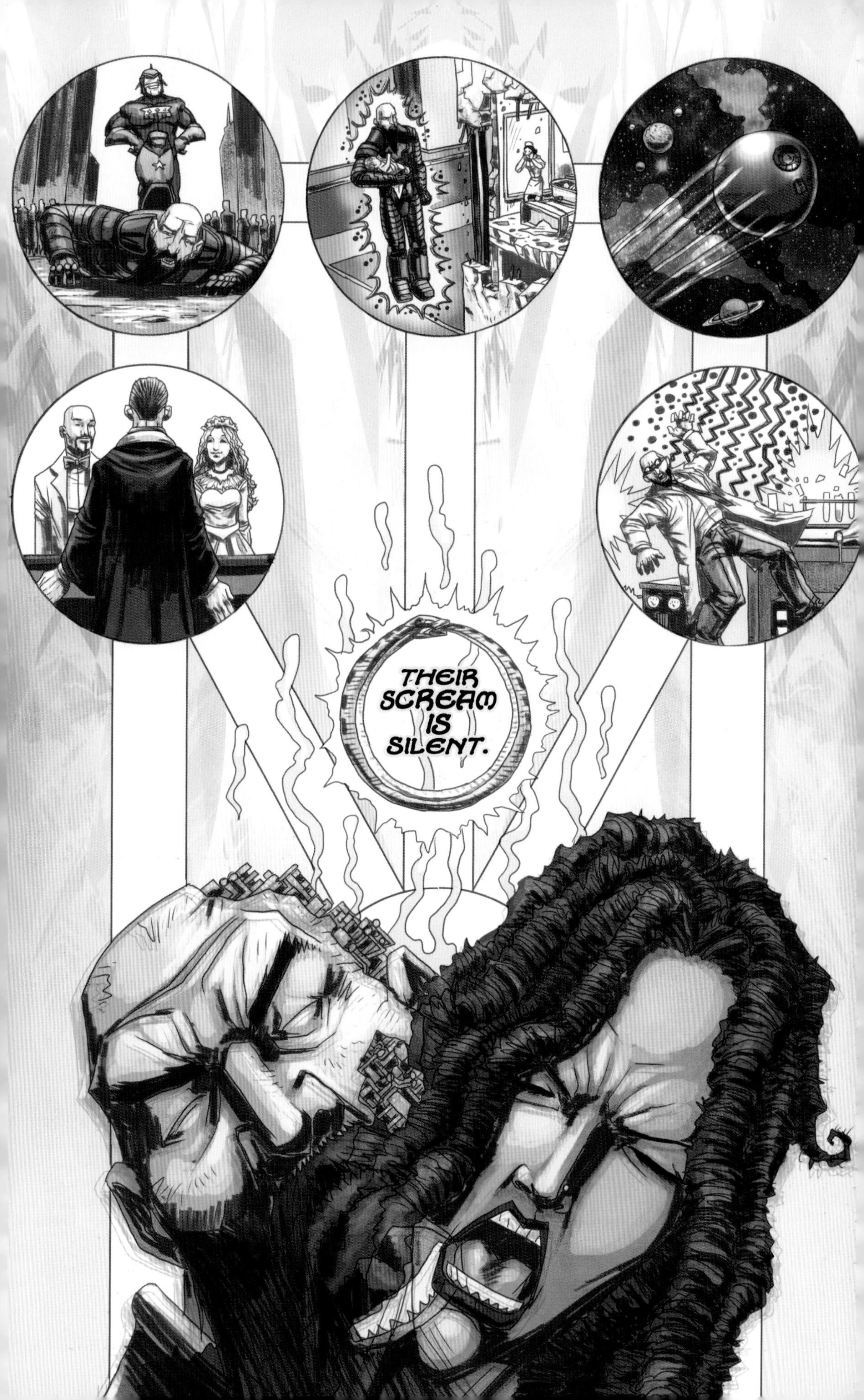
THEIR SCREAM IS SILENT.

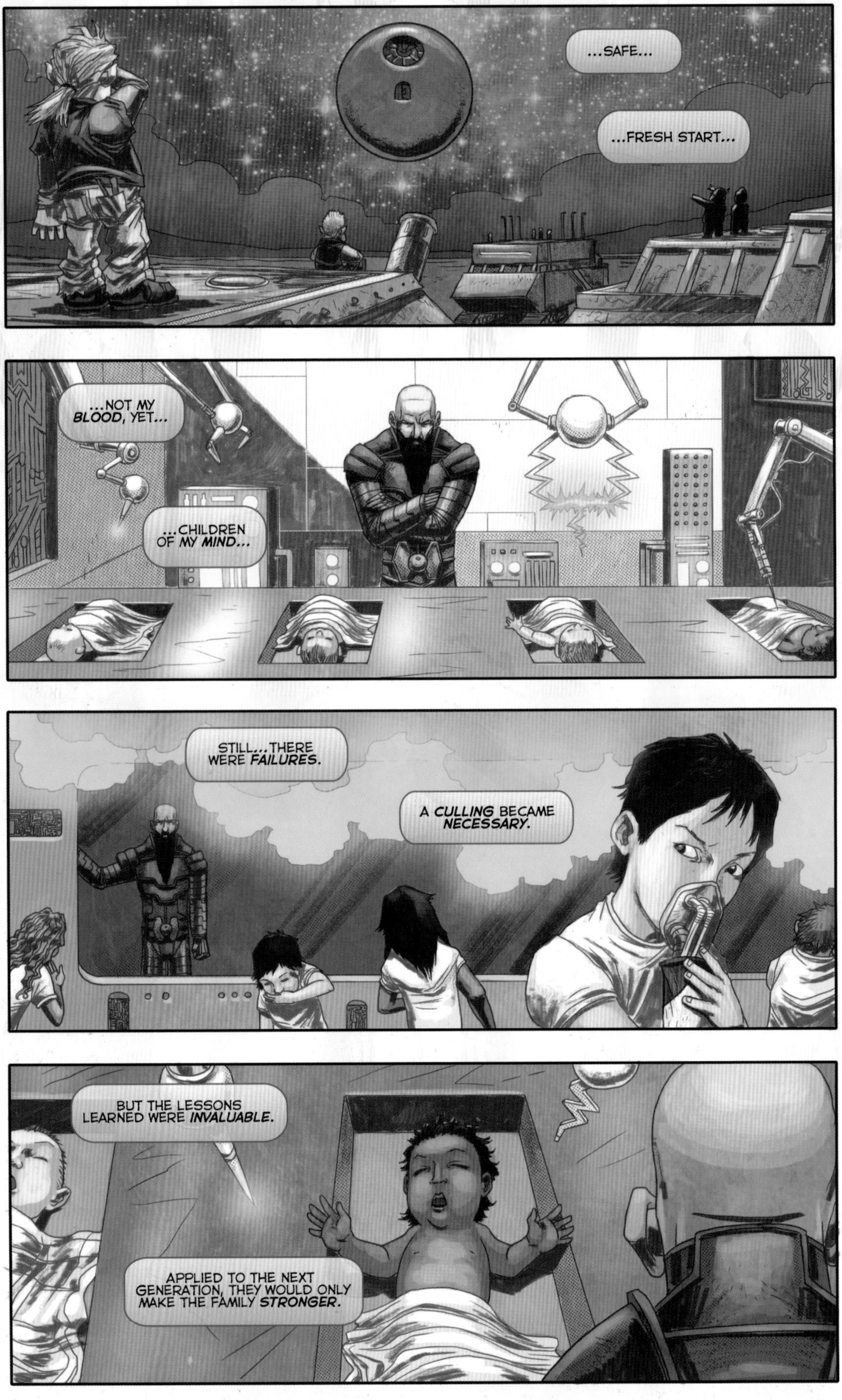
...SAFE...
...FRESH START...
...NOT MY BLOOD, YET...
...CHILDREN OF MY MIND...
STILL...THERE WERE FAILURES.
A CULLING BECAME NECESSARY.
BUT THE LESSONS LEARNED WERE INVALUABLE.
APPLIED TO THE NEXT GENERATION, THEY WOULD ONLY MAKE THE FAMILY STRONGER.

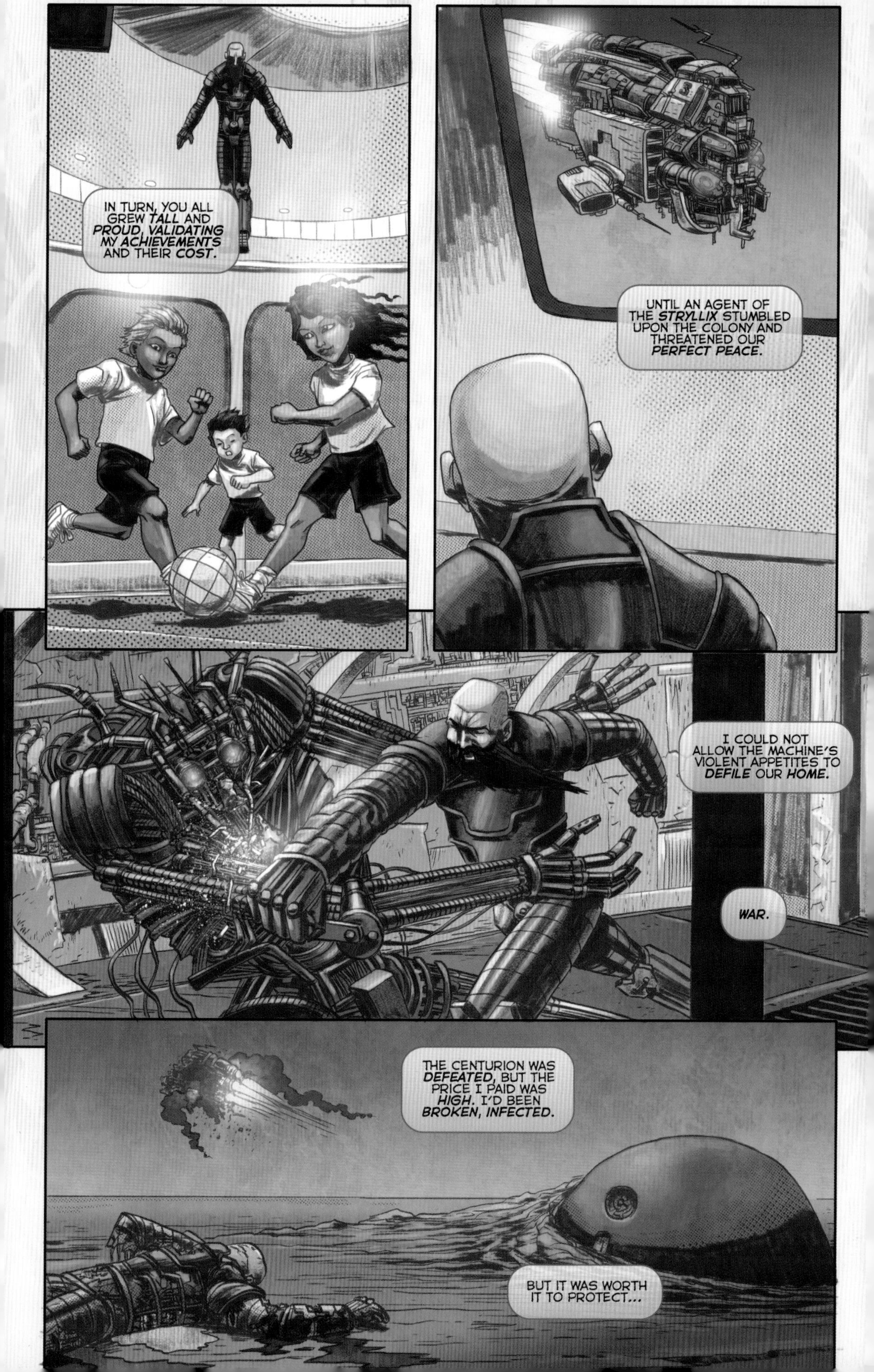
IN TURN, YOU ALL GREW TALL AND PROUD, VALIDATING MY ACHIEVEMENTS AND THEIR COST.
UNTIL AN AGENT OF THE STRYLLIX STUMBLED UPON THE COLONY AND THREATENED OUR PERFECT PEACE.
I COULD NOT ALLOW THE MACHINE'S VIOLENT APPETITES TO DEFILE OUR HOME.
WAR.
THE CENTURION WAS DEFEATED, BUT THE PRICE I PAID WAS HIGH. I'D BEEN BROKEN, INFECTED.
BUT IT WAS WORTH IT TO PROTECT...

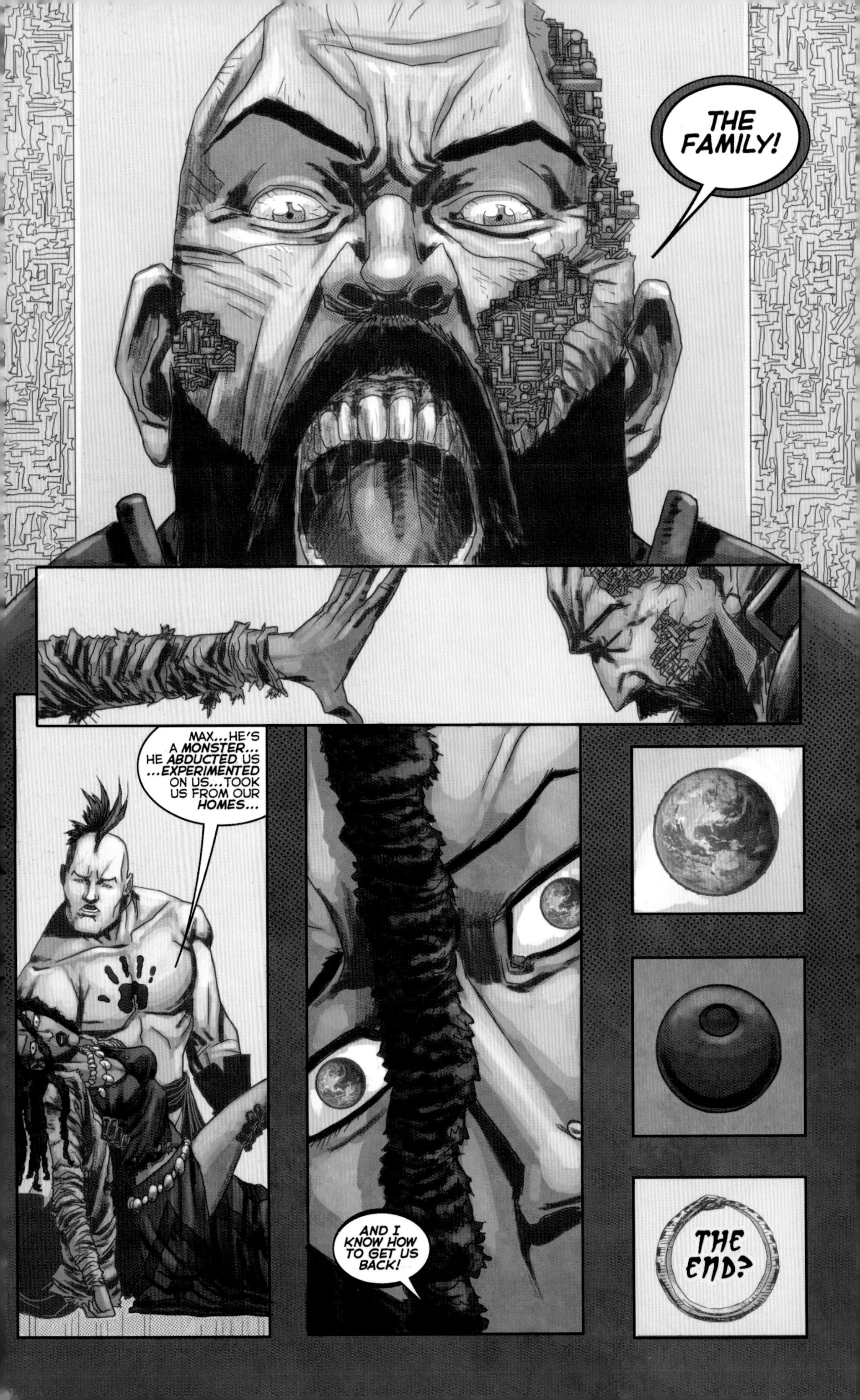
THE FAMILY!
MAX...HE'S A MONSTER... HE ABDUCTED US ...EXPERIMENTED ON US...TOOK US FROM OUR HOMES...
AND I KNOW HOW TO GET US BACK!
THE END?

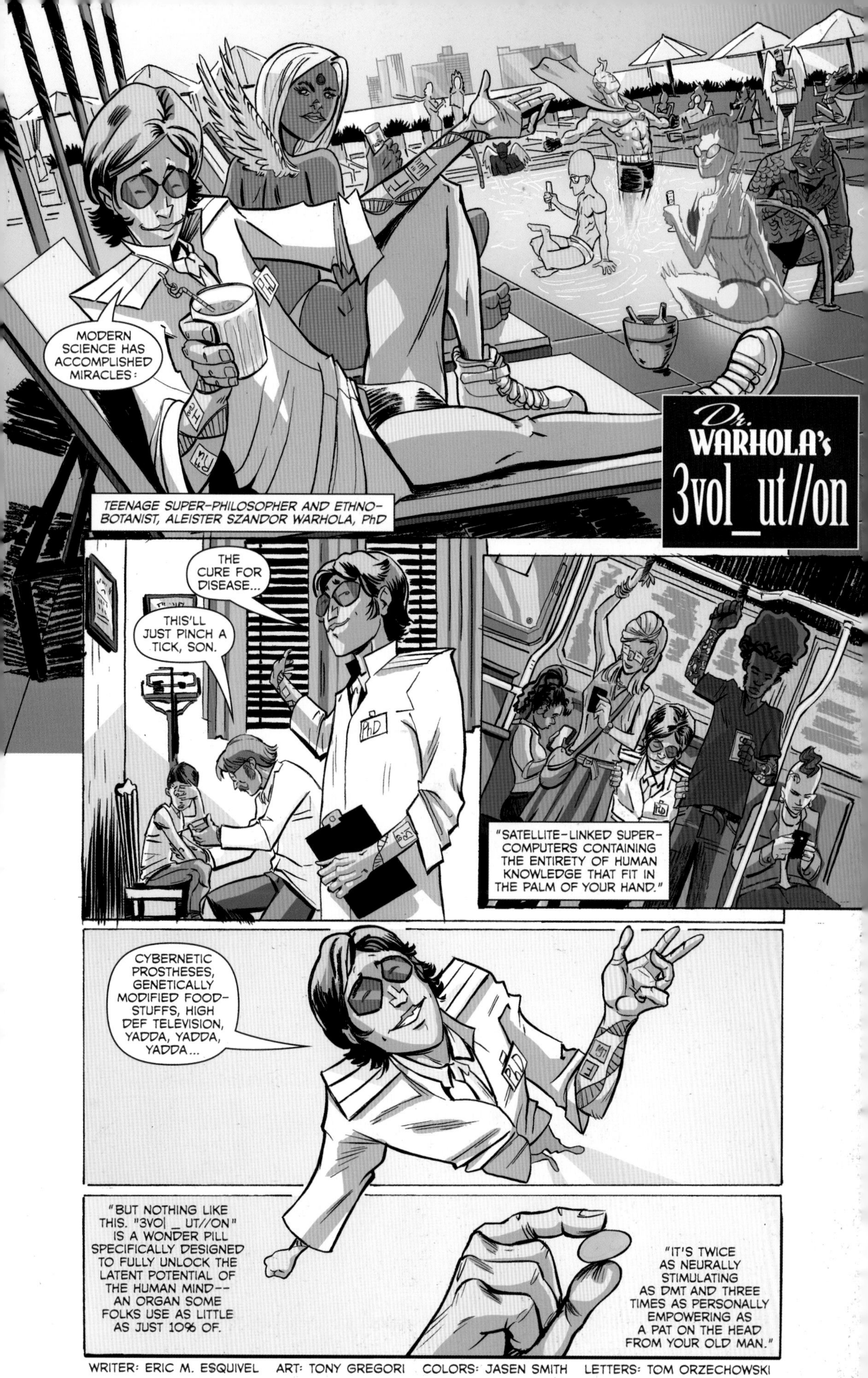
Dr. WARHOLA's
3vol_ut//on
MODERN SCIENCE HAS ACCOMPLISHED MIRACLES:
TEENAGE SUPER-PHILOSOPHER AND ETHNO-BOTANIST, ALEISTER SZANDOR WARHOLA, PhD
THE CURE FOR DISEASE...
THIS'LL JUST PINCH A TICK, SON.
"SATELLITE-LINKED SUPER-COMPUTERS CONTAINING THE ENTIRETY OF HUMAN KNOWLEDGE THAT FIT IN THE PALM OF YOUR HAND."
CYBERNETIC PROSTHESES, GENETICALLY MODIFIED FOOD-STUFFS, HIGH DEF TELEVISION, YADDA, YADDA, YADDA...
"BUT NOTHING LIKE THIS. "3VO| _ UT//ON" IS A WONDER PILL SPECIFICALLY DESIGNED TO FULLY UNLOCK THE LATENT POTENTIAL OF THE HUMAN MIND-- AN ORGAN SOME FOLKS USE AS LITTLE AS JUST 10% OF.
"IT'S TWICE AS NEURALLY STIMULATING AS DMT AND THREE TIMES AS PERSONALLY EMPOWERING AS A PAT ON THE HEAD FROM YOUR OLD MAN."

WRITER: ERIC M. ESQUIVEL ART: TONY GREGORI COLORS: JASEN SMITH LETTERS: TOM ORZECHOWSKI

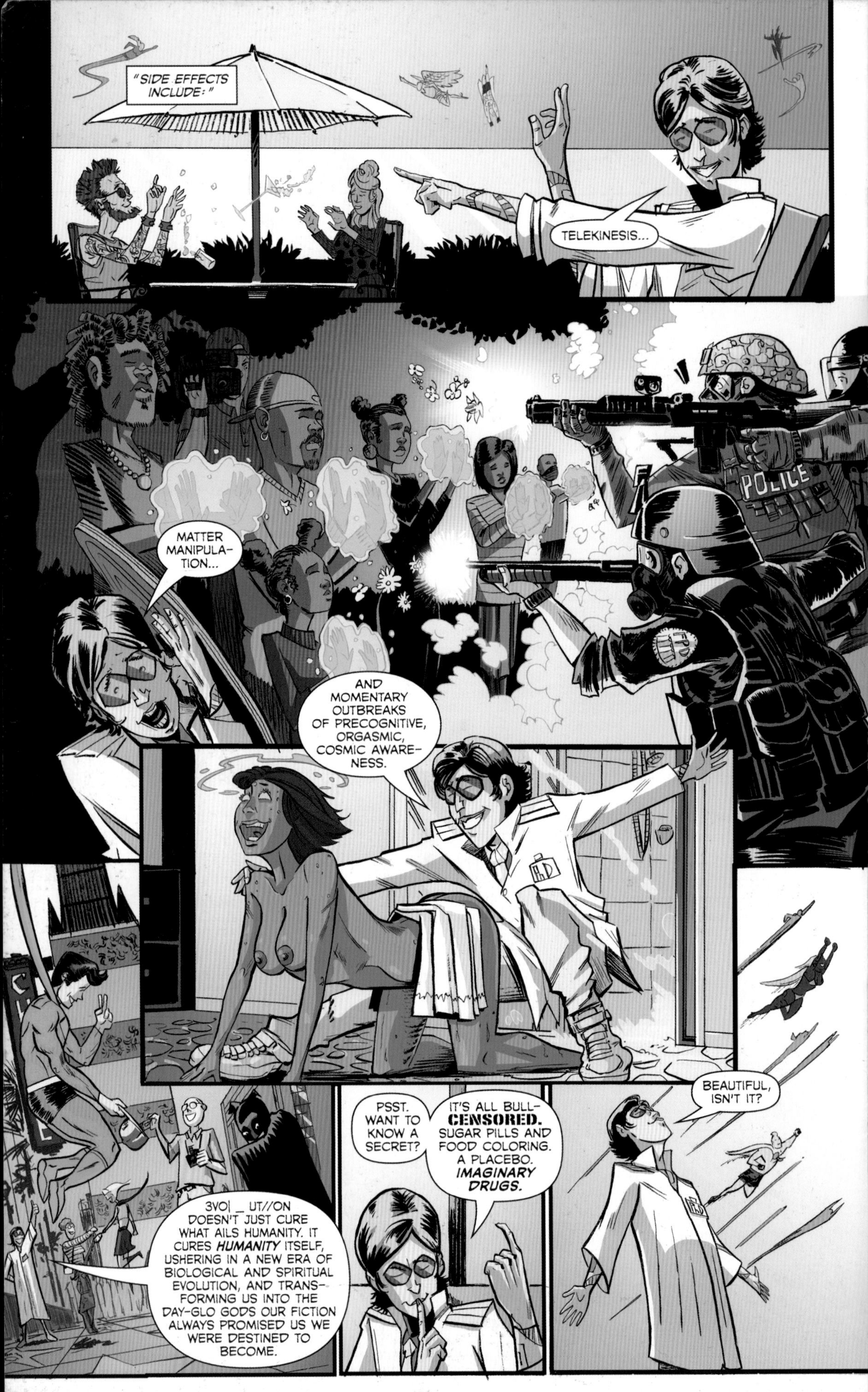
"SIDE EFFECTS INCLUDE:"
TELEKINESIS...
MATTER MANIPULATION...
AND MOMENTARY OUTBREAKS OF PRECOGNITIVE, ORGASMIC, COSMIC AWARENESS.
POLICE
3VO| _ UT//ON DOESN'T JUST CURE WHAT AILS HUMANITY. IT CURES *HUMANITY* ITSELF, USHERING IN A NEW ERA OF BIOLOGICAL AND SPIRITUAL EVOLUTION, AND TRANSFORMING US INTO THE DAY-GLO GODS OUR FICTION ALWAYS PROMISED US WE WERE DESTINED TO BECOME.
PSST. WANT TO KNOW A SECRET?
IT'S ALL BULL-**CENSORED.** SUGAR PILLS AND FOOD COLORING. A PLACEBO. ***IMAGINARY DRUGS.***
BEAUTIFUL, ISN'T IT?

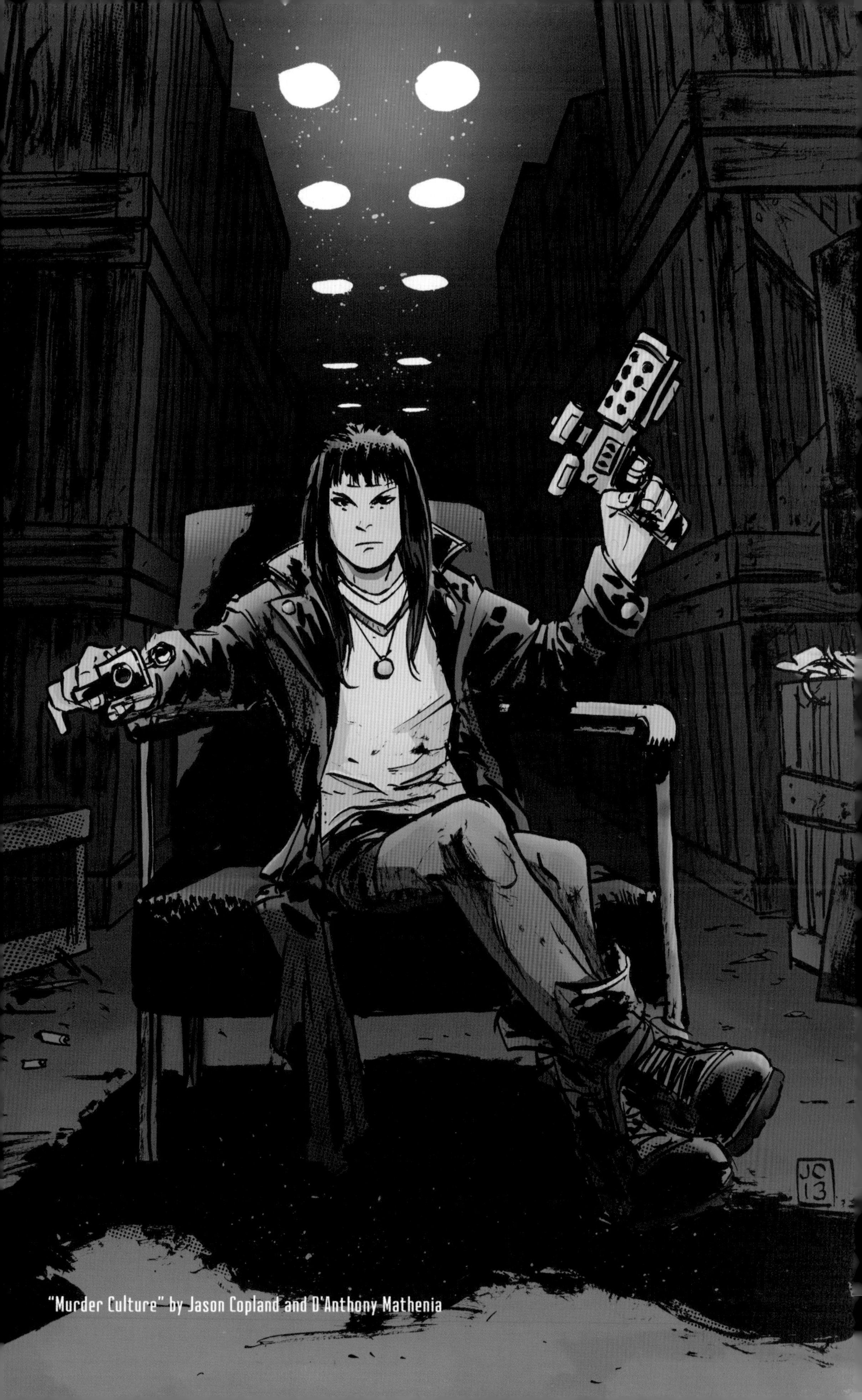
JC
13
"Murder Culture" by Jason Copland and D'Anthony Mathenia

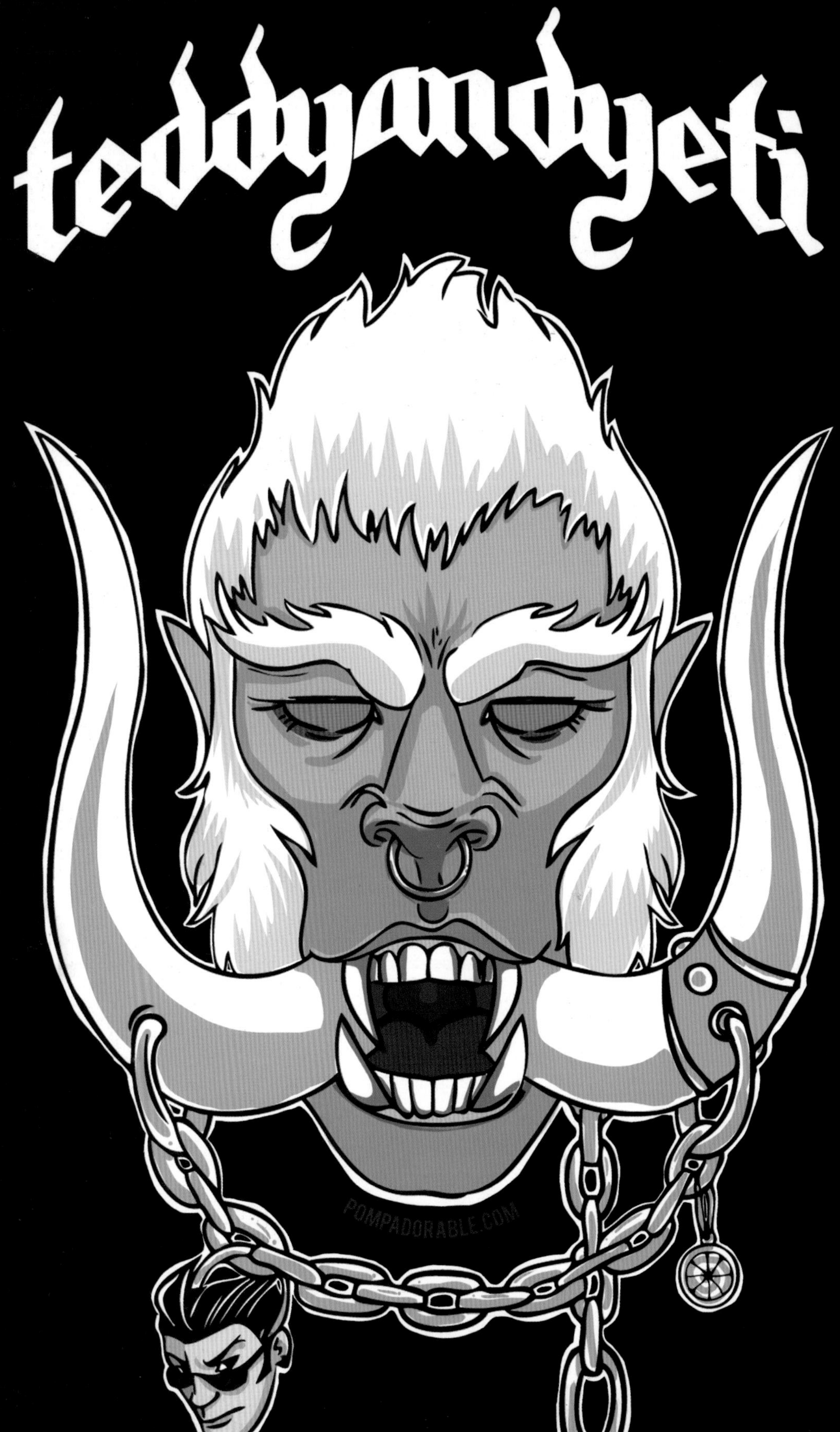
teddyandyeti
POMPADORABLE.COM

"Teddy and the Yeti" by Ally Cat

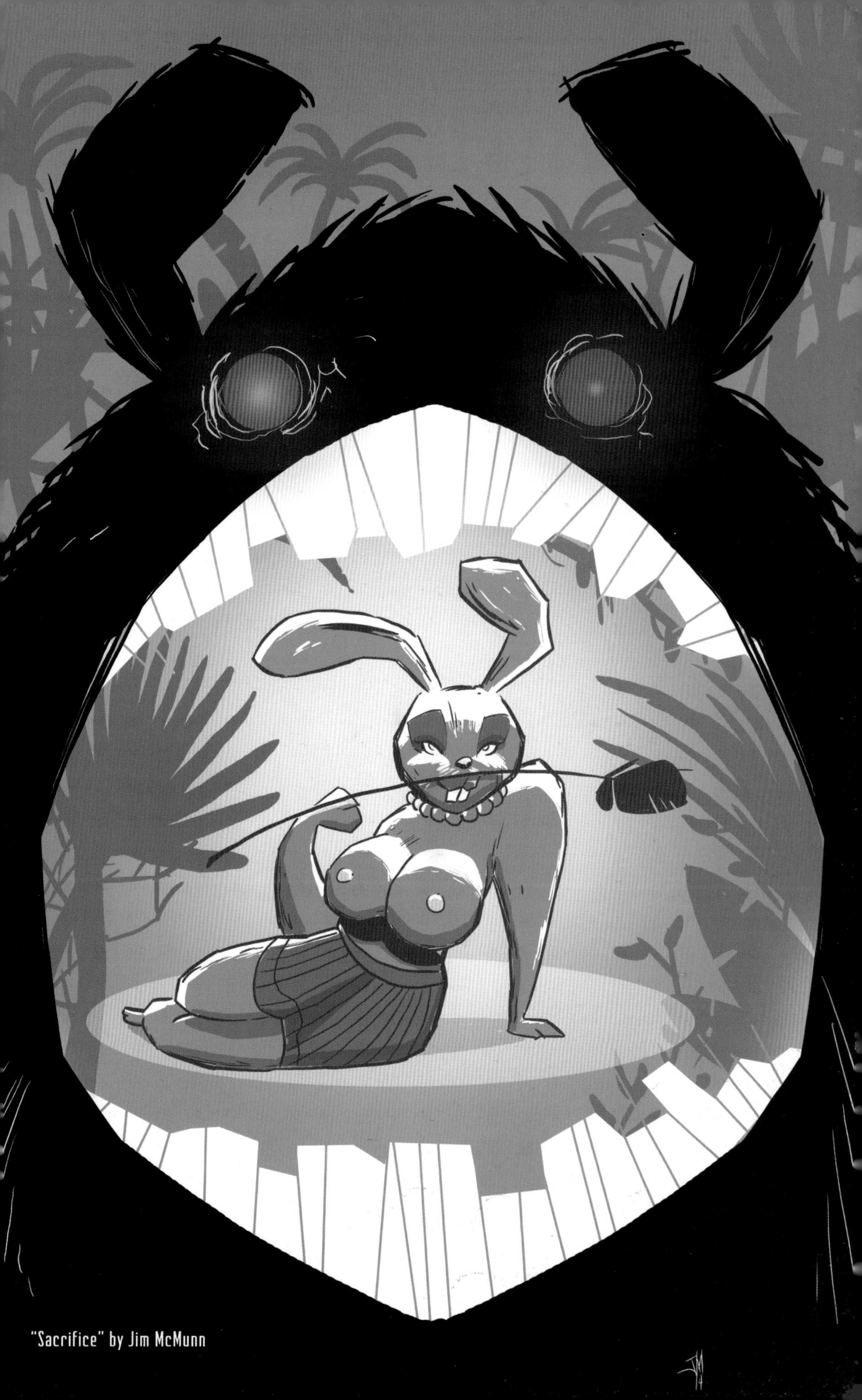

"Sacrifice" by Jim McMunn

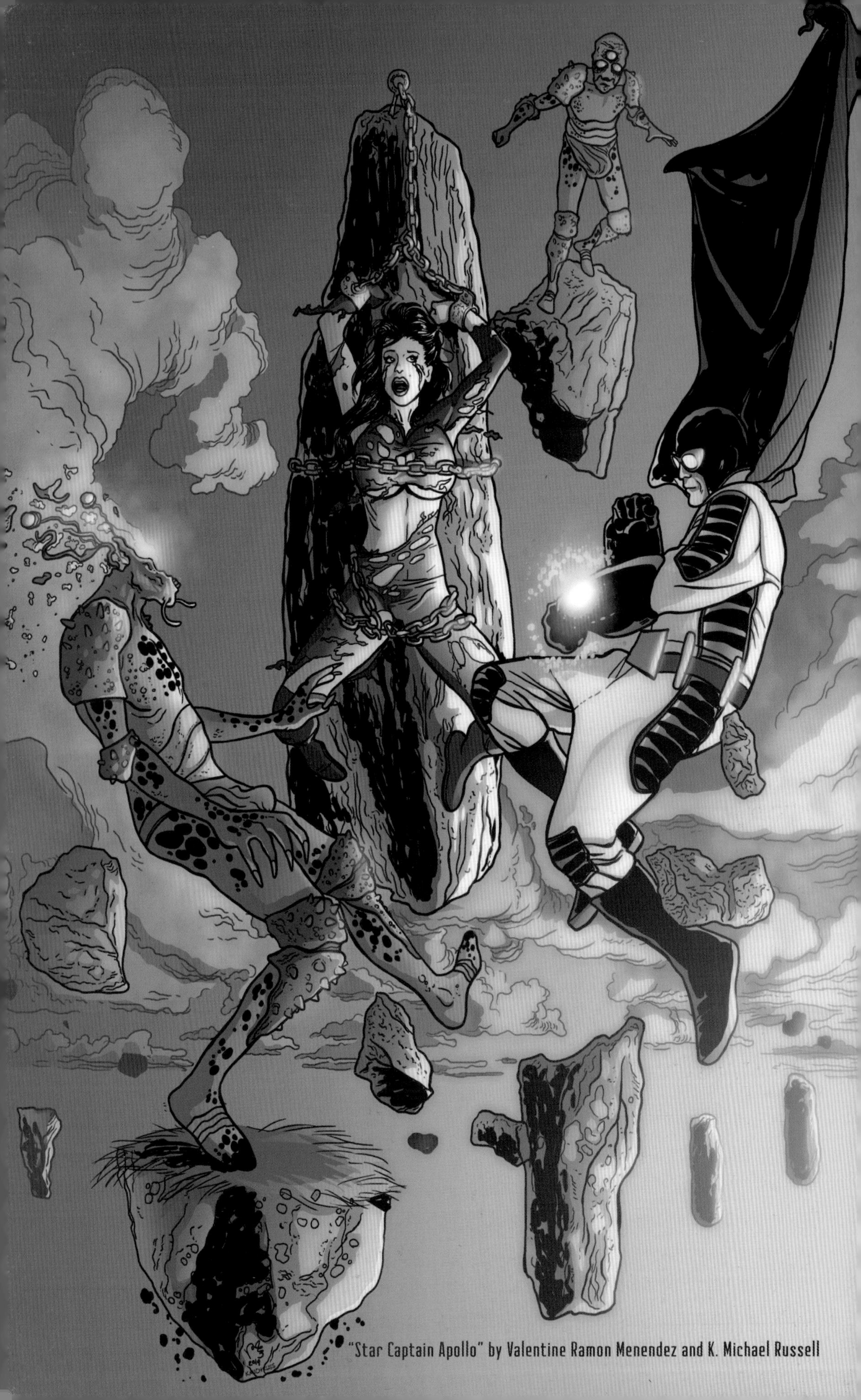

"Star Captain Apollo" by Valentine Ramon Menendez and K. Michael Russell

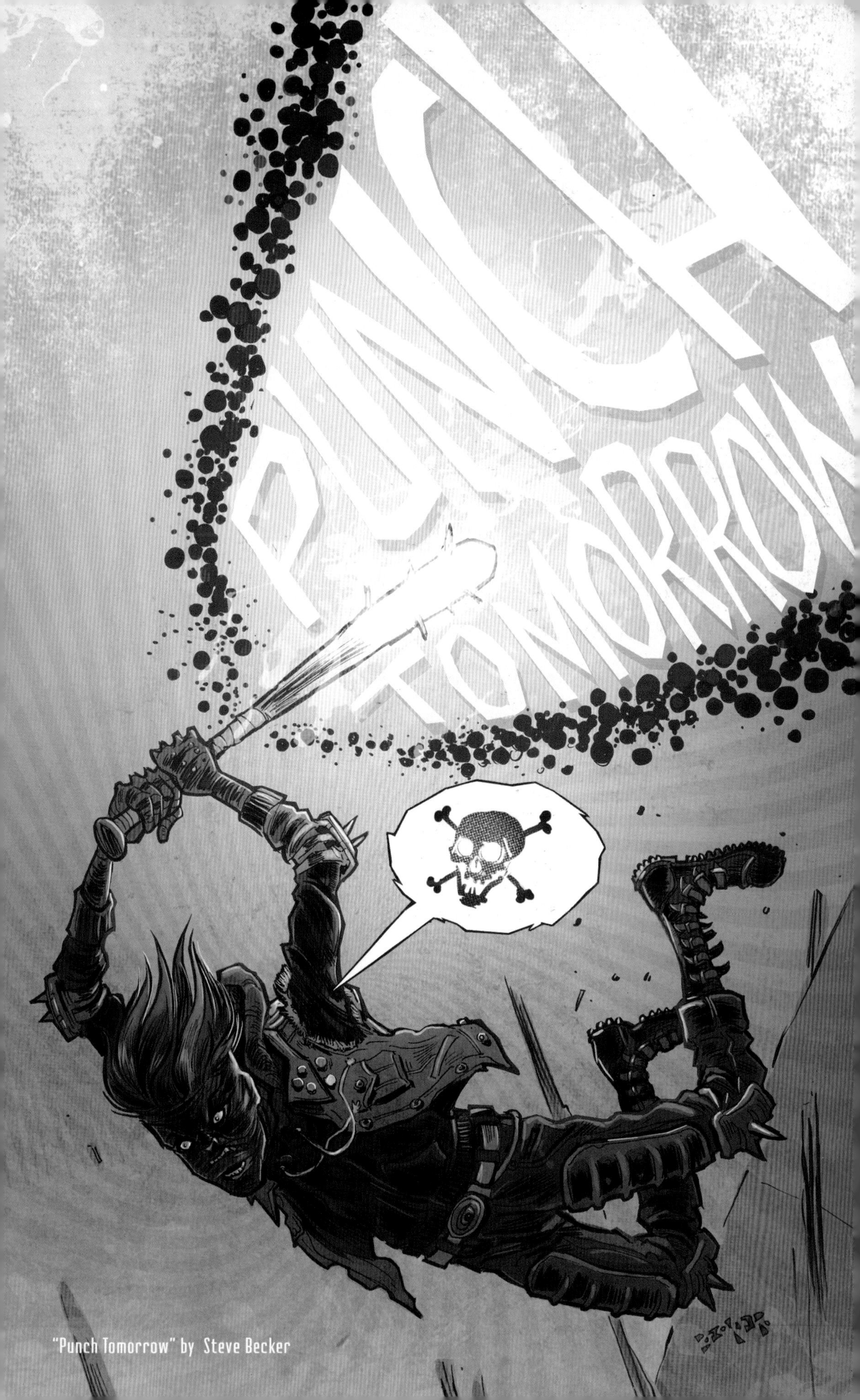
PUNCH
TOMORROW

“Punch Tomorrow” by Steve Becker

"Imaginary Drugs"
by Francesco Penzy Chippara
and K. Michael Russell

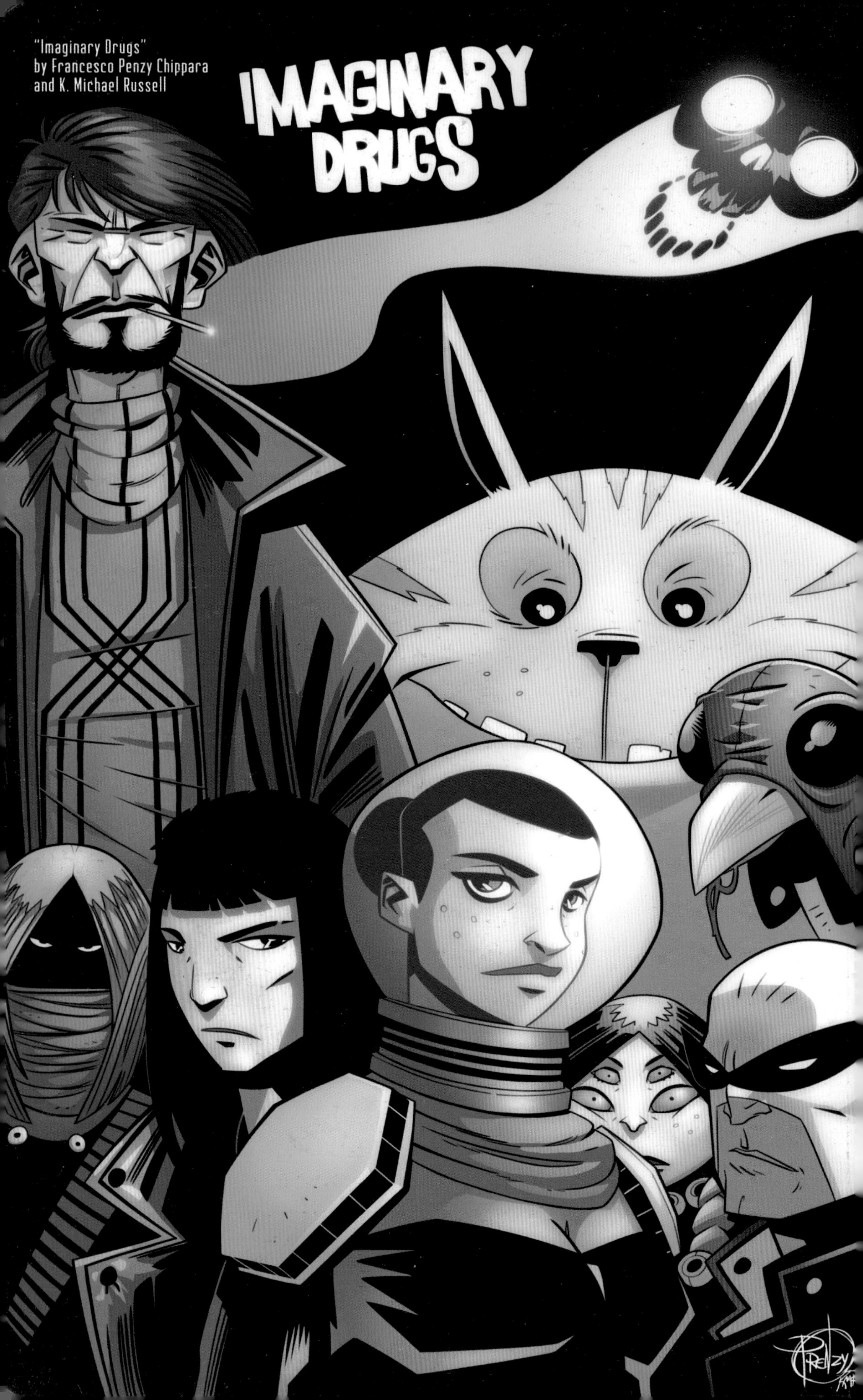
IMAGINARY
DRUGS
Penzy